The Economics of Pollution Control in the Asia Pacific

NEW HORIZONS IN ENVIRONMENTAL ECONOMICS

General Editor: Wallace E. Oates, *Professor of Economics, University of Maryland*

This important new series is designed to make a significant contribution to the development of the principles and practices of environmental economics. It will include both theoretical and empirical work. International in scope, it will address issues of current and future concern in both East and West and in developed and developing countries.

The main purpose of the series is to create a forum for the publication of high quality work and to show how economic analysis can make a contribution to understanding and resolving the environmental problems confronting the world in the late 20th century.

Titles in the series include:

The Economics of Pollution Control in the Asia Pacific

Edited by

Robert Mendelsohn
Edwin Weyerhaeuser Davis Professor, School of Forestry and Environmental Studies, Yale University, New Haven, CT, US

and

Daigee Shaw
Research Fellow, Institute of Economics, Academia Sinica, Taipei, Taiwan, ROC

New Horizons in Environmental Economics

Edward Elgar
Cheltenham, UK · Brookfield, US

Published by
Edward Elgar Publishing Limited
8 Lansdown Place
Cheltenham
Glos GL50 2HU
UK

Edward Elgar Publishing Company
Old Post Road
Brookfield
Vermont 05036
US

A catalogue record for this book
is available from the British Library

Library of Congress Cataloging in Publication Data
Mendelsohn, Robert O. , 1952-
     The economics of pollution control in the Asia Pacific / Robert
Mendelsohn, Daigee Shaw.
          (New horizons in environmental economics)
     Includes bibliographical references and index.
     1. Pollution —Economic aspects—Taiwan. 2. Pollution—Economic
aspects—Korea (South) 3. Environmental policy—Taiwan.
4. Environmental policy—Korea (South)   I. Shaw, Daigee, 1951-
II. Title. III. Series.
   HC430.5.Z9P556 1996
   338.4'336373'095—dc20   96–5865
                                                                CIP

ISBN 1 85898 307 X

Printed and bound in Great Britain by Hartnolls Limited, Bodmin, Cornwall

Contents

Tables

Figures

Contributors

Anna Alberini, *Assistant Professor of Economics, University of Colorado at Boulder, Colorado, US*

Richard C. Bishop, *Professor of Agricultural Economics, University of Wisconsin, Madison, Wisconsin, US*

Pamela Chang, *Assistant Professor of Economics, Wellesley College, Wellesley, Massachusetts, US*

Kai-Lih Chen, *Associate Professor of Agricultural Economics, National Ilan Institute of Agriculture and Technology, Ilan, Taiwan, ROC*

Youngsub Chun, *Assistant Professor of Economics, Seoul National University, Seoul, Korea*

Jonathan Coppel, *Economist, Organization for Economic Cooperation and Development, Paris, France*

Maureen Cropper, *Principal Economist, Policy Research Department, The World Bank; Professor of Economics, University of Maryland; Senior Fellow, Resources for the Future; and President, Association of Environmental and Resource Economists, Washington, DC, US*

Tsu-Tan Fu, *Research Fellow, Institute of Economics, Academia Sinica, Taipei, Taiwan, ROC*

Jerome Geaun, *Professor of Agricultural Economics, National Taiwan University, Taipei, Taiwan, ROC*

Winston Harrington, *Senior Fellow, Quality of the Environment Division, Resources for the Future, Washington, DC, US*

Wen-Hua Hsieh, *Graduate Student, Department of Agricultural Economics and Rural Sociology, Ohio State University, Columbus, Ohio, US*

Chung-Huang Huang, *Professor of Economics, National Tsing Hua University, and Research Fellow, Institute of Economics, Academia Sinica, Taipei, Taiwan, ROC*

Victor T.Y. Hung, *Assistant Professor of Economics and Finance, City University of Hong Kong, Hong Kong*

Alan Krupnick, *Senior Fellow, Quality of the Environment Division, Resources for the Future, Washington, DC, US*

Seung-Jun Kwak, *Assistant Professor of Economics, Korea University, Seoul, Korea*

Gye-Pyeong Lee, LG Economic Research Institute, Seoul, Korea

Hiro Lee, *Associate Professor, Graduate School of International Development, Nagoya University, Nagoya, Japan*

Lung-An Li, *Associate Research Fellow, Institute of Statistical Science, Academia Sinica, Taipei, Taiwan, ROC*

Jin-Tan Liu, *Professor of Economics, National Taiwan University, and Research Fellow, Institute of Economics, Academia Sinica, Taipei, Taiwan, ROC*

Alan Yun Lu, *Professor of Agricultural Economics, National Taiwan University, Taipei, Taiwan, ROC*

Robert Mendelsohn, *Edwin Weyerhaeuser Davis Professor, School of Forestry and Environmental Studies, Yale University, New Haven, Connecticut, US*

Wen-Harn Pan, *Research Fellow, Institute of Biomedical Sciences, Academia Sinica, Taipei, Taiwan, ROC*

Clifford S. Russell, *Professor of Economics and of Public Policy, and Director, Vanderbilt Institute for Public Policy Studies, Vanderbilt University, Nashville, Tennessee, US; and former president, Association of Environmental and Resource Economists*

Daigee Shaw, *Research Fellow, Institute of Economics, Academia Sinica, Taipei, Taiwan, ROC*

Hirofumi Shibata, *Professor of Policy Science and Director of Keihanna Research Center, Ritsumeikan University, Kyoto, Japan*

Michael P. Welsh, *Senior Associate, Hagler-Bailly Consulting Inc., US*

Huoying Wu, *Assistant Research Fellow, Institute of Economics, Academia Sinica, Taipei, Taiwan, ROC*

Pei-Ing Wu, *Associate Professor of Agricultural Economics, National Taiwan University, Taipei, Taiwan, ROC*

Chung-Hsin Yang, *Research Fellow, Institute of Economics, Academia Sinica, Taipei, Taiwan, ROC*

Acknowledgments

The editors wish to express their appreciation for the hard and professional work provided by the editorial team: Nancy Zigmund, Jia-Tsing Chen and Shu-Yi Lin. Nancy served as the copyeditor and compiled the index, and Jia-Tsing and Shu-Yi provided word processing and desktop publishing services.

The editors would like to thank the Institute of Economics, Academia Sinica (IEAS) for funding the original conference and the editing of this book. We especially want to thank Dr. Jia-Dong Shea, IEAS Director, for his consistent support and encouragement. We also want to thank numerous reviewers for helping us with their constructive and insightful comments during the conference and in the review process. Finally, we thank the authors for their full cooperation. This book belongs to every author.

Robert Mendelsohn
Daigee Shaw

1. Asia Pacific Environmental Economics

Robert Mendelsohn and Daigee Shaw

The Asia Pacific region provides a wide diversity of development levels and growth rates, from essentially rural countries such as Vietnam, through rapidly developing countries such as the Republics of China and Korea, to developed countries such as Japan. Corresponding to this range of development experiences is a range of environmental concerns. The least developed nations tend to be skeptical of the personal benefits of adopting environmental protection, the most rapidly developing countries struggle to get control of their environments without stifling their rapid growth, and the top income tier countries commit to protecting not only their own environments, but also the global 'commons'. To help inform the political debate, environmental economists can provide evidence about the costs and benefits of alternative environmental decisions and alternative methods of implementation.

But in every case, whether of benefit estimation or of instrument choice, the details of local cultures and conditions matter. It is not enough – and may even be misleading – to import methods, arguments, and conclusions from the US and Europe without modification.

This book includes papers selected from those delivered at an international conference organized by the Institute of Economics of Academia Sinica in Taiwan. The conference, entitled 'Economic Perspectives of Pollution Control in the Pacific Rim Countries', was held March 18-19, 1994. The papers presented in this book have subsequently been peer reviewed and edited. The collection begins the process of adapting environmental economics to the special situation of the nations of the region. In the process it demonstrates that citizens of rapidly developing countries such as Taiwan and Korea are willing to pay substantial amounts for protection and improvement of air and water quality, that they face potentially large losses from global climate change, and may, at the same time, have some cost-effective alternatives for helping to reduce global greenhouse gas emission. It also demonstrates that capturing the fine detail of Asian politico-economic systems requires complex models of the environmental policy setting.

1

This book lays the foundation for environmental policies in the region. We present evidence of the magnitude of environmental benefits of pollution control in rapidly developing countries. Given the rapid increase in pollution problems and the concurrent increase in people's income, several studies in this book demonstrate that citizens of developing countries are willing to pay substantial amounts for pollution control. Of course, these benefits must be weighed carefully against abatement costs, as pollution control can be expensive depending upon the restrictiveness of regulations. Further, the effectiveness of regulations can depend on local conditions and the nature of regulatory systems. Several contributions in the book construct theoretical models of pollution regulation and discuss how different types of regulations and conditions affect optimal policies.

The book is organized in five sections. The first includes research aiming to measure the costs and benefits of global warming for Pacific Rim countries. The second section quantifies the health impacts of air pollution in Taiwan. Efforts to measure air pollution impacts more generally are found in the third section. The fourth section is concerned with the demand for water quality. The final section of the book is a collection of theoretical papers concerning the effectiveness of pollution control policies under alternative regulatory structures and settings. These sections are further briefly described in this introduction.

The global warming section begins with an analysis by Robert Mendelsohn on the benefits of controlling greenhouse gases (GHGs) for a number of Pacific Rim countries. He uses estimates of the sectoral impacts from doubling GHGs to predict the damages which would occur in each country. The analysis indicates that while the absolute magnitude of damages is higher in developed countries, developing countries are more vulnerable to climate change because their damages as percentages of GNP are higher. Mendelsohn's assessments suggest that a sizable proportion of the expected damages from global warming will be nonmarket impacts such as ecological changes and health effects.

Jonathan Coppel and Hiro Lee provide a corresponding image of the costs of controlling GHGs. Using a global general equilibrium environment (GREEN) model, they estimate the costs of alternative GHG reduction policies such as country-specific carbon taxes, a uniform carbon tax, and tradable emission quotas. Coppel and Lee emphasize the importance of allowing carbon emission trading between OECD and Asian developing countries because it leads to an efficiency gain resulting from equalization of marginal carbon abatement costs among participating countries. They estimate that the global cost of stabilizing GHG emissions at 1990 levels for Annex I countries would fall from 1% of GDP to 0.3% of world GDP, if Annex I countries could purchase carbon reductions from the Asian countries, rather than relying upon less efficient country-specific carbon taxes.

Huoying Wu analyzes the sensitivity of rice to climate change. Analyzing rice yields throughout Taiwan over the last forty years, Wu notes that yields are higher when temperatures are slightly less than average. She estimates that a 2.5°C increase in temperature would reduce rice yields by 1.8% in Taiwan. This estimate, however, does not include the beneficial impacts of carbon fertilization which would likely offset this impact.

The next section, on health effects, begins with an epidemiological study by Daigee Shaw et al. of Taiwan, linking air pollution to chronic and acute illnesses. The study, using 83-day diaries, finds a significant relationship between particulates or sulfur dioxide and chronic illnesses. Acute illnesses are sensitive to both particulates and sulfur dioxide too. The study predicts that a 50% reduction in three air pollutants (particulates, sulfur dioxide and ozone) would eliminate 5.75 million person-days of acute illness per year in Taipei and 3.33 million person-days in Kaohsiung.

Anna Alberini et al. use contingent valuation to investigate people's willingness to pay for fewer acute illnesses in Taiwan. They find that the median willingness to pay to avoid an episode is about US$40, although this amount varies by the severity and length of the illness. The authors also find that respondents are more consistent when questions are coupled with a 90-day health diary. Coupling these results with Shaw et al. reveals that a 50% reduction in air pollution in Taipei would provide acute health benefits of approximately US$100 million per year, which is equivalent to US$37 per person per year.

The section on air pollution contains two hedonic property value studies. Chung-Hsin Yang explores the effect of airborne particulate matter on property values in Taipei, while Seung-Jun Kwak et al. explore the same approach in Seoul. Both studies include a number of traditional housing characteristics in their hedonic price equations to control for housing and neighborhood quality. They both find a relationship between particulate matter and housing prices. Yang uses a log-log functional form while Kwak et al. find the Box-Cox relationship fits their data better. Yang finds a quadratic relationship between particulates and housing value, with a threshold at $75\mu g/m^3$. Households would like to pay for the reduction of particulates if the present level is in excess of this threshold level. Kwak et al. find that additional particulates decrease housing values, at least in their sample of apartments. Both studies apply a single equation hedonic price model to estimate benefits and refrain from estimating a second stage demand equation because they are limited to single-market data. A 20% reduction in particulates results in benefits of US$950 per household in Taipei and US$227 in Seoul annually.

Pacific. The book contains several empirical measurements of the costs and especially the benefits of pollution control in the region using a variety of techniques. The book also contains some interesting theoretical papers which are relevant to the region and to other areas in the world. Finally, this book serves as an introduction to the growing body of regional talent in the Asia Pacific who will play an important future role in environmental policy-making throughout this region.

REFERENCES

Mendelsohn, Robert (1986), 'Regulating Heterogeneous Emissions', *Journal of Environmental Economics and Management*, **13**, 301-12.

2. The Impact of Global Warming on Pacific Rim Countries

Robert Mendelsohn

1 INTRODUCTION

With the widespread attention being given global warming studies in the last decade, an increasing number of studies have examined the impact of climate change on specific sectors of the economy. Although a comprehensive and reliable measure of all major climate change impacts is not yet possible, the extensiveness and reliability of studies is steadily improving.

In this paper, we extrapolate from sector-specific studies (many of which have been done for the United States) and predict the magnitude of climate change impacts on Pacific Rim countries. For each country, we predict the range of damages which might occur in each sector from the doubling of greenhouse gases. Sectors include both market and nonmarket impacts. By presenting a range of effects, we are trying to illustrate the uncertainty surrounding these estimates.

These predictions serve two useful purposes. First, they provide a benchmark of damages so that individual countries can begin to get a sense of the magnitude of climate impacts. Second, these numbers highlight the uncertainty surrounding these estimates, thus identifying countries and sectors where additional research would be helpful.

The predictions of climate impacts from the doubling of greenhouse gases are large for the 20 Pacific Rim countries, summing to $37 billion a year. However, in comparison with previous estimates which have been made just for the United States, they are relatively small. Nordhaus (1991), Cline (1992), and Fankhauser (1993) predict annual damages in the United States alone of $50–70 billion or 1 to 1.4 % of GDP. The numbers in this study are significantly lower for two basic reasons. First, more recent predictions of climate change are more moderate than the ones used by the above authors. Earlier predictions of 4–5°C increases have been replaced with a rise in temperature of only 2.5°C by 2060.[1] Similarly, the earlier predictions of sea level rising by 1 meter by 2060 have been replaced with an estimated

7

44 cm increase. Second, adaptation is expected to mitigate much of the damages from climate change. By failing to take adaptation into account, the earlier studies overestimated market damages.

This paper examines an expected climate scenario defined by the Intergovernmental Panel on Climate Change (IPCC) (1990a, 1990b, 1992). The scenario involves a 2.5°C increase in temperature and an increase in mean precipitation of 8%. We assume that carbon dioxide has increased to 550 ppm and that the remaining climate forcing is due to other gases such as methane and nitrogen oxide. We further assume that sea level rise will be equal to 44 cm. This scenario is assumed to take place in 2060.

Because the economic system has 70 years to adjust, there is every reason to believe that people will try to adapt to the new climate. The inclusion of adaptation in climate change impact research is critical. Models which assume people and systems remain rigid in the face of slow and yet conspicuous change inevitably overestimate damages. For example, many agronomic studies imply that climate change will result in yield losses of 20 to 40%. In their attempt to design careful experiments, the agronomists have inadvertently frozen farmer practices. Studies which allow farmers to adjust how they farm and what they plant, however, reveal that there will be virtually no reduction in aggregate yields as a result of the climate change scenario above.

In the next section, we summarize the preliminary results of sector-specific studies of climate change impacts (see Table 2.1). For each sector, we propose a reduced-form model to capture the most important elements of the impacts in that sector. As studies in these sectors continue to develop, these reduced-form models can be updated and improved. The focus of this effort is to determine impacts across countries. No effort is made to predict intertemporal effects either before the doubling is complete or after. The reduced-form model in this paper is not designed to predict damages with different climate scenarios, only the assumed scenario.

In Section 3, the reduced-form models are applied to each of the major countries in the Pacific Rim. We have defined the Pacific Rim broadly to include all countries in South America, North America, Western Asia, Southeast Asia, Polynesia, and Oceania which have shorelines on the Pacific Ocean. The set of 20 countries represents a diverse cross-section of the world (see Table 2.2 for a precise list).

The paper concludes with a discussion of the overall results. The study predicts that climate change will have serious impacts. Most of these damages will be nonmarket in nature, involving changing ecosystems, health, lost species, and altered animal and plant populations. The nonmarket losses are concentrated in countries with high per capita incomes. About one-fifth of the losses, however, involve market damages primarily from

Table 2.1   Sector Impact Assumptions

Sector	Assumptions* for Impact
MARKET EFFECTS	
Agriculture	-6% to +1% of agr. GDP in polar region
	-1% to +6% of agr. GDP otherwise
Coastline	0 to 2 times $[0.47 \times coast \times (GDP/area) \times 0.44^2]$
Energy	+\$4 per capita if avg. T > 22°C
	\$0 per capita if 22°C > avg. T > 16°C
	-\$16 per capita if avg. T < 16°C
Forestry	-15% to +5% of forestry GDP
Tourism	-10% to +5% of tourism GDP
NONMARKET EFFECTS	
Aesthetics	-0.2% to +0.2% of GDP
Ecosystem	0 to +0.5% of GDP
Health	+\$0 to \$4 per capita

Note

*   The impacts assume a 2.5°C temperature increase, 8% precipitation increase, and 44 cm sea level rise by 2060.

coastal impacts due to sea level rise. These losses fall most heavily on Japan with its high-valued coastal land. The remaining market effects are either neutral or beneficial.

2 IMPACT STUDIES

The following section reviews impact studies in five sectors: coastal, agriculture, tourism, forestry, and energy (see Table 2.1). Most of the studies which have been completed to date have been done in the United States. One issue which consequently pervades this study is how to extrapolate from American studies to international examples. Probably the weakest link in this analysis is this extrapolation. Hopefully, future studies will concentrate on examples in other parts of the world so that the reliability of these estimates can be enhanced.

2.1 Agriculture

There have been dozens of agronomic studies done exploring the impact of climate and carbon dioxide on crops.[2] Generally, these studies have been performed in controlled settings where only the temperature or concentration of gas varied across samples. This careful scientific approach provides an appropriately controlled setting in which to test whether the stimulant in question has an effect. However, these studies, by rigidly controlling the setting, provide systematically biased estimates of the quantitative effect of the stimulus in question. In practice, farmers will adjust to increases in carbon dioxide and temperature. Predictions of the resulting effect in the field from changing carbon dioxide or temperature must incorporate these adjustments as well. Thus, some studies such as Rosenzweig and Parry (1993), Adams, Glyer and McCarl (1989) and Adams et al. (1990) suggest large crop declines as a result of climate change. However, economic studies which include adaptation, trade, and carbon dioxide fertilization all suggest much smaller damages.[3] As studies have done a better job of including adaptation, the range of effects has fallen to between 1% beneficial to 6% harmful.[4] Countries nearer the poles will likely have strictly beneficial impacts. Few studies, however, have been conducted in tropical or subtropical settings, so that the impact of warming or increased carbon dioxide in these places is poorly understood.

In light of these findings, we adopt the following reduced-form model. The climate change scenario is assumed to cause agricultural damages in the polar regions of between -6% to +1%, and in temperate and tropical regions from -1% to +6% of agricultural GDP. The magnitude of the loss will vary by region and in proportion to the size of the agricultural sector. For example, in the United States, agricultural GDP in 1989 was $94.9 billion. Given that the US climate is temperate, annual damages are calculated to be between $-0.95 to $5.69 billion (a negative annual damage is a benefit).

2.2 Coasts

Cline (1992) estimates there would be $7.0 billion of annual damages associated with a 1 meter sea level rise in the United States. Given that sea level projections are now much lower (current best estimates from a doubling of greenhouse gases are 0.44 meters), it is important to develop a relationship between sea level rise and damage. Although the shape of this function is not known, it is suspected that coastal damages will rise with the square of sea level rise.

Cline's $7 billion estimate for a 1 meter rise for the United States, in which there are 10,373 miles of coastline, implies an average cost of $675,000 per mile. Of course, the value of land varies across the world with scarcity and economic activity. In order to control for this, we assume that the value of land is proportional to GNP per square mile. Adjusting for US figures ($1.43 million/sq. mile), the resulting formula is:

$$\Delta W_{ij} = 0.47 \times Coast \times (GDP/Area) \times M^2 \qquad (2.1)$$

where *Coast* is measured in miles, *GDP/Area* is measured in dollars per square mile and sea level rise, *M*, is measured in meters.

Future estimates of sea level rise can become more sophisticated by taking into account the heterogeneity of coastlines. The slope of the land in the vicinity of the coast provides an accurate measure of the amount of land potentially threatened by sea level rise. Thus, (2.1) could be corrected for slope by multiplying the ratio of the average US slope near coastline/ average slope of the coastline of another country. Countries such as Bangladesh with very low slope coefficients would have higher proportional damages. Countries with sea cliffs would face much lower losses.

2.3 Energy

Initial studies of energy such as Linder, Gibbs and Inglis (1987) focused on measuring the impact of global change on electricity. These studies predicted that warming would significantly increase electricity demand through increased demand for cooling. Although early analysts recognized that warming would also reduce the demand for heat, they argued that cooling is more expensive than heating and would dominate. Nordhaus (1991) estimates that warming would cause energy damages equal to $0.5 billion and Cline (1992) estimates damages of $10.4 billion in the United States alone. Comprehensive studies of all sectors and all fuels, however, have not yet been completed.

More recent studies in progress indicate that these initial findings may not be accurate. The far greater reliance on heating than cooling in the United States indicates that warming will in fact reduce expenditures on energy. Preliminary estimates suggest that warming will result in savings of from $2 to $6 billion in the United States. The models of energy use also reveal that as the base temperature rises, cooling will eventually become more important than heating. Preliminary estimates suggest the point where cooling and heating exactly offset each other is around 19°C.

The reduced-form model for energy divides the world into three regions. Regions with average temperatures below 16°C are assumed to benefit from warming. Dividing the average US benefit of $4 billion by the US population implies a value of $16 per person. A value of from $4 to $16 per capita is applied to everyone in the cooler region. Given that the United States consumes more energy per capita than other countries, this is probably an overestimate for other countries. Regions with temperatures above 22°C are assumed to be hurt by warming. Cooling has not fully penetrated in these regions to date, however, so that we assume the per capita damages are from $1 to $4. Regions between 16 and 22°C are assumed to be insensitive to the warming scenario in this paper with values of from -$1 to +$1 per person.

2.4 Forestry

The biological literature on forestry is deeply divided concerning whether warming would be beneficial or harmful to forests. Ecologists who study long-run equilibriums are predicting a world with more productive trees and more extensive forests as both tropical and boreal areas expand.[5] These models predict forest production would probably increase in magnitude. In contrast, the modelers who study forest dynamics and are focused on the current distribution of forests predict that forests would not be able to move as rapidly as the climate demands and there would be extensive 'dieback' in the warmer ranges of each species.[6] These authors predict that forest production would be reduced dramatically with warming.

In practice, neither set of authors is providing accurate measures of what would happen to the timber industry. The movement of forests to keep pace with climate change is possible for managed forests. New species could be planted wherever they would do best. With short-lived species this could be done on the basis of the most recent weather. With longer-lived species, foresters would have to anticipate climate change slightly in their planting plans. Trees which have been caught in a changing climate and are no longer thriving could be harvested early and thus salvaged rather than being lost outright. Thus, the more severe predictions of forest loss could be mitigated through management. Further, ecological long-run equilibriums which take 500 years to reach are not especially powerful tools for a system in constant change.

The reduced-form model for timber is assumed to be proportional to the magnitude of the current timber industry. Given the wide range of uncertainty from the biologists, we assume that this warming could either increase the size of the industry by 10% or reduce it by 10%. We consequently are assuming that the net expected effect of warming on forestry is zero with a wide range of either positive or negative effects. For example, the US forest industry produces $72 billion worth of forest products each year. Given the assumptions, warming may cause timber damages in the US between -$7.2 and $7.2 billion. Note that the damages are assumed to be proportional to the size of the entire industry, not just the part of the industry that grows trees.

2.5 Water

Some analysts have assumed that changes in water flows will result in significant global damages. For example, Cline estimates that 11% of total climate change impacts will be due to water shortages (Cline, 1992). There are several reasons why Cline's estimates of the importance of water are probably overestimated. First, it is unclear how the climate scenario is going to affect water runoff. The warmer temperatures will result in earlier melting and more evapotranspiration. The increase in precipitation will offset this effect slightly. However, the increase in carbon dioxide may reduce the amount of water transpired by plants and trees significantly. The net change in water runoff may therefore be slight. Second, most of the world does not fully utilize available water. It is only in certain arid locations that society has tapped into most of the available water. Thus, in wetter locations, society could respond simply by using a greater fraction of the available water. For example, it is only in California, the southern Rocky Mountains, and Texas in the US that people consume more than one-half of the available supply of water. Third, even in arid settings, a large fraction of water is used for low-valued purposes. If water shortages occur and these low-valued uses are cut off, the actual economic loss from the permanent shortage is relatively small. For example, California survived a recent three-year drought with only small agricultural losses by eliminating two low-valued water users, rice and barley. Fourth, the principle loss from water reductions is in agricultural uses. There is a serious question of double-counting with the agricultural sector.

In the absence of data concerning water supply and water uses around the world, water effects are not included in the model. However, it is likely that such effects would be small and would be concentrated in arid regions.

2.6 Tourism

The increase in temperature predicted by climatologists is likely to have an effect on tourism. Tourists tend to spend more time outdoors than residents and are more vulnerable to the weather. Tourism is consequently dependent on the season. Tourism is partially a GDP effect and partially a nonmarket effect. It is clear that some local service economies are tied closely to tourism. However, it is also clear from travel cost studies that much of the value of tourism is not captured in what tourists buy. In fact, this value is largely claimed by the tourist themselves. In this study, we measure the local GDP effect, a market impact. The nonmarket benefits of tourism, captured by the tourists themselves are not explicitly included in the model and are assumed to be captured by the ecosystem effects.

Warming increases the length of the effective summer season and decreases the length of winter seasons in the destination site. A great deal of attention has been focused on how skiing operations may be hurt with additional warming. However, what is missing in these discussions is the fact that the magnitude of summer tourism vastly outweighs winter tourism. The increase in the summer season is therefore likely to be more important than the corresponding decrease of the winter season. On net, tourism should grow. Even places which are better known for their skiing such as Norway or Austria are likely to get an increase in tourism as summer tourism expands.

The reduced-form model for tourism assumes that the climate scenario will cause damages of between -10% to +5% of tourism GDP. For example, US tourism in 1989 was equal to $41 billion. The reduced-form model predicts global warming would cause a range of damages on US tourism of between -$4.1 to $2.0 billion.

2.7   Nonmarket Effects

2.7.1   Ecosystem
There are no aggregate measures of what people are willing to pay for ecosystems. Many individual sites have been studied and several species have been valued but none of these specific studies correspond well to the system-wide changes envisioned by global warming. Ecosystem effects are one of the most uncertain measures of global warming impacts. On the one hand, one could argue that these effects are likely to be close to zero as people adapt to the ecosystem they happen to live in. For example, people in Connecticut are now quite comfortable with the forested ecosystem they have grown up in and would be greatly disturbed by any proposal to return to the farmland landscape of the previous century. As the area warms and maples are pushed out and other trees come to take their place, future Connecticut residents may adapt as readily to this new landscape.

One could also argue that tampering with large ecosystems is one of the most dangerous things humans are doing. People are clearly worried that this tampering will eventually result in an environment which is distinctly hostile and barren. When ecologists discuss ecosystems retreating and forests in dieback, the common citizen conjures up images of moonscapes and charred forest remains. These haunting images of damaged ecosystems may motivate people to make large sacrifices for the status quo. Along this line, Fankhauser estimates that ecosystem effects could be equal to 0.4% of GDP in the US (1993).

In this study, we assume that the value of ecosystem effects caused by the warming scenario could vary from 0 to 0.4% of GDP. We implicitly argue that ecosystem damages are proportional to income (ability to pay) because valuation studies suggest that environmental values increase with income. We also assume that ecosystem damages are independent of the specific ecosystems in a country. That is, we assume that everyone is equally concerned about the environment in which they live.

2.7.2 Health

There have been a number of studies of health effects from climate change in the United States.[7] The studies have focused upon the effect of daily weather on daily mortality. The data suggest that in cooler climates, especially warm days cause sharp increases in daily mortality among the elderly. The same studies report this effect to be less apparent in warmer climates. It would appear that as climates warm, people adapt their behavior and learn to protect themselves on especially hot summer days.

Cross-sectional analysis of the effect of climate on annual mortality reveals that there are no consistent relationships (Mendelsohn and Shaw, 1994). Elderly people who live in warmer climates actually live longer. Climate appears to have only minor impacts on health in developed countries.

The effect of climate change on health in developing countries is much less clear. Warmer climates may increase the pathways of human health hazards. Poorer households may have fewer ways to mitigate against higher temperatures. Health care against increased risks may be less effective.

We assume that warming will cause health damages of from 0 to $1 billion in the United States. Dividing by the US population, the average expected health effects are from 0 to $4 per person. This estimate would presumably apply to all developed countries. Less developed countries may have a much larger physical risk from warming. However, poorer countries also tend to place a much lower value on human life. We consequently assume that the estimated 0 to $4 per capita would apply worldwide.

2.7.3 Aesthetics

In addition to effects on local ecosystems, people may have direct preferences for living in one climate rather than another. For example, many people have moved from northern to southern US cities since World War II primarily to enjoy the warmer climate. As societies have learned to create more complete indoor environments, former problems with heat have lessened, making these environments relatively more attractive. There of course may be a limit to how warm people would like the climate to become. However, for small changes such as the warming scenario, it seems likely that this preference will be as much for warming as against it.

The reduced-form model once again assumes that the magnitude of the aesthetic preference is proportional to GDP. In the absence of relevant empirical studies, it is assumed that warming would either cause damages or benefits equal to 0.2% of GDP. Thus, the expected value of aesthetic damages from warming is zero.

3   RESULTS

The results of global warming for each country and each sector are presented in Table 2.2. The impacts in eight sectors are calibrated for each of the 20 countries around the Pacific Rim. A range of values is given for each sector reflecting the uncertainties surrounding each estimate.

The damages and benefits of climate change across these 20 countries vary by sector and country. The largest market damages occur in the coastal sector as a result of sea level rise. Japan, in particular, would be hit hard by sea level rise because of the extraordinary value of coastal land in that country. Countries with extensive coastlines and relatively high land values such as the United States, Taiwan, Russia, Indonesia, and the Philippines are also affected.

The largest nonmarket damages come from ecosystem effects. Because the value of ecosystem changes are assumed to be proportional to GDP, countries with relatively large economies have the largest ecosystem damages. The United States, Japan, and Russia consequently are the most sensitive.

The only other sector which is consistently harmful is health effects. These effects are assumed to be proportional to population. Countries with relatively large populations are more sensitive, including China, the former Soviet Union, and the United States.

The remaining impacts could be either harmful or beneficial depending upon the resolution of uncertainty. The single most uncertain market effect is the impact of climate change on agriculture. Each country's sensitivity to agriculture depends upon their initial climate and the size of the agricultural sector. Despite the assumption that climate change is expected to produce more negative effects in tropical and temperate settings, aggregate agricultural effects have a zero expected value. The large expected benefits of climate change for Canada and the former Soviet Union counterbalance the harmful effects in the rest of the world. Because of the magnitude of potential agriculture impacts, it is important to resolve agricultural effects, especially outside the United States.

On the basis of more recent research which reveals that heating is far more extensive than cooling, it is clear that warming will reduce net spatial heating and cooling requirements in temperate and polar climates. Tropical climates however are likely to experience an increased cooling cost. This analysis assumes these costs are distributed on the basis of population. Spatial energy costs per capita, however, also vary and this effect is not yet captured in the model. Countries with the largest sensitivity to cooling damages lie in Southeast Asia. Countries which are expected to gain large benefits from heating reductions include the former Soviet Union, the United States, and Japan.

It is not clear what direction forest impacts from climate change will take. Countries with the largest forest-related sectors are assumed to be the most sensitive to these changes. Note that this calculation includes the entire forest sector, not just the growing of timber. Japan, for example, grows little timber but is expected to have large timber impacts. Other countries sensitive to changes in the forest sector include the United States, the former Soviet Union, China, and Indonesia.

Climate change is expected to benefit tourism. The United States is expected to be the most sensitive to these changes as it is the country with the largest tourist-related industry. Canada and Mexico are also expected to be affected.

Aesthetic effects are assumed to be proportional to GDP. It is not clear, however, how different countries will respond to climate changes. As with ecosystem effects, countries with large economies are assumed to be more sensitive to aesthetic effects. These effects are thus most pronounced in the United States, Japan, and the former Soviet Union.

Summing these impacts across market and nonmarket effects yields Table 2.3. Overall, market impacts are more uncertain. Aggregate effects range from -$57 to +$72 billion for the 20 countries. In contrast, nonmarket impacts are more likely to be harmful, ranging from -$20 to +$78 billion. The countries with the largest potential impacts from climate change include the United States, Japan, the former Soviet Union, and China. These four countries appear to be the most sensitive to both market and nonmarket impacts.

Taking the average of the highest and lowest impacts yields an average effect for each country (see Table 2.3). The countries with the largest impacts include Japan, the United States, and China. Taken together, the damages from these three countries sum to $31 billion (over 80% of all damages in the Pacific Rim). The former Soviet Union stands out as a net beneficiary of climate change. The warming scenario moves territory from low-valued polar to higher-valued temperate climates.

*Table 2.2 Sectoral Impacts of Global Warming on Pacific Rim Countries**

TYPE COUNTRY	MARKET AGRICULTURE	MARKET COASTAL	MARKET ENERGY	MARKET FORESTRY
Canada	-0.78 to 0.13	0.00 to 0.38	-0.40 to -0.10	-0.27 to 0.27
Mexico	-0.13 to 0.81	0.00 to 0.25	0.09 to 0.35	-0.26 to 0.26
US	-0.95 to 5.7	0.00 to 3.0	**-4.0 to -1.0**	-7.2 to 7.2
Chile	-0.02 to 0.13	0.00 to 0.04	-0.21 to -0.05	-0.16 to 0.16
Columbia	-0.07 to 0.42	0.00 to 0.03	0.03 to 0.12	-0.08 to 0.08
Ecuador	-0.02 to 0.10	0.00 to 0.01	-0.01 to 0.01	-0.05 to 0.05
Peru	-0.03 to 0.20	0.00 to 0.02	-0.01 to 0.01	-0.04 to 0.04
Japan	-0.54 to 3.2	**0.00 to 15.9**	**-2.0 to -0.50**	-1.8 to 1.8
Russia	**-14.1 to 2.4**	0.00 to 2.8	**-4.6 to -1.2**	-3.7 to 3.7
S. Korea	-0.12 to 0.75	0.00 to 0.50	-0.40 to -0.10	-0.25 to 0.25
Taiwan	-0.44 to 0.07	0.00 to 1.8	-0.08 to 0.08	-0.01 to 0.01
China	-0.97 to 5.8	0.00 to 0.07	-0.50 to 0.50	-1.7 to 1.7
N. Korea	-0.06 to 0.34	0.00 to 0.05	-0.17 to -0.04	-0.02 to 0.02
Thailand	-0.07 to 0.44	0.00 to 0.08	0.05 to 0.22	-0.22 to 0.11
Vietnam	-0.04 to 0.22	0.00 to 0.03	0.07 to 0.27	-0.08 to 0.08
Indonesia	-0.20 to 1.2	0.00 to 0.48	0.18 to 0.72	-0.85 to 0.85
Malaysia	-0.09 to 0.54	0.00 to 0.05	0.06 to 0.25	-0.39 to 0.39
Philippines	-0.20 to 1.2	0.00 to 0.49	0.02 to 0.07	-0.13 to 0.13
Australia	-0.07 to 0.44	0.00 to 0.22	-0.27 to -0.07	-0.25 to 0.25
New Zealand	-0.02 to 0.13	0.00 to 0.29	-0.05 to -0.01	-0.15 to 0.15
TOTAL	-18.9 to 24.2	0 to 26.5	-12.2 to -0.5	-17.6 to 17.6

Note

* Values are expressed in terms of annual damages in billions of US$ from a +2.5°C temperature, +8% precipitation, and +44 cm sea level change.

Absolute impacts, however, can hide the relative burden of any distribution of impacts across countries. Although the United States and Japan have large absolute damages, these damages average 0.3% and 0.7% of GDP, respectively, implying small overall disruption. Less developed countries, such as Vietnam, the Philippines, Indonesia, China, and Malaysia are expected to suffer losses equal to a much higher fraction of their GDP. For example, Vietnam is expected to lose 3.5% of its GDP and the Philippines up to 2.9% of its GDP to coastal, agricultural, and health impacts. Developing nations average much higher impacts per unit of GDP

Table 2.2, continued

TYPE COUNTRY	NONMARKET AESTHETICS	NONMARKET ECOSYSTEM	NONMARKET HEALTH	MARKET TOURISM
Canada	-0.8 to 0.8	0 to 2.0	0 to 0.10	-0.64 to 0.32
Mexico	-0.2 to 0.2	0 to 0.75	0 to 0.35	-0.53 to 0.27
United States	-9.0 to 9.0	**0 to 22.6**	0 to 1.0	-4.1 to 2.0
Chile	-0.04 to 0.04	0 to 0.09	0 to 0.05	-0.05 to 0.03
Columbia	-0.08 to 0.08	0 to 0.18	0 to 0.04	-0.04 to 0.02
Ecuador	-0.02 to 0.02	0 to 0.05	0 to 0.04	-0.02 to 0.01
Peru	-0.06 to 0.06	0 to 0.15	0 to 0.09	-0.02 to 0.01
Japan	-3.9 to 3.9	**0 to 9.6**	0 to 0.49	-0.36 to 0.18
Russia	-3.1 to 3.1	**0 to 7.8**	0 to 1.2	-0.03 to 0.02
S. Korea	-0.23 to 0.23	0 to 0.57	0 to 0.17	-0.36 to 0.18
Taiwan	-0.41 to 0.41	0 to 1.0	0 to 0.08	-0.19 to 0.09
China	-0.60 to 0.60	0 to 1.6	**0 to 4.5**	-0.22 to 0.11
N. Korea	-0.04 to 0.04	0 to 0.10	0 to 0.09	-0.01 to 0.01
Thailand	-0.09 to 0.09	0 to 0.23	0 to 0.22	-0.44 to 0.22
Vietnam	-0.02 to 0.02	0 to 0.06	0 to 0.27	-0.01 to 0.01
Indonesia	-0.15 to 0.15	0 to 0.38	0 to 0.72	-0.21 to 0.11
Malaysia	-0.06 to 0.06	0 to 0.15	0 to 0.07	-0.20 to 0.05
Philippines	-0.07 to 0.07	0 to 0.17	0 to 0.25	-0.23 to 0.12
Australia	-0.36 to 0.36	0 to 0.90	0 to 0.06	-0.36 to 0.18
New Zealand	-0.05 to 0.05	0 to 0.13	0 to 0.01	-0.11 to 0.06
TOTAL	-19.3 to 19.3	0 to 48.5	0 to 9.8	-8.1 to 4.0

compared to developed nations.

Aggregating across all the Pacific Rim countries reveals that global warming is predicted to cause between $76 billion in benefits to $150 billion in damages. This averages to $37 billion of damages a year or 0.4% of GDP in the 20 countries analyzed.

Nonmarket damages account for over three-fourths of total impacts. Although market damages are potentially large, it is likely that adaptation will mitigate most of these effects. Nonmarket impacts through ecosystem and health effects are likely to prove more intransigent, and will probably become the primary reasons to engage in greenhouse gas control.

Table 2.3 Total Impacts of Global Warming on Pacific Rim Countries[a]

COUNTRY	MARKET ($BILLION)	NONMARKET ($BILLION)	TOTAL ($BILLION)
Canada	-2.1 to 1.0	-0.8 to 2.9	-2.9 to 3.9
Mexico	-1.0 to 2.0	-0.2 to 1.3	-1.2 to 3.3
United States	**-16.3 to 16.9**	**-9.0 to 32.6**	**-25.3 to 49.5**
Chile	-0.5 to 0.3	-0.0 to 0.2	-0.5 to 0.5
Columbia	-0.1 to 0.7	-0.1 to 0.3	-0.2 to 1.0
Ecuador	-0.1 to 0.2	-0.0 to 0.1	-0.1 to 0.3
Peru	-0.1 to 0.3	-0.1 to 0.3	-0.2 to 0.6
Japan	**-4.7 to 20.6**	**-3.9 to 14.4**	**-8.6 to 35.0**
Russia	**-22.3 to 7.7**	**-3.1 to 12.1**	**-25.4 to 19.8**
S. Korea	-1.2 to 1.6	-0.2 to 1.0	-1.4 to 2.6
Taiwan	-0.7 to 2.1	-0.4 to 1.5	-1.1 to 3.6
China	**-3.4 to 8.2**	**-0.6 to 6.7**	**-4.0 to 14.9**
N. Korea	-0.3 to 0.4	-0.1 to 0.2	-0.4 to 0.6
Vietnam	-0.1 to 0.6	-0.0 to 0.4	-0.1 to 1.0
Thailand	-0.6 to 1.0	0.3 to 0.6	-0.3 to 1.6
Indonesia	**-1.1 to 3.4**	-0.2 to 1.3	-1.3 to 4.7
Malaysia	-0.6 to 1.4	-0.1 to 0.3	-0.7 to 1.7
Philippines	-0.5 to 2.0	-0.1 to 0.5	-0.6 to 2.5
Australia	-1.0 to 1.0	-0.5 to 1.3	-1.3 to 2.3
New Zealand	-0.3 to 0.7	-0.1 to 0.2	-0.4 to 0.9
TOTAL	-57.0 to 72.1	-19.8 to 78.2	-76.0 to 150.3

Notes

a. Values are expressed in terms of annual damages in billions of US$ from a +2.5°C temperature, +8% precipitation, +44 cm sea level change.

b. Negative values imply that nonmarket impacts are the opposite sign of total effect. Market impacts exceed total impacts by the same percentage. Negative total impacts imply net benefits.

4 CONCLUSION

This study examines a specific global warming scenario and explores the distribution of effects which might occur across Pacific Rim countries.

Table 2.3, continued

COUNTRY	TOTAL EXPECTED DAMAGES ($BILLION)	% NONMARKET	DAMAGES (% GDP)
Canada	0.5	220% [b]	0.1% [b]
Mexico	1.1	55%	0.7%
United States	**12.1**	**98%**	0.3%
Chile	0.0	100%	0.0%
Columbia	0.4	25%	1.1%
Ecuador	0.0	0%	0.0%
Peru	0.2	50%	0.7%
Japan	**13.2**	40%	0.7%
Russia	-2.8	-161% [b]	-0.1% [b]
S. Korea	0.6	66%	0.5%
Taiwan	1.3	60%	0.6%
China	5.5	56%	**1.7%**
N. Korea	0.1	50%	0.5%
Thailand	0.7	71%	1.3%
Vietnam	0.4	50%	**3.5%**
Indonesia	1.7	35%	**2.2%**
Malaysia	0.5	20%	**1.7%**
Philippines	1.0	20%	**2.9%**
Australia	0.5	**80%**	0.3%
New Zealand	0.3	33%	1.2%
TOTAL	**37.3**	**79%**	**0.4%**

Although strong assumptions are required to derive these estimates, this exercise provides important insights for both policy and research. For policy purposes, the assumptions are useful starting points in order to understand the possible implications of climate change. Most analyses of climate change have focused on costs. This analysis provides some of the first country- and sector-specific impact estimates.

The calculations in this paper highlight the sectors and countries which will be the most sensitive to climate change. To the extent that global warming control is effective, it will require the cooperation of many nations. This analysis is intended to give individual countries some sense of the impacts that they will face if nothing is done.

For research, the calculations are useful in identifying which assumptions are important. That is, which assumptions lead to potentially large impacts. The calculations also reveal which sectors are poorly defined, and have wide ranges of impacts. By making all the assumptions explicit, countries and researchers who feel the assumptions are wrong can see where better and more defensible estimates are needed.

Overall, the analysis indicates that market impacts from climate change are likely to be small on average (they average about 0.1% of GDP). The analysis also indicates that there is a great deal of uncertainty about this result. Additional work, especially outside of the United States, is needed to narrow this uncertainty.

The analysis suggests that nonmarket impacts will dominate climate change damages. These results come from concerns by ecologists that natural systems will be slow to adjust to climate change and will result in substantial disruption of ecosystems. The magnitude of these effects is highly uncertain. Further, what value individual societies place upon these changes is also uncertain.

Finally, the analysis indicates that the distribution of effects across countries is not at all uniform. The developed countries are expected to endure the largest share of absolute damages. Almost two-thirds of the damages will be felt by Japan and the United States. However, these damages average only 0.5% of the incomes of these two countries. Although the remaining damages are spread across many countries, the average impact per unit of GDP will be much higher in developing countries. Further, beyond such broad categories as developed and undeveloped nations, impacts will vary widely. The former Soviet Union, for example, will likely benefit from climate change. Vietnam, the Philippines, and Indonesia, in contrast, may lose over 2% of their GDP to climate impacts. Thus, it is likely that individual countries will find their incentive to control climate impacts unique, making treaties between countries complex at best.

ACKNOWLEDGEMENT

I want to thank Hiro Lee for his valuable comments.

NOTES

1. The IPCC (1990a) predicts a temperature increase of between 1.5–4.5°C by 2060 and yet the published climate models predict an increase of between 4.5–5.5°C in temperature.

2. See, for example, Bazzaz and Fajer (1992), Idso and Kimball (1989), Kimball (1982), Mearns, Rosenzweig and Goldberg (1992), Parry, Porter and Carter (1990), Rosenzweig and Parry (1993), and Strain (1992).

3. Crosson (1993), Kaiser et al. (1993), Mendelsohn, Nordhaus, and Shaw (1994), and Shaw, Mendelsohn and Nordhaus (1994) all show that with adaptation fully modeled, climate change impacts become small and likely beneficial. Further, Kane, Reilly and Tobey (1991) show that even with large agronomic impacts, trade can result in small economic losses.

4. These results are indicated by Adams et al. (1993), Crosson (1993), and Mendelsohn, Nordhaus and Shaw (1994).

5. Strain and Cure (1985), for example, suggests that forest area will increase.

6. Botkin (1979), Davis and Botkin (1985), and Solomon and West (1986) are all concerned about the ability of forest systems to adjust to rapid climate change.

7. See Kalkstein and Valimont (1987), Kalkstein and Davis (1989) and Kalkstein (1991).

REFERENCES

Adams, R., R. Fleming, C. Chang, B. McCarl and C. Rosenzweig (1993), *A Reassessment of the Economic Effects of Global Climate Change on U.S. Agriculture*,Washington, DC: United States Environmental Protection Agency.

Adams, R., D. Glyer and B. McCarl (1989), 'The Economic Effects of Climate Change on U.S. Agriculture: A Preliminary Assessment', in J. Smith and D. Tirpak (eds), *The Potential Effects of Global Climate Change on the United States*, Washington, DC: United States Environmental Protection Agency.

Adams, R., C. Rosenzweig, R. Peart, J. Ritchie, B. McCarl, D. Glyer, B. Curry, J. Jones, K. Boote and H. Allen (1990), 'Global Climate Change and U.S. Agriculture', *Nature*, **345**(6272), 219–24.

Bazzaz, F. and E. Fajer (1992), 'Plant Life in a CO_2-Rich World', *Scientific American*, **266**(1), 68–74.

Botkin, D. (1979), 'A Grandfather Clock Down the Staircase: Stability and Disturbance in Natural Ecosystems', in R. Waring (ed.), *Forests: Fresh Perspectivesfrom Ecosystem Analysis*, Corvallis: Oregon State University Press, pp. 1–10.

Cline, W. (1992), *The Economics of Global Warming*, Washington, DC: Institute for International Economics.

Crosson, P. (1993), 'Impacts of Climate Change on the Agriculture and Economy of the Missouri, Iowa, Nebraska and Kansas (MINK) Region', in H. Kaiser and T. Drennen (eds), *Agricultural Dimensions of Global Climate Change*, Delray Beach, FL: St. Lucie Press.

Davis, M. and D. Botkin (1985), 'Sensitivityof the Cool-Temperate Forests and their Pollen to Rapid Climate Change', *Quaternary Research* **23**, 327–40.

Fankhauser, S. (1993), 'The Economic Cost of Global Warming: Some Monetary Estimates', in Y. Kaya et al. (eds), *Costs, Inputs, and Benefits of CO₂ Mitigation*,Laxenburg, Austria: International Institute of Applied Systems Analysis.

Idso, S. and B. Kimball (1989), 'Growth Response of Carrot and Radish to Atmospheric CO_2 Enrichment', *Environmental and Experimental Botany*, **29**(2).

Intergovernmental Panel on Climate Change (1990a), *Scientific Assessment of Climate Change: Report Prepared for IPCC by Working Group I*, New York: World Meteorological Organization and United Nations Environment Programme.

Intergovernmental Panel on Climate Change (1990b), *Potential Impacts of Climate Change: Report Prepared for IPCC by Working Group II*, New York: World Meteorological Organization and United Nations Environment Programme.

Intergovernmental Panel on Climate Change (1992), *Supplemental Report to the IPCC Scientific Assessment*, Cambridge: Cambridge University Press.

Kaiser, H. and T. Drennen (eds) (1993), *Agricultural Dimensions of Global Climate Change*, Delray Beach, FL: St. Lucie Press.

Kaiser, H., S. Riha, D. Wilkes and R. Sampath (1993), 'Adaptation to Global Climate Change at the Farm Level',in H. Kaiser and T. Drennen (eds), *Agricultural Dimensions of Global Climate Change*, Delray Beach, FL: St. Lucie Press.

Kalkstein, L. (1991), 'A New Approach to Evaluate the Impact of Climate on Human Mortality', *Environmental Health Perspectives*, **96**, 145–50.

Kalkstein, L. and R. Davis (1989), 'Weather and Human Mortality: An Evaluation of Demographic and Interregional Responses in the United States', *Annals of the Association of American Geographers*, **79**(44).

Kalkstein, L. and K. Valimont (1987), 'Effect on Human Health', in D. Tirpak (ed.), *Potential Effects of Future Climate Changes on Forest and Vegetation, Agriculture, Water Resources, and Human Health*, vol. V, Washington, DC: United States Environmental Protection Agency, pp. 122–52.

Kane, S.,J. Reilly and J. Tobey (1991), *Climate Change: Economic Implications for World Agriculture*,Washington, DC: United States Department of Agriculture.

Kimball, B. (1982), 'Carbon Dioxide and Agricultural Yield', *Agronomy Journal*, **75**, 779–88.

Linder, K.,M. Gibbs, and M. Inglis (1987), 'Potential Impacts of Climate Change on Electric Utilities', Report 88–2. Albany, NY: NY State Energy Research and Development Agency.

Mearns, L., C. Rosenzweig and R. Goldberg (1992), 'Effect of Changes in Interannual Climatic Variability on CERES-Wheat Yields: Sensitivity and $2\times CO_2$ General Circulation Model Studies', *Agricultural and Forest Meteorology*, **62**, 159–89.

Mendelsohn, R. and D. Shaw (1994), *The Impact of Climate Change on Mortality*, New Haven, CT: Yale School of Forestry and Environmental Studies.

Mendelsohn, R., W. Nordhaus and D. Shaw (1994), 'The Impact of Global Warming on Agriculture: A Ricardian Analysis', *American Economic Review*, **84**(4), 753–71.

Nordhaus, W. (1991), 'To Slow or not to Slow: The Economics of the Greenhouse Effect', *The Economic Journal*, **101**, 920–37.

Parry, M., J. Porter and T. Carter (1990), 'Agriculture: Climatic Change and its Implications', *Trends in Ecology and Evolution*, **5**(9), 318–22.

Rosenzweig, C. and M. Parry (1993), 'Potential Impacts of Climate Change on World Food Supply: A Summary of Recent International Study', in H. Kaiser and T. Drennen (eds), *Agricultural Dimensions of Global Climate Change*, Delray Beach, FL: St. Lucie Press.

Shaw, D., R. Mendelsohn, and W. Nordhaus (1994), *The Impact of Climate Variation on Agriculture*, New Haven, CT: Yale School of Forestry and Environmental Studies.

Solomon, A. and D. West (1986), 'Atmospheric Carbon Dioxide Change: Agent of Future Forest Growth or Decline?', in J. Titus (ed.), *Effects of Stratospheric Ozone and Global Climate*. Washington DC: United States Environmental Protection Agency.

Strain, B. (1992), 'Atmospheric Carbon Dioxide: A Plant Fertilizer?', *The New Biologist*, **4**(2), 87–9.

Strain, B. and J. Cure (eds) (1985), *Direct Effects of Increasing Carbon Dioxide on Vegetation*, Washington, DC: United States Department of Energy.

3. The Framework Convention and Climate Change Policy in Asia

Jonathan Coppel and Hiro Lee[*]

1 INTRODUCTION

The United Nations' Framework Convention on Climate Change (FCCC), signed at the Earth Summit in Rio de Janeiro in the summer of 1992, outlines greenhouse gas (GHG) abatement policies to reduce the risk of climate change. The FCCC explicitly acknowledges the global dimension of climate change and hence the importance of securing the cooperation of major GHG-emitting countries. Less-than-comprehensive country involvement would imply that the global costs of policies to limit the risk of climate change would be greater than necessary, since opportunities to reduce emissions in low-cost countries would be excluded. Similarly, with narrow participation, the potential benefits from limiting climate damages would be smaller relative to the global cost of achieving a given level of abatement.

However, appealing to economic efficiency alone will not be sufficient to unite countries to implement cost-effective policies. The major emitters of GHG are a heterogeneous group including developed countries, newly industrialized countries, developing countries, oil exporters, centrally planned economies, and formerly centrally planned economies. Asia by itself includes countries in each of these categories. Consequently, securing the cooperation of major emitting nations is complicated. The costs of abatement among a diverse group of countries are likely to vary considerably depending upon existing energy taxes and subsidies, real output, relative energy prices, the composition of energy demand, and the level of technological development. The distribution of benefits in terms of reduced risk of adverse climate change that countries derive from a GHG abatement policy is also likely to be dispersed. Greater cooperation is more likely to be forthcoming if the policy process and policy outcomes are perceived to be fair. Perhaps partly for this reason the initial FCCC commitments are limited to Annex I countries (consisting of all OECD countries except

26

Mexico, the former Soviet Union and Eastern Europe) with no specific targets for developing countries.

Two principles of great importance to the FCCC are equity and economic efficiency. The FCCC provides scope to accomplish these two objectives jointly via a provision called 'joint implementation' (JI). Specifically, Annex I countries can implement policies and measures jointly with other parties or assist other parties to achieve the objective of the convention. The principle attraction of joint implementation is that it separates the question of where abatement is undertaken, maintaining incentives for cost minimization, from the question of who should pay. In this paper we evaluate the role and relative importance of Asian developing countries in mitigating global carbon emissions using the OECD's global general equilibrium environment (GREEN) model. The focus is on the relative costs of abatement, the efficiency gains from joint implementation, and the distributional implications of participation in an international agreement.

We analyze the role which China, India and the dynamic Asian econo-mies (DAEs) can play in improving the cost-effectiveness of carbon abatement policies by jointly implementing the FCCC emission target using tradable emission quotas as a policy instrument. The analysis is not intended to recommend specific policy solutions, but to inform policy makers by identifying areas where agreement among Annex I and Asian countries to jointly mitigate carbon emissions may prove difficult and to suggest mechanisms for reaching such agreement. Our results suggest that if joint implementation can be conducted carefully, both Annex I and Asian countries may experience an improvement in their real income compared with the case where only Annex I countries curtail CO_2 emissions.

2 JOINT IMPLEMENTATION AND THE FCCC

The FCCC recognizes the potential gains from international cooperation and endorses principles which share the benefits and encourage universal implementation of net GHG abatement policies. The opening sentence of the FCCC states, 'change in the earth's climate and its adverse effects are a common concern of humankind'. It then acknowledges, in the preamble, 'the global nature of climate change calls for the widest possible coopera-tion by all countries and their participation in an effective and appropriate international response, in accordance with their common but differentiated responsibilities and respective capabilities and their social and economic conditions' (United Nations 1992).

The FCCC provides scope for a mechanism which potentially could attract broad participation in an international GHG reduction policy.

Specifically, paragraph 2a of Article 4, referred to here as the provision for joint implementation, states: 'developed country Parties and other Parties included in Annex I may implement policies and measures jointly with other Parties and may assist other Parties in contributing to the achievement of the objective of the convention'. One way of doing this would be to allow a participating country to earn credit towards its own abatement obligation by financing abatement in another country whether it is part of the agreement or not. Organized on a bilateral negotiated basis, such action is called an offset. As offset schemes develop, more sophisticated exchange mechanisms could be envisaged, perhaps evolving towards a market for tradable emission quotas. The term joint implementation has been used to characterize both ends of the spectrum. Here, joint implementation is examined using tradable quotas as the policy instrument, recognizing that a comprehensive system encompassing all GHGs would not start from scratch but could ultimately evolve to embrace an international market for emission rights. The advantage of focusing on tradable quotas is that transfer mechanisms are necessarily transparent, elegantly demonstrate the principle of JI and are straightforwardly simulated with GREEN.

The scope for joint implementation in Asia to improve the cost-effectiveness of Annex I carbon emission stabilization policies is considerable. The share of global carbon emissions in China, India and the DAEs was 15% in 1990, having grown rapidly from earlier levels. A more than five-fold increase in carbon emissions is expected between 1990 and 2050 as these economies continue to grow at significantly faster rates than the rest of the world, demanding higher energy requirements. By 2050, the share of carbon emissions in China and India alone could account for about 24% of the global total, and the DAEs for an additional 4%. Moreover, China and India have among the world's highest carbon intensities of energy consumption and energy requirements relative to GDP, reflecting the large coal reserves and pricing policies in these countries.[1] As such, the potential to reduce emissions through fossil fuel substitution and via energy efficiency improvements at a low marginal cost is large. For OECD countries, the flexibility to source emission cuts in Asia could lower the total cost of climate change policies. In the process, joint implementation could be a source of new revenues for Asia and an initial basis upon which future global climate change policies could be built.

3   BRIEF OVERVIEW OF THE GREEN MODEL

The current version of GREEN consists of twelve regional sub-models, eleven producer sectors, and four consumer sectors.[2] All pairs of regions are linked together by bilateral trade flows of each tradable good. The model is simulated over the period 1985–2050, in five steps of five-year intervals up to 2010 with two further steps of twenty-year intervals. As GREEN is a recursive dynamic model, the solution for each period can be solved independently of any future period. In other words, there is no forward-looking behavior. The periods are linked together through factor accumulation equations which can be either exogenous, as is the case for labor supply, or endogenous, as for capital supply.

Eight of the eleven sectors cover the supply and distribution of energy: coal, crude oil, natural gas, refined petroleum, electricity, and three non-conventional backstop fuels.[3] The remaining sectors are broad aggregates: agriculture, energy-intensive industries, and other industries and services. In each conventional producer sector, production technologies are modeled mainly by nested constant elasticity of substitution (CES) functions. Non-energy intermediate inputs, as well as capital and fixed factors (e.g., land in agriculture), are used in constant proportions. Within each period, capital is classified as being either old (or installed) or new. New capital is generated by the previous period's investment. This vintage structure of capital allows for differentiating the substitution possibilities across inputs by the age of capital.[4]

Each region has one representative consumer (household), which receives all labor and capital income. The model uses a static version of the extended linear expenditure system (ELES) to determine the optimal allocation of the consumer's disposable income for four broad consumer goods (food and beverages, fuels and power, transport and communication, and other goods and services) and household saving.[5] The four consumer goods are transformed from producer goods using a consumer-production technology matrix.

Trade is modeled using the so-called Armington assumption. All goods except crude oil are differentiated by region of origin. This implies a two-level nested CES structure. At the first level, each agent in the economy divides an aggregate demand for a good between a domestic component and an aggregate import component. At the second level, the aggregate import demand is distributed across different regions of the model. Crude oil is assumed to be a homogeneous commodity, and the world price is identical across all regions.

Some features of GREEN make it particularly well suited as a tool to analyze aspects of joint implementation in Asia. Despite being a global general equilibrium model, GREEN distinguishes the region's major emitters – China and India – with a consistent treatment of world trade flows and energy price distortions. The model allows for tradable quotas, where each region is allocated an initial quota of emission rights which can be traded. These features make it well suited to analyzing the effects of cooperative international agreements upon economic welfare, real output, energy consumption and international trade.

The present version of GREEN does have some limitations. GREEN, as with other models of its kind, is unable to evaluate the benefits of reducing CO_2 emissions in terms of slowing climate change. Secondly, sinks and GHGs other than CO_2 are not measured, and the menu of possible policy instruments excludes command and control measures.[6] Finally, GREEN, being a 'top-down' type of model, has limited ability to characterize the portfolio of technologies and their penetration.

4   THE BASELINE SCENARIO AND CARBON EMISSIONS IN ASIA

The baseline scenario describes the path of carbon emissions which could be expected in the absence of policies designed to reduce their growth. It is an important step in quantifying the costs and distribution of abatement in different countries since it determines the size of emission cuts needed to achieve a given target. Table 3.1 summarizes the assumptions on gross domestic product (GDP) and population growth rates over the period 1990–2050. These are based on the guidelines used for the OECD Model Comparisons Project and the Energy Modeling Forum Number 12 (EMF 12) exercise, with some modifications to the GDP projections in the former Soviet Union, Eastern Europe and China.[7]

Four key assumptions are explicitly built into the baseline scenario. First, it is assumed that any existing subsidies on oil will be gradually eliminated by 2000 and those on coal and natural gas by 2010 to reflect major price reforms that have been instigated or planned in several countries currently subsidizing the production of fossil fuels.[8] Presently, the largest subsidies are in the former Soviet Union, especially for oil and natural gas.[9] Eastern Europe, China and India also subsidize fossil fuels extensively, creating wide wedges between domestic and world prices.[10]

Second, the three backstop energy options are assumed to become available in 2010. The same backstop prices as those used in EMF 12 (1990) are assumed in GREEN. Third, while coal reserves are assumed to be unlimited over the period to 2050, oil and natural gas reserves are finite and their potential supplies depend upon the initial levels of proven and yet-to-find reserves, the rate of extraction from proven reserves and the rate of discovery of new reserves.[11] The potential oil supply constraint is projected to become binding by 2030. Finally, the baseline does not assume any discretionary policy action, except the subsidy removal already discussed, to

Table 3.1 Real GDP and Population Projections underlying the Baseline Scenario in GREEN, per annum percentage changes

	1990 Level[a]		1990-2000		2000-2010		2010-2030		2030-2050		1990-2050	
	RGDP	POP	RGDP	POP	RGDP	POP	RGDP	POP	RGDP	POP	RGDP	POP
United States	4,178	250	2.6	0.7	2.1	0.6	1.9	0.3	1.6	-0.1	2.0	0.3
Japan	1,515	123	3.7	0.3	2.7	0.1	2.5	-0.2	2.2	-0.3	2.6	-0.1
European Community	2,477	324	2.2	0.1	1.7	0.0	1.5	-0.2	1.3	-0.3	1.6	-0.1
Other OECD Countries[b]	876	127	2.2	1.2	1.7	0.9	1.5	0.6	1.3	0.2	1.6	0.6
Former Soviet Union	722	289	0.0	0.6	2.3	0.5	3.0	0.4	2.3	0.2	2.1	0.4
Eastern Europe	268	121	0.0	0.4	2.3	0.3	3.0	0.2	2.3	0.1	2.1	0.2
China	549	1,117	6.0	1.3	5.0	0.9	4.3	0.6	3.5	0.2	4.4	0.6
India	227	832	4.6	1.8	4.4	1.4	3.9	1.0	3.4	0.6	4.0	1.1
Dynamic Asian Economies	322	190	4.4	1.4	4.2	1.1	3.7	0.7	3.2	0.3	3.7	0.8
Brazil	230	150	4.4	1.7	4.2	1.2	3.7	0.9	3.2	0.5	3.7	1.0
Energy Exporting Countries	1,248	744	3.6	2.3	3.4	2.0	3.1	1.5	2.7	0.9	3.1	1.5
Rest of the world	729	994	3.5	2.6	3.1	2.3	2.7	1.9	2.4	1.2	2.8	1.8
Annex I Countries	10,035	1,234	2.4	0.5	2.1	0.3	1.9	0.2	1.7	-0.1	1.9	0.2
Asia[c]	1,099	2,139	5.1	1.5	4.6	1.1	4.0	0.8	3.4	0.4	4.1	0.8
World	13,341	5,260	2.8	1.6	2.5	1.3	2.3	0.9	2.0	0.5	2.3	1.0

Notes

a. Real GDP (RGDP) in billions of 1985 US dollars, population (POP) in million persons.

b. Mexico excluded.

c. In our definition, Asia consists of China, India, and dynamic Asian economies. Malaysia and Indonesia are aggregated into the energy exporting countries, whereas other Asian countries (e.g. Vietnam and Pakistan) are aggregated into the rest of the world category.

31

Table 3.2 CO$_2$ Emissions in the Baseline Scenario[a]

	1990	2000	2010	2020	2030	2040	2050	1990 share	2050 share	Average growth[b]
United States	1,350	1,575	1,783	1,988	2,193	2,461	2,730	22.9	16.0	1.2
Japan	333	487	512	595	678	833	989	5.6	5.8	1.8
European Community	823	961	1,030	1,121	1,212	1,371	1,530	13.9	9.0	1.0
Other OECD Countries[c]	295	354	404	457	509	573	637	5.0	3.7	1.3
Former Soviet Union	1,055	887	977	1,224	1,472	1,834	2,196	17.9	12.9	1.2
Eastern Europe	359	298	321	395	468	578	688	6.1	4.0	1.1
China	601	776	989	1,359	1,730	2,402	3,073	10.2	18.0	2.8
India	151	204	277	400	522	756	989	2.6	5.8	3.2
Dynamic Asian Economies	108	156	210	287	363	508	653	1.8	3.8	3.0
Brazil	96	128	159	210	260	377	494	1.6	2.9	2.8
Energy Exporting Countries	424	524	637	834	1,031	1,365	1,699	7.2	10.0	2.3
Rest of the wrld	310	413	544	711	877	1,120	1,362	5.3	8.0	2.5
World	5,907	6,762	7,842	9,580	11,317	14,178	17,040	100.0	100.0	1.8

Notes

a. Carbon emissions in million tons of carbon, shares and growth rates in percentages.
b. Average annual growth rates over the period 1990-2050.
c. Mexico excluded.

32

Table 3.3 Sensitivity of CO$_2$ Emissions to Different GDP Projections underlying the Baseline Scenario[a]

	1990	2000	2010	2020	2030	2040	2050	1990 share	2050 share	Average growth[b]
Benchmark Asian GDP growth rates										
OECD Countries[c]	2,802	3,376	3,729	4,160	4,592	5,239	5,886	47.4	34.5	1.2
Annex I Countries	4,217	4,561	5,027	5,779	6,532	7,651	8,769	71.4	51.5	1.2
Asia	860	1,136	1,476	2,046	2,616	3,665	4,715	14.6	27.7	2.9
World	5,907	6,762	7,842	9,580	11,317	14,178	17,040	100.0	100.0	1.8
1 percentage point higher Asian GDP growth rates										
OECD Countries[c]	2,802	3,373	3,720	4,156	4,592	5,255	5,917	47.4	28.7	1.3
Annex I Countries	4,217	4,559	5,018	5,781	6,543	7,682	8,820	71.4	42.8	1.2
Asia	860	1,238	1,749	2,752	3,755	5,943	8,131	14.6	39.4	3.8
World	5,907	6,862	8,108	10,303	12,498	16,555	20,613	100.0	100.0	2.1
2 percentage points higher Asian GDP growth rates										
OECD Countries[c]	2,802	3,370	3,710	4,153	4,595	5,275	5,955	47.4	22.4	1.3
Annex I Countries	4,217	4,556	5,010	5,785	6,560	7,722	8,885	71.4	33.4	1.2
Asia	860	1,348	2,069	3,719	5,368	9,626	13,884	14.6	52.2	4.7
World	5,907	6,970	8,421	11,296	14,170	20,381	26,592	100.0	100.0	2.5

Notes

a. Carbon emissions in million tons of carbon, shares and growth rates in percentages.
b. Average annual growth rates of carbon emissions over the period 1990–2050.
c. Mexico excluded.

33

curtail carbon emissions.

Table 3.2 presents carbon emission levels underlying the baseline scenario for the six Annex I regions, three Asian regions, Brazil, energy exporting countries, and an aggregate rest-of-the-world region of the model. World CO_2 emissions are expected to increase by 1.8% per annum, from 5.9 billion tons of carbon in 1990 to 17.0 billion tons in 2050. Carbon emissions in the three Asian regions are projected to grow at significantly higher rates (2.7, 3.2, and 3.0% for China, India, and DAEs, respectively) than Annex I countries (1.2%).[12] As a consequence, the combined share of Asian CO_2 emissions could increase from 15% of world emissions in 1990 to 28% in 2050. This contrasts with a reduction in emission shares of all six Annex I regions, with the combined share declining from 71% in 1990 to 51% in 2050.

Since a great deal of uncertainty exists concerning the real GDP growth trends assumed in the baseline scenario, we have conducted a sensitivity analysis of carbon emissions to different GDP projections for the Asian regions. Given that the projected annual growth rates for Asia appear to represent a lower bound, they are first raised by 1 percentage point and then by 2 percentage points per annum over the period 1990–2050.[13] The results, summarized in Table 3.3, indicate that the levels of carbon emissions are quite sensitive to GDP growth rate assumptions. An increase in the annual growth rates of China, India, and DAEs by percentage point per annum for the whole period could raise the combined projected CO_2 emissions in these regions from 4.7 to 8.1 billion tons of carbon and their combined share from 28 to 39% of world emissions in 2050. The results of an increase in their GDP growth rates by 2 percentage points are dramatic: the Asian regions could emit almost 14 billion tons of carbon, accounting for 52% of world emissions by 2050. The results of this exercise suggest that carbon emissions in Asia could exceed those of Annex I countries by the middle of the next century if Asian countries continue to grow at significantly higher rates than the rest of the world.

Table 3.4 shows primary energy consumption levels and shares for selected aggregate regions in the baseline scenario. Traditional fossil fuels (coal, oil and natural gas) maintain the predominant shares in all regions although their compositions differ considerably over time and across regions. The global market share of coal increases while that of oil decreases after 2010 as the oil reserves decline and the relative price of oil starts to rise. The increase in coal consumption is especially large in the former Soviet Union, China and India, and by 2050 the market share of coal would exceed 70% in these countries.[14]

Backstop options are assumed to become available with infinite supply elasticities (i.e., constant supply price) from 2010 onward.[15] The market

Table 3.4   *Total Primary Energy Consumption and Fuel Shares in the Baseline Scenario (total consumption in million tons of oil equivalent, fuel shares in %)*

	1990	2000	2010	2020	2030	2040	2050
OECD Countries'							
Total Energy							
Consumption	3,718	4,524	5,400	6,038	6,676	7,400	8,124
Coal	23.0	21.9	22.8	25.0	26.7	27.7	28.5
Oil	42.0	45.9	41.8	35.3	30.0	21.2	14.0
Natural Gas	19.5	17.9	17.5	16.7	16.2	16.5	16.8
Conventional							
Electricity	15.5	14.3	12.6	13.4	14.0	14.1	14.2
Synthetic Fuel	0.0	0.0	0.2	1.7	2.9	7.1	10.6
Carbon-free							
Electricity Backstop	0.0	0.0	5.1	7.9	10.2	13.4	15.9
FSU and Eastern Europe							
Total Energy							
Consumption	2,034	1,406	1,473	1,807	2,140	2,592	3,044
Coal	32.4	49.9	56.7	61.8	65.4	67.6	69.2
Oil	30.7	16.7	14.2	10.4	7.8	5.0	3.2
Natural Gas	30.6	25.1	19.8	17.7	16.3	16.1	16.0
Conventional							
Electricity	6.4	8.3	9.3	9.7	10.0	9.7	9.6
Synthetic Fuel	0.0	0.0	0.1	0.4	0.6	1.5	2.1
Carbon-free							
Electricity Backstop	0.0	0.0	0.0	0.0	0.0	0.0	0.0
Annex I Countries							
Total Energy							
Consumption	5,752	5,930	6,874	7,845	8,816	9,992	11,168
Coal	26.3	28.5	30.0	33.4	36.0	38.0	39.6
Oil	38.0	39.0	35.9	29.6	24.6	17.0	11.0
Natural Gas	23.4	19.6	17.9	17.0	16.2	16.4	16.6
Conventional							
Electricity	12.3	12.9	11.9	12.6	13.1	13.0	12.9
Synthetic Fuel	0.0	0.0	0.2	1.4	2.3	5.7	8.3
Carbon-free							
Electricity Backstop	0.0	0.0	4.0	6.1	7.8	9.9	11.6

Table 3.4, continued

	1990	2000	2010	2020	2030	2040	2050
Asia							
Total Energy							
Consumption	997	1,326	1,770	2,357	2,943	3,839	4,734
Coal	64.5	60.7	58.3	61.8	63.9	68.2	70.8
Oil	27.3	31.3	33.2	28.3	25.3	17.2	12.1
Natural Gas	2.3	2.4	2.8	3.1	3.2	3.4	3.4
Conventional							
Electricity	5.9	5.6	5.1	4.6	4.3	3.8	3.4
Synthetic Fuel	0.0	0.0	0.1	1.3	2.0	5.9	8.3
Carbon-free Electricity							
Backstop	0.0	0.0	0.5	0.9	1.2	1.7	2.0
World							
Total Energy							
Consumption	8,058	8,851	10,743	12,803	14,863	17,501	20,139
Coal	29.3	31.1	31.9	35.4	38.0	41.0	43.1
Oil	40.4	41.3	39.6	33.2	28.6	19.7	13.1
Natural Gas	19.1	16.2	14.9	14.7	14.6	15.3	15.9
Conventional							
Electricity	11.2	11.5	10.5	10.7	10.9	10.5	10.3
Synthetic Fuel	0.0	0.0	0.2	1.8	2.9	7.2	10.4
Carbon-free Electricity							
Backstop	0.0	0.0	2.8	4.1	5.1	6.3	7.1

Note
* Mexico excluded.

share of carbon-based synthetic fuel begins to increase much more rapidly after 2030 when the relative oil price is projected to rise sharply. Overall, backstop energy fuels make significant inroads in OECD countries, where their market share gradually increases to 27% by 2050. In Japan, conventional electricity is almost entirely replaced by the carbon-free electric backstop option by the middle of the next century. The market shares of these new energy sources would remain low in China and India while those in DAEs increase steadily from 3% in 2010 to 29% in 2050. The third backstop option, carbon-free liquid fuel, never becomes competitive in any region before 2050.

Two other carbon emission measures of policy relevance are per capita emissions and carbon intensity, which are plotted in Figure 3.1. The US has the highest per capita emissions, followed by the former Soviet Union and Eastern Europe. By contrast, all three Asian regions have low per capita emissions.[16] In particular, per capita emissions in India are one-thirtieth

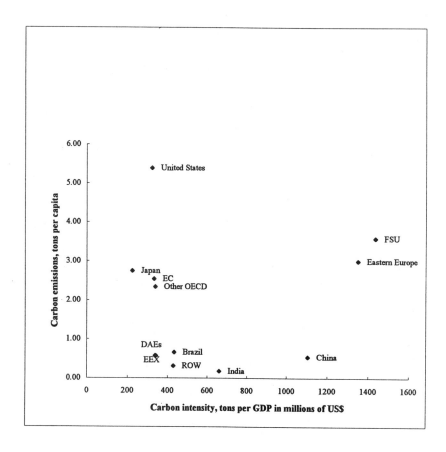

Figure 3.1 1990 Per Capita Carbon Emissions and Carbon Intensity in Countries/ Regions of the GREEN Model

those of the US. These statistics can have important implications for tradable emission quota allocation methods. Countries with high values of per capita emissions (e.g., the US and the former Soviet Union) would probably favor an allocation of quotas based on reference year emission shares, whereas those with low values (e.g., India and China) would probably favor an allocation rule based on population shares.

Carbon intensity, the ratio of carbon emissions to GDP, provides a measure of carbon efficiency and a proximate measure of energy efficiency. Using this measure, Japan is about seven times more efficient than the former Soviet Union. Among the Asian regions, there are also large disparities: DAEs are about three times as efficient as China. However, because GDP is converted from national currencies to US dollars using 1985 exchange rates, this measure is subject to some bias. If instead, purchasing power parity (PPP) measures were used for the conversion of GDP, disparities in carbon intensities in Asia would largely disappear. Among the Annex I countries, however, Japan would remain the most efficient and the former Soviet Union the least efficient, the latter emitting about four times more carbon per GDP measured in PPP than the former.

5   THE FCCC, ANNEX I STABILIZATION, AND GAINS FROM ASIAN COOPERATION

A doubling of CO_2 concentrations is a standard benchmark used by climate scientists to evaluate the climatic impact of the enhanced greenhouse effect. The IPCC reports that a doubling of CO_2 equivalent could evoke a major climatic change, increasing average global temperatures by between $1.5°C$ and $4.5°C$ with a central estimate of $2.5°C$. These estimates, in part, motivated negotiation of the FCCC, and, as such, reflect a common concern that current emission trends cannot continue indefinitely. A doubling of CO_2 concentrations can therefore be considered a useful point of reference for evaluating climate change policies in the context of the FCCC.[17]

The objective of the FCCC is to achieve a 'stabilization of greenhouse gas concentrations in the atmosphere at a level that would prevent dangerous anthropogenic interference with the climate system' (Article 2, FCCC). Currently, given the many uncertainties, it is difficult to identify a GHG abatement target which could, with confidence, ensure fulfillment of this objective. Rather, the commitments suggested in the FCCC embody a precautionary approach: Annex I countries commit themselves to take immediate action in a flexible manner as a first step towards comprehensive response strategies at the global level. In particular, Annex I countries are committed to implement policies which 'will demonstrate that developed countries are taking the lead in modifying longer-term trends in anthropogenic emissions consistent with the objective of the convention, recognizing that the return by the end of the present decade to earlier levels of anthropogenic emissions would contribute to such modification'. The base year implied by 'earlier levels' is suggested in paragraph 2b of the FCCC as 1990.

In order to simulate FCCC climate change policies with GREEN, several interpretations of the FCCC are necessary. The FCCC gives no indication of whether the commitment to stabilize emissions continues beyond the year 2000. It is however, unlikely, assuming the continued risk of climate change,

Table 3.5 Summary of Carbon Emission Results under Alternative Scenarios

	1990 Level[a]	2000	2010	2020	2030	2040	2050
		(percentage change relative to the baseline scenario)					

Scenario 1: Annex I countries stabilize their emissions at 1990 levels by country-specific carbon taxes

United States	1,350	-13	-23	-31	-38	-45	-50
Japan	333	-33	-35	-44	-50	-59	-66
European Community	823	-15	-20	-27	-32	-40	-46
Other OECD Countries[b]	295	-17	-28	-36	-42	-49	-54
Former Soviet Union	1,055	-2	-3	-19	-29	-43	-53
Eastern Europe	359	1	1	-13	-22	-37	-47
China	601	-1	-1	-1	-1	0	1
India	151	0	0	0	-1	0	0
Dynamic Asian Economies	108	5	3	2	1	1	1
Other Regions[c]	830	0	0	-1	-1	1	2
Annex I Countries	4,217	-13	-19	-28	-35	-45	-52
Asia	860	0	0	0	0	0	1
World	5,907	-9	-12	-17	-21	-24	-26

Scenario 2: Annex I countries stabilize their emissions at 1990 levels by a uniform carbon tax

United States	1,350	-7	-16	-27	-35	-44	-51
Japan	333	-4	-9	-18	-24	-35	-42
European Community	823	-4	-10	-18	-24	-33	-40
Other OECD Countries[b]	295	-8	-18	-28	-36	-44	-50
Former Soviet Union	1,055	-16	-26	-40	-50	-60	-67
Eastern Europe	359	-10	-16	-27	-35	-45	-52
China	601	0	0	0	0	1	1
India	151	0	0	0	0	0	0
Dynamic Asian Economies	108	1	1	1	0	1	2
Other Regions[c]	830	0	0	0	0	2	3
Annex I Countries	4,217	-8	-16	-27	-35	-45	-52
Asia	860	0	0	0	0	1	1
World	5,907	-5	-10	-16	-20	-24	-26

Table 3.5, continued

	1990 Level[a]	2000	2010	2020	2030	2040	2050
		(percentage change relative to the baseline scenario)					

Scenario 3: Annex I and Asian countries cooperate to reduce emissions by the equivalent of Annex I stabilization at 1990 levels by a uniform carbon tax

	1990 Level	2000	2010	2020	2030	2040	2050
United States	1,350	-5	-12	-18	-23	-27	-30
Japan	333	-2	-6	-10	-12	-16	-18
European Community	823	-3	-7	-10	-13	-17	-19
Other OECD Countries[b]	295	-6	-14	-19	-24	-28	-31
Former Soviet Union	1,055	-11	-19	-26	-31	-36	-40
Eastern Europe	359	-7	-11	-17	-21	-25	-27
China	601	-12	-20	-31	-37	-42	-45
India	151	-11	-22	-33	-39	-45	-48
Dynamic Asian Economies	108	-4	-9	-14	-18	-22	-24
Other Regions[c]	830	0	0	0	0	1	2
Annex I Countries	4,217	-6	-12	-17	-22	-26	-29
Asia	860	-10	-19	-29	-35	-40	-43
World	5,907	-6	-11	-17	-21	-24	-26

Notes

a. Million tons of carbon.

b. Mexico excluded.

c. Other regions include Brazil, energy exporting countries, and rest of the world.

that countries will abandon their commitment to prevent dangerous anthropogenic interference with the climate system. Accordingly, it is assumed that Annex I-equivalent emissions are stabilized throughout the period to 2050. Secondly, the FCCC refers to all greenhouse gases not included in the Montréal protocol. Because of the complex nature of some GHGs, such as methane (which is important in Asia), GREEN does not compute all GHG emissions. Rather, attention is focused on the GHG most important in quantity, carbon dioxide, which represents about 55% of all GHG emissions and 75% of energy-related GHG emissions.[18]

5.1 Stabilization of Annex I CO_2 Emissions under Alternative Scenarios

This section discusses the results of three alternative Annex I stabilization scenarios. In the first scenario, Annex I countries stabilize their CO_2 emissions at 1990 levels over the 1995–2050 period by adopting country-specific carbon taxes as the policy instrument. The second scenario is the same as the first except that a uniform carbon tax is imposed to attain the same emission target. In the third scenario, the agreement to reduce world emissions from baseline projections by an amount equivalent to that resulting from stabilizing emissions of Annex I countries by a uniform carbon tax is extended to include China, India, and DAEs. In all three experiments, revenue neutrality is assumed; i.e., tax revenues are recycled within the same country in a lump-sum manner.

Table 3.5 summarizes the carbon emission results. For Annex I countries to stabilize emissions at 1990 levels would require a reduction of their emissions by 52% in 2050 compared to the baseline.[19] This translates into a cut of global emissions by 26%. As shown in Table 3.5, those countries/ regions with relatively high emission growth in the baseline (e.g., Japan) would be required to reduce emissions by larger percentages than those with relatively low growth (e.g., EC and Eastern Europe). Accordingly, carbon taxes are relatively high in countries with rapid baseline emission growth (Table 3.6). Country-specific carbon taxes also depend upon other variables, including the composition of energy demand, relative energy prices, and the inter-fuel elasticities of substitution.

Different patterns of emission abatement across regions emerge when a uniform carbon tax is imposed (Scenario 2). The distribution of emission cuts shifts from countries with relatively high marginal abatement costs (e.g., Japan) to countries with relatively low marginal abatement costs (e.g., the former Soviet Union) until the marginal abatement cost in every Annex I region is equalized at the common carbon tax rate. The uniform carbon tax is significantly lower than the emission-weighted average of country-specific taxes, particularly before backstop options become available in 2010 (Table 3.6).

If the Asian countries were to participate in the agreement to stabilize the equivalent of Annex I emissions (Scenario 3), the average tax burden would be further reduced. At the same time, the burden of stabilizing emissions would shift from the OECD countries to China and India (Table 3.5). Thus, there will be both efficiency gains and distributional effects from this international agreement, both of which will be evaluated in more detail in the subsequent sections.

5.2 Welfare Effects of Annex I Stabilization and Asian Cooperation

Table 3.7 summarizes the welfare results of the three experiments. Specifically, it gives percentage changes in Hicksian 'equivalent variation' (EV) relative to the baseline scenario.[20] Levying distortionary taxes unequivocally reduces economic welfare, but it also alters the terms of trade

Table 3.6   Summary of Carbon Tax Results under Alternative Scenarios (1985 US dollars per ton of carbon)

	2000	2010	2020	2030	2040	2050
Scenario 1: Annex I countries stabilize their emissions at 1990 levels by country-specific carbon taxes						
United States	52	62	74	87	112	138
Japan	246	76	146	216	238	260
European Community	79	68	88	109	135	162
Other OECD Countries*	54	66	84	102	126	150
Former Soviet Union	0	0	14	28	48	68
Eastern Europe	0	0	21	42	78	114
Asia and Other Regions	0	0	0	0	0	0
Scenario 2: Annex I countries stabilize their emissions at 1990 levels by a uniform carbon tax						
Annex I Countries	19	34	54	74	101	129
Asia and Other Regions	0	0	0	0	0	0
Scenario 3: Annex I and Asian countries cooperate to reduce emissions by the equivalent of Annex I stabilization at 1990 levels by a uniform carbon tax						
Annex I and Asia	12	21	26	31	34	38
Other Regions	0	0	0	0	0	0

Note

* Mexico excluded.

which could either raise or lower welfare. In the first scenario, for example, favorable terms of trade movements associated with a decline in oil import demand more than offset the negative welfare effects of a carbon tax in the US in 2000. For Annex I countries as a whole, real income losses occur in every period and increase over time (from 0.3% in 2000 to 2.4% in 2050) because of the progressively tighter abatement constraint. Individually, energy exporting countries (EEX) incur the greatest loss, experiencing a 4.9% loss in real income in 2010. This loss results from reductions in their oil export demand, causing a deterioration in their terms of trade, particularly up to 2010. By contrast, Brazil gains from Annex I stabilization, largely because of the improvement in its terms of trade. For China, India, and DAEs, the welfare effects of Annex I stabilization are relatively small.

To make comparisons of welfare effects across regions more transparent, the present values (PVs) of welfare changes over the period 1995–2050 are computed assuming a 3% per annum discount rate.[21] The results are presented in Figure 3.2. In Scenario 1, Japan incurs the largest loss among Annex I countries, followed by the former Soviet Union and the EC. Abatement at the margin is more costly in Japan because it is initially the

Table 3.7 Summary of Welfare Results under Alternative Scenarios (percentage change relative to the baseline scenario)

	2000	2010	2020	2030	2040	2050	PV
Scenario 1: Annex I countries stabilize their emissions at 1990 levels by country-specific carbon taxes							
United States	0.1	-0.2	-0.4	-0.5	-1.2	-1.7	-0.5
Japan	-1.0	-2.3	-2.4	-2.5	-3.1	-3.5	-2.2
European Community	-0.2	-0.5	-0.9	-1.2	-2.1	-2.8	-1.0
Other OECD Countries*	-0.1	-0.4	-0.5	-0.6	-1.1	-1.4	-0.5
Former Soviet Union	-1.3	-1.3	-1.2	-1.2	-1.7	-2.0	-1.4
Eastern Europe	0.4	0.5	0.4	0.3	-1.6	-2.8	-0.2
China	-0.5	-0.1	-0.3	-0.3	0.1	0.3	-0.2
India	0.0	0.2	0.0	0.0	0.0	0.0	0.0
Dynamic Asian Economies	0.0	0.0	-0.2	-0.4	-0.1	0.0	-0.1
Brazil	0.7	0.7	0.4	0.3	0.6	0.8	0.6
Energy Exporting Countries	-3.9	-4.9	-3.4	-2.6	-1.2	-0.4	-3.0
Rest of the World	-0.9	-0.6	-0.6	-0.6	-0.2	0.1	-0.5
Annex I Countries	-0.3	-0.7	-1.0	-1.1	-1.9	-2.4	-1.0
Asia	-0.2	0.0	-0.2	-0.3	0.0	0.1	-0.1
World	-0.6	-1.1	-1.1	-1.1	-1.2	-1.3	-1.0
Scenario 2: Annex I countries stabilize their emissions at 1990 levels by a uniform carbon tax							
United States	0.0	-0.1	-0.4	-0.5	-1.2	-1.7	-0.5
Japan	0.0	-0.2	-0.6	-0.9	-1.7	-2.2	-0.7
European Community	0.0	-0.1	-0.5	-0.8	-1.7	-2.3	-0.7
Other OECD Countries	0.0	-0.1	-0.2	-0.3	-0.8	-1.1	-0.3
Former Soviet Union	0.3	0.1	-0.7	-1.2	-2.8	-3.9	-1.0
Eastern Europe	0.6	1.0	0.3	-0.1	-2.1	-3.3	-0.3
China	-0.2	0.0	-0.1	-0.1	0.3	0.5	0.0
India	0.0	0.1	0.0	-0.1	0.0	0.0	0.0
Dynamic Asian Economies	0.0	0.0	-0.1	-0.2	0.1	0.3	0.0
Brazil	0.1	0.3	0.2	0.2	0.7	1.0	0.3
Energy Exporting Countries	-0.8	-1.7	-1.1	-0.8	0.2	0.8	-0.7
Rest of the World	-0.2	-0.3	-0.2	-0.2	0.1	0.3	-0.1
Annex I Countries	0.0	-0.1	-0.4	-0.7	-1.5	-2.1	-0.6
Asia	-0.1	0.0	-0.1	-0.1	0.2	0.4	0.0
World	-0.1	-0.3	-0.4	-0.5	-0.8	-1.0	-0.4

Table 3.7, continued

	2000	2010	2020	2030	2040	2050	PV

Scenario 3: Annex I and Asian countries cooperate to reduce emissions by the equivalent of Annex I stabilization at 1990 levels by a uniform carbon tax

	2000	2010	2020	2030	2040	2050	PV
United States	0.0	0.0	-0.2	-0.2	-0.5	-0.6	-0.2
Japan	0.0	-0.1	-0.3	-0.5	-0.7	-0.9	-0.3
European Community	0.0	-0.1	-0.3	-0.4	-0.7	-0.9	-0.3
Other OECD Countries*	0.0	0.0	-0.1	-0.2	-0.3	-0.5	-0.1
Former Soviet Union	0.2	0.2	0.2	0.2	0.2	0.2	0.2
Eastern Europe	0.5	0.8	0.5	0.4	-0.2	-0.5	0.3
China	-0.1	-0.3	-1.1	-1.5	-2.1	-2.4	-1.0
India	0.3	0.0	-0.4	-0.6	-1.0	-1.2	-0.3
Dynamic Asian Economies	0.0	0.1	-0.2	-0.4	-0.9	-1.2	-0.3
Brazil	0.1	0.2	0.1	0.1	0.5	0.7	0.2
Energy Exporting Countries	-0.6	-1.2	-0.6	-0.2	0.6	1.0	-0.3
Rest of the World	-0.2	-0.2	-0.1	0.0	0.2	0.3	0.0
Annex I Countries	0.0	0.0	-0.2	-0.3	-0.5	-0.7	-0.2
Asia	0.0	-0.1	-0.7	-1.0	-1.6	-1.8	-0.7
World	0.0	-0.2	-0.3	-0.4	-0.5	-0.6	-0.3

Note
*   Mexico excluded.

world's most efficient energy user and has the highest energy prices. The PVs of Annex I and world welfare both decline by 1.0% compared to the baseline.

Compared with country-specific carbon taxes, a uniform tax is more efficient because it equalizes the marginal abatement costs among the participating countries. The PV of welfare changes for Annex I regions improves by 0.4 percentage points (from -1.0 to -0.6%), and that for the world increases by 0.6 percentage points (from -1.0 to -0.4%). With the exception of Eastern Europe, no Annex I region is made worse off from adopting a uniform carbon tax. Japan gains substantially, while welfare in the EC and other OECD countries is slightly improved. Again, the impact on Asia is minimal.

Participation by Asian developing countries in mitigating global CO_2 emissions equivalent to Annex I stabilization would further lower the average economic costs of emission reductions. Most notably, the PV of

percent

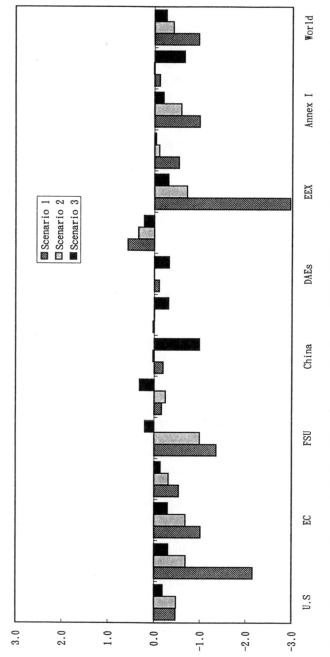

Figure 3.2 Present Value of Welfare Changes over the Period 1995–2050 under Alternative Scenario

45

welfare changes in the Annex I region improves by a further 0.4 percentage points (from –0.6 to –0.2%) while that for the world gains by 0.1 percentage points (from –0.4 to –0.3%). While Asian participation in an agreement to stabilize Annex I emissions would lead to an improvement in global welfare, Asian countries, and China in particular, would incur significant welfare losses. As participation causes welfare losses among Asian countries, part of the world welfare gains have to be used to at least offset Asian welfare losses to entice these countries to participate in the scheme. Thus, the likelihood of securing the cooperation of Asian countries depends critically on the level and form of side-payments that would be associated with such a scenario.

6   IMPLICATIONS OF JOINT IMPLEMENTATION FOR ASIA

Results from the policy simulations in the previous section demonstrated the magnitude of global efficiency gains possible when Asian countries cooperate to fulfill FCCC commitments among Annex I countries using carbon taxes as a policy instrument. From a practical point of view, however, the likelihood of implementing such a policy is negligible since the distribution of abatement costs is very unequal and disfavors Asian developing countries. Countries with the lowest marginal abatement costs – typically those which consume large quantities of coal such as China and India – account for the largest absolute emission changes. Conversely, there are smaller contributions from countries with high domestic abatement costs like Japan and the EC which consume energy relatively efficiently and rely less on coal. Without some form of side-payments or non-uniform obligations, achieving cost-effective GHG abatement policies will be elusive, especially given the large disparities in existing income levels. Developing countries have numerous other, more immediate, concerns and would typically be less enthusiastic about adopting measures which could impede their pace of development.

The FCCC outlines principles governing compensation to developing countries which implement measures to reduce the risk of climate change. The fundamental provision is that developed country parties 'provide new and additional financial resources to meet the agreed full costs incurred by developing country parties in complying with their obligations' (Article 4, paragraph 3). This wording implies that the gains from cooperation are shared by Annex I and Asian developing countries. In that case, the cost to Annex I countries would be higher than 'full compensation', and the benefit to the Asian countries would be positive. The minimum side-payments

Asian countries require for JI of the stabilization agreement are equivalent to the abatement costs Asian countries incur.[22] For Annex I countries as a group, the maximum amount of side-payments is the difference between the cost incurred under Annex I stabilization by a uniform carbon tax (Scenario 2) and the cost incurred under Asian participation (Scenario 3).

An accord based on direct transfers allocated on this principle would need to establish and agree on more precise abatement cost estimates than currently exist in each country. Yet most countries entering an agreement are likely to have only approximate information on their costs of abatement and even less idea of how these costs might evolve during the life of the agreement. Negotiations about side-payments may be less difficult if based on simple transfer mechanisms which are easy to implement and have broad appeal. In this context, the finding that the initial distribution of emission quotas can be used to reconcile the dual need for cost-effective GHG abatement with an equitable distribution of abatement costs is important. A key question therefore, is whether allocation principles exist which would be supported by countries in Asia. The evaluation hypothesis is to assume an allocation is acceptable to a country if, compared to no agreement, it maintains or improves welfare among Asian countries. In practice, due to difficulties measuring the benefits of GHG emission reductions, the approach ignores the benefits of an abatement policy which, because of their non-excludability, are enjoyed by most regions whether they participate or not.[23]

6.1 Alternative Endowments of Tradable Quotas

Many quota allocation rules have been proposed reflecting a variety of international distributional considerations. This section considers three quota distribution rules in order to evaluate the sensitivity of welfare gains and losses in the scenario where global emissions are reduced by an amount equivalent to Annex I stabilization through joint action by Annex I countries and the three Asian regions. Simulating the same emission reduction policy with different quota allocation rules substantially alters the distribution of abatement costs across countries. The rules are (1) 'grandfathering': quotas allocated in proportion to 1990 emission shares, (2) 'egalitarian': quotas allocated in proportion to 1990 population shares, and (3) a 'two-tiered' system, which combines the first two rules. Reaching a consensus as to which distribution rule best serves equity objectives is unlikely since, in contrast with efficiency, there are many equity criteria and no unanimity on which is the best definition at either the international or interpersonal level.

Table 3.8 summarizes the volume of trade in emission quotas for each of the three allocation rules and gives a broad indication of which distribution

Table 3.8   Volume of Trade in Emission Quotas (million tons of carbon)

	2000	2010	2020	2030	2040	2050
1. Allocation rule based on 1990 emission shares						
United States	-61	-48	42	132	299	467
Japan	-138	-114	-129	-144	-178	-213
European Community	-70	-44	4	52	130	207
Other OECD Countries*	-25	-25	-8	8	44	80
Former Soviet Union	306	350	361	373	425	477
Eastern Europe	101	116	115	114	124	135
China	-56	-117	-194	-272	-440	-609
India	-20	-45	-77	-109	-177	-245
Dynamic Asian Economies	-38	-74	-114	-154	-227	-300
Total Volume of Trade	814	933	1,045	1,358	2,045	2,732
2. Allocation rule based on 1990 population shares						
United States	-1,087	-1,140	-1,153	-1,166	-1,197	-1,228
Japan	-298	-286	-318	-350	-416	-482
European Community	-425	-423	-411	-399	-391	-383
Other OECD Countries*	-138	-145	-140	-135	-121	-108
Former Soviet Union	-316	-298	-353	-409	-468	-528
Eastern Europe	-88	-83	-103	-124	-149	-174
China	1,068	1,073	1,111	1,150	1,196	1,243
India	1,136	1,179	1,265	1,351	1,501	1,652
Dynamic Asian Economies	148	123	102	81	44	7
Total Volume of Trade	4,705	4,749	4,957	5,164	5,485	5,805
3. Two-tiered allocation rule						
United States	-270	-490	-634	-777	-1,002	-1,228
Japan	-170	-183	-235	-288	-385	-482
European Community	-142	-197	-231	-264	-324	-383
Other OECD Countries*	-48	-74	-83	-92	-100	-108
Former Soviet Union	188	100	-38	-177	-352	-528
Eastern Europe	64	38	-8	-53	-114	-174
China	167	358	541	725	984	1,243
India	210	443	679	914	1,283	1,652
Dynamic Asian Economies	0	5	8	11	9	7
Total Volume of Trade	1,258	1,888	2,457	3,301	4,553	5,805

Note
*   Mexico excluded.

mechanism a particular country/region would tend to support. Given the relatively high level of energy consumption in 1990 and negative growth over the period 1990–2010, grandfathering (Scenario 4.1) would allocate to the former Soviet Union and Eastern Europe a number of quotas in excess of their requirements for emission stabilization, resulting in relatively large exports of quotas. In contrast, Asia, having produced a small fraction of total emissions in 1990, receives only 17% of the quota allocation. Because of rapid industrialization, however, Asia's energy requirements increase, creating a strong demand for additional quotas. On the other hand, since more than 40% of the global population resides in Asia, the population rule (Scenario 4.2) clearly favors this region. OECD countries tend to receive a relatively large share (55%) if quotas are distributed according to historical emission levels and a relatively small proportion (24%) if based on population shares.

A striking feature of the first two allocation rules is that they emphasize the differences between the parties rather than the similarities. This could make negotiations for a jointly implemented agreement between Annex I countries and Asian developing countries problematic. The impact of two-tiered rules (Scenario 4.3) is to limit the weight given to countries which rank at the extremes of an allocation criteria, placing more focus on countries with average rankings. We have simulated a two-tiered rule which initially gives a large weight (90%) to 1990 emission shares and a small weight (10%) to 1990 population shares. Over the period, the relative weights reverse such that by 2015 the two rules are given equal importance and by 2050 the weight attached to 1990 population shares is 100%. On these assumptions, the allocation rule reduces the dispersion of initial quota shares between countries/regions.

Which countries/regions buy and sell quotas depends both on a country's marginal abatement costs and the quota allocation rule chosen. The volume of trade in emission quotas for each of the three allocation rules is summarized in Table 3.8. The egalitarian principle strongly favors the Asian developing countries. This rule results in India being the largest seller of emission quotas throughout the period, closely followed by China. The DAEs also become net sellers over the period although the volume of sales are significantly smaller. By contrast, the small number of quotas Annex I countries receive from an egalitarian rule combined with their relatively high marginal costs of abatement ensures that each Annex I country requires additional quotas. The largest demand for quotas comes from the United States, where net quota purchases reach a market value of $43 billion (at 1985 prices) per annum in 2050.[24]

The grandfathering system strongly favors the former Soviet Union, which becomes the major net seller of quotas by the turn of the century. It is able to sell a large proportion of its allocation because, since 1990 (the reference year), this region has experienced strong declines in energy consumption associated chiefly with several years of negative output growth and energy price liberalization. The grandfathering rule, however, is unlikely to attain the support of Asian developing countries since throughout the period these countries have to purchase additional quotas. In particular, quota demand in China increases rapidly as the implicit carbon constraints tighten.

With the two-tiered allocation method that was chosen here, all Asian developing countries receive quotas in excess of their requirements (with the exception of DAEs in 2000) although the volume of quota sales is smaller than under the egalitarian rule. Each OECD country/region is a net buyer of quotas, and Eastern Europe and the former Soviet Union are net sellers during the first 25 years, which affords them a longer period of adjustment as anticipated in the FCCC. The situation reverses after 2020, when it becomes increasingly costly to stabilize emissions.

6.2 Gains and Losses from Tradable Quotas

The value of quota trade is one indication of how a country could gain or lose from a carbon abatement policy based on tradable quotas. But it is not a complete picture since it ignores the full general equilibrium effects. Table 3.9 compares the welfare gains and losses from quota trading under the three initial quota allocation rules from a policy of stabilizing the ex-ante equivalent of Annex I carbon emissions with the cooperation of Asian developing countries. In contradiction to the objective of full compensation for developing countries, the grandfathering rule results in welfare losses in Asia. By 2050 real household income in China is 3.5% lower than the baseline level and in India and the DAEs welfare losses result in almost every period. The distribution of welfare changes across Annex I countries is also different. Income losses in the United States and other OECD countries are close to zero while Japanese welfare would be reduced by 1.1% in 2050. The former Soviet Union and Eastern Europe, on the other hand, are major beneficiaries from trade in quotas under this allocation rule, gaining as much as 2.9 and 2.2%, respectively, relative to the baseline.

As in Section 5.2, the present value of welfare changes over the period 1995–2050 is computed, and the results are presented in Figure 3.3. This diagram shows the welfare gains and losses across regions more clearly: small losses for OECD regions, large gains for the former Soviet Union and Eastern Europe, and large losses for Asian regions. Welfare in Annex I countries as a whole is virtually unchanged (a 0.1% loss) whereas Asia incurs a PV 1.2% in welfare loss. Given this distribution of abatement costs across countries, it is highly unlikely that the participation of the major emitters in Asia would be forthcoming under such conditions.

Asia gains under the egalitarian rule, especially over the earlier period of the simulation, when their terms of trade improve. Real household incomes in India are 7.5% higher than baseline in 2010 (Table 3.9). The gains are lower towards the end of the period as the relative oil price starts to in-

Table 3.9 Summary of Welfare Results under Alternative Tradable Quota Allocation (percentage changes relative to the baseline scenario)

	2000	2010	2020	2030	2040	2050	PV
Scenario 4.1: Cooperative emission reductions by Annex I and Asian countries with tradable quotas based on 1990 emission shares (Rule #1)							
United States	0.0	-0.1	-0.1	-0.2	-0.3	-0.4	-0.1
Japan	-0.1	-0.3	-0.5	-0.6	-0.9	-1.1	-0.5
European Community	0.0	-0.1	-0.3	-0.4	-0.6	-0.7	-0.3
Other OECD Countries*	0.0	-0.1	-0.1	-0.2	-0.2	-0.3	-0.1
Former Soviet Union	1.0	1.8	2.1	2.3	2.7	2.9	1.9
Eastern Europe	1.3	2.2	2.0	1.8	1.3	0.9	1.6
China	-0.3	-0.7	-1.7	-2.2	-3.1	-3.5	-1.5
India	0.2	-0.3	-0.9	-1.2	-1.8	-2.1	-0.8
Dynamic Asian Economies	-0.1	-0.3	-0.7	-1.0	-1.7	-2.0	-0.8
Brazil	0.1	0.2	0.1	0.1	0.5	0.7	0.2
Energy Exporting Countries	-0.5	-1.1	-0.5	-0.1	0.6	1.0	-0.2
Rest of the World	-0.1	-0.1	0.0	0.1	0.2	0.3	0.0
Annex I Countries	0.0	0.0	-0.1	-0.1	-0.3	-0.4	-0.1
Asia	-0.1	-0.5	-1.3	-1.6	-2.4	-2.8	-1.2
World	0.0	-0.2	-0.3	-0.3	-0.5	-0.6	-0.3
Scenario 4.2: Cooperative emission reductions by Annex I and Asian countries with tradable quotas based on 1990 population shares (Rule #2)							
United States	-0.4	-0.7	-0.9	-1.1	-1.3	-1.4	-0.9
Japan	-0.2	-0.5	-0.8	-0.9	-1.2	-1.3	-0.7
European Community	-0.3	-0.5	-0.7	-0.9	-1.1	-1.3	-0.7
Other OECD Countries*	-0.2	-0.3	-0.4	-0.5	-0.6	-0.7	-0.4
Former Soviet Union	-0.6	-1.1	-1.7	-2.0	-2.5	-2.9	-1.6
Eastern Europe	-0.3	-0.3	-0.9	-1.1	-1.8	-2.2	-0.9
China	2.8	3.2	2.2	1.7	0.6	0.0	2.0
India	6.4	7.5	6.7	6.3	5.2	4.7	6.2
Dynamic Asian Economies	0.4	0.5	0.1	-0.1	-0.9	-1.3	-0.1
Brazil	0.1	0.2	0.1	0.1	0.6	0.8	0.2
Energy Exporting Countries	-0.4	-0.8	-0.2	0.1	0.8	1.3	0.0
Rest of the World	-0.1	-0.1	0.0	0.1	0.3	0.4	0.0
Annex I Countries	-0.3	-0.6	-0.8	-1.0	-1.3	-1.4	-0.8
Asia	2.9	3.4	2.6	2.2	1.2	0.7	2.4
World	0.0	-0.2	-0.3	-0.3	-0.5	-0.6	-0.3

Table 3.9, continued

	2000	2010	2020	2030	2040	2050	PV
Scenario 4.3:Cooperative emission reductions by Annex I and Asian countries with tradable quotas based on gradual transition from Rule #1 to Rule #2							
United States	-0.1	-0.3	-0.6	-0.8	-1.1	-1.4	-0.6
Japan	-0.1	-0.4	-0.6	-0.8	-1.1	-1.3	-0.6
European Community	-0.1	-0.3	-0.5	-0.7	-1.0	-1.3	-0.5
Other OECD Countries*	-0.1	-0.2	-0.3	-0.4	-0.6	-0.7	-0.3
Former Soviet Union	0.6	0.7	0.0	-0.4	-1.5	-2.3	-0.2
Eastern Europe	0.9	1.2	0.4	0.0	-1.1	-1.8	0.2
China	0.4	0.9	0.6	0.5	0.1	-0.1	0.5
India	1.4	3.0	3.8	4.2	4.4	4.6	3.2
Dynamic Asian Economies	0.0	0.0	-0.3	-0.4	-1.0	-1.3	-0.4
Brazil	0.1	0.2	0.1	0.1	0.6	0.8	0.2
Energy Exporting Countries	-0.5	-1.0	-0.3	0.0	0.8	1.2	-0.1
Rest of the World	-0.1	-0.1	0.0	0.1	0.3	0.4	0.0
Annex I Countries	0.0	-0.2	-0.5	-0.7	-1.1	-1.4	-0.5
Asia	0.5	1.1	1.1	1.1	0.8	0.6	0.8
World	0.0	-0.2	-0.3	-0.3	-0.5	-0.6	-0.3

Note
* Mexico excluded.

crease sharply. The distribution of losses among OECD countries is more uniform than that implied from grandfathered quotas. Despite a weak emission growth in the former Soviet Union, the region incurs losses rising to 2.9% of household income by 2050. The PV of Annex I household income declines by 0.8% while that of Asian household income rises by 2.4% (Figure 3.3). In summary, the distribution of gains and losses favors the Asian developing countries such that they may be willing to participate in a jointly implemented Annex I carbon stabilization agreement.

A notable aspect of the egalitarian rule is its weakness in effectively targeting the level of transfers needed among countries to secure participation. The welfare calculations, ignoring the benefits which Asian countries receive from the climate change policy, suggest that the transfers are substantially greater than needed to ensure full compensation. Over-generous compensation could equally constrain the chances of a cooperative agreement. Some studies suggest that the Annex I countries like Russia and

percent

6.23.2

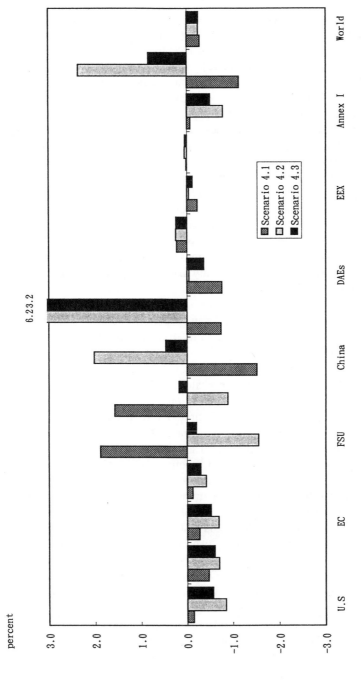

Figure 3.3 Present Value of Welfare Changes over the Period 1995–2050 under Alternative Tradable Quota
Allocation

53

Canada could even benefit from climate change and that damages from global warming could be relatively larger in non-Annex I countries. In these circumstances, there will still be an incentive to implement policies jointly, so as to achieve reductions at least cost, as well as pressure to limit the implicit level of transfers to the minimum amount necessary.

The third allocation rule – a combination of grandfathering and egalitarian – avoids some of the problems with the first two allocation methods. Real household incomes in Asian developing countries combined are still higher than those at the baseline throughout the period. The maximum gain, relative to the baseline, is 1.1% of household income over the 2010–2030 period. DAEs incur small losses from 2020, however, their per capita income is expected to increase sharply by 2020 and they are thus likely to become more willing to participate in an international agreement. Over the 1995–2050 period, India becomes the largest net seller of quotas, ensuring sufficient revenues to increase the PV of its welfare by 3.2% above baseline. Eastern Europe's PV of household income change is positive and the former Soviet Union is initially made better off. Although the PV of household income is 0.2% lower than at the baseline, the former Soviet Union is considerably better off under this rule than when Annex I stabilization is pursued without Asian cooperation, either by country-specific taxes (a 1.4% loss in PV relative to the baseline) or by uniform tax (a 1.0% loss in PV).

The choice of initial allocation rule is arbitrary and can be easily varied in GREEN to simulate other mechanisms. Simple static rules tend to place too much weight on extreme positions and consequently the implicit transfers are frequently too high or too low to ensure a more equitable distribution of abatement costs. The grandfathering rule could even produce perverse transfers. In principle, an allocation formula could be calculated which closely targets the costs and benefits of GHG abatement in individual countries. The major disadvantages, however, are the unwieldy calculations involved and the risk of losing transparency and simplicity. For these reasons, a quota allocation based simply on a weighted average of two easily interpreted allocation methods and which have some ethical basis may prove more widely acceptable. The two-tiered approach appears to ensure sufficient compensation and a more equal distribution of abatement costs among the OECD countries. Of course, the exact weights would be a question for negotiation but this type of rule seems to offer a lot of opportunities for agreement.

Perhaps the most important result of our simulation experiments, however, is that Annex I countries as a whole would benefit from Asian participation in a carbon emission abatement agreement using a two-tiered allocation rule (Scenario 4.3), compared to Annex I stabilization adopting a uniform carbon tax (Scenario 2). In the former case, the present value of Annex I equivalent variations is 0.5% lower than at the baseline, whereas in the latter it is 0.6% lower. In other words, cooperation between Annex I and Asian countries in mitigating CO_2 emissions potentially benefits both groups of countries, as well as the global economy as a whole.

7 CONCLUSIONS

Despite a great deal of uncertainty surrounding the scientific and economic evidence on global warming, the FCCC unambiguously advocates adopting measures which moderate the growth of atmospheric CO_2 concentrations for reducing the threat of climate change. Accordingly, it has defined guidelines for climate change policies in Annex I countries. In this paper, we have evaluated a number of alternative CO_2 reduction scenarios equivalent to stabilizing Annex I emissions at 1990 levels. In particular, we have estimated the potential savings and the distributional effects of participation by Asian developing countries in an international emission abatement agreement.

Our simulation results indicate that while the mitigation cost of Annex I stabilization could be lowered significantly by imposing a uniform carbon tax rather than country-specific carbon taxes, Asian cooperation could reduce the global cost even further. At the same time, however, the welfare level of Asian countries would be lowered by a non-trivial amount compared to the situation where they do not participate in the agreement. Thus, unless some form of side-payment is provided, attaining cooperation from the developing countries in Asia is unlikely.

As alternatives to a uniform carbon tax among Annex I and Asian regions which results in welfare losses in Asian countries, we have also evaluated the effects of adopting tradable emission quotas using three different allocation rules. The simulation results suggest that a two-tiered system – an allocation rule based upon a gradual transition from 1990 carbon emission shares to 1990 population shares – is most attractive. Compared with the case where Annex I countries stabilize their CO_2 emissions at 1990 levels by a uniform carbon tax, the tradable quota scenario with a two-tiered allocation rule could improve the welfare of both Annex I and Asian regions. In other words, it is possible to design a climate change policy that is both cost-effective and supportive to some of the equity issues involved.

ACKNOWLEDGEMENTS

This paper written while Lee was visiting the Resource Allocation Division of the OECD Economics Department. We thank Ching-Cheng Chang, Tom Jones, Joaquim Oliveria Martins, Dirk Pilat and Peter Sturm for helpful comments and Christophe Complainville for excellent statistical assistance. The views expressed in this paper are those of the authors and do not necessarily reflect the views of the OECD or the governments of its member countries.

NOTES

1. As indicated in Section 4, carbon intensity depends crucially upon whether GDP is measured at purchasing power parity (PPP) or official exchange rates.
2. For a detailed description of the model, see Lee, Oliveira Martins, and van der Mensbrugghe (1994) and van der Mensbrugghe (1994). The twelve regions of the model are: the United States, Japan, the EC, other OECD Countries, the former Soviet Union, Eastern Europe, China, India, the dynamic Asian economies (DAEs), Brazil, the energy exporting countries (EEX), and the rest of the world. The DAEs include South Korea, Taiwan, Singapore, Hong Kong, Thailand, and the Philippines. Two other Asian countries with high GDP growth rates, Malaysia and Indonesia, are currently aggregated into EEX.
3. The three backstop fuels are carbon-based synthetic fuel, carbon-free liquid fuel (such as that derived from hydrogen), and a carbon-free electricity backstop fuel (such as that derived from solar or wind power).
4. Typically, the substitution elasticities are lower for old capital than for new capital.
5. The ELES is similar to the more familiar LES, or the Stone-Geary demand system. The main difference is the extension of the LES to a dynamic setting. The version of the ELES used in GREEN assumes myopic behavior, so saving enters the utility function, but its determination is based only on contemporary prices (where the price of saving is assumed to be the consumer price index).
6. GREEN can, however, calculate the energy-related emissions of nitrogen oxides (NO_x) and sulfur oxides (SO_x).
7. For the decade 1990–2000, some downward adjustment to GDP growth in the former Soviet Union and Eastern Europe and an upward adjustment to Chinese growth were made to be coherent with recent GDP trends.
8. The existing energy taxes in the benchmark year (1985) in all regions are assumed to remain unchanged over the 1990–2050 period.
9. Ad valorem subsidy rates for oil, natural gas, and coal in the former Soviet Union in 1985 have been estimated to be 87.6, 88.3, and 55.9%, respectively. The same rates are assumed to prevail in 1990. These rates are estimated as

$$s = [P_w - (1+T)P_d] \,/\, (1+T)P_d$$

where P_w is the world price, P_d is the domestic producer price, and T is the ratio of transport cost to the value of shipment.

10. For example, in 1985, ad valorem subsidy rates for coal in Eastern Europe, China, and India were 51.9, 55.0, and 41.5%, respectively.

11. Modeling of finite oil and gas reserves and their exploitation is described in more detail in Burniaux, Martin, Nicoletti, and Oliveira Martins (1992). The data on oil and gas reserves are obtained from the International Energy Agency (IEA).

12. The major reason why carbon emissions in China grow at a slightly lower rate than in India or DAEs despite China's higher GDP growth projections is because coal subsidies are assumed to be phased out by 2010. Since coal is the most carbon-intensive fossil fuel, and China has a higher consumption share and subsidy rate for coal in the base year (DAEs impose taxes on coal), the removal of coal subsidies slows down the emission growth in China more than in the other two Asian regions.

13. According to estimates made by the Research Institute on the National Economy in Japan, annual economic growth in Southeast Asia, not including Japan, could average 7.7% for the rest of the decade, compared with 2.5% for the world economy (*The Yomiuri Shimbun*, November 2, 1993).

14. Although not shown in Table 3.4, the consumption share of coal in 2050 increases to 72% in former Soviet Union, 75% in China, and 85% in India. In China, the share of coal declines during the 1990–2010 period as coal subsidies are gradually removed.

15. The backstop prices used in the model are $50/barrel for coal or shale-based synthetic fuel, $100/barrel for carbon-free liquid fuel, and $75.0 mills/kwh for carbon-free electric options. These prices are consistent with EMF 12 assumptions.

16. 1990 per capita carbon emissions in China, India, and the DAEs were, respectively, 0.54, 0.18, and 0.57 tons.

17. Cohen and Collette (1991) provide a calculation of CO_2 concentrations. Our baseline scenario projects that a doubling of CO_2 concentrations from their pre-Industrial Revolution levels would occur around 2075.

18. See e.g., Houghton, et al. (1990). Other GHGs include methane (CH_4), nitrous oxide (N_2O), and chlorofluorocarbons (CFC-11 and CFC-12).

19. In the former Soviet Union and Eastern Europe, the emission levels in 2000 and 2010 are lower than their 1990 levels in the baseline scenario. Thus, stabilization of OECD countries' emissions by country-specific carbon taxes would result in an emission cut that is greater than that required for Annex I stabilization in 2000 and 2010.

20. EV is defined as the amount of real income that would have to be taken away from the representative consumer at pre-policy consumer prices to make the individual as well off as he/she would be at post-policy consumer prices.

21. There is considerable disagreement on the appropriate discount rate of for climate change policy. For example, Cline (1992) advocates a low discount rate of about 2%, while the World Bank (e.g., Birdsall and Steer, 1993) recommends rates ranging from 5% (developed countries) to 8% (developing countries).

22. This would leave the Asian countries indifferent, subtracting from any perceived gains from reducing the risk of global warming.

23. It should be noted that while atmospheric carbon concentrations are a truly public good, the resulting climate effects on economic activity and welfare may differ greatly among regions.

24. The market value is calculated as the volume of trade multiplied by the uniform carbon tax ($35 per ton of carbon in 2050).

REFERENCES

Atkinson, Scott and Tom Tietenberg (1991), 'Market failure in incentive-based regulation: The case of emissions trading', *Journal of Environmental Economics and Management*, **21**, 17–31.

Birdsall, Nancy and Andrew Steer (1993), 'Act now on global warming – but don't cook the books', *Finance and Development*, **30** (March), 6–8.

Bohm, Peter (1992), 'Distributional implications of allowing international trade in CO_2 emission quotas', *The World Economy*, **15**, 107–14.

Burniaux, J.M., J.P Martin, G. Nicoletti and J. Oliveira Martins (1992), 'GREEN – A multi-sector, multi-region dynamic general equilibrium model for quantifying the costs of curbing CO_2 emissions: A technical manual', Economics Department Working Paper No. 116, Paris: OECD.

Burniaux, J.M., G. Nicoletti and J. Oliveira Martins (1992), 'GREEN: A global model for quantifying the costs of policies to curb CO_2 emissions', *OECD Economic Studies*, **19**, 49–92.

Cline, William R. (1992), *The Economics of Global Warming*, Washington, DC: Institute of International Economics.

Cohen, B.C. and J.M. Collette (1991), 'Fossil-fuel use and sustainable development path', *International Journal of Global Energy Issues*, **3**, 132–41.

EMF 12 (1990), 'Study design for EMF 12 global climate change: Energy sector impacts of greenhouse gas emission control strategies', Energy Modeling Forum No. 12, Stanford University.

Hoeller, Peter and Jonathan Coppel (1992), 'Energy taxation and price distortions in fossil fuel markets: Some implications for climate change policy', in *Climate Change: Designing a Practical Tax System*, Paris: OECD.

Houghton, J.T., G.J. Jenkins and J.J. Ephraums (eds) (1990), *Climate Change: The IPCC Scientific Assessment*, Cambridge: Cambridge University Press.

Jones, Tom (1994), 'Joint implementation as a policy instrument for responding to climate change', a paper presented at the IPCC Working Group III Workshop on Policy Instruments and their Implications, Tsukuba, Japan, January 17–20.

Kaya, Y., N. Nakicenovic, W.D. Nordhaus and F.L. Toth (eds) (1993), *Costs, Impacts, and Benefits of CO_2 Mitigation*, Laxenburg, Austria: International Institute for Applied Systems Analysis.

Lee, H., J. Oliveira Martins and D. van der Mensbrugghe (1994), 'The OECD GREEN model: An updated overview', Technical Working Paper No. 97, Paris: OECD Development Centre.

Mann, Alan S. and Richard G. Richels (1992), *Buying Greenhouse*

Insurance: The Economic Costs of CO₂ Emission Limits, Cambridge, MA: MIT Press.

Martin, J.P, J.-M. Burniaux, G. Nicoletti and J. Oliveira Martins (1992), 'The Costs of international agreements to reduce CO₂ emissions: Evidence from GREEN', *OECD Economic Studies*, **19**, 93–121.

Nordhaus, William D. (1991), 'To slow or not to slow: The economics of the greenhouse effect', *The Economic Journal*, **101**, 920–37.

Nordhaus, William D. (1993), 'Reflections on the economics of climate change', *Journal of Economic Perspectives*, **7**, 11–25.

Peck, Steven C. and Thomas J. Teisberg (1993), 'Optimal CO₂ emissions control with partial and full world-wide cooperation: An analysis using CETA', a paper presented at the International Workshop on Integrative Assessment of Mitigation, Impacts and Adaptation to Climate Change, IIASA, Laxenburg, Austria, October 13–15.

Porteba, James M. (1993), 'Global warming policy: A public finance perspective', *Journal of Economic Perspectives*, **7**, 47–63.

United Nations (1992), United Nations' Framework Convention on Climate Change, New York.

van der Mensbrugghe, Dominique (1994), 'GREEN: The reference manual', Economics Department Working Paper No. 143, Paris: OECD.

Weyant, John P. (1993), 'Costs of reducing global carbon emissions', *Journal of Economic Perspectives*, **7**, 27–46.

4. The Impact of Climate Change On Rice Yield in Taiwan

Huoying Wu

1 INTRODUCTION

The weather and climate have influenced agricultural development in many ways. Although the agricultural output in developing countries is no longer as subject to seasonal and weather-induced fluctuations as previously, uncertainty about crop yield is still a major risk that every farmer has to confront. Thus, economists still cannot ignore the weather as a prime factor in determining the agricultural production.

Because weather affects variously the output of individual agricultural crops, what is favorable weather for one crop may be unfavorable for another. The identification of a systematic relationship between weather and crop yields would thus have significant implications for governmental agricultural policy and the direction of future research.

Weather is the state of the atmosphere at a given time and place, whereas climate is the average weather. Climate change is viewed as a paramount social issue at the century's end. As climate is a major determinant of both the location and productivity of agricultural enterprises, agriculture is identified as an area of concern in the current public debate about the causes and effects of climate change because of its importance to human welfare. Indeed, agriculture has been the central focus of several treatments of potential effects of climate change. Most authors have evaluated the sensitivity of various dimensions of agricultural activity to climate change, including yields, input use and locational patterns.

Here, I attempt to examine the impact of climate change upon agricultural productivity. As rice is the staple food of twenty million people in Taiwan, any shortage or surplus of rice production has important socio-economic and political implications in Taiwan. Hence, rice production is chosen for this work. Instead of using simulation techniques, which have often been used in previous research, I employ regression to evaluate the impact of global warming upon crop yields. Among the research about change in rice yield, Horie (1991) found that a warmer climate ($+2°C$) would decrease rice yield in most of Japan, except northern Tohoku and Hokkaido; Okada (1991) also found that warming would decrease the rice yield in Japan; Lansigan and Orno (1991) discovered that rice yield in a warmer climate would also be less in the Philippines.

The paper is organized as follows. The following section explains the characteristics of rice production in Taiwan. Section 3 depicts the model to estimate the average rice yield per hectare. Section 4 describes the data source and presents empirical results. Section 5 evaluates the impacts of climate change upon rice yield according to four scenarios. The final section summarizes the main findings.

2 RICE PRODUCTION IN TAIWAN

Rice is the single most important crop in Taiwan. Much rice produced in Taiwan is on small farms. The rice crop averaged 2,144,009 metric tons annually and was cultivated on 698,396 hectares on average for the 1952–1992 period. The production of rice per hectare doubled in this period. The average yield was 4.1 metric tons per hectare in 1992. The total planted area of rice, including first and second crops, decreased from 785,729 hectares in 1952 to a total of 397,252 hectares in 1992. The ratio of rice area to total cultivated area declined from 89% in 1952 to 45% in 1992. Even though its importance is diminishing, rice is still the leading grain crop in Taiwan.

Figures 4.1, 4.2, and 4.3 show the variations of rice production, area under rice cultivation, and average rice yield per hectare in Taiwan for the past 92 years, i.e., 1901–1992. The doubling of rice production during the 1952–1992 period can be entirely attributed to technological improvement. After 1980, rice production decreased significantly. Government policies also now encourage farmers to practice crop rotation during the second cropping season. The first crop thus becomes the primary source of rice supply. Only the first crop is analyzed in this work.

Rice is generally cultivated in warm temperate latitudes in which adequate water is available to submerge the land. The seeds of rice are first sown broadcast on well-prepared beds, and, when the seedlings are 25–50 days old, they are transplanted to paddy that is enclosed by levees and submerged under water 5–10 cm deep. The land remains submerged during most of the growing season. As rice is a crop grown under flooded conditions, irrigation is a necessary technique of water management. Irrigation channels equipped with dams are generally used to facilitate irri-

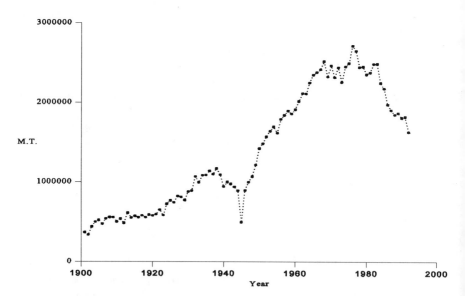

Figure 4.1 Total Rice Production in Taiwan, 1901–1992

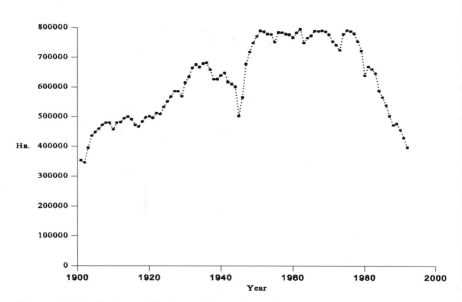

Figure 4.2 Total Area of Taiwan Planted in Rice, 1901–1992

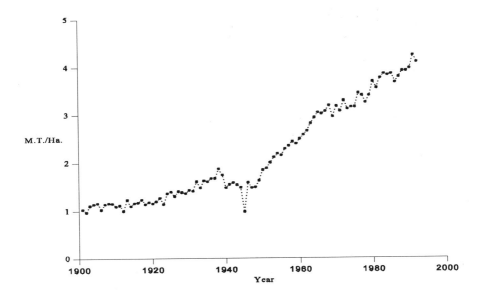

Figure 4.3 Average Rice Yield in Taiwan, 1901–1992

gation of paddies in Taiwan. Most paddy fields are doubly cropped. Some in southern Taiwan are triply cropped. The cropping season is from January to June/July for the first crop and from June to October/November for the second crop.

In general, weather affects rice production in a significant way. The major climatic factors that influence rice production in Taiwan include temperature, precipitation, duration of sunshine, and typhoons. Other extreme weather factors include flood and drought. Typhoon damage is unavoidable, but typhoons also customarily bring much precipitation that is necessary for rice production. Because rice produced in Taiwan is cultivated in paddy fields flooded with water that is supplied through well-developed waterways, precipitation during the planting period is not as critical as before. Heavy rainfall during booting and flowering causes more serious damage and makes ripening slow and unsuccessful. In any case, heavy rainfalls during flowering are the most influential.

3   THE EMPIRICAL MODEL

We regress rice yield per hectare on weather, wage, and rent to estimate the impact of weather variations upon the rice yield. For each weather variable, linear and quadratic terms are included to reflect the nonlinear relationship between weather and rice yield. The means have been taken away from the weather variables in this regression to make the quadratic weather variables easier to interpret. The linear term reflects the marginal value of weather evaluated at the mean, whereas the quadratic term shows how that marginal effect varies as one moves from the mean (see Mendelsohn et al., 1994).

As data exist in both a time series and cross-sectional form, we combine information of these two types by pooling the cross-sectional and time-series observations and estimate the weather-yield relationship according to the fixed-effects model. Dummy variables are used to capture the unobserved site-level heterogeneity: the fixed effect measured by α_i is assumed to be fixed but distinct for every i. With these data to estimate the relationship between weather and average rice yield, this model adequately allows for varying intercept terms over cross-sectional units to capture variability across sites. The parameter coefficients of explanatory variables are assumed to be constant over cross-sectional units. Thus, this model written as

$$AQ_{i,t} = \alpha_i + \beta X_{i,t} + \gamma W_{i,t} + \theta W_{i,t}^2 + \eta t + \varepsilon_{i,t},$$

$$i = 1,2,...,16, \ t = 1,...,41,$$

$$\text{with } E(\varepsilon_{i,t}) = 0, \ Var(\varepsilon_{i,t}) = \sigma^2,$$

$$\text{and } E(\varepsilon_{i,t}\varepsilon_{j,t}) = 0 \text{ if } i \neq j \ ;$$

where AQ denotes the average rice yield per hectare; W and W^2 denote the weather variables and their squared terms; X includes wage and rent; and t is used to capture the effect of technological change.

The selection of weather variables in the first analysis is related to the growth of the rice plant in three main phases: vegetative phase, reproductive phase, and ripening phase (Vergara, 1980). Among these three phases, the vegetative phase is the period from seed germination to panicle initiation (55 days); the reproductive phase occurs from panicle initiation to flowering (35 days); the ripening phase lasts from flowering to full maturity (25–35 days). Total growth takes about 120 days and the duration between sowing and harvest is about 150 days.

Water is the most important factor influencing rice growth and its yield potential. Precipitation is commonly the source of irrigation-use water. Abundant precipitation at the beginning of the rice season is beneficial as it allows timely land preparation and transplanting; too much rainfall during the ripening stages, however, damages rice growth and rice yield. During the flowering period, rainy weather, which is typically accompanied by decreased temperature, may also adversely affect normal pollination and increase the fraction of sterile spikelets. As rice cannot fully utilize the total annual rainfall, only precipitation occurring during the vegetative phase is directly beneficial. Excessive rainfall can cause crop loss if flooding cannot be controlled and crops are then inundated. As rice is adapted to warm areas with abundant sunshine, temperatures lower than 15°C generally slow seedling development, postpone transplanting, delay reproductive growth and consequently decrease grain yields.

As the weather conditions needed for the vegetative and reproductive phases are similar, we use the time of flowering to divide the rice growth process into two stages to select weather variables. In this work, the first stage is the period from seed germination to flowering and the second stage is the period from flowering to harvest. The weather variables thus include mean temperatures at both stages, their squared terms, and mean temperature variations at both stages. As water is an essential element in rice production, precipitation at the second stage, and yearly total precipitation before planting are also included in the set of explanatory variables. Average temperatures for these two stages are obtained by averaging monthly mean temperatures through the period. A detailed schedule of the first and second stage for each site is presented in Table 4.1. For instance, the first stage of the first crop is from January to April and the second stage is from May to June in the following sites: Keelung, Taipei, Taoyuan, Hsinchu, Miaoli, and Ilan. As not every site has its own weather station, some weather stations are used for several sites within the same geographic area.

4   THE EMPIRICAL RESULTS

This empirical work focuses on a 41-year period beginning in 1952 and ending with 1992. The data on rice are drawn from the Taiwan Food Statistics Book of the Food Bureau, 1952–1992. Monthly weather data on temperature and precipitation for the period 1887–1992 are obtained from the Central Weather Bureau of Taiwan. Annual data on the input costs per hectare, such as wages and rents for the period 1952–1992, are taken from the Survey of Rice Production Costs. Wages and rents are deflated by the wholesale price index (WPI) which employs 1986 as the base year. The rice

Table 4.1   Growing Seasons of Rice Production: First Crop

Site	First Stage	Second Stage	Weather stations
Keelung	January–May	May–July	Keelung
Taipei	January–May	May–July	Taipei
Taoyuan	January–May	May–July	Taipei
Hsinchu	January–May	May–July	Hsinchu
Miaoli	January–May	May–July	Hsinchu
Taichung	January–May	May–July	Taichung
Changhwa	January–May	May–July	Taichung
Nantou	January–May	May–July	Taichung
Yunlin	December–April	May–June	Tainan
Chaiyi	December–April	May–June	Tainan
Tainan	December–April	May–June	Tainan
Kaohsiung	December–April	April–May	Tainan
Pingtung	December–April	April–May	Tainan
Ilan	January–May	May–July	Ilan
Hualien	January–May	May–June	Hualien
Taitung	December–April	April–June	Taitung

Sources: various local agricultural improvement stations in Taiwan.

yield per hectare is obtained by dividing the total rice yield by the total planted area of rice. Sixteen sites in this work include Keelung, Taipei, Taoyuan, Hsinchu, Miaoli, Taichung, Changhwa, Nantou, Yunlin, Chaiyi, Tainan, Kaohsiung, Pingtung, Ilan, Hualien and Taitung. The summaries of statistics are presented in Tables 4.2 and 4.3.

We first regress weather variables, such as mean temperatures and their variations before and after flowering, and precipitation, on the average rice yield per hectare. Then we redo the regression with temperature and precipita tion in fixed months such as January, March, and July. This second analysis allows farmers to adjust by changing planting dates, whereas the first analysis fixes planting times. The estimated results are presented in Tables 4.4 and 4.5 respectively. They are quadratic models that include six measures of weather. Significant squared terms of the climate variables imply that observed relationships are nonlinear. For instance, the positive quadratic coefficient of the first-stage temperature implies that either higher or lower temperature in the first stage increases the rice yield. However, the negative quadratic coefficients of climatic variables imply that there are optimal levels of climate variables beyond which the rice yield decreases in both directions. Examples include mean temperature after flowering, mean temperature variation before flowering, and precipitation from flowering to harvest (see Table 4.4).

The result of the first analysis suggests that higher temperatures after flowering are beneficial for rice production, but that greater variation of temperature at any time, more annual precipitation, and more precipitation after flowering are all unfavorable to the first-crop rice growth. Wage and rent both act negatively as expected, although only the former is statistically significant. Although rice benefits from a flooded soil environment, more annual precipitation usually implies that typhoons have occurred more frequently during the year and is consequently harmful to rice production. Rainy weather after flowering, which damages normal pollination, is also unfavorable to rice growth.

These results indicate that weather significantly affects the production of the first-crop rice. Particularly mean temperatures, mean variation of temperature before flowering, and precipitation after flowering affect the rice yield nonlinearly.

The estimated results of the second analysis, presented in Table 4.5, show that January temperature, March temperature, July temperature, and January rainfall affect the rice yield significantly and nonlinearly. The findings suggest that higher January and March temperatures are harmful for rice; that higher July temperatures and more January rainfall are beneficial for rice. Because it allows timely land preparation and transplant- ing, abundant January rainfall is beneficial for rice. The nonlinearity of July

Table 4.2 *Summary of Statistics for the Selected Sites: First Crop*

Variable	Taipei Mean	Taipei Std. Dev.	Taichung Mean	Taichung Std. Dev.	Yunlin Mean	Yunlin Std. Dev.	Tainan Mean	Tainan Std. Dev.
rice yield/M.T.	49,495.540	9,508.480	118,254.950	12,411.680	104,314.900	45,781.310	45,784.000	31,663.920
rice area/Ha	19,611.320	8,746.930	31,775.930	4,299.310	26,209.370	6,903.630	11,565.070	5,503.490
average yield/M.T. Ha^{-1}	2.651	0.333	3.800	0.680	3.803	0.818	3.754	1.128
mean temperature: 1st stage/°C	19.050	0.636	19.968	0.611	19.758	0.730	19.758	0.730
mean temperature: 2nd stage/°C	26.949	0.638	27.132	0.450	27.766	0.571	27.766	0.571
temperature variation: 1st stage	7.024	0.964	9.204	0.856	9.797	0.996	9.797	0.996
temperature variation: 2nd stage	8.045	0.730	8.153	0.523	7.660	0.777	7.660	0.777
precipitation: 2nd stage/mm	253.616	98.794	276.754	130.764	167.878	134.701	167.878	134.701
total precipitation/mm	2,165.140	412.050	1,626.520	383.890	1,632.610	506.451	1,632.610	506.451
wage/NT$ Ha^{-1}	26,457.430	14,419.120	26,457.430	14,419.120	26,457.430	14,419.120	26,457.430	14,419.120
rent/NT$ Ha^{-1}	9,123.040	4,004.520	9,123.040	4,004.520	9,123.040	4,004.520	9,123.040	4,004.520

Table 4.2, continued

Variable	Pingtung		Ilan		Hualien		Taitung	
	Mean	Std. Dev.	Mean	Std. Dev.	Mean	Std. Dev.	Mean	Std. Dev.
rice yield/M.T.	121,893.900	46,157.910	59,528.390	11,541.750	30,367.120	7,871.090	26,776.100	6,276.030
rice area/Ha	28,900.680	9,761.780	19,303.610	2,403.180	10,320.020	1,767.500	8,675.660	1,249.040
average yield/M.T. Ha^{-1}	4.295	0.772	3.124	0.661	2.983	0.727	3.132	0.806
mean temperature: 1st stage/°C	19.758	0.730	19.244	0.555	20.485	0.632	20.803	0.664
mean temperature: 2nd stage/°C	25.833	0.735	26.315	0.461	25.850	0.596	25.888	0.503
temperature variation: 1st stage	9.797	0.996	6.485	0.420	6.286	0.558	6.696	0.511
temperature variation: 2nd stage	8.732	0.990	7.009	0.369	6.395	0.569	6.775	0.655
precipitation: 2nd stage/mm	121.591	72.034	206.615	70.890	211.511	101.911	84.771	61.528
total precipitation/mm	1,632.610	506.451	2,781.570	597.691	2,153.480	439.251	1,862.050	502.307
wage/NT$ Ha^{-1}	26,457.430	14,419.120	26,457.430	14,419.120	26,457.430	14,419.120	26,457.430	14,419.120
rent/NT$ Ha^{-1}	9,123.040	4,004.520	9,123.040	4,004.520	9,123.040	4,004.520	9,123.040	4,004.520

Notes

a. Wage and rent are national data and are deflated by WPI (1986=100).

b. First stage is from planting to booting/flowering; second stage is from booting/flowering to harvest.

Sources: Central Weather Bureau; Survey of Rice Production Costs, 1952–1992; Taiwan Food Statistics Book, 1952–1992.

Table 4.3 Summary of Statistics for the Taiwan Area: First Crop

Variable	Taiwan Mean	Std. Dev.
Temperature-1st stage/°C	19.583	0.88997
Temperature-2nd stage/°C	26.787	0.87007
Temperature Variation: 1st stage/°C	8.0363	1.8091
Temperature Variation: 2nd stage/°C	7.6087	1.0115
Rainfall: 2nd stage/mm	211.80	126.01
Total Rainfall/mm	1961.4	726.68
Temperature: January/°C	16.226	1.5968
Temperature: February/°C	16.890	1.8404
Temperature: March/°C	19.340	1.9124
Temperature: April/°C	22.793	1.6435
Temperature: May/°C	25.761	1.4368
Temperature: June/°C	27.449	0.94494
Temperature: July/°C	28.670	0.65579
Rain: January/mm	564.97	604.01
Rain: February/mm	841.62	999.34
Rain: March/mm	1000.6	986.62
Rain: April/mm	1170.1	982.65
Rain: May/mm	2001.3	1310.3
Rain: June/mm	3108.7	2125.1
Rain: July/mm	2470.2	1778.6
Average yield/M.T. Ha^{-1}	3.3465	0.9604

Notes
a. Wage and rent are national data and are deflated by WPI (1986=100).
b. First stage is from planting to booting/flowering; second stage is from booting/flowering to harvest.
Sources: Central Weather Bureau; Survey of Rice Production Costs, 1952–1992; Taiwan Food Statistics Book, 1952–1992.

Table 4.4 Coefficient Estimates of the First Model: First Crop

Variable	Coefficient	Std. Error	t-ratio
Temperature 1st stage	-0.62358E-01	0.2393E-01	-2.606
Temperature Squared 1st stage	0.30751E-01	0.1649E-01	1.865
Temperature 2nd stage	0.48988E-01	0.3285E-01	1.491
Temperature Squared 2nd stage	-0.34784E-01	0.1488E-01	-2.338
Temperature Variation 1st stage	-0.27171E-01	0.2997E-01	-0.906
Temperature Variation squared 1st stage	-0.15622E-01	0.6644E-02	-2.351
Temperature Variation 2nd stage	-0.30775E-01	0.3688E-01	-0.835
Temperature Variation squared 2nd stage	0.19156E-01	0.1398E-01	1.370
Rainfall 2nd stage	-0.40788E-03	0.1824E-03	-2.236
Rainfall squared 2nd stage	-0.13120E-05	0.7986E-06	-1.643
Total rainfall	-0.75769E-04	0.3308E-04	-2.290
Total rainfall squared	-0.26229E-07	0.1990E-07	-1.318
Wage	-0.21306E-04	0.7131E-05	-2.988
Rent	-0.79480E-05	0.1142E-04	-0.696
T	0.79344E-01	0.6550E-02	12.114

Estimated Fixed Effects

KEELUNG	0.94012	0.14717	6.388
TAIPEI	1.62840	0.08373	19.448
TAOYUAN	1.85037	0.08373	22.099
HSINCHU	1.94051	0.08278	23.442
MIAOLI	2.02411	0.08278	24.452
TAICHUNG	2.87776	0.08638	33.315
CHANGHWA	3.13262	0.08638	36.266
NANTOU	2.54878	0.08638	29.507
YUNLIN	2.85746	0.10301	27.740
CHAIYI	2.58914	0.10301	25.135
TAINAN	2.80799	0.10301	27.259
KAOHSIUNG	3.22157	0.10855	29.678
PINGTUNG	3.42462	0.10855	31.549
ILAN	2.16162	0.08420	25.672
HUALIEN	2.02775	0.09781	20.732
TAITUNG	2.12176	0.10214	20.773

Sample Size	656
R-squared	0.8607
Log-Likelihood	-257.3401
F-value (d.f. = (30,625))	128.6900

Table 4.5 Coefficient Estimates of the Second Model: First Crop

Variable	Coefficient	Std. Error	t-ratio
January temperature	-0.30958E-01	0.1441E-01	-2.149
January temperature squared	0.62695E-02	0.4253E-02	1.474
March temperature	-0.16488E-01	0.1276E-01	-1.292
March temperature squared	0.91318E-02	0.3968E-02	2.302
July temperature	0.61200E-01	0.3395E-01	1.803
July temperature squared	-0.73233E-01	0.2556E-01	-2.865
January rain	0.12999E-03	0.5029E-04	2.585
January rain squared	-0.37114E-07	0.2109E-07	-1.760
March rain	-0.35993E-04	0.3059E-04	-1.177
March rain squared	-0.15565E-08	0.8884E-08	-0.175
July rain	0.86011E-05	0.1356E-04	0.634
July rain squared	-0.61177E-08	0.4201E-08	-1.456
Wage	-0.20749E-04	0.7225E-05	-2.872
Rent	-0.50204E-05	0.1200E-04	-0.418
T	0.79525E-01	0.6489E-02	12.255

Estimated Fixed Effects

KEELUNG	0.65054	0.08040	8.091
TAIPEI	1.50864	0.08023	18.804
TAOYUAN	1.73062	0.08023	21.571
HSINCHU	1.87760	0.08807	21.319
MIAOLI	1.96120	0.08807	22.269
TAICHUNG	2.77665	0.07640	36.344
CHANGHWA	3.03151	0.07640	39.679
NANTOU	2.44766	0.07640	32.037
YUNLIN	2.79871	0.08345	33.538
CHAIYI	2.53039	0.08345	30.322
TAINAN	2.74924	0.08345	32.945
KAOHSIUNG	3.08799	0.08345	37.005
PINGTUNG	3.29104	0.08345	39.437
ILAN	2.02789	0.08945	22.671
HUALIEN	2.01157	0.08211	24.498
TAITUNG	2.12382	0.09514	22.323

Sample size	656
Adjusted R-squared	0.84905
Log-likelihood	-268.2322
F-value (d.f. = (30,625))	123.8062

Table 4.6 Predicted Effect of Global Warming on Rice Yield: First Crop (Based on the estimated results of the first model in Table 4.4)

	Scenario	Rice Yield per Hectare	Total Rice Yield
Case 1.	Temperature Increases 2.5°C		
	Precipitation Constant	-0.05863M.T.	-12,281.84M.T.
Case 2.	Temperature Increases 5.0°C		
	Precipitation Constant	-0.16768M.T.	-35,124.94M.T.
Case 3.	Temperature Increases 2.5°C		
	Precipitation Increases 8%	-0.07845M.T.	-16,433.39M.T.
Case 4.	Temperature Increases 5.0°C		
	Precipitation Increases 8%	-0.18749M.T.	-39,274.66M.T.

Note
*   The calculation of changes in total rice yield is based upon 1992 data for the total planted area of rice, i.e., 209,476 hectares.

Table 4.7 Predicted Effect of Global Warming on Rice Yield: First Crop (Based on the estimated results of the second model in Table 4.5)

	Scenario	Rice Yield per Hectare	Total Rice Yield
Case 1.	Temperature Increases 2.5°C		
	Precipitation Constant	-0.32706M.T.	-68,511.88M.T.
Case 2.	Temperature Increases 5.0°C		
	Precipitation Constant	-1.37702M.T.	-288,453.16M.T.
Case 3.	Temperature Increases 2.5°C		
	Precipitation Increases 8%	-0.55470M.T.	-116,197.13M.T.
Case 4.	Temperature Increases 5.0°C		
	Precipitation Increases 8%	-1.60466M.T.	-336,138.41M.T.

Note
*   The calculation of changes in total rice yield is based upon 1992 data for the total planted area of rice, i.e., 209,476 hectares.

temperature affects the rice yield most significantly, which implies that a small increase in July temperature is favorable, however, a big increase could be harmful to the first crop.

5 THE PREDICTED IMPACT OF GLOBAL WARMING ON RICE YIELD

Although this work has shown that weather variability significantly affects the first-crop rice yield, how climate change may affect the rice yield remains unknown. The effects of weather upon rice yield have been shown in the first analysis to be highly nonlinear and to vary with growing phases. Here, we evaluate the effects of a constant shift of temperature and rainfall on rice yield.

Projections of climate change from three-dimensional models of atmospheric general circulation (GCMs) indicate that doubling the concentration of CO_2 in the atmosphere is expected to increase the mean global temperature somewhere from 1.5 to 4.5 °C and to alter amounts of seasonal precipitation (Rosenzweig, 1988). As there is a consensus that the climatic effects of a doubling of CO_2 are likely to occur within the second half of the next century if current trends continue, it is important to project the impact of global warming on rice production. For this projection, a conventional scenario of a doubling of CO_2 is taken. According to most projections, an increase of 2.5° C in temperature will be accompanied by an average increase of 8% in precipitation (Mendelsohn et al., 1994). These changes are applied uniformly by month and site to Taiwan in our calcu-lations. The effect of fertilization with CO_2 is omitted here. Four scenarios of climate change, shown in Tables 4.6 and 4.7, were prepared. The first scenario corresponds to an increase of 2.5° C, the second scenario an increase of 5°C, the third scenario an increase of 2.5°C accompanied by an increase of 8% in precipitation, and the last an increase of 5°C accompanied by an increase of 8% in precipitation. In all scenarios, temperature variations, measured by the difference between mean maximum temperature and mean minimum temperature, are assumed to be unaltered. These results are based upon the current technology of rice cultivation.

The results in Tables 4.6 and 4.7 show that rice yield per hectare will decline as the temperature and precipitation increase above the contemporary mean level. The damages predicted by the second analysis, using temperature and precipitation figures for specific months, are generally larger than those predicted by the first analysis, which uses mean temperatures. In detail, an increase of 2.5°C in the mean temperature decreases the first-crop rice yield by 0.05863 and 0.32706 metric tons per hectare respectively for the first and second models; a 5°C increase in the mean temperature decreases the first-crop rice yield by 0.16768 and 1.37702 metric tons per hectare respectively; an 8% increase in rainfall decreases the first-crop rice yield by 0.01982 and 0.22764 metric tons per hectare respectively. Assuming that the area planted in rice remains the same as in 1992, the annual loss in the first-crop rice yield from global warming ranges from 12281.84 metric tons to 39274.66 metric tons under the first analysis.

Surprisingly, the second analysis predicts a more severe annual loss in the first-crop rice yield, which ranges from 68511.88 metric tons to 336138.41 metric tons. This result could be due to the fact that farmers may respond to warmer weather by planting one more crop, like those in southern Taiwan who plant three times in a year. They may sacrifice a little productivity in the first crop in order to get one more crop. This could be seen from the following fact. The second analysis chooses the July temperature to stand for the summer temperature, however, sites in southern Taiwan harvest rice before July. An increase in July temperature could make farmers in other more northern sites also finish their first crop before July in order to plant another crop, and thus cause greater loss in the first-crop compared to that in the first analysis.

As Horie (1991) pointed out, an increased temperature generally speeds crop development, resulting in an abbreviated vegetative stage and early maturing cultivars. The early maturing cultivars consequently have an increased the risk of floral impotency. As a result, the global warming predicted for the future would adversely affect the rice yield under current technology. As the beneficial effects of fertilization of increased CO_2 are not considered in this work, the obtained impacts of climate change on rice yield could be overestimated.

6 CONCLUSIONS

On the grounds that studying the effect of climate change on agriculture is of particular importance in showing potential costs associated with the accumulation of greenhouse gases, we assessed empirically how rice yields might be affected by climate change. Rice is chosen for this study as it is the primary crop in Taiwan. The empirical study focuses on a 41-year period beginning in 1952 and ending in 1992. A fixed-effects model is employed for estimation by pooling the time series and cross-sectional data. The results indicate that both temperature and precipitation affect the rice yield significantly and nonlinearly.

Furthermore, we projected the impact of climate change according to four different scenarios by adding 2.5°C and 5°C to the mean levels of temperature and an 8% increase in rainfall. The results indicate that rice yield per hectare in the first crop decreases as the temperature and precipitation increase above current mean levels. Hence, the global warming predicted for the future will adversely affect the rice yield under current technology. The fertilization effects of increased CO_2 are not considered in this work, therefore the obtained impacts of climate change on rice yield may be overestimated.

REFERENCES

Adams, R.M., et al. (1988) 'Implications of Global Climate Change for Western Agriculture', *Western Journal of Agricultural Economics*, **13**(2), 348–56.

Arthur, L.M. (1990), 'Potential Adjustments to Climate Change', *Canadian Journal of Agricultural Economics*, **38**(4), 711–16.

Horie, T. (1991) 'Model Analysis of the Effect of Climatic Variation on Rice Yield in Japan', in *Proceedings of Climatic Variations and Change: Implications for Agriculture in the Pacific Rim*, University of California, Davis, 159–68.

Lansigan, F.P. and J.L. Orno (1991), 'Impact of Climate Change on Rice Yield Variability in the Philippines', in *Proceedings of Climatic Variations and Change: Implications for Agriculture in the Pacific Rim*, University of California, Davis, 177–84.

Mendelsohn, R. and D. Shaw, (1994), 'The Impact of Climate Change on Human Mortality', New Haven, CT: Yale School of Forestry and Environmental Studies.

Mendelsohn, R., W.D. Nordhaus, and D. Shaw (1994), 'The Impact of Global Warming on Agriculture', *American Economic Review*, **84**(4), 753–71.

Nerlove, M. (1956), 'Estimates of the Elasticities of Supply of Selected Agricultural Commodities', *Journal of Farm Economics*, **38**(2), 496–509.

Okada, M. (1991), 'Variations of Climate and Rice Production in Northern Japan', in *Proceedings of Climatic Variations and Change: Implications for Agriculture in the Pacific Rim*, University of California, Davis, 169–76.

Rosenzweig, C. (1988), 'Potential Effects of Climate Change on Agricultural Production in the Great Plains: A Simulation Study', Report to Congress on the Effects of Global Climate Change, Washington, DC: U.S. Environmental Protection Agency.

Vergara, B.S. (1980), 'Rice Plant Growth and Development', in Bor S. Luh (ed.), *Rice: Production and Utilization*, West Port: AVI, 75–86.

Wu, H., D. Shaw, and F.T. Fu (1993), 'Climatic Change and Rice Production in Taiwan', in Central Weather Bureau of ROC (ed.), *Proceedings of the Third Symposium on the Impact of Climatic Change on Agricultural Production in the Pacific Rim*, 251–90.

5. Acute Health Effects of Major Air Pollutants in Taiwan

Daigee Shaw, Tsu-Tan Fu, Lung-An Li, Wen-Harn Pan and Jin-Tan Liu

1 INTRODUCTION

Increasing public demand for better environmental quality has pushed through a substantial reform of pollution control policies recently in Taiwan. For example, in 1992, the Legislative Yuan (the Congress) amended the Air Pollution Control Act to adopt an emission charge program and an offset program. Under the emission charge program, the control agencies of local governments are empowered to levy an air pollution emission charge on polluters based on types and quantities of air pollutants emitted. Under the offset program, polluter(s) with more than one stationary source of air pollution within the same air quality control region may request that the control agency of the local government review the situation and allow its (their) individual sources to be free from the limitations set by the emission standards. However, the details of the two new programs are left for the executive branch of the government, i.e., the Environmental Protection Administration (EPA) under the Executive Yuan, to spell out. It is, as usual, a long and tedious process of rent-seeking and consensus-building. During this process, the need for more solid information on air pollution damage assessment is strongly felt.

Since most previous air pollution epidemiological studies were conducted in the US,[1] it is a common practice to use estimates from US studies in Taiwan. However, this practice is not satisfactory, since the types, levels and sources of air pollutants in the US and Taiwan are quite different. First, ozone is regarded as the major health-related air pollutant in the US. However, in Taiwan, according to air quality data reported by the EPA's monitoring stations, particulate matter $(d \leq 10\mu m)$ (PM10), instead of ozone, tends to be the highest in sub-PSI numbers (the daily pollution standard index of a pollutant) among five air pollutants monitored.[2] Such high levels of PM10 concentrations can be attributed to the widely

78

distributed construction sites in urban areas.[3] Second, in addition to different types and sources of air pollutants, the well-documented nonlinearity of air pollutants' damage functions makes the US epidemiological estimates based on low-level concentrations inapplicable to the high-level environment in Taiwan.

This paper reports on a detailed epidemiological investigation of acute health effects on the population in Taiwan associated with daily exposure to major air pollutants, i.e., PM10, ozone, sulfur dioxide (SO_2), and nitrogen dioxide (NO_2). This epidemiological study is the first part of a comprehensive health damage assessment study in Taiwan.[4] The parameters estimated from this comprehensive research can be used to assess health damage caused by air pollution in physical and monetary terms and to design detailed regulations for the revised Air Pollution Control Act, e.g., rates and bases of emission charges.

This comprehensive health damage assessment, in general, and the first-part epidemiological study, in particular, not only combine the best features of previous work in the field, but also make several improvements. First, this is the first study to administer an epidemiological survey and a contingent valuation survey to the same group of respondents in order to obtain a better damage assessment of air pollution. A three-stage survey was conducted between October, 1991 and September, 1992 to collect socio-economic characteristics, daily health status and willingness to pay to avoid the latest episode of acute symptoms of 1,287 individuals living in five selected communities in the Taipei, Kaohsiung and Hualien areas. The study by Alberini et al. (1996) in this book, which reports on the second-part contingent valuation study, concludes that familiarity with the symptoms being valued affects the stability of responses significantly, and calls for interdisciplinary research, pairing epidemiological studies with contingent valuation studies.

Second, in order to obtain a better representation of the population in Taiwan, our survey, which will be described in detail in the next section, was conducted by a stratified random sampling approach in the five selected communities.

Third, in order to obtain a better estimate of the air quality to which the respondents are exposed, the distance between each respondent's residence and the nearest EPA air quality monitoring station had to be less than 750 meters. Then, each respondent's data were matched to their respective daily air pollution and meteorological measurements taken at these stations. According to a 1990 EPA study of the representativeness of the air quality readings at monitoring stations in metropolitan areas in northern Taiwan (EPA-79-007-06-133), the air quality readings of each monitoring station are accurate to 750 meters in distance for SO_2, 650 meters for NO_x, and 500 meters for CO. This high degree of correspondence between the quality of the air breathed by our respondents and that measured by the EPA has not been achieved in previous epidemiological studies.[5]

Next, whereas previous studies analyze either acute health effects (e.g., Korn and Whittemore, 1979; Krupnick, Harrington and Ostro, 1990; Mullahy and Portney, 1990) or chronic respiratory effects (Portney and Mullahy, 1990), our data set allows us to simultaneously analyze the links between the acute respiratory symptoms and chronic diseases on the one hand, and air pollution and other suspected risk factors on the other.

Finally, in the model specification of the acute effect function, we treat both the effects of smoking and chronic diseases as being endogenously determined using an instrumental variable approach. Although Mullahy and Portney (1990) correctly pointed out a potential bias created by treating smoking propensity as an exogenous variable in the respiratory health function, all papers still treat chronic diseases as exogenous in acute effect functions.[6] Actually, the presence of chronic illnesses is endogenous too, since Portney and Mullahy (1990) have shown that air pollutants (especially ozone and total suspended particulate matter) and smoking are significant explanatory variables of the propensity for chronic illnesses. Furthermore, whereas Krupnick, Harrington and Ostro (1990) use a Markov-process logit model developed by Korn and Whittemore (1979) to correct the auto-correlation problem from persistence of symptoms, we accommodate such problems by specifying the presence of acute symptoms as a function of pollution variables in the previous day and other explanatory variables.

In the next section, we describe the survey design and the data set collected. This is followed by a description of our approaches to data analyses designed to measure both the acute and chronic health effects of air pollutants. We then carry out regression analyses. This paper ends with conclusions and suggestions for further research.

2 DATA

The data for this study come from two sources. The air pollution and meteorological data all come from five networked and standardized EPA air quality monitoring stations located, respectively, in the five communities in question. The individual health data and socio-economic data come from a carefully designed and administered survey.

2.1 Survey Design

The survey was designed to represent the structure of the air quality and socio-economic characteristics of the population in Taiwan. The respondents were restricted to those living within 750 meters of one of five air quality monitoring stations: Sungshan in Taipei, Yungho in Taipei County, Sanmin and Fushing in Kaohsiung, and Hualien; and those living and working (or attending school) in the same metropolitan area.

These five stations were selected because they are exposed to quite different levels and types of air pollution and because they are located in cities with different socio-economic structures. Sungshan is in Taipei, which is the most populated city in Taiwan where the service sector dominates. Taipei is in the midst of an infrastructural construction boom and thus according to the 1991 EPA air pollution statistics, has higher PM10 and lower ozone levels than other cities. Sanmin and Fushing are in Kaohsiung, which is the second largest city and is the center of heavy and petrochemical industries. They have higher levels of ozone and PM10 concentrations. Yungho, a suburban town in the Taipei metropolitan area, and Hualien, a quiet town on the east coast, were selected for the study because of their lower PM10 and ozone concentrations.

The respondents were selected according to a stratified random sampling approach. The variable according to which the population was stratified is age. It is well known that the elderly and children are more prone to experience acute illness. However, at the same time, their frequency in the general population is much lower than middle-aged adults. Thus, the sampling probabilities for those above 64 years old and under 15 were set to be higher than their respective population shares. The resulting shares of the sample by age and their respective shares in the overall population were 29.1% and 27.6% for those under 15, 61.5% and 67.4% for those between 14 and 65, and 9.4% and 5% for those above 64.

There were three stages in the whole survey process: a background survey, a 92-day diary survey, and a contingent valuation survey.[7] The background survey was pretested twice by professional interviewers before the survey began. Then, in October of 1991, professional interviewers of Gallup Taiwan administered an extensive baseline interview at homes of respondents being sampled according to the stratified sampling design. Respondents were asked to answer the following four kinds of questions: (1) health status, including any chronic respiratory diseases diagnosed, (2) exposure to air pollution at home, work or school, and on the road, (3) lifestyle, including diet, smoking and exercise, and (4) standard socio-economic and demographic questions.

In the second stage, respondents were asked to fill out diaries on their daily health status, activities, medical visits and medication taken, from November 1, 1991 to January 31, 1992. This diary is similar to the questionnaire used in Krupnick, Harrington and Ostro (1990). In the diary are recorded the presence of any one of 15 air-pollutant-related symptoms (eye irritation, headache, runny nose, sinus problems, dry/scratchy throat, sore throat, dry cough, cough with phlegm, wheezing, allergy, chest pain, a cold, asthma, fever, and shortness of breath), and the severity of symptoms, including activity restrictions, medical visits or medication taken. Professionally trained interviewers interviewed respondents by telephone once a week over the three-month period to record the diary information and to remind the respondents to keep on filling out their diaries. The whole survey process was concluded with a contingent valuation survey which was administered in face-to-face interviews in September of 1992. The total sample size in the first stage was 1,287. After three months of telephone interviews, the sample size was reduced to 953. The final sample size after the three stages was 864.

2.2 Data Description

The symptom and severity data collected are used to construct one discrete dependent variable: acute respiratory disease (ARD). This variable is defined as follows:

ARD $= 1$, if presence of any one of the 15 symptoms

$\qquad = 0$ otherwise.

Table 5.1 reports the basic information on acute symptoms for the whole sample. To avoid a possible reporting bias which may result from respondents' unfamiliarity with the diary survey technique, we skipped the first 10 days' data.[8] Observations are defined in terms of 'person-days'. Constructing the sample in this manner results in a panel of 78,146 observations (953 persons multiplied by 82 days).

Table 5.1 shows that about 53.8% of persons in the sample had experienced one or more symptoms (ARD$=1$) during this 82-day period.[9] The rate of occurrence of symptoms is 5.1% of total person-days in the sample. Among the five communities, Yungho had the highest rates of occurrence in terms both of persons and symptom-days. On the contrary, Hualien had the lowest rates of occurrence. There are substantial variations in the rates of occurrence between communities.

Definitions and descriptive statistics of nonenvironmental variables are given in Table 5.2. The means and standard deviations are listed for the whole sample. Of the 953 persons in the sample, exactly 50% are male, 56% are single, 61% exercise regularly. Although 79% have air conditioning at home, only 29% own a dehumidifier. The average age is 29. The average number of years of formal education is 8. Smokers make up 18% of persons in the sample, while 44% are second-hand smokers. Seven percent of them have one or more of the five chronic diseases: asthma, chronic bronchitis,

Table 5.1 Descriptive Statistics for Acute Symptoms

Area	(1) Sample Size (Persons)	(2) Survey Period (day)	(3) Person-days = (1)×(2)	Occurrence of Symptoms		Rate of Occurrence (%)	
				(4) Persons with Symptoms[a]	(5) Symptom-Days	(6) Persons (4)/(1)	(7) Symptom-days (5)/(3)
Sungshan	172	83	14276	103	749	59.9	5.3
Yungho	160	83	13280	95	858	59.4	6.5
Sanmin	192	83	15936	105	751	54.7	4.7
Fushing	205	83	17015	118	902	57.6	5.3
Hualien	224	83	18592	92	744	41.1	4.0
All	953	83	79099	513	4004	53.8	5.1

Note
a. Presence of any one of the 15 symptoms.

Table 5.2 Descriptive Statistics: Nonenvironmental Variables, N=953

Variable	Definition	Mean	Standard
CHRONIC	= 1 if any one of the five diseases (asthma, chronic bronchitis, emphysema, heart trouble, or high blood pressure) has been diagnosed, = 0 otherwise	0.07	0.26
SMOKER	= 1 if smoking regularly, = 0 otherwise	0.18	0.38
SECOND-HAND SMOKER	= 1 if a nonsmoker usually breathing second-hand smoke staying in an office or classroom with smokers, = 0 otherwise	0.44	0.50
AGE	= years since birth	28.82	19.48
YOUNG	= 1 if age ≤ 14, =0 otherwise		
OLD	= 1 if age ≥ 65, =0 otherwise		
EDUCATION	= years of formal education	8.24	4.95
SEX	= 1 if male, = 0 if female	0.50	0.50
INCOME	= total household monthly income (NT$)	56,457	30,759
SINGLE	= 1 if single (unmarried, married but separate, divorce or widowed), = 0 otherwise	0.56	0.50
CROWD	= number of persons/ping in a household[a]	0.16	0.096
AIR CONDITIONING	= 1 if has air conditioners at home, = 0 otherwise	0.79	0.41
DEHUMIDIFIER	= 1 if has dehumidifiers at home, = 0 otherwise	0.29	0.45
EXPOSURE AT WORK	= 1 if exposed to air pollution at work or school = 0 otherwise	0.32	0.47
EXERCISE	= 1 if exercises regularly, = 0 otherwise	0.61	0.49
STUDENT	= 1 if a student in school, = 0 otherwise	0.43	0.50

Note
a. *Ping* is an area unit commonly used in Taiwan. One *ping* = 3.305078 square meters = 3.954 square yards.

emphysema, heart trouble, or high blood pressure.

Table 5.3 shows descriptive statistics for four air pollutants, PSI, temperature and humidity. Daily measures, five-year averages and ambient air quality standards of four pollutants: particulate matter (PM10), ozone, nitrogen dioxide (NO_2), and sulfur dioxide (SO_2), are reported. It is clear that PM10 is the most serious air pollutant among the four, since its ambient air quality standard has been violated in four of the five stations. The ambient standard for SO_2 has been violated in two stations. The standard for ozone has only been violated in Yungho, due to the heavy traffic there, and the readings for NO_2 are always lower than the standard. There are great differences in these variables among the five communities. It is clear that Hualien is the cleanest city, while Kaohsiung, where Sanmin and Fushing are located, is the dirtiest.

Each respondent's daily records are related to the corresponding daily measures of ambient air quality, humidity and temperature monitored at nearby stations. The daily data are superior to the temporal means of these variables because the former incorporate the information of the probability distributions.

3   STATISTICAL MODELS

In order to take the endogeneity of smoking and chronic diseases into account, we specify the simultaneous-equations model as:

$$Y_1^* = \gamma_1 X_1 + e_1 \tag{5.1}$$

$$Y_2^* = \gamma_2 X_2 + e_2 \tag{5.2}$$

$$Y_3^* = \alpha_3 Y_1^P + \beta_3 Y_2^P + \gamma_3 X_3 + e_3 \tag{5.3}$$

where

$$
\begin{aligned}
Y_i &= 1 \quad if \quad Y_i^* > 0 \quad i=1,\ 2,\ 3 \\
Y_i &= 0 \quad \text{otherwise}
\end{aligned}
\tag{5.4}
$$

$$Y_i^P = \text{Prob}(Y_i{=}1) \quad i=1,\ 2 \tag{5.5}$$

Table 5.3   Descriptive Statistics: Pollution and Meteorological Variables

Variable	Areas	Daily Readings in the 92 days				Ambient Air Q. Standards	Five-year Averages[a]
		Mean	S.D.	Minimum	Maximum		
PSI	Sungshan	80.04	29.82	44.00	187.00		
	Yungho	56.10	18.43	27.00	117.00		
	Sanmin	88.12	17.84	45.00	144.00		
	Fushing	99.21	27.75	32.00	185.00		
	Hualien	34.16	7.22	19.00	57.00		
	All	71.52	31.94	19.00	187.00		
$PM10(\mu g/m^3)$	Sungshan	112.62	62.85	41.33	332.54	$125\ \mu g/m^3$	77.75
(daily mean	Yungho	62.80	31.71	28.43	186.17	(one-hour	89.63
one-hour	Sanmin	133.89	36.89	47.46	251.58	reading)	100.72
reading)	Fushing	155.08	52.12	46.25	322.71		112.26
	Hualien	31.88	8.64	17.13	52.08		42.67
	All	98.98	62.22	17.13	332.54		84.61
$O_3(ppb)$	Sungshan	17.55	14.63	0.00	92.00	120 ppb	27.70
(daily	Yungho	30.54	19.54	9.00	125.00	(hourly	32.57
maximum	Sanmin	44.66	18.83	7.00	80.00	mean)	48.03
one-hour	Fushing	39.55	19.22	5.00	80.00		44.43
reading)	Hualien	34.56	8.42	12.00	69.00		25.28
	All	33.37	18.99	0.00	125.00		35.60
$SO_2(ppb)$	Sungshan	43.56	19.93	6.09	113.54	100 ppb	36.00
(daily mean	Yungho	30.16	20.52	5.88	99.33	(daily mean	30.80
one-hour	Sanmin	21.10	8.53	6.33	47.57	one-hour	17.05
reading)	Fushing	32.74	27.49	5.04	122.00	reading)	25.08
	Hualien	9.93	4.73	4.21	24.71		13.33
	All	27.49	21.43	4.21	122.00		24.45
$NO_2(ppb)$	Sungshan	69.35	30.24	34.00	176.00	250 ppb	26.42
(daily	Yungho	56.76	30.01	22.00	193.00	(hourly	29.21
maximum	Sanmin	67.33	32.40	9.00	242.00	mean)	24.88
one-hour	Fushing	82.11	34.68	20.00	200.00		26.90
reading)	Hualien	34.51	8.24	9.00	54.00		10.85
	All	62.01	32.77	9.00	242.00		23.65
HUMIDITY	Sungshan	77.92	9.02	56.83	96.85		75.8
(%)	Yungho	77.26	9.49	57.21	93.96		75.8
(daily mean	Sanmin	79.13	7.85	57.00	97.56		75.8
relative	Fushing	80.66	6.73	62.79	95.46		75.8
humidity)	Hualien	79.13	8.46	55.04	96.38		78.6
	All	78.82	8.41	55.04	97.56		76.7
TEMPERATURE	Sungshan	19.85	4.41	10.00	30.00		23.24
(°C)	Yungho	20.60	4.46	10.00	32.00		23.24
(daily	Sanmin	21.93	3.25	11.00	29.00		25.06
maximum	Fushing	24.24	3.28	13.00	29.00		25.06
temperature)	Hualien	22.15	3.56	12.00	28.00		23.34
	All	21.75	4.10	10.00	32.00		23.88

Note

a. Average values of 1987–1991. They are the five-year averages of yearly means which are the averages of monthly means.

Y_1^* measures the propensity to smoke, Y_2^* measures the propensity to have chronic diseases, Y_3^* measures the short-term health status. These three variables are assumed to be latent indexes. Y_1 is the observed dichotomous smoker variable, Y_2 is the observed chronic variable, Y_3 is the observed acute response variable, i.e., ARD; X_1, X_2 and X_3 are sets of independent variables; the residual variables e_1, e_2 and e_3 are assumed to be standard-normally distributed and are not independent.[10] This model says that a person's short-term health status depends on his/her probabilities of being a smoker and having a chronic disease, in addition to a set of environmental and nonenvironmental variables. His/her propensity to smoke depends on a set of nonenvironmental exogenous variables, and his/her propensity to have chronic diseases depends on a set of environmental and non-environmental exogenous variables. Thus, Y_1 and Y_2 precede Y_3.

Maddala (1983, p. 123) suggests a two-stage estimation method for this model. We first obtain the probit ML estimates of γ_1 and γ_2. We then substitute $\Phi(\gamma_i X_i)$ for Y_i^p, $i = 1,2$, in (5.3), and estimate (5.3) by the probit model. Maddala notes that the resulting estimates are consistent. During the estimation process, the probit ML estimates of γ_1 and γ_2 which are consistent and asymptotically normal will provide us with valuable information about the smoking behavior function and the epidemiological chronic illness response function.

In addition to the above two-stage method, (5.3) is also estimated by the ordinary probit model. This model fails to account for the potential endogeneity of smoking and chronic disease variables.

4   ESTIMATION RESULTS

In using the diary data, we have encountered an autocorrelation problem due to the persistence of symptoms. To deal with this problem, Korn and Whittemore (1979) developed a Markov-process logit model in which a lagged dependent variable was added as a regressor in a logit model, whereas Schwartz, Hasselblad, and Pitcher (1988) accommodate this problem by specifying an instrumental variable for the lagged dependent variable in their logit model. We have tried both approaches in our analyses. However, the results show that most risk factors previously identified become insignificant when any of the above approaches is used. To solve this problem, we adopt an instrumental variable approach suggested by Kennedy (1992, p. 139), where lagged values of pollutant variables are used as the instruments.

Table 5.4 presents the regression results using the whole sample. Regression (1) is the epidemiological chronic disease effect function. It is found

Table 5.4   Probit Regressions (Standard errors in parentheses)

Variable	CHRONIC (1)	SMOKER (2)	ACUTE (3) Simultaneous Equation	ACUTE (4) Single Equation
CONSTANT	-71.1361***	-1.9594***	-1.1634***	-1.1948***
	(24.2662)	(0.3218)	(0.1061)	(0.1048)
PM10			4.238E-4**	3.713E-4**
			(1.71E-4)	(1.72E-4)
SO$_2$			0.0012***	0.0014***
			(4.5E-4)	(4.48E-4)
O$_3$			9.592E-4	6.829E-4
			(5.87E-4)	(5.82E-4)
HUMIDITY			-0.0022**	-0.0023**
			(9.99E-4)	(9.98E-4)
TEMPERATURE			-0.0121***	-0.0113***
			(0.0025)	(0.0025)
PM10	0.0306**			
(five-year average)	(0.0151)			
SO$_2$	0.0625**			
(five-year average)	(0.0274)			
HUMIDITY	0.8810***			
(five-year average)	(0.3051)			
TEMPERATURE	-0.1024			
(five-year average)	(0.2795)			
CHRONIC			0.6897***	0.0536*
			(0.1716)	(0.0324)
SMOKER			-0.3190***	-0.1183***
			(0.0653)	(0.0298)
SECOND-HAND	0.0395		6.433E-4	-0.0064
SMOKER	(0.1502)		(0.0177)	(0.0186)
YOUNG	-0.1589	-1.4893***		
	(0.2878)	(0.4491)		
OLD	1.0519***	0.1996		
	(0.2281)	(0.2062)		
AGE			-0.0030***	-0.0018***
			(8.27E-4)	(6.27E-4)
EDUCATION	-0.0097	-0.0064	-0.0076***	-0.0116***
	(0.0245)	(0.0202)	(0.0022)	(0.0021)
SEX	0.3507**	2.0582***	0.0131	-0.0141
	(0.1506)	(0.1744)	(0.0258)	(0.0186)
INCOME	7.441E-7	3.4987E-6	-5.829E-7**	-5.628E-7**
	(2.339E-6)	(2.2E-6)	(2.791E-7)	(2.791E-7)
SINGLE	0.3111*	-0.2416	-0.0485*	0.0121
	(0.1811)	(0.1742)	(0.0270)	(0.0240)
CROWD	0.3310	0.4006	0.1374	0.1610*
	(0.6782)	(0.5771)	(0.0853)	(0.0841)

Table 5.4, continued

Variable	CHRONIC (1)	SMOKER (2)	ACUTE (3) Simultaneous Equation	ACUTE (4) Single Equation
AIR CONDITIONING	0.0253 (0.1799)	0.1411 (0.1582)		
DEHUMIDIFIER	-0.0473 (0.1750)	-0.0641 (0.1540)		
EXPOSURE AT WORK	0.1563 (0.1579)	0.3006** (0.1402)	0.0766*** (0.0186)	0.0738*** (0.0180)
EXERCISE	0.1974 (0.1608)	-0.5111*** (0.1362)	0.0151 (0.0189)	0.0469*** (0.0179)
STUDENT		-1.0521*** (0.2943)		
-2log L	47.0522	344.8668	289.6475	264.7127
N	793	802	65326	65243

Notes

* significant at 10% level

** significant at 5% level

*** significant at 1% level

that, as expected, long-term environmental variables, i.e., five-year averages of PM10, SO_2 and humidity, have significant effects on a person's propensity to have one or more of the five chronic diseases, i.e., asthma, chronic bronchitis, emphysema, heart trouble, or high blood pressure. Older people, males and single people are more prone to have chronic diseases. Variables for defensive activities, such as AIR CONDITIONER, DEHUMIDIFIER and EXERCISE, INCOME and EDUCATION are not significant explanatory variables in Regression (1).[11]

Regression (2) is the smoking behavior function. Also as expected, males and those exposed to air pollutants at work are more likely to be smokers, while young people, students and regular exercisers are less likely to smoke.

As Regressions (3) and (4) in Table 5.4 clearly show, treating smoking and chronic disease as endogenous variables has a significant effect on the coefficients of the acute response function. Specifically, the sizes and significance of the coefficient estimates of CHRONIC, SMOKER, AGE, SINGLE and EXERCISE change substantially. The two-stage method for the simultaneous equations model changes SINGLE from an unimportant variable to an important determinant of acute symptoms. It also makes the coefficient estimates of CHRONIC and SMOKER increase to more than three times the original estimates and become highly significant. On the other hand, it makes EXERCISE become an insignificant explanatory variable rather than an unexpectedly positive and significant one. It is notable that the sizes and significance of the coefficient estimates of the air pollution and climate variables are relatively stable between Regressions (3) and (4), except for OZONE.

Using the two-stage method, we could conclude that PM10 and SO_2 are positively and highly significantly correlated with the likelihood of experiencing acute symptoms, while OZONE is positively and barely significantly correlated, at the 10% level. It is less likely that one would experience acute symptoms on the higher humidity days because those days are usually rainy days and precipitation will probably reduce the amounts of most of the air pollutants.

The probability of experiencing acute symptoms responds as expected to other variables, such as TEMPERATURE (it is more likely on colder days), AGE (younger people are more likely to suffer), EDUCATION (the more educated are less likely), INCOME (those with higher incomes are less likely), SINGLE (singles are less likely), and EXPOSURE AT WORK (those exposed at work or school are more likely to experience acute symptoms).

The most surprising finding in the model estimated here is the negative association between being a smoker and the likelihood of experiencing acute symptoms, after holding other variables, including air pollutants, constant. This finding seems contrary to common prior beliefs. However, a similar result is found in Portney and Mullahy (1990). It is also found in Krupnick, Harrington, and Ostro (1990) that smokers are less acutely sensitive to air pollutants than nonsmokers are.[12] The physiological explanation provided in Krupnick, Harrington, and Ostro (1990) is that when lungs come into contact with smoke, chemicals may be formed or mucus may be secreted that have the ancillary effect of protecting the lung tissue from irritation by air pollutants. They also note that this finding is becoming accepted among health professionals. The same physiological reason can be used to explain our finding of the negative association between smoking and acute symptoms, since a smoker's lung tissue is not only protected from irritation by air pollutants but also by other uncontrolled irritants.

5   EFFECTS OF AIR POLLUTANTS

An important application of the epidemiological analysis is to predict the effects of air pollution control programs on human health. Owing to the nonlinearity of the probit models, the magnitude of the estimated parameters from probit models do not contain intuitive meaning. In order to compare across variables with different units of measurement, unitless elasticities can be used.

Table 5.5 presents the elasticities of PM10, SO_2 and ozone at three levels of magnitude. An elasticity with respect to an air pollutant represents the percentage change in the probability of ARD$=1$ given a 1% change in the daily concentration of the pollutant. For example, the elasticity at the mean PM10 of 98.98 $\mu g/m^3$ is 0.0868, implying a 0.0868% increase in the probability of ARD$=1$ being associated with 1% increase of PM10 concentration.

It is found that, using the two-stage approach, in which smoking and chronic disease status are endogenously determined, the estimated elasticities of PM10 and ozone increase relative to their single equation estimates. On the other hand, the estimated elasticity of SO_2 decreases.

Case 1 shows the elasticities of air pollutants at their prevalent levels represented by their means across the five EPA stations and the sample period. Among pollutants, PM10 has the highest elasticity which is consistent with the findings from EPA statistics that PM10 is the most serious air pollutant among the five pollutants monitored in Taiwan presently. By comparing Cases 1 and 2, it is found that pollutants' elasticities increase with respect to their respective concentrations. If the concentration of PM10 decreases by 50%, then its elasticity decreases to 0.0438.

Case 3 presents the elasticities of the three pollutants at their respective ambient air quality standards. This case is needed since it is very hard to compare the acute effects of the three pollutants on human health based on Cases 1 and 2. This is simply because their elasticities vary greatly depending on the levels of pollutants and their prevalent levels are not comparable. The three pollutants' ambient air quality standards are presumably comparable levels.

It is found in Case 3 that SO_2 and O_3 are much more health-damaging than PM10 at their ambient standards. This result has two policy implications. First, the ambient standards for SO_2 and O_3 are too lenient. They should be made more stringent. Second, it would be very beneficial for human health to reduce the number of days on which the levels of SO_2 and O_3 exceed their respective standards.

The purpose of the study is to assess health damage caused by air pollution. In order to do so, using the regression estimates of the two-stage approach, we first compute the probabilities of ARD$=1$ for a representative person living in the three cities at the sample averages of the covariates (Table 5.6). Then, we calculate non-marginal changes in the probabilities (ΔP) if the current daily air quality in each city is improved. Three cases of improvement are investigated. ΔP_1, ΔP_2 and ΔP_3 in Table 5.6 are the results

Table 5.5   Estimated Elasticities

	SIMULTANEOUS	SINGLE EQUATION
CASE I: Evaluated at the means of pollutants		
PM10 = 98.98 $\mu g/m^3$	0.0868	0.0759
SO_2 = 27.49 ppb	0.0685	0.0806
O_3 = 33.37 ppb	0.0663	0.0471
CASE II: Evaluated at 50% of the means		
PM10 = 49.49 $\mu g/m^3$	0.0438	0.0383
SO_2 = 13.74 ppb	0.0345	0.0406
O_3 = 16.68 ppb	0.0333	0.0237
CASE III: Evaluated at ambient air quality standards		
PM10 = 125 $\mu g/m^3$	0.1014	0.0891
SO_2 = 100 ppb	0.2304	0.2723
O_3 = 120 ppb	0.2204	0.1573

Table 5.6   Predicted Effects of Air Quality Improvements

	Taipei	Kaohsiung	Hualien
P(ARD=1 | covariates= means)	0.0502	0.0520	0.0444
ΔP_1 (PM10 50% off only)[a]	0.0024	0.0032	6.30E-04
ΔP_2 (SO_2 50% off only)	0.0027	0.0017	5.58E-04
ΔP_3 (O_3 50% off only)	8.6E-4	0.0021	0.0015
ΔP_4 (PM10, SO_2 and O_3 50% off simultaneously)	0.0058	0.0067	0.0027
ΔP_5 (PM10, SO_2 and O_3 are lowered to Hualien's levels simultaneously)	0.0058	0.0075	
Population in 1991	2,718,000	1,361,600	107,600
Population×365 (person-days)	992,070,000	496,984,000	39,274,000
(Population×365)×ΔP_1	2,380,968	1,590,348.8	24,742.6
(Population×365)×ΔP_2	2,678,589	844,872.8	21,914.9
(Population×365)×ΔP_3	858,140.6	1,043,666.4	58,911
(Population×365)×ΔP_4	5,754,006	3,329,792.8	106,039.8
(Population×365)×ΔP_5	5,754,006	3,727,380	

Note

a. ΔP_1 = P(ARD=1 | covariates= means) - P(ARD=1|PM10 50% off only). Other ΔPs are defined similarly.

of the first case of improving each of the three air pollutants (one at a time) by 50%. The other two cases are to improve the three air pollutants by 50% simultaneously (ΔP_4), or to improve them to their respective levels in Hualien (ΔP_5). Lastly, we calculate the total health benefits, i.e., the decrease in the total number of person-days experiencing one of the symptoms if the three cases of improvements come true in the three cities, assuming the average concentrations of pollutants over the year 1991 are the same as the averages of the 92 days we investigated in 1991 and 1992.

Table 5.6 presents the results of the calculation. First, the P values tell us that the daily probability of a representative person living in Kaohsiung experiencing acute symptoms is 5.2%, which is equivalent to 18.98 days in the year 1991. It is slightly higher than in Taipei. Hualien is the most environmentally comfortable city with an ARD probability of 4.44%. The number of days of ARD$=1$ for a representative Kaohsiung person would have decreased by 2.74 ($=0.0075 \times 365$) days in 1991 if he had moved to Hualien. Second, it is found that there is an interactive effect between the three air pollutants, since the sums of ΔP_1, ΔP_2 and ΔP_3, which are the sums of the three individual pollutants' effects given other things as constant, are slightly greater than ΔP_4, which is the effects of a simultaneous improvement of the three pollutants by 50% in Taipei and Kaohsiung. However, these two numbers are almost the same in Hualien. The interactive effects, which may be either synergism or antagonism, is a good topic for further studies using the data. Third, the total health effects of a simultaneous improvement of the three pollutants by 50% in Taipei and Kaohsiung, are 5.75 million person-days and 3.33 million person-days, respectively. The same kind of data can be calculated for different kinds of scenarios and every city in Taiwan. These data coupled with the WTP to avoid symptoms estimated in Alberini et al. (1996) can provide us with the value of a pollution control policy which would make the improvement happen.

6   CONCLUSIONS AND FURTHER RESEARCH

The EPA in Taiwan has usually opted for relying on foreign studies and standards to design pollution control strategies and to issue standards, since limited epidemiological data are available on the relationship between pollution and health in Taiwan. Although this practice of regulation transfer is cost-saving, it sometimes backfires. The long process of rent-seeking and consensus-building for formulating the air pollution emission charge program is a current example.

This study is the first carefully designed, surveyed and analyzed epidemiological investigation of daily acute health effects associated with daily exposure to air pollutants in Taiwan, using statistical techniques common in the social and natural sciences. It makes advances in methodologies such as the three-month diary survey, the close match of exposure data and illness data, the careful selection of monitoring stations taking the special features and deviation of air pollutants into account, the randomly selected sample in the vicinity of the stations, and the use of a simultaneous probit model, treating both smoking and chronic disease as being endogenously determined, to analyze the data.

However, several improvements can still be made. First, the effects of the interaction among pollutants and meteorological variables, i.e., synergism and antagonism, may be too complicated to allow use of the current regression model. Further studies of the effects are needed to derive a better air pollution index. Second, we can analyze the panel data feature of the diary survey data to advance our understanding of the dose-response function even further.

Many variables that could influence human behavior and health status are not present in the current study. This epidemiological study indicates that human behavior, such as averting behavior and income effects, are important since they can influence the effects of pollution on humans significantly.[13] Thus, those missing variables could be a source of bias in the present study. Further exploration of those variables is warranted.

APPENDIX

Appendix 5.A   Questionnaire for the Background Survey

A. The interviewer fills out:

0. Identification number:_____
   Name:_____
   Address:_____
   Telephone number:_____
1. The monitoring station number:_____
   The distance between the respondent's house and the monitoring station: _____meters
2. The width of the road outside the respondent's house:_____meters
3. Which floor does the respondent live on?_____

B. The respondent answers:

1. Are you employed at a job other than a job you work at within your own house?
   (1)___No
   (2)___Yes (please write down your office's address:_____)
2. Are you a student at school?

(1)___No
(2)___Yes (please write down your school's
address:_____)

B-1. Family information

3. How old is your house?
    (1)___less than 1 year
    (2)___1–5 years
    (3)___6–10 years
    (4)___11–15 years
    (5)___16–20 years
    (6)___over 20 years old
    (7)___don't know
4. The area of your house:_____
    The number of rooms in your house:____
5. Types of water heating equipment used? (multiple choice)
    (1)___gas, indoor
    (2)___gas, outdoor
    (3)___electric
    (4)___other (please specify _____)
6. Type of indoor cooking equipment used? (multiple choice)
    (1)___gas
    (2)___electric
    (3)___other (please specify _____)
7. Are there any air conditioners in your house?
    (1)___No
    (2)___Yes, central system
    (3)___Yes, window only
    (4)___other (please specify_____)
8. Are there any dehumidifiers in your house?
    (1)___No
    (2)___Yes, central system
    (3)___Yes, room only
    (4)___other (please specify_____)
9. What kind of water do you drink? (multiple choice)
    (1)___ tap water
    (2)___ spring
    (3)___ ground water
    (4)___ distilled water
    (5)___ mineral water
    (6)___ other (please specify_____)

10. How many persons live in your house?____

B-2. Personal Information

I. Basic information

11. Your birth year and month: _____
12. Sex: (1)___Female
                  (2)___Male
13. Height:_____cm
   Weight:_____kg
14. Marital status:
   (1)___unmarried: ___single, ___cohabiting
   (2)___married, ___married but separated
   (3)___divorced or widowed: ___single, ___cohabiting
15. Position in the household:
   (1)___Father   (2)___Mother   (3)___Grandfather
   (4)___Grandmother (5)___Child   (6)___Other (Please
                                    specify___)
16. How long have you lived at the present address:____years
17. (17-1) The house in which you live is
   (1)___rented   (2)___owned by yourself
   (17-2) If rented, the monthly rent is
   (1)_____NT$
   (2)___Unknown
   (3)___Refuse to answer
   (17-3) If you are the owner of your house, how much would you ask for
   the monthly rent?
   (1)_____NT$
   (2)___Unknown
   (3)___Refuses to answer
18. (18-1) What is the last place you lived in?_____
   (18-2) And for how long?_____years
19. (19-1) What is the largest city you lived in for three or more
     years?_____
   (19-2) And for how long?_____years
20. Highest education level completed:
   (1)___elementary school (and below)
   (2)___junior high school
   (3)___senior high school
   (4)___university or college
   (5)___graduate degree

II. Work and school environment

II-1. Work environment (skip to question 31 if the respondent has no job outside his/her own house)

21. (21-1) Which industry do you engage in?_____
    (21-2) What is your occupation?_____
22. (22-1) Do you work indoors?
    (1)___Shop
    (2)___Office
    (3)___Factory
    (4)___Other (please specify_____)
    (22-2) Do you work outdoors?
    (1)___Stationary
    (2)___Mobile
    (3)___Other (please specify_____)
    (You may work both indoors and outdoors.)
23. Are there any air conditioners in your workplace?
    (1)___No
    (2)___Yes, central system
    (3)___Yes, window only
    (4)___Other (please specify_____)
24. Are there any dehumidifiers in your workplace?
    (1)___No
    (2)___Yes, central system
    (3)___Yes, room only
    (4)___Other (please specify_____)
25. (25-1) What is the usual duration of your commute to work?
    From ____ o'clock and ____minutes to ____ o'clock and ____minutes
    (25-2) On your commute to work, how much time do you usually spend in a:
    (1)___automobile   ___hour(s)___minutes
    (2)___motorcycle   ___hour(s)___minutes
    (3)___bicycle   ___hour(s)___minutes
    (4)___bus   ___hour(s)___minutes
    (5)___train   ___hour(s)___minutes
    (6)___walk   ___hour(s)___minutes
    (7)___waiting   ___hour(s)___minutes
    (8) other (please specify)___hour(s)___minutes
26. (26-1) What is the usual duration of your commute from work?
    From ____ o'clock and ____ minutes to ____ o'clock and ____ minutes
    (26-2) On your commute from work, how much time do you usually

spend in a:
(1)___automobile   ____hour(s)____minutes
(2)___motorcycle   ____hour(s)____minutes
(3)___bicycle   ____hour(s)____minutes
(4)___bus   ____hour(s)____minutes
(5)___train   ____hour(s)____minutes
(6)___walk   ____hour(s)____minutes
(7)___waiting   ____hour(s)____minutes
(8) other (please specify)____hour(s)___minutes

27. Do you travel predominately on roads with traffic jams?
    (1)____no
    (2)____yes

28. (28-1) How many hours a day do you usually work?____ hours.
    (28-2) How many days of the week do you usually work?____ days.

29. (29-1) Are you now at your job exposed to irritating odor, smoke, dust, or fumes?
    (1)___No (skip to Question 30)
    (2)___Yes
    (29-2) Kind of irritant: (multiple choice)
    (1)____odor
    (2)____dust
    (3)____smoke and fumes
    (4)____other (please specify)_____
    (5)don't know

30. Have you been exposed to irritating smoke, dust, or fumes at your past workplaces?
    (1)___No
    (2)___Yes. For how long:_____years
    (2-1)___odor
    (2-2)___dust
    (2-3)___smoke and fumes
    (2-4)___others, _____
    (2-5)___don't know

II-2. School environment (skip to question 36 if the respondent is not a student)

31. (31-1) What is the usual duration of your commute to school?
    From ____ o'clock and ____ minutes to ____ o'clock and ____minutes
    (31-2) On your commute to school, how much time do you usually spend in a:
    (1)___automobile_____hour(s)_____minutes

(2)___motorcycle   ____hour(s)____minutes
(3)___bicycle   ____hour(s)____minutes
(4)___bus   ____hour(s)____minutes
(5)___train   ____hour(s)____minutes
(6)___walk   ____hour(s)____minutes
(7)___waiting   ____hour(s)____minutes
(8) other (please specify)___hour(s)____minutes

32. (32-1) What is the usual duration of your commute from school?
   From ____ o'clock and ____minutes to ____ o'clock and ____minutes
   (32-2) On your commute from school, how much time do you usually
   spend in a:
   (1)___automobile   ____hour(s)____minutes
   (2)___motorcycle   ____hour(s)____minutes
   (3)___bicycle   ____hour(s)____minutes
   (4)___bus   ____hour(s)____minutes
   (5)___train   ____hour(s)____minutes
   (6)___walk   ____hour(s)____minutes
   (7)___waiting   ____hour(s)____minutes
   (8) other (please specify)___hour(s)____minutes

33. Do you travel predominately on roads with traffic jams?
   (1)____no
   (2)____yes

34. (34-1) How many hours a day are you usually at school?____ hours.
   (34-2) How many days of the week are you usually at school?____ days.

35. Are you exposed to irritating smoke, dust, or fumes at your school?
   (1)___No
   (2)___Yes
   (2-1)___odor
   (2-2)___dust
   (2-3)___smoke and fumes
   (2-4)___other, _____
   (2-5)___don't know

36. Have you been frequently exposed to irritating smoke, dust, or fumes at
   your past school?
   (1)___No
   (2)___Yes. For how long:_____years
   (2-1)___odor
   (2-2)___dust
   (2-3)___smoke and fumes
   (2-4)___other, _____
   (2-5)___don't know

III. Health and medical information

37. (37-1) Do you smoke regularly in the past and/or at present?
   (1)___No
   (2)___Yes, ___pipe, ___cigars, ___cigarettes. ___Refuses to answer
   (37-2) Have you smoked a total of more than 100 cigarettes in your life?
   (1)___No
   (2)___Yes
   (3)___Don't know
   (37-3) How many cigarettes do you smoke per day?_____
   (37-4) How old were you when you started smoking regularly?_____
   (37-5) If you are an ex-cigarette smoker, how old were you when you gave up smoking regularly? _____
38. If you do not smoke, do you usually breath second-hand smoke staying in an office or classroom with smokers?
   (1)____no
   (2)____yes
39. Do you do exercise regularly?
   (1)___No
   (2)___Yes,_____hrs/week
40. Have you ever had any of the following symptoms?
   (1)___bronchitis
   (2)___pneumonia
   (3)___bronchopneumonia
   (4)___chronic bronchitis
   (5)___emphysema
   (6)___pleurisy
   (7)___heart trouble
   (8)___high blood pressure
   (9)___other lung disease (please specify_____)
   (10)___other chronic disease (please specify___)
41. (41-1) Are you troubled by shortness of breath when hurrying or walking up a slight hill?
   (1)____no (skip to 42)
   (2)____yes
   (41-2) Do you have to walk slower than people of your age because of breathlessness?
   (1)____no (skip to 42)
   (2)____yes
   (41-3) Do you ever have to stop for breath when walking at your own pace?
   (1)____no

(2)____ yes

42. (42-1) Do you usually have a cough or bring up phlegm from your chest within one hour after getting up in the morning?

Winter:(1)____ no   (2)____ yes

Summer:(1)____ no   (2)____ yes

(42-2) Do you usually bring up phlegm on most days for 3 consecutive days or more during the year?

(1)____ no (skip to 43)

(2)____ yes

(42-3)For how many years have you had trouble with phlegm?

____ year(s)

43. (43-1)Do you usually have asthma attacks?

(1)____ no (skip to 44)

(2)____ yes

(43-2)Under what circumstances, do you seem to have asthma attacks? (multiple choice)

(1)____ cold or flu

(2)____ other diseases

(3)____ after doing exercise or taking activities

(4)____ at the job exposed to smoke

(5)____ at home or at the job exposed to dust

(6)____ other (please specify)_____

(7)____ don't know

(43-3)When did the last asthma attack happen?

(1)____ last week

(2)____ one month ago

(3)____ one and a little more months ago

(43-4)Have you ever felt breathless because of an asthma attack recently?

(1)____ no

(2)____ yes

44. Have you ever had any chest injuries?

(1)____ no

(2)____ yes (please specify)_____

45. Have you ever had any chest operations?

(1)____ no

(2)____ yes (please specify)_____

46. Do you have any medical insurance?

(1)___ No

(2)___ Yes,   (2-1)____ government employee insurance

             (2-2)____ labor insurance

             (2-3)____ farmer insurance

(2-4)_____low income families subsidy

(2-5)_____life insurance

(2-6)_____student health insurance

(2-7)_____soldier insurance

(2-8)_____other (please specify)_____

47. Your food and drink intake:

(47-1) Milk drinking frequency:

(1)____one bottle or more a day

(2)____4–6 bottles a week

(3)____1–3 bottles a week

(4)____1–3 bottles a month

(5)____few

(6)____none

(7)____unknown

(47-2) Meat:

(1)____almost every day

(2)____4–6 times a week

(3)____1–3 times a week

(4)____1–3 times a month

(5)____few

(6)____none

(7)____unknown

(47-3) Fruit:

(1)____almost every day

(2)____4–6 times a week

(3)____1–3 times a week

(4)____1–3 times a month

(5)____few

(6)____none

(7)____unknown

(47-4) Green vegetables:

(1)____almost every day

(2)____4–6 times a week

(3)____1–3 times a week

(4)____1–3 times a month

(5)____few

(6)____none

(7)____unknown

(47-5) Bowls of rice each meal:_____bowl(s)

(47-6) Vitamin or other nutriment:

(1)____none

(2)____calcium tablet

(3)____cod-liver oil
(4)____multi-vitamin
(5)____multi-vitamin & minerals
(6)____vitamin C tablet
(7)____other

48. The total monthly income of your family:
(1)___ None
(2)___ less than 15,000 NT$
(3)___ 15,001 to 20,000 NT$
(4)___ 20,001 to 25,000 NT$
(5)___ 25,001 to 30,000 NT$
(6)___ 30,001 to 35,000 NT$
(7)___ 35,001 to 40,000 NT$
(8)___ 40,001 to 45,000 NT$
(9)___ 45,001 to 50,000 NT$
(10)___ 50,001 to 60,000 NT$
(11)___ 60,001 to 70,000 NT$
(12)___ 70,001 to 80,000 NT$
(13)___ 80,001 to 90,000 NT$
(14)___ 90,001 to 10,0000 NT$
(15)___ 100,001 to 120,000 NT$
(16)___ 120,001 to 140,000 NT$
(17)___ 140,001 to 160,000 NT$
(18)___ more than 160,001 NT$

Appendix 5.B   Questionnaire for the Daily Diary Survey

Dear Madam/Sir:

Please fill out the following diary before you go to bed every night.

Date: _____ _____ _____ _____
            year   month   date   weekday

1. Have any symptoms occurred today?
(1)___ yes
(2)___ no

2. Please check the symptom(s) you have had today on the following Symptoms Table.
SYMPTOMS TABLE
(1)___ eye irritation   (10)___ cough with phlegm
(2)___ headache   (11)___ chest discomfort or pain

(3)___fever

(4)___runny nose

(5)___sinusitis
or sinus problem

(6)___dry scratchy throat

(7)___sore throat

(8)___croup

(9)___dry cough

(12)___allergy attack with respiratory
symptoms

(13)___wheezing

(14)___asthma

(15)___shortness of breath

(16)___others

3. Did the illness episode cause you to spend the day in bed?

(1)___No

(2)___Yes

4. Did the illness episode prevent you from going out to work?

(1)___No

(2)___Yes

5. Did this illness episode prevent you from doing daily activities other than working?

(1)___No

(2)___Yes

6. Did you seek medical advice or visit a medical provider today because of illness?

(1)___No

(2)___Yes

7. Where did you obtain the medical advice or treatment?

(1)___drugstore

(2)___called a doctor

(3)___emergency room

(4)___hospital, (name of the hospital:_____)

(5)___clinic

8. How much did you pay for the medical advice or treatment today?

_____NT$

9. What was the doctor's diagnosis? Diagnosis was_____

(1)___ear infection

(2)___bronchiolitis

(3)___bronchitis

(4)___influenza

(5)___pneumonia

(6)___sinusitis

(7)___others

10. Did you take medication today?

(1)___No

(2)___Yes

11. Has anyone else living in the same residence as you had any symptoms today?
12. Did you exercise today?
    (1)___ as usual
    (2)___ more than usual
    (3)___ less than usual
13. Did you exercise outdoors today?
    (1)___ No
    (2)___ Yes, for _____minutes.
14. How many hours did you stay outdoors today? _____hours
15. Was the air quality in your workplace or school different from the usual air quality?
    (1)___ No
    (2)___ Yes, it was worse than usual.
    (3)___ Yes, it was better than usual.
16. How many cigarettes did you smoke today?
17. Was there any change in the number of residents living in the same household as you today?
    (1)___ No
    (2)___ Yes, more persons
    (3)___ Yes, less persons
18. Did you go to a place other than your community in the last 24 hours?
    (1)___ No
    (2)___ Yes

ACKNOWLEDGEMENTS

We are grateful to the Chiang Ching-Kuo Foundation for International Scholarly Exchange, the Institute of Economics of Academia Sinica, and the ROC Environmental Protection Administration for funding this research, although all views are the authors' alone. We also thank Drs. Alan Krupnick and Maureen Cropper at the Resources for the Future for helping us to design the study, and Robert Mendelsohn and the conference participants for their helpful comments, and Pi Chen, Ching-Yao Lai and Ming-Feng Hung for their very able research assistance.

NOTES

1. Most previous epidemiological and clinical analyses have typically dealt with ozone exposure. The following studies, however, also examine exposure to other pollutants. Schwartz, Hasselblad, and Pitcher (1988) examined effects of ozone, CO, SO_2, NO, and NO_2 on Los Angeles student nurses. Harrington and Krupnick (1985) focused on the effect of NO_2 ambient pollution levels on acute respiratory disease in children. Mendelsohn and Orcutt (1979) measured the chronic effects of sulfates, nitrates, particulates, CO, SO_2, NO_2 and O_3 on mortality rates of Caucasians. Krupnick, Harrington, and Ostro (1990) examined the effect of SO_2, NO_2, and COH (coefficient of haze) exposure, in addition to ozone. Other studies such as Chappie and Lave (1982), Krumm and Graves (1982), Whittemore and Korn (1980), Lipfert (1984), Ostro (1983) and Portney and Mullahy (1986), attempted to relate sulfates and/or various kinds of particulate matter to mortality and morbidity damages.

2. The five air pollutants monitored are PM10, ozone, SO_2, NO_2, and CO. The daily Pollution Standard Index (PSI) is the highest of the five pollutants' sub-PSI numbers in that day. According to EPA statistics, among all days with PSI > 100 in 1991, about 80% came from PM10's sub-PSI. In 1992, that percentage increased to 88%.

3. According to a recent EPA study (EPA-82-F102-09-18), 60% of PM10 emissions in ten counties in Taiwan can be traced back to sources in construction sites, whereas mobile sources and other stationary sources account for 11% and 20%, respectively.

4. The second part of the health damage assessment was conducted by the same team to elicit willingness to pay to avoid a recurrence of the illness most recently experienced by the respondent. Respondents are the same in the two parts of the research. Results are reported in Alberini et al. (1996) in this book.

5. For example, the distance between the monitoring stations and the individuals is less than one mile (1,609 meters) in Harrington and Krupnick (1985), ten miles in Mullahy and Portney (1990) and Portney and Mullahy (1986), and 20 miles in Portney and Mullahy (1990). Some earlier studies use metropolitan-wide averages for a metropolitan area, e.g., Lave and Seskin (1977), Chappie and Lave (1982).

6. See Krupnick, Harrington and Ostro (1990) and Mullahy and Portney (1990), for example.

7. The questionnaires for the background survey and the diary survey are provided in Appendix A and B. The questionnaire for the contingent valuation survey is provided in Appendix B in Alberini et al. (1996) in this book.

8. Actually we discarded the data recorded by the first telephone interview since the diary began on Friday and the first telephone interview was conducted on that Sunday.

9. Many people do not like to lose a day's work or schooling even with acute symptoms or medication. While 53.8% of the sample whose ARD=1, only 37.2% of the sample had sought medication and 23.0% had taken days off. In terms of person-days, the rates of occurrence of symptoms, of symptoms with medication, and of symptoms with work loss are 5.1%, 1.% and 0.5%, respectively.

10. The conditions for identification in this model are that u_i be independent, or else there is at least one variable in X_1 and X_2 not included in X_3.

11. Since the major purpose of this paper is to estimate the acute response function, a more detailed analysis of the epidemiological chronic response function remains to be done.

12. By partitioning the sample into smokers and nonsmokers, Krupnick, Harrington, and Ostro (1990) are able to test the sensitivity of smokers and nonsmokers to air pollutants. Since this paper and Portney and Mullahy (1990) do not partition their sample in this way, the interpretations of the regression results are slightly different.

13.   This implies that the traditional approach to estimating the damage of pollution using clinical studies would tend to overestimate the damages.

REFERENCES

Alberini, Anna, Alan Krupnick, Jin-Tan Liu, Daigee Shaw, Tsu-Tan Fu, Maureen Cropper and Winston Harrington (1996), 'What is the Value of Reduced Morbidity in Taiwan?', in Robert Mendelsohn and Daigee Shaw (eds), *The Economics of Pollution Control in the Asia Pacific*, Aldershot: Edward Elgar.

Chappie, M. and L. Lave (1982), 'The Health Effects of Air Pollution: A Reanalysis', *Journal of Urban Economics*, **12**, 346–76.

Harrington, W. and A.J. Krupnick (1985), 'Short-term Nitrogen Dioxide Exposure and Acute Respiratory Disease in Children', *Journal of Air Pollution Control Association*, **35**, 1061–67.

Kennedy, P. (1992), *A Guide to Econometrics*, 3rd edition, Oxford: Basil Blackwell.

Korn, E.L. and A.S. Whittemore (1979), 'Methods for Analyzing Panel Studies of Acute Health Effects of Air Pollution', *Biometrics*, **35**, 795–802.

Krumm, R. and P. Graves (1982), 'Morbidity and Pollution: Model Specification Analysis for Time-Series Data on Hospital Admissions', *Journal of Environmental Economics and Management*, **9**, 311–27.

Krupnick, A.J., W. Harrington and B. Ostro (1990), 'Ambient Ozone and Acute Health Effects: Evidence from Daily Data', *Journal of Environmental Economics and Management*, **18**, 1–18.

Lave, L. and E. Seskin (1977), *Air Pollution and Human Health*, Baltimore, MD: Johns Hopkins University Press.

Lipfert, F. (1984), 'Air Pollution and Mortality: Specification Searches using SMSA-based Data', *Journal of Environmental Economics and Management*, **11**, 208–43.

Maddala, G.S. (1983), *Limited-dependent and Qualitative Variables in Econometrics*, Cambridge: Cambridge University Press.

Mendelsohn, R. and G. Orcutt (1979), 'An Empirical Analysis of Air Pollution Dose Response Curves', *Journal of Environmental Economics and Management*, **6**, 85–106.

Mullahy, J. and P.R. Portney (1990), 'Air Pollution, Cigarette Smoking, and the Production of Respiratory Health', *Journal of Health Economics*, **9**, 193–205.

Ostro, B. (1983), 'The Effects of Air Pollution on Work Loss and Morbidity', *Journal of Environmental Economics and Management*, **10** 371–82.

Portney, P.R. and J. Mullahy (1986), 'Urban Air Quality and Acute Respiratory Illness', *Journal of Urban Economics*, **20**, 21–38.

Portney, P.R. and J. Mullahy (1990), 'Urban Air Quality and Chronic Respiratory Disease', *Regional Science and Urban Economics*, **20**, 407–18.

Schwartz, J., V. Hasselblad and H. Pitcher (1988), 'Air Pollution and Morbidity: A Further Analysis of the Los Angeles Student Nurses Data', *Journal of Air Pollution Control Association*, **38**, 158–62.

Whittemore, A.S. and E. Korn (1980), 'Asthma and Air Pollution in the Los Angeles Area', *American Journal of Public Health*, **70**, 687–96.

6. What is the Value of Reduced Morbidity in Taiwan?

Anna Alberini, Maureen Cropper, Tsu-Tan Fu, Alan Krupnick, Jin-Tan Liu, Daigee Shaw and Winston Harrington

1 INTRODUCTION

When estimating the benefits of health improvements in developing countries, it is common practice to use estimates from US studies, adjusted for differences in per capita incomes (Krupnick et al., 1993). This is especially true when one wishes to measure willingness to pay for reduced illness, rather than using a cost-of-illness approach.

The drawback of such a benefits transfer is obvious: without further documentation, there is no reason why the preferences of people in other countries should be presumed to be identical to preferences in the United States. Cultural factors, especially those that affect perceptions of illness, may alter people's willingness to trade income for health. This implies that one needs to conduct health valuation studies in countries outside of the United States.

What is reported here is one such study. In September of 1992 we interviewed 1,285 people in three cities in the Republic of China (Taiwan) about the value they placed on avoiding minor illness. Specifically, we asked each respondent to describe the most recent acute illness episode he had experienced. After eliciting a complete description of the episode and the efforts the individual undertook to alleviate his symptoms, we asked each person whether he would pay a stated amount to have avoided the episode altogether. The answers to this question, and to subsequent follow-up questions, enable us to estimate willingness to pay to avoid illness as a function of the characteristics of the illness episode and of the respondent.

We feel that the results are of interest for three reasons. First, they provide information that could be used to value the benefits of air pollution control programs or other health programs in Taiwan. We use our willingness-to-pay results, together with the results of an epidemiological

108

study that measures the effects of particulate matter (PM10), sulfur dioxide (SO_2) and ozone on acute illness (Shaw et al., 1996), to value reductions in these pollutants in Taiwan.

Second, our study allows us to compare the values that people in Taiwan place on avoiding minor illness with values obtained in the United States. In particular, we are interested in seeing whether, and by how much, willingness to pay to avoid acute illness is different across the two countries, holding constant income, education and health status. Using the survey data we estimate a willingness-to-pay (WTP) function for Taiwan and use it to predict WTP for a representative US household. This prediction is then compared to estimates of WTP from a US survey (Tolley et al., 1986).

Third, the design of our survey allows us to study how familiarity with the commodity valued affects the stability of responses in a contingent valuation study. It seems reasonable to assume that the more thought a respondent has given to the commodity he is asked to value, the more reliable his answer should be. Our experimental design tests the effects of familiarity with the good being valued in two ways. First, our questionnaire was administered to two subsamples. One subsample was asked to fill out daily health diaries before they were given the questionnaire for the health valuation study. This group was therefore attuned to the illness they were asked to value. The other subsample was asked to describe and value their most recent illness episode without this practice. We examine whether the willingness-to-pay function differs between the two subsamples.

In addition, we elicit information about willingness to pay using a series of yes/no questions and estimate willingness-to-pay functions based on the responses to the initial questions and from each successive round of follow-up questions. We hypothesize that estimates of WTP will be relatively stable for the subsample that previously participated in the diary study, but may change over the successive rounds of follow-ups for the other group.

The paper is organized as follows. The second section of the paper describes the health valuation survey and the samples to which it was administered. The raw data from the survey are described in Section 3. In Section 4, these data are used to estimate a statistical model of willingness-to-pay in which respondent characteristics and characteristics of the illness valued are allowed to influence willingness-to-pay. Sections 5 and 6 describe estimates of the willingness-to-pay function for the two subsamples. In Section 7, estimates of willingness-to-pay in Taiwan are used to predict willingness-to-pay of a US household and comparisons are made with estimates from a similar contingent valuation study conducted in the United States. Section 8 concludes.

2   SURVEY DESIGN

2.1 Health Valuation Questionnaire

In September of 1992 we administered an in-person survey about acute illness and the value of avoiding it to 1,285 persons in Taiwan. The goal of our questionnaire (attached as Appendix 6.B) was to have people value reductions in acute illness, primarily acute respiratory illness, such as a cold or the flu. In valuing such illness, two approaches can be taken. One is to allow the respondent to describe the illness to be valued (Rowe and Chestnut, 1985). The second, which has been used more often, is to describe for the respondent the symptoms he is to value. For example, Loehman et al. (Loehman et al., 1979; Loehman and De, 1982), in a study of willingness to pay to avoid respiratory illness in Tampa, Florida, asked people to value symptom complexes such as 'minor head conges-tion/eye/ear/throat irritation', where 'minor' was defined to mean that 'you could continue with your daily activities with little or no change'. The length of illness episode was also specified.

Tolley et al. (1986) employed a similar approach in a study, conducted in Denver, Colorado, of willingness to pay to avoid seven symptoms of illness. Both the length of the illness episode and its severity were defined. A day of headache, for example, was described as follows: 'Two rather painful, splitting headaches will strike some time during the day. Each period of headache will last two hours'.

The advantage of describing symptoms for the respondent is that the commodity he is asked to value is well defined. One drawback is that such descriptions leave little room for averting behavior. For example, is the headache description in Tolley et al. *before* or *after* medicine is taken? If the symptoms can be mitigated at low cost, this should influence how much a person will pay to avoid the illness. Another disadvantage is that respon-dents who have never experienced the symptoms exactly as stated may find the valuation exercise meaningless.

To circumvent this problem, we allowed respondents to define the illness episode they were asked to value. Specifically, we asked each respondent to recall the last time he was acutely ill and to check on a card all the symptoms he experienced.[1] The respondent was also asked to indicate on a time line how long each symptom lasted. To capture severity of illness, we asked people if the illness episode had caused them to miss work or school, stay in bed, or in any other way interrupt their normal activities. The associated numbers of work loss days, bed disability days and restricted activity days were recorded by the interviewer.[2]

In theory (Harrington and Portney, 1987), an individual's willingness to pay to avoid illness should consist of three components: the value of the disutility (discomfort) suffered while the individual is ill, the value of time lost while he is ill, and the amount he spends to relieve his discomfort. The latter would include the out-of-pocket costs of medication, and doctor and hospital visits.

So that the individual would consider each of these components of willingness to pay, we asked if time was missed from work, whether income was lost as a result, and what activities the respondent undertook to relieve his symptoms, including purchasing over-the-counter medicine, increasing his intake of fruits and vegetables, and visiting a hospital or a doctor. If any of these activities were undertaken, we asked whether it was effective and how much money the respondent spent on it.

After describing his illness episode in detail, the respondent was given the following valuation question:

> We are now going to ask you a hypothetical question. Suppose you were told that, within the next few days, you would experience a recurrence of the illness episode you have just described for us. What would it be worth to you — that is, how much would you pay — to avoid the illness episode entirely?
>
> Remember that you are paying to eliminate all of your pain and suffering, your medical expenditure, the time you spent visiting the doctor or clinic, your missed work, leisure or daily activities.
>
> Bear in mind if you pay to completely avoid being ill this time, you have to give up some other use of this money. For example, you may reduce your expenditures for entertainment or education.
>
> Would you pay [FILL X1] NT dollars to avoid being sick at all?
>
> [If NO] Would you pay [FILL X2] NT dollars to avoid being sick at all?
>
> [If YES] Would you pay [FILL X3] NT dollars to avoid being sick at all?

Two focus groups conducted prior to developing the final version of the survey instrument suggested that respondents accepted the hypothetical nature of the valuation exercise, and that it was not necessary for the scenario to provide more specific information on how the illness would be remedied. A small pretest survey was also conducted using initial and follow-up WTP amounts derived from previous US studies of willingness to pay to avoid illness. Some revisions were made in the structure of the WTP amounts available to the respondents, based on the responses from the pretest.

Willingness-to-pay values for all six versions of the final questionnaire are

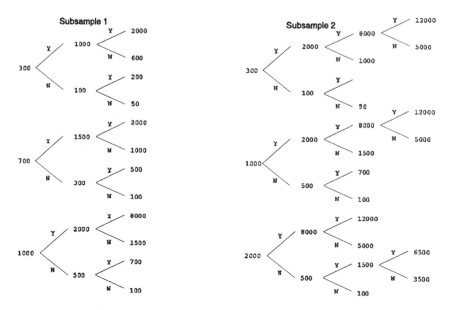

Figure 6.1 Structure of the Bids in the Taiwan CV study (NT$)

given in Figure 6.1. Respondents 1 to 864 were given one of three initial willingness-to-pay (WTP) values [FILL X1] in order to test for starting point bias. This was followed by *two* follow-up questions. The value stated in a follow-up question was higher than the value in the immediately preceding payment question if the response to the latter was a 'yes', and lower if it was a 'no'. All respondents who received the same FILL X1 value received identical follow-ups; hence there were three different sets of WTP values. A similar design was used in the questionnaires assigned to respondents 865 to 1285; however, respondents in this group received *three* follow-up questions, depending on their responses.

The valuation question was followed by standard demographic questions, questions about income, the respondent's attitude about health and pollution issues, his health history and environmental quality in the home and at the workplace.

2.2 Sampling Frame

Respondents 1 to 864 ('Subsample I') consisted of adults who also participated in an epidemiological study of the health effects of particulate matter and ozone.[3] In the epidemiological study, respondents were asked to fill out daily health diaries from November 1, 1991–January 31, 1992 and

Table 6.1   *Percentage of Respondents Reporting at least One Day of Each Symptom (based on complete samples)*

Symptom	Subsample I (n=865)	Subsample II (n=421)
Headache	39.1	42.3
Runny Nose	33.3	36.6
Sore Throat	27.1	37.8
Dry Cough	19.9	28.3
Cough with Phlegm	19.1	15.9
Fever	14.8	15.2
Dry/Scratchy Throat	13.7	19.7
Eye Irritation	12.5	12.6
Croup	9.3	12.8
Sinus Problem	9.0	7.4
Aching Muscles	6.7	6.4
Chest Pain	5.6	6.2
Allergy	2.4	2.9
Rash	2.2	2.1
Shortness of Breath	2.1	2.1
Wheezing	1.0	0.5
Asthma	0.7	0.2
Other Symptoms	6.8	1.0

from August 1, 1992–October 31, 1992. The health diary consisted of a matrix with the symptoms listed in Table 6.1 as columns and days of the week as rows. The respondent was asked to check off symptoms as they occurred and received weekly telephone calls to record the diary information. Participants in the epidemiological study were not told why they were asked to keep the health diaries.

The participants in the epidemiological study lived either in Taipei, the capital of Taiwan, Hualien, an unpolluted city on the east coast of the country, or Kaohsiung, an industrial center on the southwest coast of Taiwan, which is quite polluted. Respondents in Subsample I received the health valuation questionnaire in September of 1992, in the middle of their second round of health diaries. We would therefore expect these respondents to be very focused on questions relating to their health.

The second subsample, consisting of 421 respondents (respondents 865 to 1285), was drawn from the same geographic areas as the epidemiological study. These respondents had no experience filling out health diaries and

Table 6.2   Characteristics of Illnesses Experienced by Participants in the Taiwan CV Study (based on complete samples)

Variable	Subsample I (n=864)		Subsample II (n=421)	
	Mean	Median	Mean	Median
Duration of Episode (Days)	6.82	4	7.42	4
Number of Symptoms per Episode	2.22	1	2.49	2
Episode is a Cold	68.5%		64.6%	

were, therefore, unfamiliar with the task of recording symptoms. They thus served as a control group.

Because of the emphasis we place on acute morbidity, subjects who had reported spells longer than 30 days were not included in the sample we used for regression purposes. Responses that were incomplete or that we deemed implausible were also eliminated, bringing the size of the sample used in regression analyses from 1285 down to 1206.[4]

3   SURVEY RESPONSES

3.1 Symptoms Experienced

Since it is up to respondents to define the illness they are valuing, our first order of business is to examine the acute illnesses reported in the questionnaire. Table 6.1 gives the frequency distribution of symptoms reported for each subsample. The symptoms most frequently experienced for each subsample were, in order, headache, runny nose, sore throat and cough. It is not, therefore, surprising that two-thirds of each subsample characterized their illness as a cold (Table 6.2). With a few exceptions — sore throat, the two types of cough and dry/scratchy throat — the two subsamples do not appear to differ meaningfully in terms of incidence of symptoms.

We define the duration of the illness episode as the time from the beginning of the first symptom to the end of the last symptom experienced. The median duration of an episode was four days for both subsamples (see Table 6.2). The distribution of duration of the spell is shown in Figure 6.2.

Although the median duration is four days for both groups, the histogram

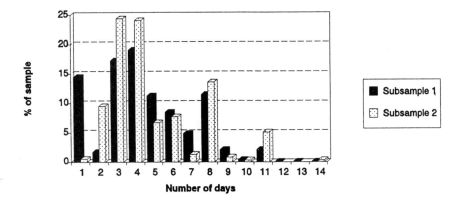

Figure 6.2 Distribution of Length of Episode of Illness

shows that there are some differences between the two subsamples, with Subsample I subjects recalling very short episodes (one-day spells) much more frequently than Subsample II respondents (14% versus only 1.2%), and more Subsample II respondents reporting two-, three- and four-day episodes. The Kolmogorov-Smirnov test of the null hypothesis of identical distributions in the two groups yields a test statistic equal to 0.1329, which rejects the null hypothesis at the 1% level.[5]

During the episode, the median number of symptoms experienced was one for Subsample I and two for Subsample II, the difference being significant at the 1% significance level.[6] The distribution of the number of symptoms of the episode is depicted in Figure 6.3. The Kolmogorov-Smirnov test statistic has a value of 0.1023, which rejects the null hypothesis of identical distributions at the 1% significance level. These findings lend support to the notion that the two groups of respondents value episodes of different severity and suggest that it might be best to fit separate WTP functions to the two subsamples.

Table 6.3, which also characterizes severity of illness, suggests that these cold or flu-like symptoms inconvenienced people, but did not keep them from going about their daily routine. Only a quarter of each subsample experienced at least one restricted activity day (RAD) — a day on which their normal activities had to be curtailed. Subsample I reports more RADs than Subsample II, with a few individuals reporting relatively high counts of RADs. Approximately 10–12% of each group were confined to bed for at least one day. Of those persons who worked, 12.6% of Subsample I and

Table 6.3 Activity Impairment Due to Illness (based on cleaned dataset)

Activity Impairment	Percent of Cleaned Dataset		Statistics for Respondents with Positive Counts (after excluding respondents who reported counts of RADs, BDDs and WLDs greater than the duration of the illness)	
	Subsample I	Subsample II (n=816)	Subsample I[b] (n=390)	Subsample II[c]
Restricted Activity Day (RAD)	25.3	24.1	Mean: 3.44 Median: 2.00	Mean: 2.20 Median: 1.00
Bed Disability Day (BDD)	12.5	10.2	Mean: 2.68 Median: 1.00	Mean: 1.57 Median: 1.00
Work Loss Day[a] (WLD)	12.7	12.6	Mean: 2.18 Median: 1.00	Mean: 1.28 Median: 1.00

Notes

a. Percent of those respondents who reported being employed at the time of the survey (574 subjects for Subsample I and 390 subjects for Subsample II).

b. Inconsistent records were detected for 4, 4 and 4 respondents for RADs, BDDs and WLDs, respectively.

c. Inconsistent records were detected for 2, 0 and 4 respondents for RADs, BDDs and WLDs, respectively.

12.7% of Subsample II missed at least one day of work due to illness.

Further evidence of severity of illness is provided in Table 6.4, which describes activities taken to relieve symptoms. Approximately thirty to thirty-two percent of each sample took over-the-counter drugs during their illness. A higher percentage changed their diet or went to the doctor. While approximately 45% of Subsample II engaged in each of these activities, 54% of Subsample I changed their diets and 55% consulted a doctor.

We interpret both taking medication and visiting a doctor as indicators of illness severity. Probit analyses of these actions indicate that they are unrelated to income, age, gender or having health insurance. This is confirmed by introspection: while the *number* of symptoms experienced need be only weakly related to severity of illness (it depends on what the symptoms are), whether one is 'sick enough to go to a doctor' or 'sick enough to take medication' are truer indicators of how ill one feels.

While we do not know the average out-of-pocket cost of a doctor's visit, we do know the extent of insurance coverage for each subsample. Twenty percent of the respondents in Subsample I and 33% of the respondents in Subsample II incurred no out-of-pocket cost for doctor's visits; whereas 34% of Subsample I and 29% of Subsample II paid all of the cost themselves.

Table 6.4 Effects of Illness on Behavior and Income (based on cleaned dataset)

Change in Behavior Due to Illness	Percent of Respondents Affected (based on cleaned dataset)		Costs Incurred by Respondents who Change Behavior (statistics obtained after excluding those respondents whose reported expenditures or lost income are greater than the upper bound on WTP) (number of valid observations in parentheses)			
			Subsample I		Subsample II	
	Subsample I (n=816)	Subsample II (n=390)	Mean in NT$	Median in NT$	Mean in NT$	Median in NT$
Missed Work [a]	12.7	12.6				
Lost Income Because of Missed Work [a]	2.6	1.8	1825.00 (8)[b]	1000.00 (8)[b]	470.00 (10)[b]	300.00 (10)[b]
Changed Diet	53.6	44.6				
Incurred Costs Because of Diet Change	24.1	39.2	330.43 (172)	200.00 (172)	207.23 (116)	120.00 (116)
Took Non-prescription Drugs	30.5	32.1				
Incurred Costs for Non-prescription Drugs	29.2	31.8	254.74 (209)	120.00 (209)	344.24 (106)	100.00 (106)
Consulted Doctor	55.0	43.9				
Was Prescribed Medication	52.9	42.2				
Went to Hospital	2.2	0.9				

Notes
a. Percent of the 574 subjects of subsample I and 390 Subjects of Subsample II who were employed at the time of the survey.
b. Respondents whose reported count of work loss days was greater than the duration of the illness were excluded when calculating mean and median lost income due to the illness.

Respondent characteristics, including age, sex, and household income, are summarized in Table 6.5.

3.2   Willingness to Pay to Avoid Illness

For each of the six versions of the questionnaire, Table 6.6 gives the percen-

Table 6.5 Summary of Respondent Characteristics

Individual Characteristic	Subsample I	Subsample II
Age (years)	42.36	35.83
Sex (male)	46.9%	48.5%
Years of Schooling	11.07	12.33
Home Air Conditioner	79.3%	79.6%
Home Dehumidifier	37.4%	29.7%
Exercise Often	58.4%	60.6%
Currently Employed	69.7%	100.0%
Is a Resident of ...		
TAIPEI	41.2%	39.4%
HUALIEN	17.4%	19.5%
KAOHSIUNG	41.4%	41.4%
Sick Leave Plan *	30.2%	41.8%
Smoke	23.7%	25.7%
Monthly Household Income:		
mean	NT$ 58,875	NT$ 62,008
median	NT$ 47,500	NT$ 47,500
Has ever had a serious lung disease	26.0%	622.3%
Has had other chronic disease	13.5%	10.2%

Note
* Percentage of those respondents who report being employed.

tage of respondents whose willingness-to-pay falls in a specified interval. The table combines the information about WTP provided by the responses to the initial and follow-up payment questions.

As is usually done in contingent valuation surveys, the starting WTP 'bid' value was varied to test for starting point bias and for other abnormal response effects (see Mitchell and Carson, 1989).[7] Table 6.6 does suggest that there are differences in the implied WTP values between the two subsamples. The median WTP for Subsample I respondents is NT$1000 and is consistent across questionnaire versions, whereas Subsample II's median WTP amounts vary with the questionnaire versions and are lower than NT$1000 for two of the three questionnaire versions. Since Figures 6.2 and 6.3 suggest that the illnesses of Subsample II are no less severe than those

Table 6.6 Distribution of Responses Based on First, Second and Third Rounds of Questions (implied willingness-to-pay intervals in parentheses)

Questionnaire Version (Count of Respondents)	NNN (%)	NNY (%)	NYN (%)	NYY (%)	YNN (%)	YNY (%)	YYN (%)	YYY (%)	Implied Median WTP
1 (288)	11.1 (0,50)	8.68 (50, 100)	4.17 (100, 200)	2.78 (200, 300)	13.19 (300, 600)	10.07 (600, 1000)	15.28 (1000, 2000)	34.72 (2000+)	NT$ 1000
2 (289)	12.80 (0,100)	13.15 (100, 300)	6.92 (300, 500)	5.54 (500, 700)	12.46 (700, 1000)	11.42 (1000, 1500)	6.23 (1500, 2000)	31.49 (2000+)	NT$ 1000
3 (287)	16.03 (0,50)	21.60 (100, 500)	5.23 (500, 700)	6.97 (700, 1000)	9.06 (1000, 1500)	8.36 (1500, 2000)	14.63 (2000, 8000)	18.12 (8000+)	NT$ 1000
4 (126)	15.87 (0,100)	4.76 (50, 100)	-	-	35.71 (300, 1000)	11.11 (1000, 2000)	12.70 (2000, 8000)	14.29 (8000+)	less than NT$ 1000
5 (130)	32.31 (0,100)	13.85 (100, 500)	0.77 (500, 700)	3.08 (700, 1000)	16.15 (1000, 1500)	3.85 (1500, 2000)	13.08 (2000, 8000)	16.15 (8000+)	NT$ 1000
6 (165)	31.52 (0,100)	13.94 (100, 500)	11.52 (500, 500)	7.27 (1500, 2000)	13.33 (2000, 5000)	4.24 (5000, 8000)	4.85 (8000, 12000)	13.33 (12000+)	between NT$500 and 1500

of Subsample I, this is a puzzling finding. It is possible that the experience of filling out health diaries has made Subsample I respondents more aware of their health and more focused on what they were asked to value. It is also possible that duration and number of symptoms do not adequately capture the seriousness of illness experienced by Subsample II respondents, especially if the symptoms were perceived as minor and if subjects found it difficult to successfully recall their illnesses.

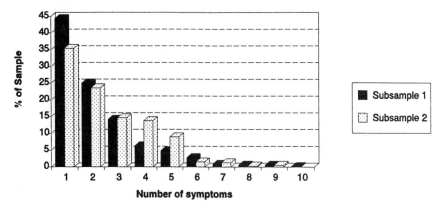

Figure 6.3 Distribution of Number of Symptoms Per Episode

4   A HEDONIC MODEL OF WILLINGNESS TO PAY

What the information in Table 6.6 does not reveal is how willingness to pay
to avoid illness varies with the characteristics of the illness episode (e.g., its
severity and duration) and with respondent characteristics (e.g., income). To
measure the effects of covariates on willingness-to-pay we assume that the
logarithm of willingness-to-pay is a linear function of these characteristics
or transformations of them. Formally,

$$\log WTP_i = z_i\beta + x_i\gamma + \varepsilon_i \tag{6.1}$$

where z_i is a vector of episode attributes, x_i is a vector of individual
characteristics, and β and γ are vectors of coefficients. ε_i, which represents
unmeasured characteristics of the episode or the respondent, is assumed to
be independently and identically normally distributed for all respondents,
with variance σ^2. Because the attributes of the symptom complex, z_i, are
included among the regressors, (6.1) defines a *hedonic* model of WTP.[8]

Because respondents do not report their WTP values directly, we cannot
apply simple least squares techniques to estimate the vectors of parameters
of (6.1). Model (6.1) is estimated by the method of maximum likelihood,
using the assumption that, after answering the follow-up questions,
respondent i's willingness-to-pay lies between two values, WTP_i^L and WTP_i^U,
which are determined by the amounts stated in the payment questions and
by the responses given by the subject.[9] Respondent i's contribution to the

likelihood function is thus the probability that his WTP amount falls in the interval bracketed by WTP_i^L and WTP_i^U, or $\Pr(WTP_i^L \leq WTP_i \leq WTP_i^U)$. Formally, the likelihood function to be maximized is given by:

$$\log L = \sum_{i=1}^{n} \log \left\{ \Phi\left[\frac{\log WTP_i^U - x_i\beta - z_i\gamma}{\sigma}\right] \right.$$
$$\left. - \Phi\left[\frac{\log WTP_i^L - x_i\beta - z_i\gamma}{\sigma}\right] \right\} \tag{6.2}$$

where $\Phi(\bullet)$ is the standard normal cumulative density function (cdf).

If our model of willingness-to-pay is reasonably specified and an individual's valuation of the spell of illness is stable over the successive rounds of payment questions, the maximum likelihood estimates of β and γ obtained from the successive rounds of responses should be quite close to one another. They should also become more statistically efficient with each additional follow-up response to reflect the gain in information about WTP.[10]

4.1 The Effect of Episode Characteristics on WTP

Other things equal, we would expect the disutility of the illness episode and, hence, the respondent's willingness to pay to avoid it, to increase with the length of the episode and its severity. It should also be greater for people who missed time from work, or otherwise had to restrict their activities, and for persons who did something to mitigate their symptoms.

To measure the duration of the illness episode, we recorded the number of days between the time the first symptom began and the time the last symptom ended. Severity is measured in two ways: by the number of symptoms experienced (i.e., a simple symptom count) and by a dummy variable indicating whether or not the episode was a cold.[11]

Whether the respondent missed time from his regular activities because of his illness is measured in our regressions by a dummy variable, equal to one if the respondent suffered at least one restricted activity day. We chose to use a dummy instead of the actual count of restricted activity days because of its higher degree of statistical significance as a predictor of willingness to pay. A variable indicating the count of work loss days is also included in the WTP equation.

To measure mitigating behavior, we use two dummy variables indicating, respectively, whether the respondent visited a doctor or purchased over-the-counter medication. Ideally, we would have liked to measure the cost to the individual of these activities, but were unable to do so since we do not have the out-of-pocket cost for people whose insurance paid for part of their medical expenses.

We report specifications of the WTP equation in which no curvature restrictions are imposed on the continuous independent variables associated with the episode of illness — number of symptoms and duration of illness — i.e., they appear in logarithmic form. The predicted WTP values and most of the estimated coefficients are essentially unchanged when this specification is replaced by a semi-log specification in which number of symptoms and duration of the spell are entered linearly (Alberini et al., 1994).

4.2 The Effect of Respondent Characteristics on WTP

Economic theory suggests that persons with higher incomes and with a greater 'taste' for good health should be willing to pay more to avoid illness. To capture the importance people place on health, we have included years of education in the WTP equation. We also tried dummy variables indicating whether the respondent exercises regularly and whether he is a smoker, but they did not appear to affect WTP.

The respondent's baseline health status should also influence willingness to pay. Persons with a history of chronic illness, especially chronic respiratory illness, should be willing to pay more to avoid an illness episode, assuming increasing marginal disutility of illness. We used two dummy variables to capture these effects — one indicating that the respondent has at some time suffered from serious lung disease (pneumonia, chronic bronchitis, emphysema), the other indicating that he suffers (or has suffered) from a chronic illness that is not related to the lungs.

We also included in our WTP equation other variables that are supposed to capture the respondent's budget set and the price of health care faced by the respondent. An example of the first type of regressors are dummies for the respondent's place of residence: holding nominal household income constant, differences in *real* disposable income which may affect WTP can arise if the cost of living is different in Taipei, Kaohsiung and Hualien. An example of the other type of covariate is the availability of health insurance.

Other variables we used in our regressions, such as owning a home dehumidifier and air conditioning device, and the type of water the respondent drinks, may be interpreted as proxies for the respondent's taste for health. Standard demographic variables, such as age and gender, may influence willingness to pay, although there is no compelling reason why they should.[12]

5   WILLINGNESS TO PAY FOR REDUCED ILLNESS BY SUBSAMPLE I

5.1 The Effect of Illness Characteristics on WTP

Results for Subsample I, which are reported in Table 6.8 for the equation that combines the responses to *all* rounds of follow-up questions, are encouraging. They support the hedonic specification of willingness-to-pay by indicating that WTP increases with duration of illness, with the number of symptoms experienced and with severity of illness. Willingness-to-pay increases with duration of illness in all of the specifications of the equation, although the coefficient of log duration is significant at only the 0.08 level. This fact, combined with a coefficient on log duration of about 0.16, suggests that WTP increases with duration at a decreasing rate.[13] The elasticity of WTP with respect to the number of symptoms is about 0.27, implying that WTP also increases at a decreasing rate with the number of symptoms experienced.

Both of these results accord with studies conducted in the US. Tolley et al. (1986) report that mean WTP for a combination of symptoms is always less than the sum of the WTPs for the individual symptoms, holding duration constant. Both Tolley et al. and Loehman et al. (1979) find that WTP increases with duration of illness at a decreasing rate.

In the WTP equation, seriousness of illness is captured by five variables: whether the episode was a cold, whether the respondent's activities were impaired, the count of workdays lost, whether he went to a doctor and whether he purchased medicine. Except for the cold dummy, all of these variables indicate more serious illnesses and should therefore increase WTP. This is indeed the case. All dummies that measure severity of illness have the expected sign and, with the exception of work loss days, are significant at conventional levels. The magnitude of the coefficients is also noteworthy. Having a cold (as opposed to a more serious illness) reduces WTP by about 36%. Buying drugs raises WTP by 39%, as does experiencing some activity limitation, while going to a doctor raises WTP by 85%.

5.2 The Effect of Respondent Characteristics on WTP

The effect of respondent characteristics on WTP is also reasonable. WTP increases with household income, with years of education, with chronic illness and with two 'taste' variables — the fact that the respondent drinks bottled or ground water (tap water being the baseline) and the fact that he has a dehumidifier in his home (Specification (1)).

Indeed, these taste variables appear to have a large impact on WTP: in

Table 6.7 Definition of Variables Used in WTP Equation and Values of the Regressors Used for Predicting WTP [a]

Acronym	Description of Variable	Sample Average:	
		Subsample I	Subsample II
duration	Duration in days of the episode of illness	5.3064	5.3333
symid	Number of symptoms	2.2255	2.2154
cold	Dummy=1 if illness is a cold	0.6948	0.6641
actintp	Whether daily activities were restricted	0.2537	0.2487
wlday	Number of lost workdays	0.2083	0.2359
drug	Dummy=1 if over-the--counter drugs were purchased	0.3051	0.3205
doctor	Dummy=1 if doctor was visited	0.5368	0.5384
fincome	Monthly household income (in thousands of NT$)	58.249[b]	63.200[b]
edu2	Years of education	11.1131	12.4153
taipei	Dummy=1 if respondent is a resident of Taipei	0.4167	0.4238
kaohsiung	Dummy=1 if respondent is a resident of Kaohsiung	0.4142	0.3949
hualien	Dummy=1 if respondent is a resident of Hualien	0.1690	0.1923
tap	Dummy =1 if respondent drinks tap water	0.7978	0.7615
bottled	Dummy=1 if respondent drinks bottled water	0.3297	0.2948
ground	Dummy=1 if respondent drinks ground water	0.0233	0.0692
kaosbott	kaohsiung*bottled	0.2500	0.2538
hualbott	hualien*bottled 0.0502	0.0256	
taipbott	taipei*bottled	0.0294	0.0153
airfilt	Dummy=1 if dehumidifier in respondent's home	0.3669	0.2974
sickleave	Number of sick leave days	1.2718	1.9948
lungs	Dummy=1 if subject has ever had lung illnesses	0.2598	0.2231
sk	Dummy=1 for other chronic illnesses	0.1311	0.1026

Notes
a.   Based on samples of 816 and 390 respondents respectively.
b.   The imputed household income is the midpoint of the range reported by the respondent.

Table 6.8 *WTP Equations for Subsample I Based on the Third Round of Responses. Dependent variable:*log *WTP. Asymptotic t-statistics in parentheses.*

Regressor	Specif. (1)	Specif. (2)	Specif. (3)	Specif. (4)	Specif. (5)
intercept	3.7606(7.095)	3.7994(7.161)	3.9442(7.630)	4.0869(8.003)	5.0353(16.92)
log(duration)	0.1730(1.736)	0.1654(1.659)	0.1620(1.626)	0.3556(3.546)	0.3158(3.238)
log(symid)	0.2572(2.009)	0.2701(2.106)	0.2798(2.189)	0.2899(2.373)	
cold	-0.4457(-2.781)	-0.4552(-2.839)	-0.4674(-2.916)		-0.3563(-2.326)
actintp	0.3215(1.972)	0.3196(1.962)	0.3160(1.941)		
wlday	0.0906(1.740)	0.0885(1.701)	0.0930(1.801)		
drug	0.3314(2.112)	0.3250(2.079)	0.3186(2.309)		0.3728(2.367)
doctor	0.6153(4.157)	0.6063(4.096)	0.6077(4.108)		0.6702(4.493)
log(fincome)	0.3377(2.643)	0.3340(2.617)	0.3242(2.547)	0.3480(2.635)	
edu2	0.0537(2.723)	0.0547(2.773)	0.0533(2.706)	0.0562(2.835)	0.0693(3.600)
kaohsiung	-0.1860(-1.010)	-0.3103(-1.504)	-0.3934(2.013)		0.0248(0.154)
hualien	0.0856(0.407)	0.1512(0.633)			0.3062(1.473)
ground	1.6048(3.361)	1.5570(3.245)	1.6326(3.522)		1.3821(2.812)
bottled	0.5553(3.309)				
kaosbott		0.7203(3.441)	0.7319(3.444)		
hualbott		0.2876(0.800)			
taipbott		0.2362(0.572)			
airfilt	0.3423(2.257)	0.3377(2.227)	0.3153(2.091)		0.4697(3.043)
sickleave	0.0377(2.296)	0.0391(2.377)	0.0421(2.510)		
lungs	0.2965(1.904)	0.3027(1.943)	0.3129(2.009)		
sk	0.3323(1.587)	0.3430(1.635)	0.3449(1.647)		
σ	1.7818(31.480)	1.7796(31.485)	1.7820(31.485)	1.8928(31.492)	1.8612(31.815)
sample size	794	794	794	798	812
loglikelihood	-1493.28	-1492.37	-1493.47	-1544.84	-1555.25

(1), Table 6.8, respondents who drink bottled water are willing to pay 75% more than the baseline respondent. Subjects who drink ground water appear to have WTP values almost *five times* as large as the baseline respondent. This result is particularly puzzling, since only a very small fraction of Subsample I (19 subjects) reports drinking ground water. Further exami-

Table 6.9 Type of Drinking Water by Location of Residence of Subsample I Respondents

Count of Respondents Drinking	Tap	Ground	Bottled (mineral, distilled or bottled spring water)	Total Respondents
Taipei	329	3	24	340
Kaohsiung	224	0	204	338
Hualien	98	16	41	138
Total	651	19	269	816

nation of the data shows that these interviewees reside primarily in Hualien (16 out of 19) and do not report particularly high incomes, but do have high implied WTP amounts.[14] Table 6.9 also shows that almost all residents of Taipei drink tap water and that a large proportion of the residents of Kaohsiung drink bottled water instead of or as well as tap water. This is explained by the unreliable quality of piped water in Kaohsiung, a fact that has received extensive media coverage in Taiwan and is also witnessed by the respondents in the survey.

In order to disentangle the effect of a supply of water that is unfit for drinking, in Specifications (2) and (3) we kept the city dummies and the ground water dummy, and introduced three variables capturing the interaction between place of residence and drinking bottled water. The results indicate that residents of Kaohsiung are willing to pay significantly less to avoid illness, but those residents of Kaohsiung who also drink bottled water bid significantly *higher* amounts to avoid their episodes of illness. The ground water dummy remains highly significant, while the Hualien location dummy and the interaction terms between being a Hualien or Taipei resident and drinking bottled water are not significant and are, therefore, excluded from Specification (3), Table 6.8.

Having a dehumidifier in one's home has a strong impact, increasing WTP by 45%. This effect is comparable in magnitude to the two health history variables, although suffering from a chronic non-respiratory illness is significant at only the 0.10 level. Subjects who previously had a serious lung disease were willing to pay about 36% more to avoid their illness episode than persons who had not experienced such a disease. We also checked for the possibility that having a home dehumidifier might be correlated with suffering from chronic or lung illness. The proportion of persons owning a dehumidifier or an air conditioner is approximately the same for chronics and non-chronics, and persons who have and have not been affected by serious respiratory illnesses (see Tables 6.A.1 and 6.A.2 in Appendix 6.A), suggesting that the home humidifier dummy, which is significant in all of the specifications of the WTP equations, does capture a taste variable. (The percent of the households owning air conditioners or dehumidifiers is, however, higher in Taipei than in the other cities.)

The income elasticity of WTP is of special interest. It has been argued that environmental amenities, including good health, are not luxury goods (Kanninen and Kriström, 1993).[15] This fact is borne out in all of the specifications of Table 6.8, which indicate that the income elasticity of WTP to avoid illness is about 0.33. This value is, in fact, in the range of income elasticities reported by Loehman and De (1982) in their study of WTP to avoid acute illness in Tampa, Florida.[16]

In addition to the specifications reported in Tables 6.8 and 6.10, specifications including other respondent characteristics were tried and rejected. In particular, whether the respondent was a smoker or had medical insurance, the amounts spent on mitigating activities, the number of bed disability days, various measures of environmental quality and environmental risks as subjectively perceived by the respondent, as well as the respondent's age and sex, were not significant correlates of WTP. These characteristics originally reported in Table 6.5 are omitted from Tables 6.8 and 6.10.

5.3 Additional Econometric Issues

At each round of estimation we checked the adequacy of the assumption of a log normal distribution for WTP. After estimating first-round models of WTP, we calculated Pearson chi-square tests based on the differences between the actual counts of 'yes'/'no' responses to the initial payment questions and the counts predicted by the fitted models. In all cases, at the conventional levels the tests failed to reject the null hypothesis of adequate fit of the log normal distribution.[17] We also compared our second- and third-round log normal models with analogous models of WTP based on the Weibull, exponential and log logistic distributions. Based on the values of the respective log likelihood functions, we concluded that the fit of the log normal distribution was better than that of the exponential and log logistic distribution, and approximately as good as that of the Weibull.

We also estimated a variant of Specification (3) that tests for possible starting point biases by including questionnaire version dummies. The estimated coefficients for these variables are not significant.[18] It is also comforting to note that the coefficients of the WTP equation, which are reported in Table 6.10 for our preferred specification, (3), remain relatively stable over successive rounds of bidding.[19] A Hausman test for the difference between the first-round and the second-round slope coefficients does

Table 6.10 Comparison of WTP Equations for Subsample I from all Rounds of Responses. Dependent variable: logWTP. Asymptotic t-statistics in parentheses.

Regressor	First Round	Second Round	Third Round
intercept	3.3798(4.888)	3.8186(7.422)	3.9442(7.630)
log(duration)	0.0830(0.680)	0.2040(2.076)	0.1620(1.626)
log(symid)	0.4945(2.855)	0.3162(2.505)	0.2798(2.189)
cold	-0.5778(-2.694)	-0.4135(-2.603)	-0.4674(-2.916)
actintp	0.5160(2.358)	0.2174(1.365)	0.3160(1.941)
wlday	0.1183(1.038)	0.0825(1.594)	0.0930(1.801)
drug	0.2870(1.447)	0.2480(1.606)	0.3186(2.309)
doctor	0.6691(3.233)	0.6093(4.160)	0.6077(4.108)
log(fincome)	0.4009(2.355)	0.3534(2.800)	0.3242(2.547)
edu2	0.0711(2.716)	0.0526(2.712)	0.0533(2.706)
kaohsiung	-0.4115(-1.706)	-0.4374(-2.267)	-0.3934(2.013)
ground	1.0274(1.635)	1.5196(3.254)	1.6326(3.522)
kaosbott	0.7006(2.502)	0.6601(3.147)	0.7319(3.444)
airfilt	0.2241(1.192)	0.3512(2.364)	0.3153(2.091)
sickleave	0.0202(0.926)	0.0303(1.902)	0.0421(2.510)
lungs	0.2944(1.496)	0.2701(1.764)	0.3129(2.009)
sk	0.2217(0.846)	0.3782(1.828)	0.3449(1.647)
σ	1.6884(17.221)	1.6356(23.81)	1.7820(31.485)
log likelihood	-458.59	-965.47	-1493.47

not reject the null hypothesis that the coefficients are identical (the value of the statistic is 26.11, which is within the acceptance region for a chi-square with 17 degrees of freedom).[20] The second- and third-round coefficients are within at most 25% of each other.

These tests, together with the results reported above, suggest the responses of Subsample I meet criteria of internal validity. Willingness to pay varies as expected with characteristics of the illness episode and of the respondent. Responses are stable over successive rounds of bidding and there is no evidence of starting point bias. This is in sharp contrast to the results that we report below for Subsample II.

6 WILLINGNESS TO PAY FOR REDUCED ILLNESS BY SUBSAMPLE II

We began our analysis of the Subsample II data by fitting to those data (1) and (2) of Table 6.8. The results, which are reported in the first and second columns of Table 6.11, reveal marked differences between the two sub-samples. Consider first the effect of characteristics of the illness episode on willingness-to-pay. While the log of duration is significant at the 10% level, the log of the number of symptoms reported is not significant. Of the variables measuring the activity impairment caused by the illness, the restricted activity day dummy (ACTINTP) approaches significance at the 5% level, but has the wrong sign. The coefficient of work loss days (WLDAY) has the correct sign but is insignificant.[21]

Similar anomalies occur regarding respondent characteristics. The coefficient of log income is not significant. Of the two variables summarizing the respondent's health history, only the dummy for respiratory illness is significant.

Those variables that are significant in Table 6.11 often have unbelievably large coefficients. Purchasing over-the-counter drugs, for example, almost triples willingness-to-pay. The Hualien dummy suggests that people in that city are willing to pay seven times the amount that citizens of Taipei are willing to pay to avoid illness.

In the next equation (Specification (3)), we excluded income and the RAD dummy and allowed other correlated covariates to capture their effects.[22] Because log duration appeared to exhibit a stronger relationship with log WTP, we also excluded log symptoms, as well as the dummy for chronic disease, but included the dummy for serious respiratory disease. Unfortunately, matters do not improve much. In Specification (3), Table 6.11, log duration is still not fully significant at the conventional levels, nor is the count of work loss days, which, in a separate regression analysis, we had found to vary systematically with the presence of restricted activities. Instead, the dummy for serious respiratory disease is very strongly significant, suggesting that perhaps individuals put more weight on their health history than on the attributes of their most recent case of illness when they form their WTP amounts. The results also suggest that Subsample II respondents poorly recalled the duration and number of symptoms they experienced, and that the severity of the illness is better captured by the suffering it inflicted or by the effort required to seek relief from the illness, such as visiting a doctor or purchasing medication. These variables are in fact significant predictors of WTP.

However, since we are interested in establishing the relationship between WTP and the episode of illness recalled by the individual, in Specification

Table 6.11 *WTP Equations for Subsample II Based on the Fourth Round of Responses. Dependent variable:* log*WTP. Asymptotic t-statistics in parentheses.*

Regressor	Specif. (1)	Specif. (2)	Specif. (3)	Specif. (4)	Specif. (5)
intercept	2.8126(2.301)	3.0906(2.535)	3.0977(4.100)	2.8557(3.770)	2.7066(3.562)
log(duration)	0.4378(1.885)	0.4438(1.924)	0.3873(1.703)	0.4790(2.111)	0.5030(2.205)
log(symid)	0.0662(0.297)	0.0817(0.369)			
cold	-0.6660(-2.297)	-0.6945(-2.377)	-0.6630(-2.406)	-0.6927(-2.491)	-0.6512(-2.325)
actintp	-0.5873(-1.885)	-0.5919(-1.885)			
wlday	0.0742(0.678)	0.0750(0.689)	0.0236(0.223)	0.0397(0.372)	
drug	0.9650(3.456)	0.9866(3.523)	0.9654(3.486)	1.0862(3.941)	1.0835(3.976)
doctor	0.4391(1.593)	0.3981(1.450)	0.3471(1.292)	0.3911(1.446)	0.4540(1.678)
log(fincome)	-0.0212(-0.082)	-0.0621(-0.240)			
edu2	0.1026(2.059)	0.1015(2.052)	0.0849(1.782)	0.0981(2.051)	0.1025(2.126)
kaohsiung	1.3905(3.494)	1.2684(3.003)	1.2748(3.221)	1.3973(3.522)	1.3479(4.406)
hualien	2.1465(4.852)	1.8792(4.028)	1.8042(4.077)	1.9174(4.312)	2.2093(5.336)
ground	-1.6310(-2.804)	-1.5075(-2.582)	-1.4326(-2.456)	-1.4485(-2.460)	-1.6165(-2.770)
bottled	-0.0668(-0.191)				
kaosbott		-0.0335(-0.082)	-0.0339(-0.083)	-0.1415(-0.345)	
hualbott		0.8394(1.030)	0.8569(1.048)	0.8620(1.044)	
taipbott		-2.1470(-1.762)	-1.6828(-1.564)	-1.6985(-1.558)	
airfilt	0.8307(2.957)	0.7818(2.764)	0.8462(2.993)	0.8187(2.872)	0.8351(2.958)
sickleave	0.0227(0.638)	0.0249(0.703)	0.0260(0.741)	0.0392(1.116)	
lungs	0.7854(2.471)	0.7863(2.488)	0.7707(2.462)		
sk	0.2898(0.701)	0.3360(0.815)			
σ	2.2526(20.676)	2.2352(20.673)	2.2482(20.704)	2.2712(20.693)	2.2968(20.690)
sample size	366	366	367	367	368
log likelihood	-699.35	-697.19	-700.79	-703.81	-707.56

(4) we excluded LUNGS, and finally obtained a significant coefficient for log duration. The elasticity of WTP with respect to duration of illness is somewhat higher than with Subsample I. Specification (5) removed other insignificant variables, such as the location–bottled water interaction terms, the days of paid sick leave, and the count of work loss days.[23] This equation confirms that the effects of most of the dummy variables on willingness-to-pay are generally very large, much more so than with Subsample I, as is confirmed by comparing Specification (5) in Table 6.11 and the identical equation for Subsample I, Specification (5) in Table 6.8.[24]

The preceding results suggest that subjects in Subsample II did not produce reliable responses. This result is confirmed if one examines the stability of responses across successive follow-up questions. The large changes in the values of the estimated coefficients from one round to another (see Table 6.13) suggest that respondents did not have well-defined values for WTP. A possible explanation is that respondents were not fami-

Table 6.12 Type of Drinking Water by Location of Residence of Subsample II Respondents

Count of Respondents Drinking:	Tap	Ground	Bottled (mineral, distilled or bottled spring water)	Total Respondents
Taipei	152	0	6	161
Kaohsiung	103	1	99	154
Hualien	42	26	10	75
Total	295	27	115	390

Table 6.13 Comparison of WTP Equations for Subsample II from All Rounds of Responses. Dependent variable: logWTP. Asymptotic t-statistics in parentheses.

Regressor	First Round	Second Round	Third Round	Fourth Round
intercept	4.9431(7.060)	3.6874(5.301)	2.9103(3.867)	2.7066(3.562)
log(duration)	0.2527(1.256)	0.4473(2.203)	0.4428(1.963)	0.5030(2.205)
cold	-0.5466(-2.216)	-0.5239(-2.129)	-0.6485(-2.379)	-0.6512(-2.325)
drug	0.4054(1.675)	0.6776(2.775)	0.9355(3.460)	1.0835(3.976)
doctor	0.3668(1.560)	0.5393(2.265)	0.4897(1.856)	0.4540(1.678)
edu2	0.0657(1.524)	0.0862(1.979)	0.1069(2.238)	0.1025(2.126)
kaohsiung	0.7221(2.583)	0.9297(3.442)	1.3580(4.547)	1.3479(4.406)
hualien	1.4566(3.655)	1.7379(4.725)	2.1309(5.208)	2.2093(5.336)
ground	-1.5988(-2.748)	-1.4620(-2.760)	-1.6926(-2.885)	-1.6165(-2.770)
airfilt	0.6558(2.497)	0.6853(2.750)	0.8621(3.112)	0.8351(2.958)
σ	1.5880(11.000)	1.9611(17.428)	2.3177(21.221)	2.2968(20.690)
sample size	389	389	389	368
log likelihood	-224.09	-458.79	-702.99	-707.56

liar with the commodity being valued because they had difficulty recalling their last illness episode. This suggests that respondents who have not been filling out health diaries should perhaps be asked to value an illness episode that is described for them.

Because of the unreliable responses from Subsample II, we focus henceforth on Subsample I in computing willingness to pay to avoid illness.

7   WTP TO AVOID ILLNESS IN THE UNITED STATES AND IN TAIWAN

7.1 Willingness to Pay for Reduced Illness in Taiwan

Using Specification (3) of Table 6.8, we calculated median WTP for Subsample I at the sample averages of the covariates for each successive round of payment questions.[25] The median WTP to avoid a recurrence of the episode is NT$1220.75 or US$48.83 (s.e. 6.9581) after the first round of responses, NT$1019.75 or US$40.79 (s.e. 3.0280) after the second round of responses, and NT$991.75 or US$39.67 (s.e. 2.9822) after the third and final round of responses. A Hausman test fails to reject the null hypothesis that the median WTP does not change between the first and the second rounds.[26] The difference between the second- and the third-round WTP estimates is very small.

We remind the reader that the figure of US$40 represents willingness to pay to avoid an episode of about 5.3 illness days and 2.2 symptoms. For the results of our survey to be useful for policy purposes, it is important to distinguish the type of illness that respondents are valuing and to see how WTP varies with the nature of the illness episode.

Most studies in the US distinguish illnesses by the nature of the symptoms experienced, the length of the illness and its severity. In Table 6.14, we report WTP for illnesses that were colds and those that were not, and for one-day and 5-day episodes. We use two measures of severity – whether the episode involved a restricted activity day (RAD), and whether the respondent visited a doctor.

Table 6.14 shows that WTP varies considerably with the nature of the illness valued. For a one-day, one-symptom episode, WTP ranges from $17 (for a cold that was not a RAD and did not result in a doctor's visit) to $70 (for a non-cold RAD that entailed a visit to the doctor). For average illness episodes – those of 5.3 days and 2.2 symptoms – WTP per day is much lower than for one-day episodes.

Table 6.14 has two implications for valuing the benefits of air pollution reduction in Taiwan. First, the value of reducing illness by a given number of days will depend on the length of the illness episodes reduced. Willingness to pay to avoid a day of illness is much higher for a one-day episode than for each day of a 5-day episode. Second, severity, as defined in Table 6.14, significantly affects WTP values.

To illustrate how Table 6.14 could be used in a benefit-cost analysis, we use it to estimate the benefits of lowering pollution levels in urban areas of Taiwan. Shaw et al. (1996) in their analysis of the effects of air pollution on

Table 6.14 Willingness to Pay to Avoid Illness in Taiwan (in September 1992 US$). Standard Errors in Parentheses.

	Doctor Visited				Doctor Not Visited			
	Episode is a Cold 1 Day, 2.2 Sympts.	Average Episode	Episode is not a Cold 1 Day, 2.2 Sympts.	Average Episode	Episode is a Cold 1 Day, 2.2 Sympts.	Average Episode	Episode is not a Cold 1 Day, 2.2 Sympts.	Average Episode
RAD	$44.02 (9.86)	$57.59 (8.56)	$70.26 (17.99)	$92.08 (8.21)	$23.97 (5.28)	$31.42 (5.58)	$38.26 (9.39)	$50.15 (10.31)
No RAD	$32.10 (6.35)	$42.06 (4.81)	$51.22 (12.05)	$25.66 (5.11)	$17.48 (3.07)	$22.90 (2.91)	$27.89 (5.82)	$35.56 (6.07)

acute illness in Taiwan, calculate that reducing the concentrations of PM10, SO_2 and O_3 in Taipei and Kaohsiung from existing levels to their respective levels in Hualien would have eliminated 9.5 million person-days of acute illness in 1992. If we treat this as a reduction of 9.5 million one-day colds that did not entail a doctor's visit or a RAD, the morbidity value of the pollution reduction is approximately US$166 million. This value, however, falls to US$40.96 million if the 9.5 million days represent 1.79 million average episodes of the same type (colds with no RADs and no doctors' visits). In this case, the value of the illness reduction is much lower, since the value per day of avoiding an average episode is only $4.32.

7.2 Benefits Transfer

An important question when performing benefit-cost analyses of pollution control in developing countries is whether estimates of WTP computed in the United States can be transferred to other countries. The simplest approach to benefits transfer predicts WTP in Country A by multiplying US WTP by the ratio of average household income in Country A to average household income in the US (Krupnick et al., 1993). This is clearly an oversimplification: it assumes either that income is the only relevant factor affecting WTP and that the elasticity of WTP with respect to income is 1, or that treating the income elasticity of WTP as unity captures all other factors (e.g., education levels) that may influence WTP.

To see how well the simple approach works in the present instance, Table 6.15 presents estimates of WTP to avoid one day of head cold from two contingent valuation studies conducted in the US, one by Tolley et al. (1986) and the other by Loehman et al. (1979), together with household income for each study. (All figures are in 1992 US dollars.) Multiplying each US WTP estimate by the ratio of income in Subsample I to income in the US study predicts Taiwanese WTP to avoid one day of head cold.

For one restricted activity day of head cold, the predictions of Tolley's study ($28.01) and of Loehman's ($15.23) fall within the confidence interval for Subsample I for a one-day cold with no doctor's visit ($13.62,$34.32).[27] For a day of head cold that is not a RAD, Loehman's prediction ($7.08) falls below the lower endpoint of the 95% confidence interval of Subsample I. Indeed, her figure for the US, $8.91,is below the lower endpoint of the confidence interval for Taiwanese WTP.

We conclude from this limited evidence that the simple approach to extrapolating WTP values works fairly well in the case of the US and Taiwan. We caution, however, against generalizing this finding. We estimate that the income elasticity of WTP to avoid acute illness in Taiwan is about 0.33,while Loehman et al. estimate that this elasticity ranges between 0.26 and 0.6.The assumption of the simple approach, that it is 1.0,which should cause us to underpredict WTP in Taiwan, may work well here because education levels, which increase WTP, are lower in Taiwan than in the US. The unitary elasticity assumption thus captures differences between the two countries in other factors that affect WTP.

8   CONCLUSIONS

This study has investigated the value of reducing illness in Taiwan and has focused on related methodological implications.

Previous studies that value reductions in acute illness have asked respondents to value a set of symptoms that are described for them. This study approached the matter somewhat differently, allowing the respondent to describe his most recent episode of acute respiratory illness. We felt that this would make the commodity valued more meaningful to the respondent, resulting in more reliable WTP estimates and estimates that better represent values for average illness episodes. The drawback of this approach is that it may be difficult for a respondent to recall his most recent illness episode. If this is the case, WTP values obtained from self-described illness episodes may be unreliable.

Using the approach of administering the survey to a subsample that had participated in a health diary study and one that had not, we conclude that providing respondents with the experience of keeping a health diary results in WTP values that are 'robust', i.e.,internally valid. For this group, willingness to pay to avoid illness increased with duration of illness, with the number of symptoms experienced and with severity of illness. Furthermore,

Table 6.15   Willingness to Pay to Avoid a Head Cold: US v. Taiwan
(September 1992 US$)(95% confidence intervals in brackets)

	No RAD		RAD		Household Income	
	US	Taiwan	US	Taiwan	US	Taiwan
Tolley et al. (1986) (one day of severe head congestion and throat irritation)	–	–	$40.32	$28.01	$40,583[a]	
Loehman et al. (1979) (one day of head congestion, eye, ear and throat irritation)	$8.91	$7.08	$19.15	$15.23	$28,675[b]	
Taiwan CV Survey (one day and average number of symptoms; doctor not visited)	$17.48 [$11.46 –23.50]		$23.97 [$13.62 –34.62]		$28,260[a] $22,800[b]	

Notes

a.   Mean household income.

b.   Median household income. Predictions for Taiwan from the US study were obtained by multiplying the US figures by the ratio of median household income of the Taiwan-based sample to median household income of the US-based sample. If mean household income, but not median household income, was reported in the US study, predictions for Taiwan were formed using the ratio of mean household incomes. Estimates for Taiwan from the Taiwan study were based on (3), Table 6.8.

people who went to a doctor or took medication for their illness had higher WTPs than those who did not. In contrast, the willingness-to-pay equation for the subsample that did not participate in the epidemiological study performed poorly. The WTP to avoid illness did not vary as expected with many episode or respondent characteristics. WTP was not significantly related to the number of symptoms reported, to the severity of activity limitations, or to the respondent's income.

Overall, these results support a call for interdisciplinary research, pairing diary-type epidemiological studies of acute health outcomes with contingent valuation studies seeking values for avoiding such outcomes. Performing such health studies would add significantly to the cost of obtaining WTP estimates if the health studies were not valued in their own right. But, understanding of the causes of acute health outcomes is still rudimentary enough to justify major epidemiological studies. At the same time, it might not be necessary to mount full-blown health studies to obtain robust contingent valuation (CV)-based WTP estimates. Some other means of involving respondents in following their day-to-day health status might work just as well in addressing the recall problem.

Finally, we have tried to shed light on the issue of benefits transfer by comparing WTP estimates from our survey with predictions of Taiwanese WTP based on US studies. The simplest method of predicting WTP is to multiply a point estimate from the US by the ratio of average household income in Taiwan to average household income in the US. Using the results of two US studies that estimate willingness to pay to avoid a restricted activity day of head cold, we find that the simple predictions from both studies fall within the 95% confidence interval of median WTP for Subsample I in Taiwan.

The simple approach to benefits transfer thus works fairly well in the case of the US and Taiwan. We caution, however, against generalizing this finding. The assumption of the simple approach, that the income elasticity for WTP is 1.0, which should cause us to underpredict WTP in Taiwan, may work well here because education levels, which increase WTP, are lower in Taiwan than in the US. This result is most likely an artifact of these offsetting influences and may not hold in general.

APPENDIX

Appendix 6.A

Table 6.A.1   Home Air Conditioner by Location of Residence and Health Profile of Respondents

	Total Count of Respondents		Percent with Home Air Conditioning Units	
	Subsample I	Subsample II	Subsample I	Subsample II
Taipei	340	161	86.2	87.6
Kaohsiung	338	154	74.3	74.7
Hualien	138	75	75.4	73.3
Lung=1	212	87	75.9	71.3

Table 6.A.1, continued

	Total Count of Respondents		Percent with Home Dehumidifier	
	Subsample I	Subsample II	Subsample I	Subsample II
Lung=0	604	303	80.6	82.2
sk=1	107	40	77.6	72.5
sk=0	709	350	79.7	80.5

Table 6.A.2 Home Dehumidifier by Location of Residence and Health Profile of Respondents

	Total Count of Respondents		Percent with Home Dehumidifier	
	Subsample I	Subsample II	Subsample I	Subsample II
Taipei	340	161	53.2	34.8
Kaohsiung	338	154	19.8	21.4
Hualien	138	75	36.9	36.0
Lung=1	212	87	39.6	29.9
Lung=0	604	303	35.6	29.7
sk=1	107	40	42.0	30.0
sk=0	709	350	35.9	29.7

Appendix 6.B Contingent Valuation Stionnaire Questionnaire

PART I ILLNESS EPISODES

The purpose of this interview is to discuss an illness that you have had recently, and to discuss what you would be willing to pay to avoid this type of illness episode. What we stress is the illness episode that you have had recently. Please don't think it must be a serious illness, the illness episode just describes the situation in which you felt discomfort or sick the last time. You can point out the symptoms that you have had, such as eye irritation or headache, on the symptoms table.

We are interested in a short-term illness episode, such as a cold or the flu, or even a day of coughing. We are not interested in chronic disease or injury due to an accident, such as chronic back pain or bone fracture.

Now, please answer the following questions about the illness episode that you have had most recently.

Questionnaire type_____

County or city_____

Replacement sample_____

Id Number _____

1. When did this occur?_____(year month)
2. How many symptoms on the Symptoms Table 1 did you have ? Please write down the number of days the episode lasted on Table 1, and figure out the symptoms' duration on Table 2. If a symptom did not occur, leave the space blank.

SYMPTOMS TABLE 1

(1) eye irritation____days

(2) headache____days

(3) fever____days

(4) runny nose____days

(5) sinusitis____days
or sinus problem

(6) dry scratchy throat ____days

(7) sore throat____days

(8) croup____days

(9) dry cough____days

(10) cough with phlegm____days

(11) chest discomfort or pain____days

(12) allergy____days

(13) wheezing ____days

(14) asthma____days

(15) shortness of breath ____days

(16) rash____days

(17) aching muscle____days

(18) others____days

SYMPTOMS TABLE 2

Please recall the days that symptoms started and ended for the illness episode that you have had recently.

Days

1 2 3 4 5 6 7 8 9 10 11 12 13 14

Symptoms

----

(1) eye irritation

(2) headache

(3) fever

(4) runny nose

(5) sinusitis
or sinus problem

(6) dry scratchy throat

(7) sore throat

(8) croup

(9) dry cough

(10) cough with phlegm

(11) chest discomfort or pain

(12) allergy

(13) wheezing _____

(14) asthma _____

(15) shortness of breath _____

(16) rash _____

(17) aching muscle _____

(18) others _____

3. Which symptom bothered you the most?_____

4. Was the illness episode a cold?

    (1)___No

    (2)___Yes. It lasted___days

5. Did the illness episode cause you to spend the day in bed?

    (1)___No

    (2)___Yes. How many days did you spend in bed?__days

          [GO TO QUESTION 6-(2)-A]

6. Did the illness episode prevent you from going out to work?

    (1)___No, Did you feel tired or less productive than usual?

          (a)___No

          (b)___Yes

    (2)___Yes. (A) How many days did this illness episode prevent you from going to work? ___days

        (B) Did you lose any income because of not working?

          (a)___No [GO TO QUESTION 7-(2)]

          (b)___Yes,How much income did you lose?_____NT$

        [GO TO QUESTION 7-(2)]

7. Did this illness episode prevent you from doing daily activities except working?

    (1)___No

    (2)___Yes. How many days did it prevent you doing daily activities except working? ___days

8. Did you eat more vegetables, drink more water or take vitamins, or anything else to relieve the symptoms?

    (1)___No

    (2)___Yes. (A) How much money did you spend? _____NT$

        (B) Was this helpful to your symptoms?

          (a)___No

          (b)___Yes

9. Did you take any patent medicine that was bought from the drugstore to relieve symptoms or cure the disease?

    (1)___No

    (2)___Yes. (A) How much money did you spend? _____NT$

        (B) Was this helpful to your symptoms?

          (a)___No

    (b)___Yes

10. Did you go to a doctor?

    (1)___No

    (2)___Yes. (A) What was doctor's diagnosis? Diagnosis was_____

        (B) Did he prescribe any medicine?

          (a)___No

          (b)___Yes

        (C) Did you get an injection?

          (a)___No

          (b)___Yes

11. Did you go to a hospital?

    (1)___No

    (2)___Yes. How many nights did you stay?___nights

12. How did you pay the bills for doctor visits?

    (1)___You paid the fee entirely.

    How much did you pay?_____NT$

    (2)___The fee was covered entirely by insurance.

          It is (They are)(1)___government employee insurance

                    (2)___labor insurance

                    (3)___farmer insurance

                    (4)___low income families subsidy

                    (5)___life insurance

                    (6)___student health insurance

                    (7)___soldier insurance

                    (8)___other (please specify)_____

    (3)___The fee was covered partly by insurance.

        (A) It is (They are)(1)___government employee insurance

                    (2)___labor insurance

                    (3)___farmer insurance

                    (4)___low income families subsidy

                    (5)___life insurance

                    (6)___student health insurance

                    (7)___soldier insurance

                    (8)___other (please specify)_____

        (B) How much did you pay?_____NT$

13. How long did it take you to recover from the previous illness? ___days

14. We are now going to ask you a hypothetical question. Suppose you were told that, within the next few days, you would experience a recurrence of the illness episode you have just described for us. What would it be worth to you – that is, how much you would pay – to avoid the illness episode entirely?

Please read the prompt carefully before you answer the following questions.

[PROMPT] Remember that you are paying to eliminate all of your pain and suffering, your medical expenditure, the time you spent visiting the doctor or clinic, and your missed work (or lost productivity), leisure, or daily activities. Bear in mind if you pay to completely avoid being ill this time, you have to give up some other use of this money. For example, you may reduce your expenditure for entertainment or education.

[QUESTIONS] – *Example provided for Questionnaire Version 1*
Would you pay 300 NT$ to avoid being sick at all?
(1)___No. Would you pay 100 NT$ to avoid being sick at all?
    (A)___No. Would you pay 50 NT$ to avoid being sick at all?
        (a)___No. Why?_____[PLEASEWRITE DOWN]
        (b)___Yes [END OF PART I QUESTIONS]
    (B)___Yes. Would you pay 200 NT$ to avoid being sick at all?
        (a)___No [END OF PART I QUESTIONS]
        (b)___Yes [END OF PART I QUESTIONS]
(2)___Yes. Would you pay 1000 NT$ to avoid being sick at all?
    (A)___No. Would you pay 600 NT$ to avoid being sick at all?
        (a)___No [END OF PART I QUESTIONS]
        (b)___Yes [END OF PART I QUESTIONS]
    (B)___Yes. Would you pay 2000 NT$ to avoid being sick at all?
        (a)___No [END OF PART I QUESTIONS]
        (b)___Yes [END OF PART I QUESTIONS]

PART II   Personal Information
1. Your birth year: _____
2. Sex: (1)___Female
        (2)___Male
3. Ethnic Group: (1)___aboriginal
          (2)___the Ku-Chia people
          (3)___mainlander
          (4)___the Ming-Nan people
4. Highest education level completed:(1)___elementary school
                              (and below)
                            (2)___junior high school
                            (3)___senior high school
                            (4)___university or college
                            (5)___graduate degree
5. Marital status:(1)___single
               (2)___married
               (3)___divorced or widowed

6. How long have you lived at the present address:____years
7. How old is your house?   (1)___less than 1 year
                              (2)___1–5 years
                              (3)___6–10 years
                              (4)___11–15 years
                              (5)___16–20 years
 8. The size of your house:_____
    The number of rooms in your house:____
 9. How many persons live in your house?____
10. Are there any air conditioners in your house?
    (1)___No
    (2)___Yes, central system
    (3)___Yes, window only
11. Are there any dehumidifiers in your house?
    (1)___No
    (2)___Yes, central system
    (3)___Yes, room only
12. Do you do exercise often?
    (1)___No
    (2)___Yes,_____hrs/week
13. From the 17 symptoms on symptoms table 1, which of them may be
    caused by air pollution?_____
14. What kind of water do you drink?
    (1)___ tap water
    (2)___ spring
    (3)___ ground water
    (4)___ distilled water
    (5)___ mineral water
    (6)___ other   (please specify)_____
15. How much money does your household pay for tap water?
    _____NT$/month
    How much money does your household pay for distilled water or
    mineral water?
    _____NT$/month
16. Do you think the tap water you drink endangers your health? Please
    cite the risk index between 1 and 10, no danger at all to very dangerous.
    Risk index = _____.
17. Do you have a job now?
    (1)___No
    (2)___Yes, (A) working place:_____
                (B) industry:_____
                (C) occupation:_____

(D) work hours:_____hr/day

(E) work days:_____days/week

(F) sick leave days:_____days/year

(G) income loss for sick leave:_____NT$/year

(H) the transportation mode of your commute to work:

    (a)___automobile

    (b)___motorcycle

    (c)___bicycle

    (d)___bus

    (e)___train

    (f)___walk

(I) Are there any air conditioners in your work place?

    (a)___No

    (b)___Yes, central system

    (c)___Yes, window only

(J) Are there any dehumidifiers in your working place?

    (a)___No

    (b)___Yes, central system

    (c)___Yes, room only

(K) Are you exposed to irritating smoke, dust, or fumes at your working place?

    (a)___No

    (b)___Yes, it is: (b-1)___fumes

                       (b-2)___dust

                       (b-3)___smoke

                       (b-4)___others, _____

                       (b-5)___don't know

18. Do you smoke?

    (1)___No

    (2)___Yes. (A) Have you smoked a total of more than 100 cigarettes in your life?   (a)___No

                                   (b)___Yes

        (B) How many cigarettes do you smoke per day?_____

        (C) How old were you when you started smoking regularly?_____

        (D) If you are an ex-cigarette smoker, how old were you when you gave up smoking regularly? _____

19. How many people do you think may get lung cancer among 100 regular smokers?_____

20. Have you ever had any of the following symptoms?

    (1) ___bronchitis

(2) ___pneumonia
(3) ___bronchopneumonia
(4) ___chronic bronchitis
(5) ___emphysema
(6) ___pleurisy
(7) ___heart trouble
(8) ___high blood pressure
(9) ___other lung disease
(10)___ other chronic disease

21. Do you have any medical insurance?
(1)___No
(2)___Yes, (A)_____government employee insurance
(B)_____labor insurance
(C)_____farmer insurance
(D)_____low income families subsidy
(E)_____life insurance
(F)_____student health insurance
(G)_____soldier insurance
(H)_____other (please specify)_____

22. The total monthly income of your family:
(1) ___ None
(2) ___ less than 15000 NT$
(3) ___ 15001 to 20000 NT$
(4) ___ 20001 to 25000 NT$
(5) ___ 25001 to 30000 NT$
(6) ___ 30001 to 35000 NT$
(7) ___ 35001 to 40000 NT$
(8) ___ 40001 to 45000 NT$
(9) ___ 45001 to 50000 NT$
(10)___ 50001 to 60000 NT$
(11)___ 60001 to 70000 NT$
(12)___ 70001 to 80000 NT$
(13)___ 80001 to 90000 NT$
(14)___ 90001 to 100000 NT$
(15)___ 100001 to 120000 NT$
(16)___ 120001 to 140000 NT$
(17)___ 140001 to 160000 NT$
(18)___ more than 160001 NT$

23. Your own monthly income :
(1) ___ None
(2) ___ less than 15000 NT$
(3) ___ 15001 to 20000 NT$

(4) ___ 20001 to 25000 NT$
(5) ___ 25001 to 30000 NT$
(6) ___ 30001 to 35000 NT$
(7) ___ 35001 to 40000 NT$
(8) ___ 40001 to 45000 NT$
(9) ___ 45001 to 50000 NT$
(10)___ 50001 to 60000 NT$
(11)___ 60001 to 70000 NT$
(12)___ 70001 to 80000 NT$
(13)___ 80001 to 90000 NT$
(14)___ 90001 to 100000 NT$
(15)___ 100001 to 120000 NT$
(16)___ 120001 to 140000 NT$
(17)___ 140001 to 160000 NT$
(18)___ more than 160001 NT$

ACKNOWLEDGEMENTS

The authors would like to thank Jesse David, Carter Hood, Pallavi Shah and Nathalie Simon for outstanding research assistance, and the participants in the IEAS International Conference on Economic Perspectives of Pollution Control in the Pacific Rim Countries, Taipei, Taiwan, March 1994, and the Eastern Economics Association meetings, Boston, March 1994, for helpful comments. This research was supported by the Chiang Ching-Kuo Foundation, Academia Sinica and by the US Environmental Protection Agency.

NOTES

1. The symptoms on the card are listed in Table 6.1.
2. A restricted activity day is any day on which a person's normal activities are impaired, although the impairment need not be so severe as to restrict the individual to bed or prevent him from going to work.
3. The epidemiological study was designed by the authors of this paper. The results of this study are reported in Shaw et al. (1996). A total of 953 persons participated in the epidemiological study, and 89 of them refused to participate in the contingent valuation survey. Both surveys were administered by Gallup Taiwan.
4. Some respondents simply could not recall their most recent illness episode. Others refused to answer the willingness-to-pay questions, or gave willingness-to-pay values that were unbelievably large in light of their income. Respondents were eliminated if their willingness to pay to avoid the illness episode exceeded one percent of their yearly income. This criterion caused only 10 respondents to be deleted from the sample.

5. The Kolmogorov-Smirnov test is based on the comparison between the empirical distribution functions of the data in the two subsamples. The expression for the two-tailed statistic we used is $D = \max |S_n - S_m|$ where S_n and S_m are the values of the empirical cdf for a certain observation estimated from the first and the second samples, respectively. For large sample sizes m and n, under the null hypothesis the quantity $4D^2 nm/(n+m)$ converges in distribution to a chi-square with two degrees of freedom.

6. This systematic difference was established using a nonparametric test of the null hypothesis that the median values of the observations from the two subsamples are equal. The test statistic is calculated by first pooling the two samples and finding the median value for the pooled samples. The observations that are smaller and greater than the pooled-sample median are then counted for both subsamples and the counts arranged in a two-by-two table. Finally (using a Pearson chi-square test) one tests the null hypothesis that there is no difference between the actual counts and the predicted counts had the two samples come from a common distribution. See Siegel (1956).

7. The percentage of 'no' responses should increase monotonically with the stated WTP value, whereas the percentage of 'yes' responses should decrease monotonically with the stated WTP value. The empirical distribution of WTP, which is calculated as the fraction of the sample falling in a specified WTP interval, should be approximately the same across the different questionnaire versions.

8. Hedonic models have been extensively used with housing and labor market data to estimate how the attributes of a dwelling influence its market value and the attributes of a job are reflected in the wage rate. Such attributes may include local environmental quality and occupational hazards. See Freeman (1993) for a survey.

9. For instance, if the initial payment question states NT$300, the associated response is a 'yes', and the response to the follow-up amount of NT$1000 is a 'no', $WTP^L = 300$ and $WTP^U = 1000$. WTP^L and WTP^U may be equal to 0 and $+\infty$, depending on the sequence of 'yes' and 'no' responses to stated WTP amounts.

10. Cooper and Hanemann (1994) ran Monte Carlo simulations to assess the gain in efficiency of WTP estimates when moving from single-bounded models based on the responses to the initial payment questions to double- and triple-bounded models (corresponding to Round 2 and Round 3 in the present CV survey). Using mean WTP as the statistic of interest, they determined that moving from a single-bounded to a double-bounded model caused large changes in the point estimates of WTP and a marked reduction in the variance of the estimates. An additional round of follow-up questions was found to have only a small effect on the bias and the efficiency of the estimates.

11. As part of the initial specification searches, we tried including among the regressors of the WTP equation the number of days of each individual symptom (cough, headache, etc.). However, only a few of the individual symptoms thus measured turned out to be significant predictors of WTP. Other symptom-days had coefficients that were not statistically significant, or of the wrong sign. We therefore moved to a more aggregate description of the illness.

12. We report the acronyms and definitions of the variables used in our regressions in Table 6.7.

13. The duration and the number of symptoms of the episode tend to be correlated. We ran a least squares regression of log duration on an intercept term and log symptoms, and obtained a positive and strongly significant coefficient of log symptoms, even though the adjusted R-square of the regression was only about 0.08.

14. The median monthly household income for the group of respondents who drink ground water is lower than NT$47,500, the median figure for the whole of Subsample I. Seventy percent of these respondents have WTP higher than NT$2000, whereas only about 35%

of Subsample I have WTP higher than NT$2000.

15. Flores (1994) points out that the reference to luxury goods is not informative in this context, because the quantity of the commodity being purchased (health) cannot be adjusted as the respondent becomes wealthier, as is assumed in the standard definition of a luxury good. The relevant question is whether wealthier respondents are willing to pay more than less wealthy respondents for a fixed quantity of the good.

16. Loehman and De fitted separate equations to model log*WTP* for each of the symptoms or symptom complexes valued. They included the length of the spell and log income among the regressors in each equation. The coefficient of log household income is the elasticity of WTP with respect to income, and is found to range between 0.26 (minor coughing and sneezing/eye irritation complex) and 0.60 (severe shortness of breath).

17. See Alberini (1995) for a description of the Pearson chi-square testing procedure and a discussion of the power of this test with first-round estimates.

18. We treated questionnaire version 3 as the baseline. The coefficients for the version 1 and version 2 dummies were -0.0977 and -0.0960, respectively, and had t-statistics of -0.599 and -0.587.

19. Each round of bidding alters the upper and lower bounds of the respondent's WTP. Estimates labeled Round 1 are based on the WTP^L and WTP^U values obtained after one round of bidding. Estimates labeled Round 2 are based on the WTP^L and WTP^U values obtained after two rounds of bidding, etc.

20. The 95% critical level is 27.6.

21. The much smaller sample size for Subsample II does not appear to be the reason for such a weaker statistical relationship: we randomly drew several subsamples of 390 observations from Subsample I and found that log duration, log symptoms, log income and all the other regressors of the equations reported in Tables 6.7 and 6.8 remained significant even at the reduced sample size.

22. Auxiliary regressions show that log(*duration*) = 1.4182 + 0.1673*log(*symptoms*), and log (*duration*) = 1.4795 + 0.0481*SK* + 0.2385*LUNGS*, where *SK* and *LUNGS* are the dummies for chronic and respiratory illnesses, respectively (t-statistics 43.644, 0.513 and 3.496). Furthermore, the severity of the illness does not appear to be systematically affected by the city of residence of the respondent.

23. Table 6.12 reports the distribution of Subsample II respondents by their source of drinking water.

24. We also tried an additional variant of (5) which allowed for questionnaire version effects (not reported), but the questionnaire dummies were not significant at conventional levels. We treated questionnaire version 6 as the baseline, and obtained estimated coefficients of 0.1653 and -0.5334 for the version 4 and version 5 dummies. The t-statistics were 0.548 and 1.630 respectively.

25. The expression for the estimated median is $\exp(\bar{x}\hat{B}_r)$, with $\hat{B}_r$ the estimated slope coefficient from the r-th round of estimation and $\bar{x}$ the vector of the sample means of the regressors. We use median, rather than mean, WTP because it provides a robust lower bound to the mean and is not particularly sensitive to the presence of large WTP amounts. We also tried another approach based on predicting individual median WTP values using our WTP equation, and taking the average of these imputed values. Because the resulting average tended to be quite high relative to the median WTP of the sample, which is NT$1000, we decided against this latter approach.

26. The test statistic is distributed as a chi-square with one degree of freedom under the null hypothesis of no systematic change between the first- and the second-round median WTP. The value of the statistic in our sample, 1.64, is less than the 5% critical value of 3.84.

27. We use the WTP of Subsample I assuming no doctor's visit, since there is no mention

of a doctor's visit in either the Tolley et al. or the Loehman et al. surveys.

REFERENCES

Alberini, Anna (1995), 'Testing Willingness-to-Pay Models of Discrete Choice Contingent Valuation Data', *Land Economics*, **71**(1), 83–95.

Alberini, Anna, Alan Krupnick, Maureen Cropper and Winston Harrington (1994), 'Air Quality and the Value of Health in Taiwan', a paper presented at the Annual Meeting of the Eastern Economics Association, Boston, MA.

Cooper, Joseph and W. Michael Hanemann (1995), 'Referendum Contingent Valuation: How Many Bounds Are Enough?', a paper presented at the Annual Meeting of the American Agricultural Economics Association, San Diego, CA, August.

Flores, Nicholas (1994), 'The Effects of Rationing and Valuation Elasticities', draft manuscript, UCSD Department of Economics, La Jolla, CA.

Freeman, A. Myrick (1993), *The Measurement of Environmental and Resource Values: Theory and Methods*, Washington, DC: Resources for the Future.

Harrington, Winston and Paul R. Portney (1987), 'Valuing the Benefits of Health and Safety Regulation', *Journal of Urban Economics*, **22**(1), 101–12.

Kanninen, Barbara J. and Bengt Kriström (1993), 'Welfare Benefit Estimation and Income Distribution', *Beijer Discussion Paper Series* No. 20, Second Revision.

Krupnick, Alan, Kenneth Harrison, Eric Nickell and Michael Toman (1993), 'The Benefits of Ambient Air Quality Improvements in Central and Eastern Europe: A Preliminary Assessment', *Resources for the Future Discussion Paper* #ENR93-19, Washington, DC: Resources for the Future.

Loehman, E.T., S.V. Berg, A.A. Arroyo, R.A. Hedinger, J.M. Schwartz, M.E. Shaw, W. Fahien, V.H. De, R.P. Fishe, D.E. Rio, W.F. Rossley, and A.E.S. Green (1979), 'Distributional Analysis of Regional Benefits and Cost of Air Quality Control', *Journal of Environmental Economics and Management*, **6**, 222–43.

Loehman, Edna and Vo Hu De (1982), 'Application of Stochastic Choice Modeling to Policy Analysis of Public Goods: A Case Study of Air Quality Improvements', *The Review of Economics and Statistics*, **64**(3), 474–80.

Mitchell, Robert C. and Richard T. Carson (1989), *Using Surveys to Value Public Goods: The Contingent Valuation Method*, Washington, DC:

Resources for the Future.

Rowe, Robert D. and Lauraine G. Chestnut (1985), 'Oxidants and Asthmatics in Los Angeles: A Benefits Analysis', Energy and Resource Consultants, Inc., Report to the US EPA. NTIS No. PB85-228997/AS.

Siegel, S. (1956), *Nonparametric Statistics for the Behavioral Sciences*, New York: McGraw-Hill.

Shaw, Daigee, Tsu-Tan Fu, Lung-An Lee, Wen-Harn Pan and Jin-Tan Liu (1996), 'Acute Health Effects of Major Air Pollutants in Taiwan', in Robert Mendelsohn and Daigee Shaw (eds), *The Economics of Pollution Control in the Asia Pacific*, Aldershot: Edward Elgar.

Tolley, George, Lyndon Babcock, Mark Berger, Anthony Bilotti, Glenn Blomquist, Michael Brien, Robert Fabian, Gideon Fishelson, Charles Kahn, Austin Kelly, Don Kenkel, Ronald Krumm, Tracy Miller, Robert Oshfeldt, Sherwin Rosen, William Webb, Wallace Wilson and Martin Zelder (1986), 'Valuation of Reductions in Human Health Symptoms and Risks', Report for US EPA grant #CR-811053-01-0, United States Environmental Protection Agency, Washington, DC.

7. Hedonic Housing Values and Benefits of Air Quality Improvement in Taipei

Chung-Hsin Yang

1 INTRODUCTION

In the last two decades, many efforts have been made to examine the effect of air pollution on housing values. Typically, these studies employ Rosen's (1974) hedonic price technique, and most of them find that air pollution has a significant negative effect on housing values (Ridker and Henning, 1967; Sonstelie and Portney, 1980; Graves et al., 1988; Harrison and Rubinfeld, 1978; Nelson, 1978; Bender, Gronberg and Hwang, 1980; Brookshire et al., 1981). In addition to examining the effect of air pollution on housing values, some studies (Harrison and Rubinfeld, 1978; Nelson, 1978; Bender, Gronberg and Hwang, 1980; Brookshire et al., 1981) proceed to the second step of hedonic price analysis to estimate willingness-to-pay equations to measure the benefits of air quality improvement.[1]

The effect of air pollution on housing values (rents) in the Taipei metropolitan area has been investigated by Lu (1987) using a hedonic price approach. He found that air pollution did not have a significant effect on the rental rate of housing in the Taipei metropolitan area. However, Lu used a linear functional form, which implies that the housing attributes are all separable and that the hedonic prices are constants. Thus, Lu's findings are of questionable validity. The purpose of this paper is to re-investigate the effect of air pollution on housing values in the Taipei metropolitan area, and to evaluate the benefits of air quality improvement by estimating a non-linear hedonic price equation.

Section 2 below briefly describes the hedonic price technique and the nonlinear hedonic function employed in this study. Section 3 explains the variables and sources of data used. Section 4 presents the estimation of the hedonic housing value equation and examines the properties of the marginal willingness-to-pay function. Section 5 estimates the benefits of air quality improvement.

2 HEDONIC PRICE TECHNIQUE

The hedonic price technique (Rosen, 1974; Freeman, 1974a, 1974b, 1979a, 1979b, 1993) is employed in this paper. As it is becoming a standard procedure, the hedonic price technique is usually applied step by step as follows:

The first step is to estimate a hedonic housing value equation by regressing the observed housing values on environmental variables such as air pollution, housing attributes and neighborhood characteristics.

The second step is to derive the marginal willingness-to-pay function by taking the derivative of the hedonic housing values and using this function to calculate each household's marginal willingness to pay for air quality improvements.

The third step is to estimate this willingness-to-pay function (inverse demand function) by regressing the marginal willingness-to-pay variable on air pollution level and household characteristics such as household income and household size.

The final step is to integrate the willingness-to-pay function (the inverse demand function) over a specified range to obtain the benefits of air quality improvements.

It has been shown by Rosen (1974) that a hedonic housing value function is a reduced-form equation reflecting both supply and demand influences. Thus, there is no theoretical guidance as to the choice of proper functional form. The lack of a firm theoretical basis for the choice of functional form makes the application of the hedonic price technique difficult and makes the empirical results depend critically on the selected functional form. Freeman (1979b), Halvorsen and Pollakowski (1979), Goodman (1978), Bender, Gronberg and Hwang (1980), Cassel and Mendelsohn (1985), Cropper, Deck and McConnell (1988), Graves et al. (1988) and others have stressed this empirical issue and some of them recommend using the flexible Box-Cox functional form for hedonic analyses and further recommend measuring best performance with a goodness-of-fit test. For example, Goodman (1978), and Cropper, Deck and McConnell (1988) suggest the use of the linear Box-Cox transformation, which provides for explicit likelihood testing of commonly used functional forms such as linear, log-linear, and semi-log functional forms. Halvorsen and Pollakowski (1979) introduce the quadratic Box-Cox transformation which yields all other functional forms of interest as special cases (a total of 10 special cases), and suggest using the likelihood ratio test to test the appropriateness of alternative functional forms.

Although the quadratic Box-Cox function is general enough to avoid the imposition of the theoretically unwarranted restrictions, it is quite complicated. Employing this kind of complicated functional form may move the analysis away from a transparent answer to the problem at hand, which should be to explore the effects of pollution on housing values. Moreover, the quadratic Box-Cox analysis chooses the model which best explains housing prices, which is not necessarily the model which best explains how housing prices are affected by air pollution (Cassel and Mendelsohn, 1985). In the existing literature, the log-linear model appears to fit the data closely and it is therefore frequently chosen.[2]

With these arguments in mind, we employ a nonlinear logarithmic specification of the hedonic housing value equation as follows:

$$\ln P = \alpha_0 + \alpha_1 \ln TSP + \alpha_2 (\ln TSP)^2 + \Sigma \beta_i \ln A_i + \Sigma \gamma_i D_i \qquad (7.1)$$

where P = housing value; TSP = total suspended particulates (air pollution); A = a vector of housing and neighborhood characteristics; D = a vector of dummy variables. Notice that the log-linear hedonic housing value function is a special form of (7.1) with $\alpha_2 = 0$.

Since our analysis deals with one market (i.e., the Taipei metropolitan area), it is very difficult to identify the willingness-to-pay function in this case. Instead of estimating the willingness-to-pay function, we employ the set of marginal willingness-to-pay estimates obtained from steps 1 and 2 to approximate the benefits of air quality improvements. In other words, we shall assume that all households in the Taipei metropolitan area have the same preferences and incomes, and based on the marginal willingness-to-pay information, we can derive an approximate indication of the willingness to pay for air quality improvement in the Taipei metropolitan area.

3   DATA AND VARIABLES

The study area, the Taipei metropolitan area (TMA), covers Taipei City and Taipei County. Taipei City and Taipei County are subdivided into li^3 (as shown on Figure 7.2 in Appendix 7.1). The housing and household data used in this study were derived from the Housing Condition Survey, a supplementary survey of the Human Resource Survey conducted by the Directorate-General of Budget, Accounting & Statistics, Executive Yuan (DGBAS) in 1989. A total of 2,005 individual houses in the Taipei metropolitan area (898 units located in Taipei City and 1,107 units located in Taipei County) are used in this study.

The air pollution data for this study comes from the Monitoring Report on Air Quality compiled by the Environmental Protection Administration (EPA), Executive Yuan. It consists of total suspended particulates (TSP), carbon monoxide, nitrogen oxides, etc. as measured by 39 monitoring sta-

Table 7.1   Frequency Distribution of TSP in the Taipei Metropolitan Area (1989)

TSP ($\mu g/m^3$)	Frequency (# of obs)	Percent (%)	Cumulative (%)
Below 40	15	0.7	0.7
40–50	49	2.4	3.2
50–60	121	6.0	9.2
60–70	24	1.2	10.4
70–80	271	13.5	23.9
80–90	256	12.8	36.7
90–100	358	17.9	54.6
100–110	392	19.6	74.1
110–120	270	13.5	87.6
120–130	155	7.7	95.3
130–140	63	3.1	98.5
140–150	25	1.2	99.7
above 150	6	0.3	100.0

tions in the area. However, since only the TSP dataset is complete, we use *TSP* as a general measure of air pollution in this study. Further, we employ a spatial interpolation technique to estimate the *TSP* level in each li based on the levels of *TSP* read from the monitoring stations within and around the Taipei metropolitan area. The interpolation procedures are described in Appendix 7.1. Table 7.1 shows the frequency distribution of *TSP* in the Taipei metropolitan area.

The dependent variable of the hedonic housing value equation is the adjusted present value of each house (property), denoted by P. The housing price data of the Housing Condition Survey is the transaction price of the house at the time of purchase. To adjust the price at the purchasing year to the present price (capitalized value), we use a formula developed by Liu (1992) which takes the changes of housing appreciation and commodity prices into account. The formula is as follows:

$$P_t = BV_t + LV_t$$
$$= (BV_{to} \times AI_{to} + BV_{to} \div CPI_{to}) \times 0.4 \times (1 - DR_{to})^{t-to}$$
$$+ (LV_{to} \times AI_{to} + LV_{to} \div CPI_{to}) \times 0.6$$

where

   P_t = Adjusted housing value at time t.
   BV_t = Adjusted building value at time t.
   LV_t = Adjusted land value at time t.
   BV_{t_0}, LV_{t_0} = The values of building and land, respectively, at time t_0.
   t = 1989.
   t_0 = The purchasing year.
   AI = Appreciation index.
   CPI = Consumer price index.
   DR = Building depreciation rate.

The distribution of the adjusted housing values is shown in Table 7.2.

The explanatory variables to be included in the hedonic housing value equation consist of one spatial dummy, seven housing attributes, eight neighborhood attributes, and one air pollution variable. The spatial dummy variable (D_1) is introduced to control for market segmentation, where $D_1 = 1$ if the house is in Taipei City, and $D_1 = 0$ otherwise.

The housing attributes are as follows:

(1) The floor area of the house (*FA*) in pings (1 ping$=3.3\,m^2$).

(2) Two dummy variables (D_2 and D_3) introduced to differentiate houses by building materials. $D_2 = 1$ if the building is made of reinforced concrete, otherwise $D_2 = 0$; $D_3 = 1$ if the building is made of brick, otherwise $D_3 = 0$.

(3) Building types consists of single house (detached house), row house, and apartment. Two dummy variables (D_4 and D_5) are introduced here. $D_4 = 1$ if it is a single house or detached house, otherwise $D_4 = 0$; $D_5 = 1$ if it is a row house, otherwise $D_5 = 0$.

(4) Uses of buildings include residential use only, mixture of residential and commercial use, mixture of residential and industrial use, and mixture of residential and other uses. Three dummy variables (D_6, D_7 and D_8) differentiate the uses of buildings. $D_6 = 1$ if the house is for mixed residential and commercial use, otherwise $D_6 = 0$; $D_7 = 1$ is for mixed residential and industrial use, otherwise $D_7 = 0$; $D_8 = 1$ is for the combination of residential and other uses, otherwise $D_8 = 0$.

(5) Age of the house (D_9): $D_9 = 1$ for buildings more than 10 years old, otherwise $D_9 = 0$.

(6) Toilet (D_{10}): $D_{10} = 1$ if the house is equipped with more than one toilet, otherwise $D_{10}=0$.

(7) Natural gas (D_{11}): $D_{11}=1$ if the house has natural gas supply, otherwise $D_{11}=0$.

The neighborhood attributes to be included in the hedonic housing value equation are as follows:

Table 7.2 Distribution of the Adjusted Housing Values

Value (NT$1,000)	TMA* Number of households	%	Taipei City Number of households	%	Taipei County Number of households	%
Below 2,500	319	15.9	50	5.6	269	24.3
2,500–5,000	682	34.0	192	21.4	490	44.3
5,000–7,500	450	22.4	232	25.8	218	19.7
7,500–10,000	252	12.6	176	19.6	76	6.9
10,000–15,000	207	10.3	169	18.8	38	3.4
15,000–20,000	55	2.7	47	5.2	8	0.7
20,000–30,000	32	1.6	27	3.0	5	0.5
above 30,000	8	0.4	5	0.6	3	0.3
Total	2005	100.0	898	100.0	1107	100.0

Note
* TMA = Taipei metropolitan area.

(1) Accessibility to retail market (D_{12}): $D_{12}=1$ if the distance from the house to the nearest retail market is less than 0.5 km, otherwise $D_{12}=0$.
(2) Accessibility to hospital (D_{13}): $D_{13}=1$ if the distance from the house to the nearest hospital is less than 0.5 km, otherwise $D_{13}=0$.
(3) Accessibility to workplace (D_{14}): $D_{14}=1$ if the commuting distance is more than 10 km, $D_{14}=0$ otherwise.
(4) Transportation convenience (D_{15}): $D_{15}=1$ if transportation is convenient, $D_{15}=0$ otherwise.
(5) Noise (D_{16}): $D_{16}=1$ if the surrounding area is noisy, $D_{16}=0$ otherwise.
(6) Quality of tap water (D_{17}): $D_{17}=1$ if the quality of tap water is bad, $D_{17}=0$ otherwise.
(7) Drainage (D_{18}): $D_{18}=1$ if poorly drained, $D_{18}=0$ otherwise.
(8) Accessibility to the central business district (CBD) in terms of the distance from the house to the CBD: $D_{19}=1$ if it is between 2–4 km, $D_{19}=0$ otherwise; $D_{20}=1$ if it is in 4–6 km, $D_{20}=0$ otherwise, $D_{21}=1$ if it is in 6–8 km, $D_{21}=0$ otherwise; $D_{22}=1$ if it is in 8–10 km, $D_{22}=0$ otherwise; $D_{23}=1$ if it is in 10–15 km, $D_{23}=0$ otherwise; $D_{24}=1$ if it is more than 15 km, $D_{24}=0$ otherwise.

Table 7.3 summarizes the variables used in the hedonic housing value equation.

Table 7.3 List of Variables

Variable	Definition
Dependent Variable	
P	Adjusted housing value (NT\$1,000).
Air Pollution	
TSP	Total suspended particulates.
Building Size	
FA	Floor space (ping, 1 ping$=3.3$ m^2).
Spatial Dummy	
D_1	$D_1=1$ if Taipei City, $D_1=0$ otherwise.
Building Material	
D_2	$D_2=1$ if reinforced concrete (RC), $D_2=0$ otherwise.
D_3	$D_3=1$ if reinforced brick, $D_3=0$ otherwise.
Building Type	
D_4	$D_4=1$ if single or detached, $D_4=0$ otherwise.
D_5	$D_5=1$ if row house, $D_5=0$ otherwise.
Building Use	
D_6	$D_6=1$ if mixed residential and commercial use, $D_6=0$ otherwise.
D_7	$D_7=1$ if mixed residential and industrial use, $D_7=0$ otherwise.
D_8	$D_8=1$ if mixed residential and other uses, $D_8=0$ otherwise.
Building Age	
D_9	$D_9=1$ if less than 10 years, $D_9=0$ otherwise.
Toilet	
D_{10}	$D_{10}=1$ if more than 1 toilet, $D_{10}=0$ otherwise.
Natural Gas	
D_{11}	$D_{11}=1$ if with natural gas supply, $D_{11}=0$ otherwise.
Accessibility to Retail Market	
D_{12}	$D_{12}=1$ if within 0.5 km, $D_{12}=0$ otherwise.
Accessibility to Hospital	
D_{13}	$D_{13}=1$ if within 0.5 km, $D_{13}=0$ otherwise.
Accessibility to Workplace	
D_{14}	$D_{14}=1$ if more than 10 km, $D_{14}=0$ otherwise.
Transportation Convenience	
D_{15}	$D_{15}=1$ if convenient, $D_{15}=0$ otherwise.
Noise	
D_{16}	$D_{16}=1$ if noisy, $D_{17}=0$ otherwise.
Quality of Tap Water	
D_{17}	$D_{17}=1$ if bad, $D_{17}=0$ otherwise.
Drainage	
D_{18}	$D_{18}=1$ if poorly drained, $D_{18}=0$ otherwise.

Table 7.3, continued

Variable	Definition
Accessibility to CBD	
D_{19}	$D_{19}=1$ if 2 to 4 km, $D_{19}=0$ otherwise.
D_{20}	$D_{20}=1$ if 4 to 6 km, $D_{20}=0$ otherwise.
D_{21}	$D_{21}=1$ if 6 to 8 km, $D_{21}=0$ otherwise.
D_{22}	$D_{22}=1$ if 8 to 10 km, $D_{22}=0$ otherwise.
D_{23}	$D_{23}=1$ if 10 to 15 km, $D_{23}=0$ otherwise.
D_{24}	$D_{24}=1$ if over 15 km, $D_{24}=0$ otherwise.

4 HEDONIC HOUSING VALUE EQUATION

The nonlinear logarithmic hedonic housing value equation with variables as specified in the previous section can be written as

$$\ln P = \alpha_0 + \alpha_1 \ln FA + \alpha_2 \ln TSP + \alpha_3 (\ln TSP)^2 + \Sigma \beta_i D_i + \varepsilon \qquad (7.2)$$

where ε is the error term.

The estimates of the nonlinear logarithmic equation reveal that among the 28 variables included, 15 coefficients are significant at the 1% level, one coefficient is significant at the 5% level, and all the significant coefficients have the expected sign (see Table 7.A.1 in Appendix 7.2). The adjusted R^2 (0.48) is moderately high, indicating that the variables in the equation account for a moderately high percentage of the variation in housing values observed in the Taipei metropolitan area. A log-linear hedonic housing value equation was also estimated and shown in Table 7.A.2 in Appendix 7.2. It should be noted that the $\ln TSP$ variable in the estimated log-linear equation is not significant, and the adjusted R^2 is lower than that of the nonlinear specification. Thus the nonlinear logarithmic equation is superior to the log-linear equation, and is therefore used to examine the effect of *TSP* on housing values. However, as shown in Table 7.A.1, many variables in the nonlinear logarithmic equation are not statistically significant; that is, many variables in the equation have no significant effects on the variation of housing values in the Taipei metropolitan area. Consequently we deleted those insignificant variables and re-estimated the nonlinear logarithmic hedonic housing value equation. The estimates of the nonlinear logarithmic hedonic housing value equation shown in Table 7.4 are used in the remainder of the paper to examine the effect of *TSP* on housing values and to generate estimates of the willingness to pay for the reduction of *TSP* in

Table 7.4   Estimates of the Nonlinear Logarithmic Hedonic Price Equation (Dependent Variable = lnP)

Variable	Coefficient	t-value	Prob.-value
lnFA	0.69332**	16.169	0.00000
lnTSP	5.66068**	6.229	0.00000
$(\ln TSP)^2$	-0.65434**	-6.323	0.00000
D_2(RC)	0.10871**	4.131	0.00007
D_4(Single House)	-0.19043**	-2.788	0.00541
D_6(Res. & Comm.)	0.52453**	11.228	0.00000
D_7(Res. & Factory)	0.31186**	4.015	0.00011
D_8(Res. & Others)	0.24148**	3.184	0.00166
D_9(Age)	-0.30887**	-12.104	0.00000
D_{10}(Toilet)	0.11143**	3.605	ˊ0.00043
D_{11}(Nat. Gas)	0.14851**	5.840	0.00000
D_{18}(Drainage)	-0.07706*	-2.492	0.01231
D_{20}(CBD 4–6 km)	-0.17973**	-4.525	0.00002
D_{22}(CBD 6–10 km)	-0.28430**	-7.559	0.00000
D_{23}(CBD 10–15 km)	-0.58164**	-14.056	0.00000
D_{24}(CBD 15 km+)	-0.58673**	-14.696	0.00000
Constant	-7.92250	-3.949	0.00013
R^2=0.4751	Adj. R^2=0.4709	DW=1.4523	
Lmax=-13870.8	N=2005		

Notes

a. Significant at 1% level; *=Significant at 5% level.

b. D_{22} is redefined as follows: D_{22}=1 if 6–10 km, D_{22}=0 otherwise.

the Taipei metropolitan area.

All estimated coefficients in the equation shown in Table 7.4 except Drainage are significant at the 1% level (drainage is significant at the 5% level). The lnTSP has a positive sign, while $(\ln TSP)^2$ has a negative sign. Owing to the nonlinear specification, the quantitative importance of the change in TSP on housing values requires some calculation. To calculate it, we first arrange the estimated equation as

$$P = e^{f\,(TSP,\cdots)}$$

where e is the base of the natural logarithm; $f(TSP, \ldots)$ is the right-hand side (RHS) of the estimated hedonic housing value equation as shown in Table 7.4. Next, we derive the marginal willingness-to-pay function (denoted by W) by taking the derivative of the estimated housing value (P)

Table 7.5 Frequency Distribution of Marginal Willingness to Pay

W (NT$10,000)	Frequency (#of obs)	Percent (%)	Cumulative (%)
Below 0	398	19.9	19.9
0–5	59	2.9	22.8
5–10	108	5.4	28.2
10–15	189	9.4	37.6
15–20	288	14.4	52.0
20–25	307	15.3	67.3
25–30	201	10.0	77.3
30–35	146	7.3	84.4
35–40	96	4.8	89.4
40–45	70	3.5	92.9
45–50	36	1.8	94.7
above 50	107	5.3	100.0

with respect to *TSP*

$$W \equiv -\frac{\partial P}{\partial TSP} = e^{f(TSP,\cdots)} \left[\frac{1.30868 \ln TSP - 5.66068}{TSP}\right] \quad (7.3)$$

Using (7.3) we can calculate each household's marginal willingness to pay for the reduction of *TSP*. Table 7.5 displays the frequency distribution of the marginal willingness to pay. The table shows that 80.1% of the included households reveal positive values of their willingness to pay for a small reduction in air pollution levels, while only 19.9% of the households have a negative valuation of a marginal improvement in air quality. Accordingly, we may claim that air pollution has a negative effect on housing values in general and hence most of the households would pay for improving air quality.

Next, from (7.3) one can see that there exists a *TSP* threshold such that some households would pay for the reduction of *TSP* if the level of *TSP* is greater than the threshold. The threshold of *TSP* (denoted by TSP_T) can be calculated by setting the numerator in the brackets in the RHS of (7.3) equal to zero; that is, let $1.30868 \ln TSP_T - 5.66068 = 0$. Solving for TSP_T, we obtain $TSP_T = 75.6$. Households would therefore be willing to pay for a small reduction of *TSP* if the level of *TSP* surrounding their houses were higher than $75.6 \mu g/m^3$. Furthermore, from (7.3) we can show that

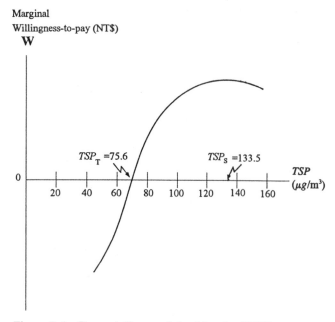

Figure 7.1   General Shape of the Marginal Willingness-to-pay Function

$$\frac{\partial W}{\partial TSP} = e^{f\,(TSP,\,\cdots)}[\frac{6.96936-1.30868\ln TSP-(1.30868\ln TSP-5.66068)^2}{TSP^2}]$$

(7.4)

From (7.4) we can further show that there exists a *TSP* (denoted by *TSP$_s$*) such that

$$\frac{\partial W}{\partial TSP} \overset{>}{\underset{<}{=}} 0 \quad as \quad TSP \overset{<}{\underset{>}{=}} TSP_s$$

where *TSP$_s$* can be determined by setting the numerator in the brackets in the RHS of (7.4) equal to zero. Solving for *TSP$_s$*, we obtain *TSP$_s$* = 133.5. Accordingly, the general shape of the marginal willingness-to-pay equation (7.3) can be shown as in Figure 7.1.

Summing up, we have seen that air pollution measured by *TSP* levels has significant negative effects on housing values. Households would be willing to pay for the improvement of air quality (a small reduction of *TSP*) whenever the concentration of *TSP* is greater than the threshold level

(TSP_T), and their marginal willingness to pay for reduction of TSP level increases with the level of TSP at a decreasing rate within a certain range of TSP levels.

5 BENEFITS OF AIR QUALITY IMPROVEMENT

In the previous section, we derived the marginal willingness-to-pay function by taking the derivative of the estimated hedonic housing value equation. The marginal willingness to pay calculated for each household represents each household's benefits from a marginal improvement in air quality. However, it is widely known that the benefits of non-marginal changes in air quality cannot in general be determined by using each household's marginal willingness to pay. One way to estimate the benefits of non-marginal changes in air quality is to estimate an (inverse) demand function, i.e., a willingness-to-pay function for air quality, by regressing the marginal willingness-to-pay variable on the level of air pollution, household income, household size and other household characteristics, and then integrate the willingness-to-pay function between two levels of environmental quality in order to derive expected benefits. However, as shown by Mendelsohn (1984, 1985), it is very difficult to identify the demand function with data from a single market. Thus, we do not attempt to estimate the inverse demand function since the Taipei metropolitan area is virtually a single market. Nevertheless, as indicated by Freeman (1979a, 1979b) and others, if all households have identical utility functions and incomes, the marginal willingness-to-pay function (W) can be interpreted as an inverse demand function for air quality. For this reason, we use the marginal willingness-to-pay function to estimate the benefits of air quality improvements and treat the benefit estimates as first approximations. Specifically, we shall estimate the average benefit per household in the Taipei metropolitan area of uniform reductions of TSP levels by 10%, 20% and 50%, respectively. To compute the average benefits of air quality improvement, we will treat the negative marginal willingness-to-pay as zero. This treatment is logical, since no payment can be collected from those households with negative willingness-to-pay for the reduction of air pollution. Accordingly, there are two measures of average benefits per household which can be defined. One is defined for all observations (with negative willingness-to-pay estimates replaced by zero), and the other is defined only for those households with a positive willingness-to-pay. Algebraically, they are defined as follows:

$$AB_1 = \frac{1}{N}\sum_{i=1}^{N}\int_{(1-\alpha\%)TSP_0}^{TSP_0} W_i(TSP)\mathrm{d}TSP$$

$$AB_2 = \frac{1}{M}\sum_{i=1}^{M}\int_{(1-\alpha\%)TSP_0}^{TSP_0} W_i(TSP)\mathrm{d}TSP$$

where let $W_i(TSP)=0$, if $W_i(TSP)<0$; N=total number of households; M=the number of households with a positive willingness to pay. The AB_1 and AB_2 are the average capitalized benefits per household. We assume that the capital recovery factor (CRF) (that is, the rate necessary to transform an initial capital investment into a series of equivalent annual charges including payment of both capital and interest) is equal to 0.0995, which corresponds to a 0.0925 interest rate and a payback period of 30 years. The estimated average benefits per household for 10%, 20% and 50% reductions of *TSP* levels, respectively, in the Taipei metropolitan area are shown in Table 7.6. As shown in Table 7.6, the average capitalized benefits per household measured by AB_1 from the reduction of *TSP* levels by 10%, 20% and 50% in the Taipei metropolitan area are NT$149,178, NT$254,304, and NT$330,164, respectively. In annual, monthly and daily terms, the average benefits per household from the 10%, 20% and 50% reduction in *TSP* are NT$14,843, NT$25,303, and NT$32,851 per year; NT$1,237, NT$2,109 and NT$2,738 per month; and NT$41, NT$69 and NT$90 per day. On the other hand, the average capitalized benefits per household measured by AB_2 from the reductions of *TSP* by 10%, 20% and 50% in the area are NT$185,202, NT$315,715 and NT$413,478, respectively. In annual, monthly and daily terms, the average benefits per household from the 10%, 20% and 50% reduction in *TSP* are NT$18,428, NT$31,414 and NT$41,141 per year; NT$1,536, NT$2,618, and NT$3,428 per month; and NT$50, NT$86 and NT$113 per day, respectively.

6 CONCLUDING REMARKS

Hedonic price techniques were employed to estimate a hedonic housing value equation for the Taipei metropolitan area, Taiwan. The 1989 Housing Condition Survey and *TSP* monitoring data are used for estimations. The major findings are as follows:

(1) Households are willing to pay for air pollution reduction only when the present pollution levels surrounding their houses are above some thres-

Table 7.6   Estimated Average Benefits of TSP Reductions in the Taipei Metropolitan Area   Unit: NT$/per home

TSP Reduction		Capitalized Benefits	Annualized Benefits	Monthly Benefits	Daily Benefits
10%	AB_1	149,178	14,843	1,237	41
	AB_2	185,202	18,428	1,536	50
20%	AB_1	254,304	25,303	2,109	69
	AB_2	315,715	31,414	2,618	86
50%	AB_1	330,164	32,851	2,738	90
	AB_2	413,478	41,141	3,428	113

Notes

a. The capital recovery factor (CRF) is assumed to be 0.0995, which corresponds to a 0.0925 interest rate and a payback period of 30 years.

b. If the willingness-to-pay is negative, then it is treated as zero.

hold level.

(2) The marginal willingness to pay for reductions of *TSP* levels increase with the level of *TSP* at a decreasing rate within a certain range of *TSP* levels.

(3) The average benefits per household for a 10% reduction in *TSP* levels are NT$14,843 per year, NT$1,237 per month, or NT$41 per day.

(4) The average benefits per household for a 20% reduction of *TSP* levels are NT$25,303 per year, NT$2,109 per month, or NT$69 per day.

(5) The average benefits per household for a 50% reduction of *TSP* levels are NT$32,851 per year, NT$2,738 per month, or NT$90 per day.

The above findings are established based on the nonlinear logarithmic specification of the hedonic housing value equation and the estimates of marginal willingness to pay for air quality. In order to obtain more accurate estimates, future study should emphasize the problems of choosing a more appropriate functional form, of identifying the inverse demand function by using multiple market data, and of choosing more meaningful housing and neighborhood characteristics.

APPENDIX

Appendix 7.A Interpolation of TSP levels

The housing condition survey data set covers samples in 113 li, while the *TSP* data set contains only 39 sample points within the TMA and some sample points surrounding the TMA. In order to make both sets of data compatible, we used GENAMAP software to interpolate *TSP* levels. Figure 7.2 shows the study area, the Taipei metropolitan area, which contains Taipei City and Taipei Prefecture. Figure 7.3 shows the locations of monitoring stations, including dummy stations. The results of smoothed interpolation are shown in Figure 7.4.

Figure 7.2 Taipei Metropolitan Area

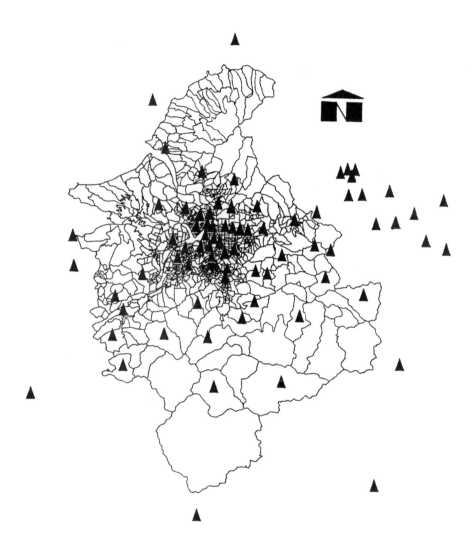

Figure 7.3   Distribution of Air Pollution Monitoring Stations in TMA

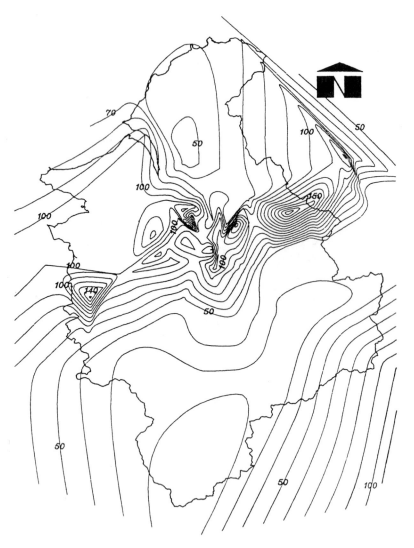

Figure 7.4 Estimated Contour Lines of TSP in TMA

Appendix 7.B Estimates of the Hedonic Housing Value Equation

Table 7.B.1 Estimates of the Nonlinear Logarithmic Hedonic Price Equation (Dependent Variable=lnP)

Variable	Coefficient	t-value	Prob-value
lnTSP	5.58589**	5.859	0.00000
lnFA	0.698775**	16.047	0.00000
(lnTSP)^2	-0.649323**	-5.916	0.00000
(lnTSP)*D_1	0.997315E-01	1.013	0.31242
D_1(Taipei)	-0.887398E-01	-0.198	0.82374
D_2(RC)	0.949987E-01**	3.337	0.00102
D_3(Brick)	0.266106E-01	0.374	0.70828
D_4(Single House)	-0.199184**	-2.850	0.00451
D_5(Row House)	-0.785771E-01	-1.893	0.05542
D_6(Res. & Comm.)	0.539600**	11.468	0.00000
D_7(Res. & Factory)	0.357271**	4.531	0.00002
D_8(Res. & Others)	0.227703**	3.009	0.00282
D_9(Age)	-0.306001**	-11.982	0.00000
D_{10}(Toilet)	0.114243**	3.693	0.00032
D_{11}(Nat. Gas)	0.139915**	5.401	0.00000
D_{12}(Retail market)	0.214721E-01	0.648	0.52469
D_{13}(Hospital)	0.330904E-01	1.333	0.17918
D_{14}(Working 10 km+)	0.439118E-02	0.160	0.84739
D_{15}(Transportation)	0.102899E-01	0.258	0.78542
D_{16}(Noise)	-0.323827E-01	-1.352	0.17286
D_{17}(Tap Water)	0.484055E-01	1.336	0.17808
D_{18}(Drainage)	-0.105584**	-3.260	0.00131
D_{19}(CBD 2–4 km)	-0.274182E-02	-0.048	0.91453
D_{20}(CBD 4–6 km)	-0.146997*	-2.528	0.01118
D_{21}(CBD 6–8 km)	-0.197217**	-3.107	0.00210
D_{22}(CBD 8–10 km)	0.948948E-01	1.011	0.31305
D_{23}(CBD 10–15 km)	-0.231639**	-2.569	0.00998
D_{24}(CBD 15 km+)	-0.231012**	-2.596	0.00927
Constant	-8.07438	-3.870	0.00018

$R^2 = 0.485183$ Adj. $R^2 = 0.477888$ DW = 1.464564

Notes
** Significant at 1% level; * Significant at 5% level.

Table 7.B.2 Estimates of the Log-Linear Hedonic Price Equation (Dependent Variable=lnP)

Variable	Coefficient	t-value	Prob-value
lnTSP	-0.363710E-01	-0.469	0.64381
lnFA	0.706265**	16.088	0.00000
(lnTSP)*D_1	-0.260357E-01	-0.268	0.77851
D_1(Taipei)	0.468903	1.060	0.28933
D_2(RC)	0.664962E-01*	2.350	0.01796
D_3(Brick)	0.790989E-02	0.110	0.87733
D_4(Single House)	-0.253801**	-3.633	0.00039
D_5(Row House)	-0.116834**	-2.825	0.00486
D_6(Res. & Comm.)	0.543788**	11.460	0.00000
D_7(Res. & Factory)	0.381034**	4.797	0.00001
D_8(Res. & Others)	0.215128**	2.820	0.00492
D_9(Age)	-0.301320**	-11.704	0.00000
D_{10}(Toilet)	0.115740**	3.710	0.00030
D_{11}(Nat. Gas)	0.139465**	5.338	0.00000
D_{12}(Retail Market)	0.567681E-01	1.726	0.08051
D_{13}(Hospital)	0.284991E-01	1.139	0.25375
D_{14}(Workplace 10 km+)	0.697296E-02	0.252	0.78945
D_{15}(Transportation)	0.160495E-03	0.004	0.94482
D_{16}(Noise)	-0.417790E-01	-1.733	0.07932
D_{17}(Tap Water)	0.263293E-01	0.724	0.47572
D_{18}(Drainage)	-0.101042**	-3.095	0.00218
D_{19}(CBD 2–4 km)	-0.211593E-01	-0.369	0.71182
D_{20}(CBD 4–6 km)	-0.230581**	-4.053	0.00009
D_{21}(CBD 6–8 km)	-0.257581**	-4.077	0.00009
D_{22}(CBD 8–10 km)	0.184527E-01	0.197	0.82434
D_{23}(CBD 10–15 km)	-0.295485**	-3.273	0.00125
D_{24}(CBD 15 km+)	-0.295846**	-3.322	0.00108
Constant	4.05168	10.291	0.00000

R^2=0.476065 Adj. R^2=0.468909 DW=1.464564

Notes
** Significant at 1% level; * Significant at 5% level.

ACKNOWLEDGEMENTS

This research has been supported by the Chiang Ching-Kuo Foundation for International Scholarly Exchange which is gratefully acknowledged. The author is also grateful for helpful comments by Robert Mendelsohn and Sun-Tien Wu on an earlier draft of this paper.

NOTES

1. See Freeman (1979a, 1993), Bartik and Smith (1987), Follain and Jimenez (1985) and Palmquist (1991) for excellent surveys of the literature.
2. I am indebted to Robert Mendelsohn for this comment.
3. Li is the smallest administrative unit in Taiwan.

REFERENCES

Bartik, T.J. and V.K. Smith (1987), 'Urban Amenities and Public Policy', in E.S. Mills (ed.), *Handbook of Regional and Urban Economics*, Vol. 2, Amsterdam: North-Holland, 1207–54.

Bender, B., T.J. Gronberg and H.-S. Hwang (1980), 'Choice of Functional Form and the Demand for Air Quality', *Review of Economics and Statistics*, **62**, 638–43.

Brookshire, D.S., R.C. d'Arge, W.D. Schulze and M.A. Thayer (1981), 'Experiments in Valuing Public Goods', in V.K. Smith (ed.), *Advances in Applied Microeconomics*, Vol. 1, Greenwich, Connecticut: JAI Press Inc., 129–72.

Cassel, E. and R. Mendelsohn (1985), 'The Choice of Functional Forms for Hedonic Price Equations: Comment', *Journal of Urban Economics*, **18**, 135–42.

Cropper, M.L., L.B. Deck and K.E. McConnell (1988), 'On the Choice of Functional Form for Hedonic Price Functions', *Review of Economics and Statistics*, **70**, 668–75.

Follain, J.R. and E. Jimenez (1985), 'Estimating the Demand for Housing Characteristics: A Survey and Critique', *Regional Science and Urban Economics*, **15**, 77–107.

Freeman, A.M. III (1974a), 'Air Pollution and Property Values: A Further Comment', *Review of Economics and Statistics*, **56**, 554–6.

Freeman, A.M. III (1974b), 'On Estimating Air Pollution Control Benefits from Land Value Studies', *Journal of Environmental Economics and Management*, **1**, 277–88.

Freeman, A.M. III (1979a), *The Benefits of Environmental Improvement: Theory and Practice*, Baltimore, MD: Johns Hopkins University Press.

Freeman, A.M. III (1979b), 'Hedonic Prices, Property Values and Measuring Environmental Benefits: A Survey of the Issues', *Scandinavian Journal of Economics*, **81**, 154–73.

Freeman, A.M. III (1993), *The Measurement of Environmental and Resource Values: Theory and Methods*, Washington D.C.: Resources for the Future.

Goodman, A.C. (1978), 'Hedonic Prices, Price Indices and Housing Markets', *Journal of Urban Economics*, **5**, 471–84.

Graves, P., J.C. Murdoch, M.A. Thayer and D. Waldman (1988), 'The Robustness of Hedonic Price Estimation: Urban Air Quality', *Land Economics,* **64**(3), 220–33.

Halvorsen, R. and H.O. Pollakowski (1981), 'Choice of Functional Form for Hedonic Price Equations', *Journal of Urban Economics*, **10**, 37–49.

Harrison, D., Jr. and D.L. Rubinfeld (1978), 'Hedonic Housing Prices and the Demand for Clean Air', *Journal of Environmental Economics and Management*, **5**, 81–102.

Liu, S.L. (1992), 'The Effect of Housing Quality on Housing Price in Taipei City', Master's thesis, Graduate Institute of Urban Planning, National Chung-Hsing University, Taipei, unpublished.

Lu, A.Y. (1987), 'Benefits of Air Pollution Control in the Taipei Metropolitan Area', a paper presented at the Chinese Economic Association Annual Meeting, Taipei, December.

Mendelsohn, R. (1984), 'Estimating the Structural Equations of Implicit Markets and Household Production Functions', *Review of Economics and Statistics*, **66**, 673–7.

Mendelsohn, R. (1985), 'Identifying Structural Equations with Single Market Data', *Review of Economics and Statistics*, **67**, 525–9.

Nelson, J.P. (1978), 'Residential Choice, Hedonic Prices, and the Demand for Urban Air Quality', *Journal of Urban Economics*, **5**, 357–69.

Palmquist, R.B. (1991), 'Hedonic Methods', in J.B. Braden and C.D. Kolstad (eds), *Measuring the Demand for Environmental Quality*, North-Holland: Elsevier Science Publishers B.V., 77–120.

Ridker, R.G. and J.A. Henning (1967), 'The Determinants of Residential Property Values with Special Reference to Air Pollution', *Review of Economics and Statistics*, **49**, 246–57.

Rosen, S. (1974), 'Hedonic Prices and Implicit Markets: Product Differentiation in Pure Competition', *Journal of Political Economy*, **82**, 34–55.

Sonstelie, J.C. and P.R. Portney (1980), 'Gross Rents and Market Values: Testing the Implications of Tiebout's Hypothesis', *Journal of Urban Economics*, **7**, 102–18.

8. Estimation of the Benefit of Air Quality Improvement: An Application of Hedonic Price Technique in Seoul

Seung-Jun Kwak, Gye-Pyeong Lee and Youngsub Chun

1 INTRODUCTION

Hedonic price technique has been widely used to estimate the benefits of environmental quality improvement such as cleaning up local shorelines and improving air quality in the US and much of Northern Europe (Brown and Pollakowski, 1977; Freeman, 1993; Harrison and Rubinfield, 1978). Recently, Smith and Huang (1992) proved with meta-analysis that a hedonic model could value air quality successfully. This technique is appropriate when environmental quality varies with a given market, and access to its various levels is obtained by purchasing some private goods. A typical example is residential real estate. For example, people can choose an air quality level by deciding on their residential location, therefore housing prices might include and reflect the implicit price of air quality.

An important part of the technique is to investigate the housing market. South Korea has a long history, but a very different cultural and regional background, and it is at a different stage of economic development from the US. Therefore, the structure of the housing market in Seoul, South Korea's capital and main city, might be different from that in cities in the US. Further, the variables affecting housing price and their signs would also be different.

The research reported in this paper has two major goals. The first is to explore the structure of the housing market in Seoul, and to consider the changes necessary in order to apply the hedonic price technique in the Seoul context. The second goal is to obtain at least a preliminary indication of the benefits to be expected from air quality improvement in Seoul. As it happens, the research also gives us a chance to experiment with various

171

forms of hedonic function because the results are sensitive to the assumption of functional form.

This paper proceeds as follows. Section 2 analyzes the structure of the housing market in Seoul. Section 3 describes the theoretical model and explains the variables and data used in this research. A discussion of the results appears in Section 4. Conclusions and suggestions for further research will be found in the final section.

2   INVESTIGATION OF THE SEOUL HOUSING MARKET AND ANTICIPATED NEED FOR ADJUSTMENTS

2.1 Housing Styles: Apartments and Houses

The characteristics of apartments and houses (detached dwellings) are quite different in Seoul. Consumers also show different consumption behavior depending on these two styles of housing.

First, it was not until the late 1970s that the Korean housing market faced an apartment construction boom. This boom, caused by an urban redevelopment plan of the government, contributed a great deal to solving the housing problem in Korea. It was at this point in time when people in Seoul began to think about the environment.

Second, an apartment in Korea, in general, is recognized as being more modern and convenient than a house. For example, almost all apartments are equipped with an indoor bathroom, while many houses are not. All apartment complexes display a model apartment before actual construction is completed, which allows consumers to have an opportunity to compare housing characteristics. According to one housing survey, more than 80% of people in Korea who had a plan to move wanted an apartment. Therefore, turnover of apartments is faster, and locating genuinely comparable housing in relevant neighborhoods is easier with apartments. Consequently, market data sufficient for reliable estimation are also easier to obtain for the apartment market.

Third, the residents of the two housing styles show different income distributions. Despite the fact that the redevelopment plan of the government was designed in part to supply housing for low-income households, households with above average income eventually moved into even those apartments. Because they either lacked the money to pay for the balance, or because they sold the right to move in for a premium, low-income households failed to become the actual tenants. Consequently, mostly middle or upper-middle class households now live in apartments. On the other hand, the upper-high-income households and low-income households tend to live in houses. The result is that the income distribution of residents of houses goes to both extremes while the average household income of apartment dwellers and of house residents are almost the same. In low-income households, it is common for several families to live together in one house and share facilities. Therefore, it is hard to obtain reliable data.

Finally, it is apartments, rather than houses, that are considered as assets for the future. During the past decade, people speculated on apartments so that the price of apartments surged in Seoul. When housing is considered as an investment for the future, people give more serious consideration to variables affecting housing price such as housing location, characteristics, and environment, etc. This fact also contributes to making the turnover of apartments faster than of houses.

The reasons above become the starting point for the empirical analysis of the two markets, which are to be carried out separately. The implicit prices of housing characteristics incorporated in the prices of the two different housing styles are different.

2.2 Variables Considering Regional and Cultural Background

Traditionally, Koreans have been very zealous about the education of their children. The quality of the schools in the area, therefore, is an important variable affecting the price of housing. The parental determination to send their children to college is probably stronger here than in any other country. In Seoul, a student cannot choose his or her own high school. The institution he or she will attend is decided by drawing lots among the schools within their 'school zone'. The so-called 'Eighth School Zone' is a sector where many people desire to live just because there are several high-quality high schools in the region. As a result the prices of housing here are higher. A 'high-quality high school' in Seoul is judged by the number of students who pass on to college from a given school. To consider such characteristics of a district, the ratio of students who go on to university to the total number of students in the graduating class can be expected to be the most appropriate variable which demonstrates the quality of education, which in turn, influences the price of housing.

Secondly, whenever there is a plan to construct a large hospital in a given area, there is usually strong resistance from the local residents. Residents protesting against the building of a hospital in their neighborhood is probably a rare scene, witnessed only in Seoul. Besides the possibility that the facility can cause traffic jams, the main reason is that there are mortuaries in large hospitals. In Korea, when someone dies, the body is placed in the hospital mortuary and for three days condolences are received.

Families and relatives of the dead moan and watch over the mortuary night and day, thus causing a small commotion in residential areas around the hospital. In the city, where there is a high density of population, the presence of a mortuary in a given area will probably have an undesirable effect on the price of housing. Research shows that apartments near large hospitals with mortuaries are relatively cheaper than those that are not (Planning Information Bulletin, 1991). Therefore, inclusion of a factor representing a large hospital will have a negative effect on the price of housing. This could be regarded as a reflection of the regional and cultural distinctiveness of Seoul.

Thirdly, another characteristic of apartments in Seoul is that these buildings are grouped into housing complexes, and the larger the complex, the higher the price. It is also found that the prices of houses (detached dwellings) around a large apartment complex are relatively higher than other houses. Taking into consideration that most apartments are in highrise buildings, of ten stories or more, the larger the apartment complex, the higher the population density. Therefore, the neighborhood's population density will also be an important variable reflecting the housing price in this special region called Seoul.

3   BASIC MODEL

3.1 Theoretical Background[1]

Housing is composed of a product class such as number of rooms, neighborhood, and environment. We assume that the price of housing is a function of those characteristics. If there exist enough models with different combinations of rooms and air quality, it would be possible to estimate an implicit price relationship as a function of the quantities of the various characteristics, and the coefficients of those characteristics can be regarded as implicit price. For example, the difference in price between two dwellings with different air quality but identical in all other components is interpreted as the implicit price of air quality.

More specifically, let S represent a vector of structural characteristics of housing such as number of rooms and scale of the housing, let N be a vector of the neighborhood area characteristics such as the quality of the schools and public parks, and let Q be a vector of environmental characteristics such as air quality. The housing price, P, is represented by the function of those characteristics. That is,

$$P(H) = f (S, N, Q) \tag{8.1}$$

The function *P(H)* is the hedonic or implicit price function. Based on this equation, we estimate the demand function for air quality in two stages. In the first stage, the marginal implicit price of air quality can be calculated by differentiating the implicit price function with respect to air quality (*Q*). That is,

$$\frac{\partial P(H)}{\partial Q} = P_Q(Q) \tag{8.2}$$

The next stage is to derive the inverse demand function. In order to use the estimates of characteristics' demand as an applied welfare measure, we solve the problem by identifying the marginal willingness-to-pay function (Mendelsohn, 1984, 1985; Bartik, 1987; Freeman, 1993). The most reliable approach to solving the identification problem is to find cases where the marginal implicit prices of characteristics vary independently of the other demand shift variables (Freeman, 1993). However, sufficient multiple market data for the implementation are not available in Korea. In this study, we, therefore, apply a single hedonic price model to estimate benefits of improving air quality and refrain from estimating the second-stage demand function because we are limited to single-market data.

3.2 Variable Definitions

Our theoretical model for benefit estimation of air quality using hedonic price technique comes from the equations in the previous subsection. The estimation procedure was not able to separate out the independent influence of each air pollutant. Thus, only one pollution measure, total suspended particulates (TSP), was utilized to describe the level of air quality. The estimation models of implicit price functions are defined as follows.

Dependent variables
    PAPT: sales price of apartment (1991), unit = million won
    PHUS: sales price of house (1991), unit = million won

Explanatory variables
    CONST: constant term
    SPACE: square of housing, unit = pyung (1.8 meter × 1.8 meter)
    NROOM: number of rooms
    NEIBOR: dummy for average income of neighborhood
            1 = below middle
            0 = middle and upper

QSCH: quality of schools (the ratio of students who go on to university versus number of high school students, unit = %)
PARK: ratio of parks (square of park per total district area, unit = %)
DIST: distance between CBD and housing (unit = km)
HOSBED: number of beds located in hospitals
POPDEN: population density (unit = population per km^2)
TSP: total suspended particulate matter (unit = μg)

SPACE, NROOM, QSCH and POPDEN are each expected to have a positive effect on housing prices. NEIBOR, DIST, HOSBED and TSP are all expected to have a negative relation with housing prices. The anticipated sign of PARK is not obvious. Parks are usually restricted to the green-belt zone. The real estate prices in this area are relatively low. When regarding housing as an asset for the future rather than as place of dwelling, the negative effect would offset the positive effect.

3.3 Data

The data on housing price and housing characteristics used in this analysis come from the *Survey on Housing Finance and Market* (1991) by the Korea Research Institute for Human Settlements. This survey contains relatively detailed materials about structural characteristics of the dwellings of surveyed households, like the number of rooms and other information such as the income level and number of family members of each of the 665 households that were surveyed. Sampling was restricted to households within the Seoul metropolitan area. The data used in this analysis include 269 observations of apartments and 227 observations of houses. The data on regional characteristics are obtained from the *Seoul Statistical Yearbook* (1992). The data on air quality in each area are obtained from the *Korean Environmental Yearbook* (1992).

4   REGRESSION   RESULTS

Marginal implicit prices of characteristics are sensitive to the form of the hedonic price function used to estimate them (see Cropper et al., 1988). Errors in measuring marginal implicit price vary with the form of hedonic price function used. We assume three functional forms: double-log, semi-log and the Box-Cox transformation function. The Box-Cox transformation form is defined as follows:

*Table 8.1 Estimation Results using Data for Apartments**

Variable	Double-Log	Semi-Log	Box-Cox
CONST	2.3343	3.4022	5.8805
	(1.055)	(8.555)	(3.111)
SPACE	0.5217	0.0076	0.1006
	(4.296)	(1.711)	(4.765)
NROOM	0.8327	0.4293	1.9671
	(5.072)	(7.010)	(6.759)
NEIBOR	-0.1378	-0.1607	-0.9036
	(-2.164)	(-2.466)	(-2.919)
QSCH	0.8195	0.0257	0.1223
	(3.463)	(4.490)	(4.493)
PARK	-0.1551	-1.3329	-7.6946
	(-2.691)	(-2.941)	(-4.341)
DIST	-0.2178	-0.0259	-0.1537
	(-2.691)	(-2.941)	(-3.675)
HOSBED	-0.2519	-0.0003	-0.0013
	(-4.724)	(-4.676)	(-4.699)
POPDEN	0.0458	0.0001	0.0001
	(0.340)	(1.463)	(0.993)
TSP	-0.2918	-0.0022	-0.0109
	(-2.577)	(-2.425)	(-2.545)
R-SQUARE	0.6104	0.5947	0.7042

Note
* t-statistics are in parentheses below coefficient estimates.

$$Y^{(\lambda)} = \alpha + \beta X + \varepsilon \qquad (8.3)$$

where, $Y^{(\lambda)} = Y^{\lambda} - 1/\lambda$. In our analysis, λ is estimated by maximum likelihood estimates (MLE) in the Box-Cox regression of LIMDEP. Using iterative procedures, we find that the regressions under $\lambda = 0.35$ for apartment and $\lambda = 0.30$ for house produce the best results.

The estimation results of the TSP equations using data from apartments are shown in Table 8.1 and the results using data from houses are shown in Table 8.2. In Table 8.1, the result under the Box-Cox function provides a bigger R^2 than the other estimations and all coefficients are significant at a 5% level. With the goodness-of-fit criterion suggested by Rosen (1974) and Goodman (1978), the Box-Cox functional form is the most accurate form in our case.[2]

*Table 8.2 Estimation Results using Data for Houses**

Variable	Double-Log	Semi-Log	Box-Cox
CONST	-4.7610	2.2569	2.3549
	(-1.183)	(3.036)	(0.837)
SPACE	0.5915	0.0024	0.0148
	(3.873)	(0.892)	(1.471)
NROOM	0.3272	0.1120	0.4058
	(1.810)	(3.473)	(3.323)
NEIBOR	-0.1601	-0.2909	-1.0899
	(-1.321)	(-2.365)	(-2.340)
QSCH	0.8063	0.0338	0.1049
	(1.820)	(2.929)	(2.402)
PARK	0.0900	1.0838	5.1128
	(0.825)	(1.317)	(1.641)
DIST	0.0613	-0.0023	0.0212
	(0.373)	(-0.133)	(0.318)
HOSBED	-0.1763	-0.00006	-0.0001
	(-1.553)	(-0.464)	(-0.205)
POPDEN	0.4618	0.00004	0.0001
	(1.832)	(2.914)	(2.341)
TSP	0.2149	0.0001	0.0015
	(0.840)	(0.054)	(0.184)
R-SQUARE	0.2757	0.2149	0.2334

Note
*   t-statistics are in parentheses below coefficient estimates.

The estimation results using data for houses in Table 8.2 produce many insignificant coefficients and low goodness-of-fit. The prices of houses are not sensitive to the housing characteristics we chose. Specifically, the air quality variables are not significant. This fact coincides with the argument presented in Section 2. In application of hedonic price techniques to the Seoul housing market, house prices are not a good example. Therefore, in this analysis, we use the Box-Cox functional form of the hedonic price function with data from apartments for measuring the benefits of TSP improvement.

As discussed in the previous section, we use the estimated hedonic price function (Table 8.1) directly to measure benefit because we are limited to single-market data. We take the characteristics of the actual sample and apply the experiment by changing the TSP level (3, 5, 10, 15, 20, 50% reduc-

Table 8.3 Average Benefit per Household (TSP Improvement)

Reduction of TSP	Capital Value	Annual Value
3%	1,317,476 won (US$1,646)	117,027 won (US$146)
5%	2,199,208 won (US$2,749)	195,349 won (US$224)
10%	4,415,475 won (US$5,515)	392,213 won (US$490)
15%	6,648,839 won (US$8,311)	590,596 won (US$738)
20%	8,899,375 won (US$11,124)	790,505 won (US$988)
50%	22,766,870 won (US$28,458)	2,022,313 won (US$2,527)

tion) of the entire sample and then take the mean response. Table 8.3 shows the estimated results. The average benefit (capital value) of a 5% reduction in TSP from the current level is 2,199,208 won (US$2,749), and for a 10% reduction the benefit is 4,415,475 won (US$5,519). Average annual benefits are 195,349 won (US$244) for the 5% reduction, and 392,213 won (US$490) for the 10% reduction. The annual values are estimated under the assumption that the discount rate is 8%, and the investment's life is 30 years.

5   CONCLUSIONS AND FURTHER RESEARCH

Beyond the intrinsic interest of our results in relation to the estimation of the benefits of improved air quality, this paper has several implications for application of the hedonic price technique in countries where regional and cultural backgrounds are different from those of the US.

We found that the application of a hedonic price technique in a Korean context was more than a matter of translating suitable research from the US. Investigating the structure of the local housing market and choosing proper variables reflecting regional and cultural characteristics, both key parts of such a study, required significant adjustment to fit the situation of Seoul.

Along the way we were able to experiment with various functional forms of the hedonic price function in Seoul, and found that a Box-Cox function was more suitable than either a linear or a log function.

However, we did not consider the approach of solving the identification problem with observations taken from several different housing markets, for example, in different cities, because of the lack of data availability in Korea. Such an approach involves finding cases where individuals with the same preferences and income face different marginal implicit prices. This can occur if similar individuals choose housing in markets with different hedonic price functions. In further research, it would be interesting to find an appropriate instrument for investigating several different housing markets and compare the results with those presented in this paper.

NOTES

1. This section is based on Mendelsohn (1985) and Freeman (1993).
2. Linear or log-linear form is actually rejected with the test using a likelihood ratio statistic.

REFERENCES

Bartik, T. (1987), 'The Estimation of Demand Parameters in Hedonic Price Model', *Journal of Political Economy*, **14**, 111–30.

Brown, G. and H. Pollakowski (1977), 'Economic Valuation and Shore Line', *Review of Economics and Statistics*, **59**, 272–8.

Cropper, M., L. Deck, and K. McConnel (1988), 'On the Estimation of Structural Hedonic Price Function', *Review of Economics and Statistics*, **70**, 668–75.

Freeman, A. III (1993), *The Measurement of Environmental and Resource Values: Theory and Methods,* Washington DC: Resources for the Future.

Goodman, A. (1978), 'Hedonic Prices, Price Indices and Housing Markets', *Journal of Urban Economics*, **5**, 471–84.

Harrison, D. and D. Rubinfield (1978), 'The Distribution of Benefits from Improvements in Urban Air Quality', *Journal of Environmental Economics and Management*, **5**, 313–32.

Korean Environmental Yearbook (1992), Seoul, Korea: Ministry of the Environment.

Mendelsohn, R. (1984), 'Estimating the Structural Equations of Implicit Markets and Household Production Function', *Review of Economics and Statistics,* **66**, 673–7.

Mendelsohn, R. (1985), 'Identifying Structural Equations with Single Market Data', *Review of Economics and Statistics*, **67**, 525–9.

Planning Information Bulletin (1991), Korea Research Institute for Human Settlements, Seoul, Korea.

Rosen, S. (1974), 'Hedonic Prices and Implicit Markets: Product Differentiation in Pure Competition', *Journal of Political Economy*, **84**, 34–55.

Seoul Statistical Yearbook (1992), Seoul, Korea: Seoul Metropolitan Government Press.

Smith, V.K. and J. Huang (1992), 'Can Hedonic Models Value Air Quality?: a Meta-analysis', Unpublished working paper.

Survey on Housing Finance and Market (1991), Seoul, Korea: Korea Research Institute for Human Settlements.

9. Measuring the Benefits of Air Quality Improvement in Taipei: A Comparison of Contingent Valuation Elicitation Techniques

Alan Yun Lu, Richard C. Bishop and Michael P. Welsh

1 INTRODUCTION

The contingent valuation method (CVM) has been widely used for the past two decades in the valuation of nonmarket commodities such as public goods and environmental resources. In Taiwan, CVM, together with other nonmarket valuation methods, started being applied during the late 1980s as continuing environmental degradation and the mounting demand for environmental protection created a need to estimate the benefits of environmental improvements. For example, Lu (1987) applied CVM to study air quality improvement and noise reduction, Liu (1990) and Wu and Tsai (1993) used it to investigate water quality improvement, and Chen and Wen (1993) applied CVM to evaluate a proposed forest recreational site. However, these studies focused on the derivation of benefit estimates rather than on the basic issues of the implementability and validity of applying CVM in Taiwan, i.e., in a non-American and non-European cultural context. For example, no empirical comparison of different CVM elicitation techniques, such as that by Boyle and Bishop (1988), was tried under local conditions. Only individual elicitation techniques were applied in the respective endeavors, including a bidding game approach (Lu, 1987) and a dichotomous choice approach (Liu, 1990; Chen and Wen, 1993; Wu and Tsai, 1993).

One potential obstacle to applying CVM in a Chinese cultural context is that Chinese people traditionally think that money cannot, and should not, be used to measure the value or importance of many things. Thus they are, in particular, not used to giving values in monetary terms, as in other capitalist economies, for commodities for which they do not have previous valuing experiences. On the other hand, as in many newly industrialized or developing countries, price bargaining not only still exists as a way of trading at traditional markets, in the countryside, or for small groceries, but sometimes also for commodities with price tags, price bargaining is still possible and allowed.

When these cultural differences are considered, it seems that the selection of an appropriate elicitation technique might be of particular importance in obtaining reliable estimates of resource values in Taiwan. This is because each elicitation technique has its unique characteristics which will make its application in certain cultures more relevant. For example, the CVM dichotomous choice (DC) approach simplifies the task for respondents by only asking them to make a single incentive-compatible decision (Hoehn and Randall, 1987) which resembles the judgment performed by consumers, while the bidding game (BG) approach enables respondents to more fully consider the value of the amenity (Mitchell and Carson, 1989) and its iteration process resembles price bargaining. The payment card (PM) approach, on the other hand as Mitchell and Carson (1989) indicated, offers the respondents reference information about the payments that households currently make for other public goods.

Mitchell and Carson (1989) also point out that in-person survey is the method of choice for most CVM studies because interviewers can motivate respondents to make a greater effort to give dollar values, control the pace and sequence of the interview, explain complex scenarios, etc. This explains why personal interview has been the most popular way to do CVM in Taiwan, except for the survey by Chen and Wen (1993). On the contrary, a mail survey also has its own virtues such as cost saving, no interviewer bias, etc. In fact, as the DC approach becomes more popular, mail surveys are being used more frequently since the DC approach can be easily implemented by a mail survey. However, few comparisons have been made between mail DC and personal interview DC surveys in CVM studies.

This paper, therefore, compares the empirical results of using different CVM elicitation techniques which include mail and personal interview surveys applied to a case study in Taiwan with a Chinese cultural background. The five elicitation techniques to be tested are a mail DC survey, a DC survey done by personal interview, a PM survey by mail, a personal interview PM survey, and a BG survey, which can only be done by personal interview. Since the BG approach can be applied jointly with the personal interview DC or the personal interview PM approaches when the offers of the latter two approaches are used as the starting bids of the iterating process, two BG results can be obtained. Thus a total of six estimates from five elicitation techniques are to be compared in this empirical study.

The case used in this study is the improvement in air quality in Taipei, the capital city of the Republic of China on Taiwan. The air quality in Taipei has been deteriorating during recent decades due to fast growth in personal income and booming business activities, both of which raise energy consumption. Generally speaking, the air pollutants come from three major sources: a huge fleet of motor vehicles, numerous construction projects and factories. According to Taiwan's Environmental Protection Administration, emissions from cars and motorcycles contribute over 90% of the air pollution in Taipei (Environmental Protection Administration, 1992).

Taipei residents have been complaining about the poor air quality. As a matter of fact, air pollution has been one of the major campaign issues in past elections. Our surveys for this study also showed that over 96% of Taipei respondents are not satisfied with the air quality, all of them are bothered by air pollution, 93% to 98% worry about the detrimental effects of air pollution on their health and on the health of their household members, and 51% to 69% feel their health problems are aggravated by or caused by air pollution. These results indicate that Taipei residents are very aware of and familiar with the air pollution problem. And especially in Taiwan, where a potential obstacle might exist in using CVM in a Chinese cultural context, this familiarity of the problem is of critical importance in helping to derive reliable conclusions for our empirical comparison of the alternative CVM elicitation techniques.

The second section will introduce the survey design used in this study. Section 3 will describe the sampling and survey procedures adopted. Then Section 4 will report the survey results. The findings of this study will be discussed in the last two sections.

2   SURVEY DESIGN

The benefit to be measured for air quality improvement in this study can be expressed as

$$V(p, y, q_0) = V(p, y-B, q_1) = U,$$

where $V(.)$ is the indirect utility function of the respondents, p is a vector of market prices, y is income, q_0 is the existing air quality, B is the value of improved air quality, q_1 is the improved air quality, and U is the current utility levels of respondents. In this way, B is a Hicksian compensating surplus measure of the benefits that respondents receive from air quality improvement, which represents the willingness to pay (WTP)[1] of the respondents.

A 50% reduction of the air pollution in Taipei was used as the improvement in air quality. To help substantiate respondents' understanding of this extent of improvement, the air quality of Taipei and that of seven other major cities in Taiwan in 1989, i.e., Keelung, Hsinchu, Taichung, Tainan, Kaohsiung, Ilan and Hualien were reported in the air quality scenario of the survey instrument, where air quality is measured as concentration of total suspended particulates (TSP, $\mu g/m^3$).[2] Since the current air quality in Taipei is 226.74 $\mu g/m^3$, respondents can easily identify from this datum that the improved air quality in Taipei would be close to the air qualities in Keelung (112.87 $\mu g/m^3$), Hsinchu (120.08 $\mu g/m^3$) and Ilan (109.84 $\mu g/m^3$). Respondents' past experiences of visiting or living in these cities could further impress them with the assumed improvement in air quality in Taipei.

To help respondents to realize that costs are incurred in air quality improvement, the following statement was included in the questionnaire before the valuation question was asked:

If steps are taken to reduce air pollution, you will have to pay more for goods and services, and the taxes you pay may go up. If you buy an automobile or motorcycle, it may cost more because of required air pollution equipment. Installing and maintaining pollution control equipment on trucks will increase the transportation costs of goods and services you consume. The cost of other goods and services would increase to cover the costs of pollution control equipment for factories. Bus fares would increase so that equipment can be added to reduce the pollutants from bus exhaust. Taxes would increase to cover various governmental costs.

The benefits of the 50% improvement in air quality were also explicitly mentioned before the valuation question was asked. These included, 'one-half as much dirt in the air, one-half as many bad smells, one-half as much irritation to eyes and breathing passages, one-half the risk of health effects, etc. This would also mean one-half as much time as we now have to spend washing faces and hands, one-half as much time as we now need to spend cleaning house, one-half as much dirt on clothes, etc.' All these different benefits were initially identified in a pretest and were later listed in the form of damages to be identified in the survey by the respondents in association with the words 'air pollution' before interviewers proceeded to the valuation section of the survey.

Following this prologue, the valuation question was then asked. For DC surveys, where six different bids, NT$5, $50, $100, $1,000, $2,500 and $5,000 were used, based on the pretest of the survey instrument, the question was phrased as follows:

Suppose that the cost to your household in the form of higher prices and taxes for reducing air pollution would be NT$____ each month. Would you be in favor of a 50 percent reduction in air pollution in Taipei if the cost to you was this amount each month?

For PM surveys, an unanchored payment card was adopted[3] where the payment figures ranged from NT$0 dollars to as high as NT$4,000 dollars and above, based on the pretest of the survey instrument. The valuation question is stated as follows:

For this 50 percent reduction in air pollution in Taipei, would your household be willing to pay some amount of money each month in the form of higher prices and taxes if it is needed for the reduction?

If the answer is yes, then the next question is:

Please circle the amount that your household would be willing to pay on the following payment card. If there is no appropriate amount on the payment card for your choice, please write your amount in the blank space provided below.

$ 0	$ 500	$ 1,000	$ 2,000	$ 4,000
$ 50	$ 550	$ 1,100	$ 2,200	or over
$ 100	$ 600	$ 1,200	$ 2,400	
$ 150	$ 650	$ 1,300	$ 2,600	
$ 200	$ 700	$ 1,400	$ 2,800	
$ 250	$ 750	$ 1,500	$ 3,000	
$ 300	$ 800	$ 1,600	$ 3,200	
$ 350	$ 850	$ 1,700	$ 3,400	
$ 400	$ 900	$ 1,800	$ 3,600	
$ 450	$ 950	$ 1,900	$ 3,800	

My household is willing to pay NT$_____ each month.

For BG surveys, the payment choices made by the respondents in either the personal interview DC or personal interview PM surveys were used as the starting bids. Increments (or decrements) of either NT$50 or NT$100 were used to iterate bidding by the interviewers.

3   SAMPLING AND SURVEY PROCEDURES

A sample of two thousand households was used in the survey and was equally divided among mail DC, personal interview DC, mail PM, and personal interview PM surveys. That is, for each of these four elicitation techniques there was a sample of five hundred households. The two BG surveys, using the final payments from either the personal interview DC or the personal interview PM survey as starting bids, would thus each have the same sample as the corresponding personal interview DC or PM survey. Stratified two-stage random sampling was used to get the 2,000-household sample. That is, 87 li[4] were randomly chosen from the total 440 li of Taipei City, and from the 168,644 households of these 87 li, 2,000 households were randomly selected. The Department of Budget, Accounting and Statistics (DBAS) of the Taipei City government assisted with the sampling.

The survey instruments used went through examinations by three focus groups of 20 randomly selected Taipei residents and were then tried out in a pretest involving 100 households during February and March in 1992. The formal survey started subsequently in late March and was completed in early July of the same year. A greeting letter was first sent to the heads of the sample households one week to ten days in advance of the scheduled surveys. In this letter we stated the purpose and importance of the survey and the reason that he or she had been chosen as one of the respondents. We also identified the person to be the interviewer in the case of personal interview surveys, specified the date of the proposed visit or mailing of the questionnaire, the small gift to be given to the respondents (i.e., a photo frame worth NT$70 for personal interview surveys or NT$50 in cash which would be enclosed in the mail), a telephone number that could be used to reach the survey coordinator, etc. For mail surveys, three reminder letters were sent to the sample households that had not responded, with the last letter enclosing a new questionnaire. For personal interview surveys, on the other hand, when nobody answered the door for the house visit, interviewers were instructed to pay the visit again two more times to make sure that nobody was available there. Backup samples located in the same neighborhood were then used to replace the unvisited households. These backup samples were provided by DBAS of the Taipei City government and were obtained using the same stratified two-stage random sampling method used to select the original sample.

Twenty-seven interviewers who were university students in agricultural economics, rural sociology, statistics and economics were hired to do the personal interview surveys. Among them, three were female and most were the first author's students. Before they started the surveys they received intensive training during which they were asked to fill in the questionnaires themselves. Then, the survey purpose, the principles governing the design of the survey instrument, interviewing techniques, possible interviewer bias and thus the importance of interviewer training were explained. In the question and answer session afterwards, each survey question was gone through carefully again and questions discussed and answered. This training session took about one and half to two hours. When the interviewers

Table 9.1 Sample Sizes and Response Rates

Treatment	Initial Sample	Undeliv- erable	Valid Sample	Completed Surveys	Response Rate as Percent of Valid Sample
Mail DC	500	74	426	306	71.8
Mail PM	500	88	412	291	70.6
Personal Interview DC	500	NA*	500	376	75.2
Personal Interview PM	500	NA*	500	393	78.6

Note
* If the residence selected in the initial sample was determined to be unoccupied at the time of the interview, a backup residence located in the neighborhood was used as a replacement sample point.

returned their first questionnaires in the first weekend of the survey, another short help session was held to solve problems they had experienced.

4   SURVEY RESULTS

For the mail PM survey, 306 valid responses were obtained, for a response rate of 71.8%. The mail PM survey had 291 responses, and a response rate of 70.6%. The DC survey conducted by personal interviews had 376 valid responses, or a 75.2% response rate, while the personal interview PM got 393 responses, a 78.6% response rate (Table 9.1). The response rates are calculated based on the number in the initial sample minus the number from whom responses were not obtained. For personal interview surveys, when the households initially selected were determined to be unoccupied they were then replaced by the backup households provided by the DBAS of the Taipei City government. This practice thus increased the response rates of the personal interview surveys. The socioeconomic characteristics of the respondents for the four completed surveys are shown in Table 9.2.

Identical distributions of bids were used in the design of both the mail and personal interview DC surveys. That is, 50 surveys used the NT$5 and

Table 9.2 Socio-economic Characteristics of Respondents

| | Mail Surveys | | Personal Interviews | |
	Dichotomous Choice	Payment Card	Dichotomous Choice	Payment Card
Percent Male	68	72	70	72
Age (%)				
18-25 years old	6	6	5	4
26-35 years old	35	43	38	42
36-45 years old	10	8	10	9
46-55 years old	26	19	21	21
56-65 years old	17	20	22	19
66 years old				
or older	5	4	4	5
Education (%)				
Less than senior				
high school	20	17	23	21
Senior high school	28	29	25	25
Junior college	21	23	25	24
University or				
college	24	23	21	25
Graduate school or				
other	7	8	6	5
Average Household Size	5	5	5	5
Employment (%)				
Full-time	78	80	74	82
Homemaker	10	10	11	8
Other	12	10	15	10
Average Household				
Income (NT$)	55,300	56,000	53,200	58,900

NT$5,000 bids and each of the NT$50, NT$100, NT$1,000 and NT$2,500 bids were used in 100 survey questionnaires. This makes a total number of 500 questionnaires for either kind of survey. However, because of non-responses in the mail survey and the use of backup respondent households in the personal interview survey, the bid distributions of the completed mail and personal interview DC surveys were slightly different. The distributions of bids and responses for these two DC surveys are shown in Tables 9.3 and 9.4.

Simple logistic regression models were fit to the data from the mail and personal interview DC surveys and the combined data of these two surveys.[6] The estimated coefficients are reported in Table 9.5. A test of likelihood on these models leads to rejection of the hypothesis that the distribution of

Table 9.3 Distribution of Bids in Completed Surveys in the two DC Treatments

Amount of Bid	Mail DC Treatment		Personal Interview DC Treatment	
	No.	% of Completions	No.	% of Completions
$5 NT	29	9.5	43	11.4
$50 NT	65	21.2	62	16.5
$100 NT	61	19.9	77	20.5
$1,000 NT	63	20.6	82	21.8
$2,500 NT	54	17.6	77	20.5
$5,000 NT	34	11.1	35	9.3

Table 9.4 Distribution of Responses in the two DC Treatments

Amount of Bid	Mail DC Treatment				Personal Interview DC Treatment			
	Yes		No		Yes		No	
	No.	%	No.	%	No.	%	No.	%
$5 NT	24	92.3	2	7.7	43	100.0	0	0.0
$50 NT	55	87.3	8	12.7	51	82.3	11	17.7
$100NT	46	82.1	10	17.9	71	92.2	6	7.8
$1,000 NT	39	68.4	18	31.6	39	47.6	43	52.4
$2,500 NT	25	49.0	26	51.0	26	33.8	51	66.2
$5,000 NT	10	33.3	20	66.7	5	14.3	30	85.7
Total	199	70.3	84	29.7	235	62.5	141	37.5

implied willingness to pay (WTP) from the mail survey is the same as the implied distribution from the personal interview survey. The two models produce different estimates of mean WTP. Since positive probability for negative WTP could be imputed from the estimated models, a 'conditional' mean WTP was calculated based on Hanemann (1989). The conditional mean from the mail DC survey is NT$3,301 and that from the personal interview DC survey is NT$1,981. The medians of the WTPs that derived from the mail and personal interview DC surveys are NT$2,969 and NT$ 1,793, respectively (Table 9.5). Since the medians reflected the imputed negative WTPs and the conditional mean estimates do not, the median WTP will typically be less than the conditional mean WTP.

To further confirm the difference in the results from the mail and personal interview DC techniques, confidence intervals for the conditional

Table 9.5 Logistic Models for Individual and Combined DC Treatments

	Mail DC	Personal Interview DC	Mail & Personal Interview Combined
n	283	376	659
Constant	1.62	1.66	1.60
	(0.1918)*	(0.1766)	(0.1277)
Bid	-0.00055	-0.00093	-0.00072
	(0.000089)	(0.00011)	(0.000068)
Percent Yes Overall	70.3%	62.5%	65.8%
-2 Log Likelihood	300.50	380.21	693.81
Median	NT$2,969	NT$1,793	
95% Confidence Interval	(2262, 3676)	(1487, 2100)	
Mean	NT$3,301	NT$1,981	
95% Confidence Interval	(2655, 4398)	(1699, 2369)	

Note
* Asymptotic standard error.

means and medians are also calculated and reported in Table 9.5. The 95% confidence intervals for the median estimates were calculated using an analytic estimate of the standard deviation of the median (Cameron, 1991). The 95% confidence intervals for the conditional mean estimates were calculated using a re-sampling technique. In the re-sampling, a distribution of conditional mean WTPs was constructed, where 1,000 random draws from the estimated variance-covariance matrix of the estimated parameters were used (Krinsky and Robb, 1986). For each of these 1,000 random draws a new conditional mean was calculated. These intervals further indicate that the WTPs for the 50% improvement in air quality of respondents in the mail DC survey are higher than those from the personal interview DC survey.

The distributions of responses for both the mail and personal interview PM surveys are reported in Table 9.6. For these two surveys only simple analysis of mean WTPs was carried out on the completed data. The same analysis was performed on the BG data obtained using as starting bids payments from the personal interview DC and PM surveys. All four means and their respective standard errors and ranges are reported in Table 9.7. It shows that the two PM techniques produced the lowest WTPs for the 50% improvement of air quality, NT$403 for the mail survey and NT$482 for the personal interview. The former is significantly lower than the latter at the 95% level. For the BG technique, the two WTP estimates are close,

Table 9.6 Distributions of Responses in PM Treatments

Amount of Bid	Mail PM Treatment		Personal Interview PM Treatment	
	No.	%	No.	%
$0 NT	49	18.4	53	14.0
$50 NT	12	4.5	9	2.4
$100 NT	47	17.6	26	6.9
$150 NT	3	1.0	8	2.1
$200 NT	24	9.0	47	12.4
$250 NT	3	1.0	5	1.3
$275 NT	1	0.4	0	0.0
$300 NT	13	4.9	38	10.0
$350 NT	2	0.8	5	1.3
$400 NT	4	1.5	11	2.9
$500 NT	57	21.4	87	23.0
$600 NT	2	0.8	6	1.6
$700 NT	0	0.0	3	0.8
$750 NT	1	0.4	3	0.8
$800 NT	2	0.8	6	1.6
$850 NT	0	0.0	1	0.3
$900 NT	0	0.0	3	0.8
$950 NT	0	0.0	2	0.5
$1,000 NT	34	12.7	46	12.1
$1,100 NT	1	0.4	0	0.0
$1,500 NT	6	2.3	8	2.1
$2,000 NT	5	1.9	7	1.8
$2,500 NT	0	0.0	1	0.3
$3,000 NT	0	0.0	2	0.5
$3,600 NT	1	0.4	0	0.0
$4,000 NT	0	0.0	2	0.5
Total	267	100.0*	379	100.0*

Note
* rounding error exists.

NT$713 and NT$763, and the ones obtained from the DC survey are higher. For the four WTPs, the two from the BG surveys are significantly higher than those from the PM surveys.

Table 9.7 Mean and Median WTPs from PM and BG Surveys (NT$)

	n	Mean	Standard Error of Mean	Minimum	Median	Maximum
Mail PM	267	403	29	0	250	3,600
Personal Interview PM	379	482	27	0	350	4,000
BG from Personal Interview PM	379	713	39	0	500	7,000
BG from Personal Interview DC	366	763	49	0	500	7,000

5 SUGGESTED EXPLANATION

It was indicated earlier that application of the CVM in a Chinese cultural context requires consideration of two factors: that traditionally Chinese people feel that an amount of money cannot, and should not, be used to measure the importance or value of many things, and that price bargaining is still a part of trading in daily life. It was also mentioned that in obtaining WTP values, the three main CVM elicitation techniques and the mail survey and personal interview all have their respective strengths and weaknesses. Thus, the disparity in mean WTPs obtained in this study, given other conditions, might reflect the impact of Chinese culture and this difference in the elicitation methods adopted. Considering this, we shall try to explain these WTP differences in this section. Of course, the following arguments put forth to explain the wide discrepancy among the four mean WTPs need to be tested by further cross-cultural empirical work. In addition, it is also possible that other causes, such as a flaw in the survey instrument, could be responsible for this disparity.

It was expected that the DC technique might produce the highest estimates of WTPs. One possible reason might be the 'yea-saying tendency' of Chinese respondents.[6] That is, when faced with a valuation decision with which they are not familiar, people tend to say yes, either to show interviewers courtesy or to express cooperative agreement with the researcher's question in the case of the mail DC survey. This implies that in deriving reliable estimates, the advantageous incentive-compatible property of the DC approach may be challenged by the yea-saying tendency caused by the unfamiliarity of valuation. For this reason, even though the

DC approach can ease the task of making valuation decisions for respondents and still, in a statistical sense, be able to produce in the Chinese context the logical conclusion that as higher prices are proposed, fewer yes responses will be elicited from respondents, the application of the DC approach in Taiwan might result in higher WTPs. But an unanchored PM approach, since it does not offer a price for respondents to choose, does not have this 'anchoring' effect. In the BG approach, on the other hand, the extent of this yea-saying tendency would be restrained by the iterative process. That is, through iteration (bargaining) people start to seriously consider the true value of the commodity they are being asked to value. As to the reason why the BG approach produces larger estimates than the personal interview PM approach, the reason is obvious: the payment selected in the PM survey is used as the starting bid of the BG survey, which intends to elicit the maximum WTP.

The observation that the mail DC survey produces a higher mean WTP than the personal interview DC might be due to strategic behavior of the respondents, or sample selection bias, or the presence or absence of interviewers. Strategic behavior means that a mail survey allows individuals receiving questionnaires to use their time to formulate an optimal strategic response (Mitchell and Carson, 1989). In this case of reducing air pollution in Taipei, the favored strategy for individuals might be to say yes to the proposed prices even though these prices are higher than individuals' true WTPs. But if the survey is carried out by personal interview, respondents can't formulate their optimal strategy as easily as in mail surveys because interviewers control the flow of information and the sequence of the survey. Sample selection bias simply indicates that in the mail survey, those who have strong negative feelings toward air pollution in Taipei may be more inclined to fill out and return questionnaires asking them to value the benefits of air quality improvement. The presence of interviewers in the personal interview survey, on the other hand, may reduce the respondents' unfamiliarity with valuation and therefore would reduce the yea-saying tendency which might exist in a DC survey. These explanations suggest that the mail DC survey should give a higher ratio of yes answers to the offers, especially to higher offers, for the improvement in air quality than the ratio from the personal interview DC survey. This certainly contributes directly to the higher WTP obtained from the mail DC survey. Table 9.4 reports that the percentages of yes ratios for the higher offers in the survey were higher for the mail DC than for the personal interview DC. In addition, the overall percentage of yes ratios for the mail DC was 70.3% while that for the personal interview DC was 62.5%, a difference of 7.8% (Table 9.5).

The finding that the mail PM survey produces a WTP which is 16.39% lower than that from the personal interview PM survey contradicts the results from the mail and personal DC surveys. One suggested explanation for this outcome is that the issue of yea-saying does not exist in PM surveys, since it was the 'unanchored' payment card that was used in the study. Thus, the effect of the presence or absence of interviewers on WTP estimates for the PM surveys is different from that for the DC surveys. To be more specific, using the unanchored payment card without interviewers to explain the function of the payment cards to respondents, though avoiding the possible starting point bias or relational bias associated with an anchored payment card, might create a new confusion or uncertainty for respondents who, being Chinese, are already not used to giving values to environmental quality. And this new confusion or uncertainty might have a downward effect on WTPs. But when the PM survey is conducted in a personal interview, the unfamiliarity of respondents to valuation could be reduced, as in the DC survey. And in addition, any confusion associated with the unanchored payment card could also be reduced by the presence of interviewers. That is, the presence of interviewers, in a sense, could provide an 'anchoring' effect which makes respondents feel more comfortable to use the unanchored payment card to choose their true WTPs. And their chosen WTPs could thus best reflect their dissatisfaction with the air quality. Thus, the presence of interviewers would have a positive effect on the magnitude of WTPs. A mail survey, on the contrary, can't help make any clarification about using the unanchored payment card and the resultant new confusion. In this case, it is suspected that the positive effects of the strategic behavior and sample selection bias on WTP that we would expect from the mail PM survey would not be as large as that in the mail DC survey when new confusion or uncertainty was added by using an unanchored payment card.

The fact that the mean WTP obtained from the BG survey that used the payments of the personal interview PM survey as starting bids is less than that of the BG survey that used the payments of the personal interview DC survey is consistent to the well-documented starting point bias (e.g., Lu, 1987). This is because the average WTP figure of the PM survey was NT\$482 while that of the DC survey was NT\$1,227.77.[7] The fact that the difference between the two BG results is very small, i.e., one is only 6.55% less than the other, might also indicate that the iterative process was not only useful for Chinese respondents to help themselves to overcome their difficulty with giving values, but was also helpful in reducing the effects of starting point bias inherent in the BG approach.

6 EPILOGUE

Using three CVM elicitation techniques and both personal interview and mail surveys, this paper empirically compares the welfare estimates of air quality improvement in a Chinese cultural context. Both the discrepancy in the WTP estimates derived and the suggested possible causes for that discrepancy indicate that further empirical studies and cross-cultural comparisons are needed. Based on the arguments made above and the experiences obtained from this study, we feel that in a Chinese cultural context all three elicitation techniques, i.e., dichotomous choice, payment card and bidding game, should be given equal attention in future CVM endeavors in Taiwan. And considering the much higher estimates derived from our DC approach and other previous DC studies in Taiwan,[8] we feel that the concern for future DC studies in Taiwan might have to be placed more on the design of the survey instrument than on the other aspects of the DC approach which have been the focus of concern in the past.

ACKNOWLEDGEMENTS

The research has been supported by the Chiang Ching-Kuo Foundation for International Scholarly Exchange which is gratefully acknowledged.

NOTES

1. As mentioned earlier, over 90% of the air pollution in Taipei is caused by the emissions from automobiles and motorcycles. According to the statistics of the Bureau of Transportation of Taipei City government, every household in Taipei had an average of 1.90 motor vehicles at the end of 1993. Considering this popularity of motor vehicles, we think that willingness to pay is the appropriate measure, rather than willingness to accept, to be adopted in this study to measure the interest in air quality improvement.
2. Past empirical experience shows that respondents are more responsive to the change in air quality measured in TSP than other air pollutants such as carbon monoxide in giving their willingness to pay (Lu, 1987).
3. The unanchored payment card was adopted in the PM approach to avoid relational bias (see Mitchell and Carson, 1989).
4. 'Li' is an administrative district adopted in cities in Taiwan. Usually, a li has a population of 5,000 to 10,000.
5. A probit model could be estimated instead, but it would be very surprising to observe a big difference between the logit and probit models. Within the logit model a logarithmic specification for the bid could be used, too. However, for both personal interview and mail surveys the log transformation did not provide a good fit. In addition, it dramatically increased the estimated WTPs in both the personal interview and mail DC surveys because

of the very thick right hand tail of the distribution.

6. If this 'yea-saying tendency' does exist, we should be able to expect, ceteris paribus, a higher percentage of yes replies to given bids in Taiwan than other western countries. In this study the yes percentages were 70.3% and 62.5% for mail and personal interview DC surveys, respectively (see Table 9.5).

7. This is calculated from the bid distribution of the completed surveys in the personal interview DC survey.

8. Chen and Wen (1993) used three methods to estimate the recreational benefits of a proposed forest recreational site. The range of benefits derived by travel cost method (TCM) was from NT$8.92 to NT$31.76. By using combined data from CVM and TCM, the range was from NT$10.61 to NT$33.28. But using the DC technique, they derived a range of benefits from NT$32,264 to NT$104,453. Apparently, these DC estimates were too large to be realistic and reliable.

REFERENCES

Boyle, Kevin J. and Richard C. Bishop (1988), 'Welfare Measurements Using Contingent Valuation: A Comparison of Techniques', *American Journal of Agricultural Economics*, **71**(1), 20–8.

Cameron, T.A. (1991), 'Interval Estimates of Nonmarket Resource Values from Referendum Contingent Valuation Surveys', *Land Economics*, **67**, 413–21.

Chen, Kai-Lih and Yue-Fang Wen (1993), 'Evaluation of the Economic Benefits of a Newly Developed Recreation Area – Combining Contingent Valuation and Travel Cost Data', *Taiwan Agricultural Economic Review*, **1**, 87–116 (in Chinese).

Environmental Protection Administration (1992), *Environmental Information of Cities and Prefectures of Taiwan Area, ROC, 1992*, June (in Chinese).

Hanemann, W.H. (1989), 'Welfare Evaluations in Contingent Valuation Experiments with Discrete Responses: Reply', *American Journal of Agricultural Economics*, **71**(4), 1057–61.

Hoehn, John P. and Alan Randall (1987), 'A Satisfactory Benefit Cost Indicator from Contingent Valuation', *Journal of Environmental Economics and Management*, **14**(3), 226–47.

Kanninen, Barbara (1993), 'Optimal Experimental Design for Double-Bounded Dichotomous Choice Contingent Valuation', *Land Economics*, **69**(2), 138–46.

Krinsky, I. and A.L. Robb (1986), 'On Approximating the Statistical Properties of Elasticities', *Review of Economics and Statistics*, **68**, 715–9.

Liu, Jin-Tan (1990), 'The Benefit Estimation of Water Quality Improvement in Tamsui River – The Application of Closed-Ended Contingent Valuation Approach', *Academia Economic Papers*, **18**(2) (in Chinese).

Lu, Alan Yun (1987), 'The Benefit Estimation of Air Quality Improvement and Noise Reduction Related to Highway Vehicles', *Proceedings of the 1987 Annual Meeting of the Chinese Energy Economic Association*, 290–304 (in Chinese).

Lu, Alan Yun (1990), 'Valuation of Environmental Resources: A Study of the Issues of the Main Nonmarket Valuation Techniques', *Academia Economic Papers*, **18**(1), 93–135 (in Chinese).

Mitchell, Robert Cameron and Richard T. Carson (1989), *Using Surveys to Value Public Goods: The Contingent Valuation Method*, Washington, DC: Resources for the Future.

Wu, Pei-Ing and Huei-Wen Tsai (1993), 'The Estimation of Compensated Demand Function for Water Quality: The Application of Closed-Ended Contingent Valuation Method', a paper presented at a seminar sponsored by the Chinese Rural Economics Society, Taipei, October 9th (in Chinese).

10. Exploring the Value of Drinking Water Protection in Seoul, Korea

Seung-Jun Kwak and Clifford S. Russell

1 INTRODUCTION

While well over 30 years old in applied welfare economics, the contingent valuation method (CVM) or direct questioning technique for trying to obtain willingness-to-pay (WTP) values for public goods has really only become respectable in the last decade. This new respectability reflects the results of many applications and experiments that collectively seem to show that people can answer the necessarily hypothetical questions, and that they will try to do so truthfully, contrary to the expectations of our profession. (See, for example, Bohm, 1972 and 1984; Schneider and Pommerehne, 1981; Mitchell and Carson, 1989; and the 'blue ribbon' NOAA Committee, 1993.) CVM has been used to measure various benefits: for example those of improvements in visibility (Brookshire et al., 1976; Rowe et al., 1980); improvement of national ambient water quality (Mitchell and Carson, 1981, 1984); reduction of risk from motor vehicle accidents (Blomquist, 1982); and avoiding the loss of 'passive use' values due to oil spills (Carson et al., 1992). Another development of great relevance to this paper has been work on applying CVM in other cultural settings than the US and northern Europe (Whittington et al., 1987, 1988, 1990, 1991, 1992).

The essence of CVM is to ask people who will be affected by a policy or event what they would be willing to pay for a carefully specified change in availability of the public good in question, often an aspect of environmental quality. Because this exercise involves constructing population samples, crafting questions for the survey instrument, and actually interacting with those being questioned (either directly or indirectly, as in a mail survey) it is clear that simply transplanting methods that work in Europe and the US is unlikely to be a successful strategy. This paper emphasizes the adjustments to standard CVM techniques that were necessary to examine a public good question in the Korean context.

Korea has a long history but very different cultural background from the

US and Europe. Recently, Korea has undergone dramatic economic development and political change, and Koreans have begun to realize that substantial environmental damage has resulted from this high-speed growth. The particular public good examined in this study was a water quality monitoring and related water storage capacity program inspired by one damage episode, a widely publicized pair of water supply contamination incidents, called the 'phenol accidents' that occurred along the Nak-Dong River, in the south of South Korea. In these incidents, industrial phenol spills into the river were not detected until they had contaminated the water supply of a major city, Taegu, contamination that lasted two days. While no serious health effects have been reported (the contaminants smelled so bad that drinking or cooking with tap water was discouraged) there was great disruption, as emergency water had to be provided until the system was flushed out.[1]

The city of Seoul and its 10 million inhabitants are currently vulnerable to just such an accident in the Han River, which provides water for the city, mainly from instream reservoirs. The Korean government has announced plans to try to prevent this by installing in the Han River, upstream of the city's water intakes, continuously operating, automated, instream water quality monitors. The purpose of these is to give warning of a 'slug' of pollutants from a spill in time to allow the intakes to be closed until the slug has passed. During the period of closure, the city will be served from small off-stream reservoirs constructed for the purpose in the hills around the city. These plans to add protection will be expensive, and it is of some interest to see how valuable the projected results are to the intended beneficiaries. So, using the CVM, this research set out to estimate Seoul households' WTP to have their drinking water supply protected by the government's monitoring and storage plan.

The paper proceeds as follows. Section 2 discusses Korean cultural characteristics and the anticipated need for adjustments to the CV methodology. Section 3 describes these adjustments. Results related to the adjustments are provided in Section 4. Results related to policy choice appear in Section 5. Some methodological conclusions can be found in the final section.

2 KOREAN CULTURAL CHARACTERISTICS AND ANTICIPATED NEED FOR ADJUSTMENTS TO 'USUAL' CV METHODS

2.1 Elicitation Method

There are four principal elicitation methods used in CVM studies: the bidding game (rather like an auction), the direct question, the payment card, and the take-it-or-leave-it format (rather like a referendum). With the bidding game, evidence of starting point bias has been found (Desvousges et al., 1987). Moreover, Koreans are not familiar with auctions. Generally, in the direct question format, it is difficult for the respondent to answer willingness-to-pay questions concerning the services of goods with which he or she is not familiar. With the take-it-or-leave-it format, since, in effect, only a 'yes' or 'no' is required, it is easier for the respondents to answer. However, a troublesome problem is how to decide the predetermined range of 'prices' from which specific 'offers' to respondents are chosen. The data-gathering efficiency of the method is reduced if the take-it-or-leave-it numbers on offer have to be drawn from a very wide range. Because ours was an initial attempt to use the method and because no other evidence was available that allowed us to infer a fairly narrow range from which to draw, and finally because the pilot project budget limited us to about 300 interviews, we felt this choice would have been problematic.

2.2 Sampling Method

The study area of this research is restricted to Seoul, the capital of Korea since 1392. Today Seoul is a big city, with a population of around ten million people (two and one half million households). Seoul is comprised of 22 wards (called 'gu'), and each 'gu' in turn contains 364 to 1,081 'tong'. In total, there are 14,956 'tong' in Seoul. There are approximately 170 households in one 'tong'.

Our goal, of course, was to draw a random sample of this population. In the US or northern Europe if one wanted to sample randomly from such a city, it would be common to begin with the phone book or even to go directly to random digit dialing. In Seoul, the incidence of household phone ownership is much lower, however. It is common there for several families living in one building to share a single phone, with the instrument appearing in the phone book under only one name, typically that of the building's owner. And even if we had sampled names from the phone book, there would have been some difficulty in actually locating the chosen households because street addresses tend to be either unreliable or nonexistent in

Seoul, while the actual street system involves many alleys connected in complicated ways.

2.3 Whom to Survey

Picking a household is not the end of the sample-selection matter. There must be a rule for picking a person from the household to interview. The objective of our study was to estimate the social benefit of improving the security of drinking water quality. We therefore needed to interview the person who was most likely to be familiar with matters touching on drinking water – from decisions about buying bottled water, to knowledge about the cost of water service to the household. In Korea, traditionally, the housewife makes small spending decisions and sets up the budget for her family. We checked that this was still the case with our focus groups (see below).

2.4 Language

The original drafts of the questionnaire were written in English to allow for maximum input from a survey expert at the Vanderbilt Institute for Public Policy Studies. But in the focus groups and the actual interviews in Korea, a Korean survey instrument had to be used. The translation problem had to be considered carefully.

3 ADJUSTMENTS AND TECHNIQUES CHOSEN IN RESPONSE TO THE ABOVE CHALLENGES

3.1 Choice of Payment Card Method

For a combination of cultural and practical reasons, Mitchell and Carson's payment card style format (1981, 1984) seemed likely to be the best choice. This choice in turn implied that a person-to-person interview would be necessary. The advantages of the payment card format are that it reduces the difficulty of providing a WTP response in the direct question format; reduces, if it does not entirely avoid, the starting point bias of the bidding game format; and does not require any guesses about the likely range of WTP.[2]   The payment card for our Korean research was designed by combining a matrix of amounts (in won) with identification of certain won amounts as the average tax payments of households in various income categories for other public and publicly provided goods and services. We identified payment amounts for sanitary services, public health, traffic control, publicly provided housing and education, and defense in our payment card.[3] (An example of a card, in English, is provided in Appendix 10.A)

3.2 Sampling Plan Using the Tong Jang's House

Our sample of 304 households was first allocated to the wards or gu in proportion to each gu's population, resulting in 8 to 15 households being assigned to each gu. Then, we selected 3–5 tong randomly from each gu. A total of 106 tongs were selected.

Within each tong, there is a head resident, known as the 'tong jang' who works part-time on neighborhood affairs. Most tong residents will know how to locate their tong jang's house, so this house becomes a natural and convenient starting point for a spatial sampling frame. In our study, in each sampled tong we selected the 5th and 6th houses to the right, and the 7th to the left of the tong jang's house as units to be sampled. (In cases where several families were living in one sampled house, we randomly chose only one household.) The interviewers visited the sampled houses and told the person who answered the door that they were doing research about water. While it is not customary to open the door to strangers in Korea, many respondents took the interviewers to be government officers from the city water service and opened the door readily. Once an interview was underway, the interviewers introduced themselves clearly and explained the specific objects of the survey as set out in the survey instrument.

3.3 Focus Group Interviews and the Decision to Interview Housewives

Twenty-five Korean households in Seoul and Nashville, including both husbands and wives, participated in our in-depth focus interviews before the actual field survey. Among other things, we asked them who would decide questions about drinking water in their families and asked the husband whether he would follow his wife's decision. Most of them said that the wife determines the budget for the family and, further, specifically decides whether or not to buy drinking-water-related goods such as bottled water. No husband in our groups knew his family's monthly water bill or its total expenditure for water, including bottled water and filtration. As it happens, in Korea the housewife is invariably the person with this knowledge, and thus appeared to be the appropriate individual to interview for this research.[4]

3.4 Double Translation

We translated the English version of the survey instrument into Korean with the assistance of two Korean faculty members at Vanderbilt University. We used easy, short, and concise Korean sentences as much as possible, and tested our instrument with our Korean focus groups to see how much they understood. The final version reflected these groups' input as well as advice from experts at the survey firm employed to organize the actual field administration (Seoul Marketing Data, Inc). The revised Korean version instrument was retranslated into English to check that no distortion had been introduced. (The final English language version of the questionnaire is included as Appendix 10.B) The final Korean version was refined by a specialist at the survey company to make it appear more professional.

4   RESULTS AS RELATED TO ADJUSTMENTS

4.1 The Surveys

Our survey procedure combined person-to-person interviews, conducted in January and February of 1992, with a follow-up telephone check. The interviewers told us that it was not difficult to do the initial interviews because most respondents were interested in the subject. Tap water is very familiar to Korean housewives and, fortunately, the phenol incidents along the Nak-Dong River were selected as one of the top ten domestic news stories of 1991 in Korea.[5] Therefore, most respondents had been reminded of them recently.

The follow-up telephone check was done to reduce the number of skipped questions and to verify the results of the survey, both of which tend to increase the reliability of our data. Besides obtaining answers for the skipped variables, a randomly selected 96 observations among telephone-equipped households were verified. We asked by phone whether the interviewer performed her job properly, whether the interviewers used the payment card properly, and whether the respondents understood our payment cards. We also checked the consistency of the respondent's answers by asking several questions again. Perhaps remarkably, respondents in Seoul understood the payment cards easily with the help of the interviewer. In the process of verification only 6 observations from the original total of 304 interviewed were removed from the sample. For one, we could find no one by the given name at the telephone number given. For two questionnaires, the answers given over the phone were inconsistent with the answers given in the interview. And, for three survey results, there were too many skipped variables to make up over the phone.

4.2 The Sample Characteristics

Thus, we successfully interviewed 298 households in Seoul. An important question is whether the spatial sample frame actually reflects with reasonable accuracy the characteristics of the population of Seoul. This turns out to be a difficult question to come to grips with in a definitive way because of the paucity of publicly available data on the characteristics. We are reduced to three reasonably good comparisons and one other that is much less satisfactory. All are, however, at least modestly encouraging.

In Table 10.1 we show data on the distributions of characteristics of the sample: (A) income; (B) family size; (C) age; and (D) education. The mean monthly household income (after tax) of our sample was 1,031,000 won. At 780 won to the US dollar, this amounted to about $1320 at the time of the interviews. The reported mean income (after tax) in Seoul for 1991 was 1,050,000 won. Therefore, at least the mean income of our sample approximates the reported mean income of the population very closely. The average number of persons per household in our sample was 4.06. The actual average family size in Seoul is reported to be 3.97. So our average family size was also close to that of the population at large.

In the matter of age, we show a comparison of our sample of housewives with the distribution of the Seoul female population aged 20 and older. We see that our sample has fewer very young women and fewer very old ones. This reflects the fact that we interviewed housewives, cutting down the number of very young women. In addition, at the upper end of the age scale, the custom is for parents to live with their oldest son, and for his wife to be officially the housewife. This reduces the likelihood of picking up very old women in our sample.

As for education, only a small proportion of our sample had either zero or elementary level. The proportion of those with some college or with some graduate training was only slightly larger. The median person in the sample had some high school. The only data we have found on this characteristic is for 38-year-old females in Seoul. For these individuals, the median level is also some high school.

4.3 The Explanation of Willingness-to-Pay Responses

Success in the choice of whom to survey, of translation and of payment card format are all reflected in the results of tests of the theoretical validity of a CVM study. Mitchell and Carson (1989) define theoretical validity of CVM as the degree to which the findings of a study are consistent with theoretical expectations, and suggest that it may be tested by regressing the WTP amounts on independent variables that are expected to influence an

Table 10.1 Sample Characteristics and Population Comparisons

A.		Sample	
Income ranges	n	(%)	
I < 500,000	15	(5.0%)	
500,000 ≤ I < 1,000,000	127	(43.0%)	
1,000,000≤ I < 1,500,000	95	(32.0%)	
1,500,000≤ I < 2,000,000	30	(10.0%)	
2,000,000≤ I < 2,500,000	20	(7.0%)	
2,500,000≤ I	11	(3.0%)	
Total respondents	298		
Sample mean	1,031,000		
Median	1,000,000		
Mean Seoul income[a]	1,050,000		

B.		Sample	
Number in Family	n	(%)	
1	2	(0.7%)	
2	17	(5.5%)	
3	65	(22.0%)	
4	121	(41.0%)	
5	69	(23.0%)	
6	17	(5.5%)	
7 ≤	7	(2.3%)	
Total respondents	298		
Sample mean	4.06		
Median	4		
Mean Seoul family size[a]	3.97		

individual's WTP for the good being valued. An unexpected sign or low
significance of one or more coefficients would be regarded as evidence that
the study is not consistent with the theory, and therefore questionable.

Our theoretical model for explaining individuals' WTP comes from the
income compensating function (Willig, 1976). When we take WTP as the
desired benefit measure, the income compensating function is referred to

Table 10.1, continued

C. Age Ranges	Sample n	(%)	Seoul Females Over 20 Years Old[b] (%)
20s	79	(27.0%)	34.9%
30s	102	(34.0%)	28.6%
40s	73	(24.0%)	20.6%
50s	44	(15.0%)	12.7%
60s	0	(0%)	3.2%
Total respondents	298		Median in 30s
Sample Mean	37.8		
Median	36		

D. Education Ranges	Sample n	(%)	38 Year Old Seoul Females[b]
No education (0)	5	(1.7%)	1%
Elementary (1-6)	25	(9.0%)	11%
Middle School (7-9)	65	(22.0%)	28%
High School (10-12)	141	(47.0%)	43%
Junior College (13-14)	9	(3.0%)	
College Grad. (13-16)	49	(16.0%)	17%
Post Grad. (16-18)	4	(1.3%)	
Total respondents	298		Median: some high school
Sample Mean	11.5		
Median: some high school			

Sources:

a. Seoul Statistical Year Book, 1991.

b. Report of Housing and Population Census, 1992.

as the WTP function, and we hypothesize that the arguments are elements of a vector of the respondent's tastes or personal characteristics as well as variables representing both the respondent's environmental and economic situations. Thus:

$$WTP(q_1) = f(P_0, q_1, q_0, Q_0, Y_0, T) \qquad (10.1)$$

where P_0 is the price level of private goods, q_i is tap water quality before (0) and after (1), Q_0 represents other environmental goods, Y_0 is income, and T is a vector of the respondents' tastes or characteristics. In what follows, P_0 and Q_0 are assumed constant across all respondents.

The definitions of q_0 and q_1 were both keyed to the Nak-Dong phenol accidents. In effect, we allowed each respondent to define for herself a subjective probability of a spill incident affecting Seoul's water supply. We prompted this with a question that asked how many such incidents the woman thought there would be in the absence of the government's proposed intervention over the next five years. While recognizing the problems even quite sophisticated people have with subjective probabilities, we really had no other choice, since there was no data on which to base an objective estimate. Then, to define the endpoint, q_1, we asserted that the goal of the government's plan was to reduce that probability to zero or very close to zero. We asked for *WTP* for the change from q_0 to q_1.

Our specific econometric model to explain the *WTP* amounts expressed in our drinking water survey in terms of respondent characteristics is:

$$
\begin{aligned}
WTP^* = a_0 &+ a_1\ ATT + a_2\ FILT + a_3\ BOTL \\
&+ a_4\ TSPW + a_5\ NAC + a_6\ AGE \\
&+ a_7\ EDU + a_8\ NCHD + a_9\ YRS \\
&+ a_{10}\ BILL + a_{11}\ PINC + U
\end{aligned}
\tag{10.2}
$$

where U is the error term and the other variables are defined – and sample means and standard deviations reported – in Table 10.2. The distribution of stated *WTP* is summarized in Table 10.3.

ATT, *FILT*, *BOTL*, *TSPW*, *NAC*, *EDU NCHD*, *BILL*, and *PINC* are all expected to have positive relationships with *WTP*. The anticipated signs of *AGE* and *YRS* are not obvious. However, older people in Korea may take their health more seriously than younger people. Therefore, older respondents may be willing to pay more. We can also guess that respondents Table 10.1, continued who have lived in Seoul for a long time would be used to publicly provided tap water and more blasé about its quality, while those who recently moved from rural areas would miss pure drinking water, such as that from the springs of their hometown. *YRS* might thus have a negative sign.

Table 10.2. Variable Definition and Sample Statistics

		Sample Mean	Std Deviation
WTP*	Stated willingness to pay per month (unit = won)	2560	176.3
ATT:	The respondent's judgment of current tap water quality 1 = Very good 2 = Good 3 = Average 4 = Bad 5 = Very bad	3.60	0.77
FILT:	Monthly expenditure for home water filtration system (unit = 1,000 won)	1.57	3.60
BOTL:	Monthly expenditure for bottled water (unit = 1,000 won)	1.86	5.52
TSPW:	Dummy for having taken a trip to obtain spring water only for drinking water during last five years 1 = Yes 0 = No	0.36	0.48
NAC:	Subjective estimate of the number of drinking water accidents that might occur in next five years if the government takes no action.	3.87	3.14
AGE:	Age of the respondent	37.8	9.43
EDU:	Education level of the respondent in years from 0 = no education to 18 = postgraduate	11.5	3.22
NCHD:	Number of children in the respondent's household under 13 years old	0.92	0.88
YRS:	Number of years respondent has been a resident of Seoul	19.5	13.1
BILL:	Monthly combined bill for water and sewerage service (unit = 1,000 won)	4.82	2.33
PINC:	Monthly household total income divided by number in the family living in the household (unit = 1,000 won)	274.9	185.2

Table 10.3   The Distribution of Stated Willingness to Pay (in won)

INTERVAL	COUNT
WTP = 0	28
0 < WTP < 2,000	111
2,000 < WTP < 4,000	93
4,000 ≤ WTP < 6,000	45
6,000 ≤ WTP < 8,000	3
8,000 ≤ WTP < 10,000	3
10,000 ≤ WTP < 12,000	12
12,000 ≤ WTP < 14,000	0
14,000 ≤ WTP < 16,000	1
16,000 ≤ WTP < 18,000	0
18,000 ≤ WTP < 20,000	0
20,000 ≤ WTP < 30,000	1
30,000 ≤ WTP	1
Total	298

In Table 10.4, we show the regression results for our willingness-to-pay equation under two model formulations.[6] In Model I, all the variables listed in Table 10.2 were included in the equation. In Model II, the subjective variables, number of accidents and attitude toward drinking water, were both omitted. (The argument here is that significant coefficients on these 'explanatory' variables may simply reflect a nexus of misunderstanding or excessive anxiety about the water quality problem.) The coefficients of all the variables in Model I are significantly different from zero at the level of at least 5% and their signs are as expected. (Nine coefficients of the 12 are significant at the 1% level.) For Model II, 9 of 10 coefficients are significant, 5 of them at the 1% level. (The coefficient on *AGE* drops to insignificance.) The signs remain correct, and none of the coefficients are dramatically different in size, though education, number of children, and water bill size now have smaller marginal effects. We believe these results provide evidence of theoretical validity.

5   RESULTS RELATED TO POLICY CHOICE

The average monthly *WTP* of our sample per household is 2,560 won (US $3.28). The average water bill of Seoul households is approximately 5,000

Table 10.4 WTP Equation Estimation Results using Symmetrically Trimmed (Censored) Least Squares Estimation

Variable	MODEL I Coefficient	t-ratio	MODEL II Coefficient	t-ratio
CONST.	-11.45	-4.02(**)	-3.12	-2.56(*)
ATT	0.83	2.80(**)	--	--
FILT	0.14	2.47(*)	0.15	2.77(*)
BOTL	0.11	3.46(**)	0.10	3.12(**)
TSPW	1.21	3.42(**)	1.23	4.37(**)
NAC	0.28	3.42(**)	--	--
AGE	0.07	2.41(*)	0.02	1.11
EDU	0.26	2.57(*)	0.15	2.49(*)
NCHD	0.71	3.42(**)	0.44	2.86(**)
YRS	-0.05	-2.87(**)	-0.04	-2.82(**)
BILL	0.18	2.90(**)	0.13	2.60(*)
PINC	0.01	5.64(**)	0.01	5.38(**)
N=298				

Notes
* Significant at the level of five percent.
** Significant at the level of one percent.

won per month. The average private payment to insure drinking water quality (monthly cost of purchased bottled water and of water filtration systems) is around 3,430 won. As a household's reported expenditures on bottled water and water filtration systems increase, its *WTP* grows.

Using Model I from Table 10.4, the 95% confidence interval for the average *WTP* of the population is between 2,211 won (US$2.83) and 2,902 won (US$3.72). Approximately 2.7 million households live in Seoul. So the aggregate *WTP* of all Seoul households is estimated to be $6,912 \times 10^6$ won per month (about US$8.86 million). The annual *WTP* is then $82,944 \times 10^6$ won (about US$106 million), and its 95% confidence interval is between $71,304 \times 10^6$ won (US$91.4 million) and $94,024 \times 10^6$ won (US$120.5 million).

The cost of the proposed new monitoring system is reported by the Ministry of Environment to be approximately US$30 millon. Besides the new automatic system, to achieve the described security of drinking water quality, it is necessary to increase storage capacity. In the case of the 'phenol accident', the city's water supply was disconnected for about 2 days. Therefore, in order to supply water continuously in even the worst case, the government must increase the storage capacity downstream of the raw water intake by building auxiliary reservoirs to store 1 or 2 days' water for emergency use. Currently, there are 4 hours' worth of such reservoir capacity in Seoul.

Daily tap water consumption in Seoul is approximately $4,570,000 \, m^3$. The cost to build one set of reservoirs whose capacity is $40,000 \, m^3$ is estimated to be $2,546 \times 10^6$ won (US\$3.26 million).[7] To have in storage one day's consumption of tap water for Seoul's residents, 114 sets of reservoirs will be needed. (We assume that it is not possible to build one very large reservoir for this purpose and thus there are no economies of scale beyond those captured in the unit costs.) Therefore the total cost of providing storage would be approximately $290,244 \times 10^6$ won (US\$372.1 million). Consequently, in order to guarantee the stated 'goal', the capital cost would be at least US\$402.1 million (the cost of the monitoring system plus the cost to build reservoirs). If more days of storage are required, the capital costs increase linearly.

In Table 10.5 we provide a comparison based on extremes for costs and benefits, using dollar values for convenience. Not surprisingly, we find the policy implications of the study to be quite sensitive to assumptions about costs. It is tempting to conclude, however, that the policy passes the cost-benefit test. Thus, if two days of storage are required to achieve the stated goal, the capital recovery factor is as high as 10%, and operating costs are 20% of annual capital costs, total annual cost becomes \$92.9 million, roughly the same as the benefits at the lower end of the 95% percent confidence interval. More favorable cost assumptions coupled with a benefit number from the upper end of the confidence interval give an estimate of net benefits equal to about \$95 million per year.

6   METHODOLOGICAL   CONCLUSION

This paper has emphasized both the adjustments to standard CVM techniques that we felt were necessary to apply this technique in the Korean context and the results of undertaking the adjusted survey, both in terms of sample characteristics and of a check for theoretical validity. We have also reported briefly the implications of the survey results for policy choice.

We found that the translation of CV studies into the Korean context was more than a matter of translating a suitable English questionnaire. Overall, creating a sampling frame and choosing a target respondent, both key parts of such a study, required significant adjustment to the realities of Seoul. Focus groups and the local technical assistance of the survey firm became especially important in the more general 'translation' exercise.

Table 10.5   Costs and Benefits under a Variety of Assumptions

Favorable Assumptions
1. Storage for one day required.
2. Capital recovery factor = 0.06.
3. Operation and management costs equal to 5% of annual capital cost.
4. Benefits valued at upper end of 95% confidence interval.

Annual benefits:	US$121 $\times$ 10^6
Annual costs: Capital:	$24.1 $\times$ 10^6
O&M:	$ 1.2 $\times$ 10^6
Total annual costs:	US$25.3 $\times$ 10^6
Net annual benefits:	$95.7 $\times$ 10^6

Unfavorable Assumptions
1. Storage for two days required
2. Capital recovery factor = 0.10.
3. Operation and management costs equal to 20% of annual capital cost.
4. Benefits valued at lower end of 95% confidence interval.

Annual benefits:	US$91.4 $\times$ 10^6
Annual costs: Capital:	$77.4 $\times$ 10^6
O&M:	$15.5 $\times$ 10^6
Total annual costs:	US$92.9 $\times$ 10^6
Net annual benefits:	$-1.5 $\times$ 10^6

Among various elicitation methods, we chose the payment card style survey instrument. Nearly all respondents understood the payment card. The random sample, spatially based on the tong jang's house, reflected with reasonable accuracy the characteristics of the population of Seoul. The sample mean approximated the reported population mean for income and family size, and age and education distributions are quite similar, given that we are dealing here with married women.

The theoretical validity of our responses seems confirmed by the excellent results obtained for our *WTP* equation estimation. And finally, the benefit estimates themselves have the reassuring quality of being of the same order of magnitude as the costs of the proposed protection plan. Whether or not our survey is taken to confirm the wisdom of that plan depends heavily on cost assumptions, but even under a very conservative (low benefit/high cost) set of such assumptions, benefits were roughly equal to costs.

All in all, we are optimistic about the prospects of successful application of CV techniques in non-US, non-northern European settings. But we stress that substantial care must be taken to adjust for the special features of the local setting.

As a final observation we offer the following: The CV technique may prove especially useful in settings like the Korean one, situations in which previous neglect of environmental quality is combined with a lack of data that might be useful for application of indirect benefit estimation techniques. This lack of data may well often be attributable to the same cause as the environmental neglect – a history of highly centralized and autocratic government which, though ostensibly committed to increasing welfare via economic growth, was anxious not to find out much about its citizenry, and certainly not to make public what it did find out.

APPENDIX

Appendix 10.A   Payment Card 5

Monthly Household Income after Taxes
900,000–1,100,000 Won

(Average Monthly Amount in Taxes
Paid for Some Public Programs)

0	24,000	
100	26,000	
250	28,000	⇐Education
500	30,000	
750	⇐ Sanitary Service	35,000
1,000	40,000	
1,500	45,000	⇐Defense
2,000	50,000	
3,000	55,000	
4,000	⇐ Health care	60,000
5,000	65,000	
6,000	70,000	

7,000	⇐ Roads & Highways		75,000
8,000			80,000
9,000			85,000
10,000			90,000
12,000	⇐ Housing		95,000
14,000	⇐ Social Security & Welfare		100,000
16,000			120,000
18,000			140,000
20,000			160,000
22,000			200,000

Appendix 10.B   Questionnaire

Section A

Hello, I'm _____.I'm with the Vanderbilt Institute for Public Policy Studies in the USA and Seoul Marketing Data, Inc. in Seoul.

The Institute is conducting a research study in order to find out how people feel about the quality of drinking water in Seoul and what should be done to improve it.

Your household was drawn in a random sample of Seoul residents. Your views will be analyzed along with those of other households, and the results of this survey will help local government here and in other Korean cities make better decisions about the supply and quality of their drinking water. Your help is essential to obtaining an accurate picture of how people feel about the quality of Seoul's drinking water and whether efforts should be taken to improve it. This interview will take less than 30 min.

First, let me begin by saying that most of the questions have to do with your opinions, and there are no right or wrong answers. You can help us get the best possible information for the study by thinking carefully about each question and taking your time to answer. If a question is unclear, tell me and I will read it again.

This interview is completely confidential; your name will never be associated with your answers.

Interviewer I.D.:
Time started:
Time Ended:
Interview length:

Section B

This section asks about your attitudes toward several issues that relate to water quality in Seoul.

B-1: What is your opinion about current tap water quality in Seoul? Tap water quality in Seoul is:
1. very good
2. good
3. average
4. bad
5. very bad

B-2: How important to (you/household members) is tap water quality? Would you say it is:
1. very important
2. somewhat important
3. not at all important
4. don't know

B-3: How concerned are you about water pollution in general?
1. very concerned
2. somewhat concerned
3. not very concerned
4. not concerned at all

B-4: It is possible that your household may have done some things to increase its own drinking water quality. In the last five years have you done any of the following things: installed water filters, purchased bottled water, boiled tap water, or gone to a spring to obtain spring water for the purpose of increasing drinking water quality?

    a. Installed water filter
       1. Yes   2. No
    b. Purchased bottled water
       1. Yes   2. No
    c. Boiled tap water regularly
       1. Yes   2. No
    d. Gone to a spring to obtain spring water regularly
       1. Yes   2. No

(If 'Yes', ask for the month and year each action was begun and ended. For action 'a', probe for the units purchased during the last 5 years, the cost per unit and the cost of filter per month. For action 'b', probe for the number of units purchased per month and the cost per unit.)

action	number of units	unit cost	cost of filter
a. Installed water filter	_____	_____	_____
b. Purchased bottled water	_____	_____	_____

(If 'No', ask again.)

Do you have any plans to do any of them within one year?

a. Install water filter   _____

b. Purchase bottled water   _____

c. Boil tap water   _____

d. Make a trip to obtain spring water   _____

B-5: Do you recall reading any news articles or hearing on radio or television about the phenol accident on the Nak-Dong River in the spring of 1991?

1. Yes

2. No

B-6: What is the monthly combined income your household (you, your husband, and any other members of your household) received after taxes in last year? Include wages, salaries, income from your business, pensions, dividends, interest, and any other income after taxes.

_____(won)

(If they do not respond, remind them again this interview is completely confidential and response on the income question is very important in this study. If they still do not respond, go to B-7.)

B-7: If you don't want to respond with your exact household income, could you tell me the number that best describes your monthly household income?

1. under 300,000 won

2. 300,000 won – 500,000 won

3. 500,000 won – 700,000 won

4. 700,000 won – 900,000 won

5. 900,000 won – 1,100,000 won

6. 1,100,000 won – 1,400,000 won

7. 1,400,000 won – 1,700,000 won

8. 1,700,000 won – 2,000,000 won

9. 2,000,000 won or more

Section C

The questions in this section are about how much the improvement of tap water quality is worth to you (and all your family).

In these questions, I will not be talking about any drinking water – bottled water, spring water, or water made with your private filtration system. For the remainder of interview, I will always be referring to the tap water supplied by civil water service as it comes from the pipe supplying your house.

First, let me remind you of the phenol accident on the Nak-Dong River in the spring of 1991.

A big electronics company accidently discharged 30 tons of phenol in 8 hours into the Nak-Dong River. Phenol entered the water supply system by way of the water purification plants and contaminated the tap water for 2 million citizens in the Taegu area. Many residents unknowingly drank contaminated tap water. Particularly, pregnant women worried about damage to the babies they were carrying. (Show visual cards of phenol accident and read the headlines.)

The critical problem was that the public water system did not detect the phenol immediately, either in the river or at the water purification plant. In less than one month, the same company discharged phenol again. However, at that time, the company reported it immediately to all relevant institutions. With the knowledge of the pollutant, the government set up proper emergency treatment action. Therefore, residents did not experience the contaminated tap water directly.

Currently, the quality of water sources used to supply drinking water in Korea is monitored manually once a month. This occasional monitoring system cannot detect accidental or intentional massive inflows of pollutants immediately. It can also fail to detect the changes in water source quality that happen during rainy season floods that bring animal waste and other run off pollutants to the river. Thirty-one percent of all companies that can potentially discharge pollutants into sources of Korean drinking water are located along the Han River, which is the source of drinking water for Seoul. Twenty-two percent of them are located along the Nak-Dong River. In addition, the Ministry of Environment reports that the percentage of pollution sources still in violation of environmental laws is around 17% of the total inspected. There still exists the possibility of an accident similar to the Nak-Dong phenol accident occurring on the Han River.

C-1: If government takes no action, how many times do you think you might experience an accident similar to the Nak-Dong phenol accident in next five years?
    1. None
    2. Once in five years
    3. Twice in five years
    4. Three times in five years
    5. Four times in five years
    6. Once in every year

7. Twice in every year
8. More than twice in every year
   ⇒ How many? _____
9. I don't know ⇒ go to C-1-1.

C-1-1: A general expectation, if the government does not take any action, is that you will experience tap water quality similar to that during the phenol accident at least twice in next five years, considering the speed of industrial development, the number of companies along the river, and the occurrence of floods.

In order to offer greater assurance of pure and safe drinking water, the government is adopting a new plan. They are going to install an automatic, continuous, and remote monitoring system, and increase the storage capacity downstream of the raw water intake in the Han by building auxiliary reservoirs to store 1 or 2 days' water for emergencies.

This automatic system will monitor water quality continuously, 24 hours a day, and be able to detect unexpected inflows of pollutants immediately, allowing the water system to initiate proper emergency treatment actions. Consequently, you can be supplied with a safe quality of drinking water continuously.

The goal of this new automatic monitoring system is <u>to reduce the possibility that, in your life, you will experience an accident similar to the phenol accident in the Nak-Dong River to zero or very close to zero. Imagine, for example, the possibility that you will be a president of Korea.</u>

Next, I am going to ask you how much this goal is worth to you. (Read the goal again.) Since this is not something we usually think about, it may be helpful for you to know what the average household like yours pays in taxes and higher prices for some other types of public programs.

(Give Respondent appropriate payment card for income range of her household.)

Monthly Income	# of Payment Card
under 300,000 won	1 & 1-A
300,000 won – 500,000 won	2 & 2-A
500,000 won – 700,000 won	3 & 3-A
700,000 won – 900,000 won	4 & 4-A
900,000 won – 1,100,000 won	5 & 5-A
1,100,000 won – 1,400,000 won	6 & 6-A
1,400,000 won – 1,700,000 won	7 & 7-A
1,700,000 won – 2,000,000 won	8 & 8-A
2,000,000 won or more	9 & 9-A

The payment card I have given you lists many different amounts. It also gives an monthly estimate of how much households in your income range paid in taxes in 1990 for programs like sanitary services, health care, roads & highways, housing, social security & welfare, education, and defense.

I remind you that the amounts shown on the payment card are not voluntary payments. You do not need to be constrained by the number or by the order of items on the payment card.

Before you think about your willingness to pay for the new automatic monitoring system and the described goal (read the goal again) you must keep in mind that if the apparent willingness to pay of Seoul water customers is small and not enough to finance the cost, the attainment of the goal will be very uncertain. Stating your actual willingness to pay is very important in this survey.

C-2: What amount on the payment card, or any amount in between, is the most you (your household) would be willing to pay in tax and higher water bills each month for the new automatic monitoring system (including storage capacity) and the described goal, provided that the success of this goal is guaranteed (read the goal again).

    1. _____ won
    2. zero   ⇒ go to C-2-1
    3. Refused   ⇒ go to C-2-1

C-2-1: People have different reasons for saying zero won or refusing to answer at all. I'm going to read you some reasons. Please choose the number(s) that best describes your reasons.

    1. My current water bill is too high and should be a large enough contribution to attaining this goal.

    2. The government should be able to meet this goal with the money they already get through taxes. ⇒ go to C-2-2

    3. I have suffered from bad tap water, therefore government should compensate me.

    4. I have a good water filter installed or buy bottled water for our drinking water.

    5. I do not believe that this accident will happen again.

    6. I don't understand the question. ⇒ go to C-2-3

    7. other reasons_____

C-2-2: It is very important to us to learn what value you (your household) place on tap water quality goals when you are given the chance to make the choice yourself. Would you be willing to answer the question if I noted that government does not have enough money to achieve this goal?
(If yes, go back to C-2.)

C-2-3: (If they don't understand the question, go back to Section C again, repeat the explanation of the question more carefully.)

Section D

Interviewer's Use Only

D-1: (If the respondent's willingness to pay is too high for her income level – approximately higher than the payment on education in her income group – ask her again.)

I am going to give you some information about other respondents' mean willingness to pay. Other respondents' mean willingness to pay is approximately _____ won (suggest to her any amount higher than what she answered first). This mean willingness to pay will be your additional payment for better service through taxes or your water bill.

At this point in the interview, I want to give you a chance to make adjustments and changes.

Will you change the amount you are willing to pay for this goal?

1. No

2. Yes ⇒ (read again question C-2)

          How much? _____ won

D-2: (Irrespective of whether or not the respondent answered the questions in Section C, in your judgment, how well did the respondent understand what she was asked to do in these questions?)

1. Understood very well

2. Understood well

3. Understood somewhat

4. Did not understand very much

Section E

Background Questions

E-1: What is your age? _____ years old

E-2: What was the last grade of regular school that you completed – not counting specialized schools like secretarial or trade schools?

1. No school (0)

2. Elementary school (Grade 1–6)

3. Middle school (Grade 7–9)

4. High school (Grade 10–12)

5. Junior college (Grade 13–14)

6. College graduate (Grade 13–16)

7. Postgraduate (Grade 17–18)

(write exact number)

Wife:_____ Husband:_____

E-3: How many people live in your household including yourself?
_____persons

E-4: If you have children (under 13 yrs old), or are a legal guardian of anyone, how many such dependents currently live with you? _____

E-5: How many years have you been a resident of Seoul?
_____years

E-6: Do you share your house with any other household?

1. No

2. Yes ⇒ How many?_____

E-6-1: Do you have your own water meter or not?

1. Yes _____

2. No _____

E-7: What is your average monthly payment on water bills and sewerage bills?

water bill _____won   sewerage bill _____won

If you pay for hot water separately from your water bill, what is your average monthly hot water payment?

_____won. Price per ton _____won

Finally, I need your telephone number in order for my supervisor to confirm that this interview was conducted properly and that I performed my job in a courteous and business-like fashion. No one else will ever have access to your number.

Telephone number:

Name of the respondent:

Address:

Thank you for your cooperation.

ACKNOWLEDGEMENTS

The authors gratefully acknowledge the advice and assistance of their colleagues, Professors Georgine Pion and Junsoo Lee; the financial support of the Korean Environmental Protection Agency; and the comments of two referees. The usual disclaimer, of course, applies.

NOTES

1. Some women, pregnant at the time of the spills, have demanded compensation for alleged damages, either miscarriages or children born alive but with some identifiable problem. Doctors cannot agree on a cause-effect relationship here, but the responsible company has paid compensation nonetheless.
2. 'Range bias' is the label given by Mitchell and Carson (1989, pp. 241-3) to a set of potential difficulties with payment cards that are closely analogous to starting point bias. These difficulties include having too low an upper limit or too high a bottom limit on the card to accommodate true WTP of the respondents and thus encouraging inaccurate statements. We do not believe our instrument suffered from these flaws. Certainly our responses were almost all reassuringly 'interior' to the card ranges.
3. The data on amounts spent by income class were supplied by the Korean Institute for Industrial Economics and Trade in Seoul.
4. Several experienced survey companies in Korea, which had surveyed the bottled water market, supported this decision as well.
5. The phenol accidents in the Nak-Dong River were widely publicized, and we expected that a very high percentage of the country's population was aware of them and had a fairly clear idea of their effects. Certainly all members of our Seoul focus group had good information about this accident. In addition, in the actual field survey, some visual cards, with newspaper front pages reproduced on them, were used to remind respondents about the accident.
6. The estimation was done using symmetrically trimmed least squares estimation. This estimator is consistent and asymptotically normal for a wide class of distributions of the error term, and is robust to heteroskedasticity. For more detail, see Powell (1986).
7. The construction company of the Hyundai group in Korea estimated this cost for us.

REFERENCES

Blomquist, Glenn C. (1982), 'Estimating the Value of Life and Safety: Recent Developments', *The Value of Life and Safety*, Amsterdam: North-Holland.

Bohm, Peter (1972), 'Estimating Demand for Public Goods: An Experiment', *European Economic Review*, **3**, 111–30.

Bohm, Peter (1984), 'Revealing Demand for Actual Public Goods', *Journal of Public Economics*, **24**, 135–51.

Brookshire, David S., Berry C. Ives, and William D. Schulze (1976), 'The Valuation of Aesthetic Preference', *Journal of Environmental Economics and Management*, **3** (4), 325–46.

Carson, Richard T., Robert C. Mitchell, W. Michael Hanemann, Raymond J. Kopp, Stanley Presser and Paul A. Ruud (1992), 'A Contingent Valuation Study of Lost Passive Use Values Resulting from the Exxon Valdez Oil Spill', A Report to the Attorney General of the State of Alaska.

Desvousges, William H., V. Kerry Smith and Ann Fisher (1987), 'Option

Price Estimates for Water Quality Improvements: A Contingent Valuation Study for the Monongahela River', *Journal of Environmental Economics and Management*, **14**, 248–67.

Mitchell, Robert Cameron and Richard T. Carson (1981), 'An Experiment in Determining Willingness to Pay for National Water Quality Improvement', Draft Report to the United States Environmental Protection Agency, Washington DC.

Mitchell, Robert Cameron and Richard T. Carson (1984), 'A Contingent Valuation Estimate of National Freshwater Benefits: Technical Report to the United States Environmental Protection Agency', Resources for the Future, Washington DC.

Mitchell, Robert Cameron and Richard T. Carson (1989), 'Using Surveys to Value Public Goods: Contingent Valuation Method', Resources for the Future, Washington DC.

NOAA (1993), 'Natural Resource Damage Assessments Under the Oil Pollution Act of 1990', *Federal Register*, **58**(10).

Powell, James L. (1986), 'Symmetrically Trimmed Least Squares Estimation for Tobit Models', *Econometrica*, **54**, 1435–60.

Report of Housing and Population Census (1992), Office of Statistics, Seoul, Korea.

Rowe, Robert D., Ralph C. D'Arge and David S. Brookshire (1980), 'An Experiment on the Economic Value of Visibility', *Journal of Environmental Economics and Management*, **7**, 1–19.

Schneider, Friedrich and Werner W. Pommerehne (1981), 'Free Riding and Collective Action: An Experiment in Public Microeconomics', *Quarterly Journal of Economics*, **97**, 689–702.

Seoul Statistical Year Book (1991), Seoul Metropolitan Government Press, Seoul, Korea.

Whittington, Dale, John Briscoe and Xinning Mu (1987), 'Willingness to Pay for Water in Rural Area: Methodological Approaches and An Application in Haiti', Prepared for the Office of Health, Bureau for Science and Technology, United States Agency for International Development, Washington, DC, Field Report No. 213.

Whittington, Dale, Donald T. Lauria and Xinming Mu (1991), 'A Study of Water Vending and Willingness to Pay for Water in Onitsha, Nigeria', *World Development*, **19**, 179–98.

Whittington, Dale, Mark Mujwahuzi, Gerald McMahon and Kyeongae Choe (1988), 'Willingness to Pay for Water in Newala District, Tanzania: Strategies for Cost Recovery', Prepared for the USAID Mission to the Government of Tanzania and the UNICEF Tanzania Mission, Washington, DC, Field Report No. 246.

Whittington, Dale, Apia Okorafor, Augustine Okore and Alexander Mcphail

(1990), 'Strategy for Cost Recovery in the Rural Water Sector: A Case Study of Nsukka District, Anambra State, Nigeria', *Water Resources Research*, **26**, 1899–913.

Whittington, Dale, V. Kerry Smith, Apia Okorafor, Augustine Okore, Jin Long Liu and Alexander Mcphail (1992), 'Giving Respondents Time to Think in Contingent Valuation Studies: A Developing Country Application', *Journal of Environmental Economics and Management*, **22**, 205–25.

Willig, R.D. (1976), 'Consumer Surplus without Apology', *American Economic Review*, **66**, 587–97.

11. Demand for Environmental Quality: Comparing Models for Contingent Policy Referendum Experiments

Pei-Ing Wu and Wen-Hua Hsieh

1 INTRODUCTION

Contingent valuation has become widely used as a method for assigning a value to a resource or commodity when the relevant market does not exist, as is often the case for a public good, and in particular for the valuation of environmental quality. Among the elicitation methods in contingent valuation technique, the contingent policy referendum approach, in which each individual is asked whether or not he would pay a specified price for the proposed improvement, has gained favor in recent years. Despite the fact that it generates less information per observation than other approaches, the popularity of the technique arises from its methodological simplicity. Moreover, Hoehn and Randall (1987) have proved that strategic biases are eliminated from the contingent policy referendum approach to the extent that the proposed price is perceived as a credible policy option.

The situation posed by the contingent policy referendum resembles that of a consumer faced with a real purchase decision, and lends itself to standard methods of estimating discrete-choice models (such as probit and logit) from disaggregate data. Bishop and Heberlein's study (1979) of goose hunting in the Horicon zone of east central Wisconsin is the first research which analyzes the individual's yes or no response with a logit model. However, the procedure employed by Bishop and Heberlein is criticized by Hanemann because it is not strictly compatible with utility theory. Hanemann (1984) then suggests a methodology which explicitly recognizes the utility-maximizing choice underlying the individuals' responses to the experiment, in which a utility difference model is then derived for analyzing data from survey responses. The application of this method is found in research by Bowker and Stoll (1988), Loehman and De (1982), Sellar, Chavas and Stoll (1986) and Sellar, Stoll and Chavas (1985), to name a few.

Cameron and James (1987a and 1987b) and Cameron (1988), however,

226

have offered an alternative interpretation of individuals' responses. They emphasize that referendum data are not discrete-choice data in the conventional sense. Additional information can be extracted from the data, and the resulting model allows an inverse Hicksian demand function to be much more easily derived. The variability of the proffered price across respondents allows the willingness to pay to be modelled as a censored latent continuous variable. Their response function is interpreted as the expenditure difference or variation function.

McConnell (1990), in a theoretical analysis of Hanemann's and Cameron's approaches, has shown that the deterministic portions of both types of response functions are dual to each other. Furthermore, when the marginal utility of income is constant the same function will be estimated in both the utility difference and the expenditure difference model. Park and Loomis (1992) have empirically tested the conditions identified by McConnell for the linear utility difference model and the linear variation function model. However, a comprehensive discussion of these two competing models in the analysis of contingent policy referendum data is lacking in the literature. It is the motivation of this study to fill this gap.

The purpose of this paper is therefore to present a complete comparison of Hanemann's and Cameron's models. The comparison, an expansion of earlier work, will be made under different specifications of utility and expenditure difference functions. The welfare measure of mean willingness to pay and the corresponding confidence intervals are estimated. To determine the optimal level of environmental goods provision, the demand function of the environmental goods is useful. The Hicksian demand function for each specification will also be derived. A set of data with 540 households from a contingent policy referendum experiment, a study conducted on the improvement of water quality in Tung-kang Creek of Ping-tung County in Taiwan, is employed for our purpose.

1.1 Response Function Derived from Utility and Expenditure Functions

Respondents are asked to consider some proposed policies which would influence the state or condition of the environment, and increase the quantity or improve the quality of the environmental goods from an initial level, Q^0, to some alternative level, Q^1. The amount of willingness to pay, denoted as *WTP*, that situates an individual at the initial level of well-being, U^0, is the compensating measure of welfare gain. The arguments of the utility function include income level, Y^0, and other sociodemographic factors, X, of the individual. In utility function format this is expressed as

$$U^0 = V(Y^0, Q^0; X) = V(Y^0 - WTP, Q^1; X) \qquad (11.1)$$

We can assume that the individual knows his utility V with certainty and the individual is rational in the sense that he makes choices that maximize his perceived utility subject to an expenditure constraint. However, there are some components, such as imperfect perception, optimization and inability of the analyst to exactly measure all the relevant variables, which make utility a random function.

When confronted with a proffered price T in the contingent policy referendum experiment, the individual's choice between remaining at the initial environmental goods level Q^0 and holding income Y^0, and enjoying a higher level of environmental goods Q^1 while paying the proposed price T, is a comparison between the following two situations

$$U^0 = V^0(Y^0, Q^0; X) + \varepsilon^0 \tag{11.2}$$

$$U^1 = V^1(Y^0 - T, Q^1; X) + \varepsilon^1 \tag{11.3}$$

where ε^0 and ε^1 are independent and identically distributed with zero means and extreme value distributions. The individual consents to pay the price only if the utility level from paying the price T and enjoying Q^1 is higher than or at least equal to the utility level from consuming initial levels of Q^0 and Y^0. That is,

$$U^1 \geq U^0 \tag{11.4}$$

or equivalently,

$$V^1(Y^0 - T, Q^1; X) + \varepsilon^1 \geq V^0(Y^0, Q^0; X) + \varepsilon^0 \tag{11.5}$$

By rearranging the terms, we obtain the following relationship

$$\Delta V(Y^0, T, Q^1, Q^0; X) + \Delta\varepsilon \geq 0 \tag{11.6}$$

where $\Delta V(\cdot) = V^1(Y^0 - T, Q^1; X) - V^0(Y^0, Q^0; X)$ and $\Delta\varepsilon = \varepsilon^1 - \varepsilon^0$. Hanemann (1984) interprets the response function $\Delta V(\cdot)$ as the utility difference.

Alternatively, Cameron's (1988) interpretation of the response function is based on an expenditure function. Similar to the assumptions made for the utility function, for the expenditure function it is assumed that the amount of money needed for an individual to reach a certain level of utility is composed of a deterministic and a stochastic component. When confronted with the price T, the individual's decision on whether to pay the price T is a decision based on the comparison between the amounts required to consume Q^1, and Q^0, while remaining at the initial level of utility U^0

$$E^0 = e^0[U^0(Q^0, Y^0; X), Q^0]+\eta^0 \qquad (11.7)$$

$$E^1 = e^1[U^0(Q^0, Y^0; X), Q^1]+\eta^1 \qquad (11.8)$$

If the individual consents to pay the price, it must be that paying an amount T, which is no more than his compensation amount, allows him to enjoy a higher level of environmental goods Q^1, i.e.

$$E^0-E^1 \geq T \qquad (11.9)$$

equivalently,

$$\Delta e(Y^0,Q^0,Q^1; X) + \Delta\eta \geq T \qquad (11.10)$$

where $\Delta e(Y^0,Q^0,Q^1;X)=e^0[U^0(Q^0,Y^0; X),Q^0]-e^1[U^0(Q^0,Y^0; X),Q^1]$ and $\Delta\eta=\eta^0-\eta^1$. $\Delta e(\cdot)$, the response function, is the expenditure difference (variation) function defined by Cameron (1988).

1.2 Duality of the Utility and Expenditure Functions

Different formulations and interpretations of the response function do not contradict each other. On the contrary, the distinction between the utility difference model and expenditure difference model disappears under certain conditions. One such condition occurs when no random component is appended to the response function. And the other occurs when the marginal utility of income is constant. A given level of utility U^0 can be reached while enjoying the level of environmental goods Q^0 and holding income level Y^0, or enjoying Q^1 and holding Y^1. That is,

$$U^0(Y^0, Q^0; X) = U^0(Y^1, Q^1; X) \qquad (11.11)$$

Without random components, a 'yes' response indicates one of the following two settings

$$U^1(Y^0-T, Q^1; X) \geq U^0(Y^0, Q^0; X) \qquad (11.12)$$

or

$$e^0[U^0(Q^0, Y^0; X),Q^0]-e^1[U^0(Q^0, Y^0; X),Q^1] \geq T \qquad (11.13)$$

Substituting (11.11) into (11.12), then

$$U^1(Y^0-T,\ Q^1;\ X) \geq U^0(Y^1,\ Q^1;\ X) \qquad (11.14)$$

The compensating amount can be calculated directly from the expenditure function in (11.13). If the utility function is nondecreasing in income and the marginal utility of income is nonnegative, then relationship (11.14) implies that

$$Y^0-Y^1 \geq T \qquad (11.15)$$

which is identical to (11.9).

On the other hand, duality between the utility and expenditure functions exists when the marginal utility of income is constant. That is,

$$V_Y + \varepsilon_Y = K \qquad (11.16)$$

where $V_Y=\partial V/\partial Y$, $\varepsilon_Y=\partial \varepsilon/\partial Y$, and K is a constant. Since the stochastic term ε does not include an argument of Y, the constant marginal utility of income implies that

$$U_Y = V_Y = K \qquad (11.17)$$

where $U_Y=\partial U/\partial Y$. (11.17) indicates that utility is a linear transformation of expenditure, i.e.,

$$U = KY + c \qquad (11.18)$$

By substituting (11.18) into (11.12), we obtain

$$K(Y^0-T) + c \geq KY^1 + c \qquad (11.19)$$

The relationship implied in this inequality is the same as (11.15).

Moreover, the constant marginal utility of income in (11.17) also implies

$$U_{YY} + U_{YQ} + U_{YX} = 0 \qquad (11.20)$$

where $U_{YY} = \partial^2 U/\partial Y^2$, $U_{YQ} = \partial^2 U/\partial Y \partial Q$, and $U_{YX} = \partial^2 U/\partial Y \partial X$. McConnell (1990, p.28) concludes that when all three conditions hold, i.e., the marginal utility of income is independent of income, $\partial^2 U/\partial Y^2=0$, constant across the level of environmental goods, $\partial^2 U/\partial Y \partial Q=0$, and constant across individuals, $\partial^2 U/\partial Y \partial X=0$, then the utility difference model and the expenditure difference model are linear transformations of one another. This is, however, the most restrictive case.

The duality between the utility and expenditure difference functions in fact exists as long as one of the three conditions holds and the sum of these three terms does not violate the relationship in (11.20). The condition in (11.20) allows the testable hypothesis to be constructed under a specific formulation of the utility function.

1.3 Inverse Hicksian Demand Function

The demand curve is useful for policy analysis with respect to the optimal provision of environmental goods. The recovery of the estimated quantity demand is possible under both types of formulation of the response function, though the derivation of this curve from the expenditure model is more straightforward than from the utility model.

In the case of a divisible environmental good, the amount of money that an individual is willing to pay for various levels of provision of that good, while remaining at the utility level U^0, is the difference between initial and alternative income levels. Figure 11.1 describes this trade-off between income and environmental goods. If the initial situation is Q^0 and Y^0, and if the provision of environmental goods increases to the level of Q^1, then the distance between B and D, which is equal to the distance between Y^0 and Y^1, is the individual's willingness to pay for Q^1. Similarly, EF is the amount of willingness to pay for a level of Q^2.

Taking A, from Figure 11.1, as the origin, *WTP* as the vertical axes and Q as the horizontal axes, the curve in Figure 11.2 is the individual bid curve or valuation function proposed by Bradford (1970). Points A, B, and D in Figure 11.1 correspond to the points $A(Q^0, Y^0)$, $B(Q^1, Y^0)$ and $D(Q^1, Y^1)$ in Figure 11.2.

The derivative of the bid function with respect to Q is the marginal bid curve. An aggregate bid curve can be obtained by vertical summation, in diagrammatic analysis, of the affected population's marginal bid curves. The derived aggregate bid curve can therefore be used for the purpose of determining the optimal provision of environmental goods. That is, if the aggregate marginal cost function is known, then the optimal level of environmental goods, Q^*, can be determined as shown in Figure 11.3.

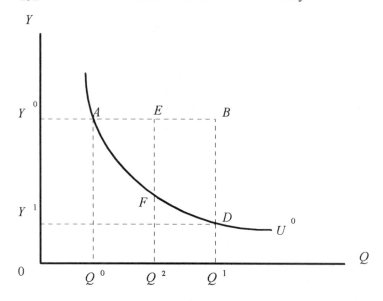

Figure 11.1 Indifference Curve of Income and Environmental Good

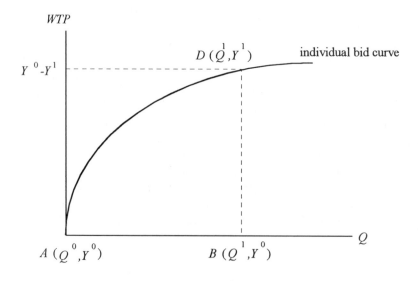

Figure 11.2 Individual Bid Curve

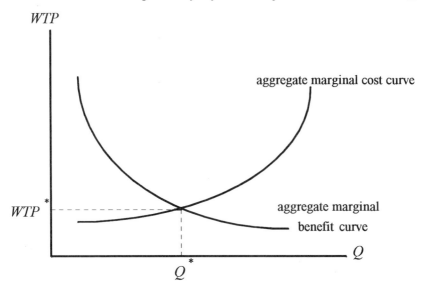

Figure 11.3. Optimal Level of Environmental Good Provision

2   MODEL   SPECIFICATION

2.1 The Utility Difference Model

Estimation of the response function requires functional forms specified both for the utility difference model and the expenditure difference model. The divergence of the specification for the utility difference, $V(Q^1, Y-T; X)-V(Q^0,Y; X)$, arises in research conducting contingent policy referendum experiments.   Bishop and Heberlein's (1979) first application of a dichotomous choice contingent valuation survey in valuing goose hunting permits is representative of one type of research which specifies the utility difference directly. Without knowing the underlying indirect utility function, flexible functional forms for the utility differences are allowable. Since then, many studies which employ the direct specification of utility difference in valuing various environmental goods and natural resources fall into this category, such as studies by Bowker and Stoll (1988), Park, Loomis and Creel (1991), and Sellar, Chavas and Stoll (1986), and Sellar, Stoll and Chavas (1985), to name a few. Four of the most commonly used functional forms for the utility differences, linear, linear-log, semilog, and double-log, will be estimated here and are listed below

$$\Delta V = \alpha + \beta Q + \gamma Y + \delta X \qquad (11.21)$$

$$\Delta V = \alpha + \beta \ln Q + \gamma \ln Y + \delta \ln X \qquad (11.22)$$

$$\ln \Delta V = \alpha + \beta Q + \gamma Y + \delta X \qquad (11.23)$$

$$\ln \Delta V = \alpha + \beta \ln Q + \gamma \ln Y + \delta \ln X \qquad (11.24)$$

Hanemann, however, criticizes this by saying that the direct specification of utility difference is not strictly compatible with utility theory. That is, no explicit utility model can be generated from ΔV. He argues that if the binary response model is to be interpreted as the outcome of a utility-maximizing choice, the condition that is the analogue of the integrability conditions in conventional demand theory is needed. This condition gives a criterion for determining whether a given statistical model is compatible with the utility maximization hypothesis. He has suggested two indirect utility functional forms for the baseline and proposed situations, then the utility differences are derived accordingly.

Two functional forms for the indirect utility functions are specified here. Linear functional forms for two choice alternatives are written explicitly as follows

$$V(Q^1, Y-T; X) = \alpha_1 + \beta_1 Q^1 + \gamma_1(Y-T) + \delta_1 X \qquad (11.25)$$

$$V(Q^0, Y; X) = \alpha_0 + \beta_0 Q^0 + \gamma_0 Y + \delta_0 X \qquad (11.26)$$

The other form is linear-logarithmic and expressed as

$$V(Q^1, Y-T; X) = \alpha_1 + \beta_1 \ln Q^1 + \gamma_1 \ln(Y-T) + \delta_1 \ln X \qquad (11.27)$$

$$V(Q^0, Y; X) = \alpha_0 + \beta_0 \ln Q^0 + \gamma_0 \ln Y + \delta_0 \ln X \qquad (11.28)$$

The correspondent utility difference function derived from specification (11.27) is expressed as

$$\Delta V = \alpha' + \beta' Q - \gamma' T \qquad (11.29)$$

and from specification (11.28) is approximated as

$$\Delta V \approx \alpha' + \beta' \ln(Q^1/Q^0) - \gamma'(T/Y) \qquad (11.30)$$

where Q in (11.29) is the difference between the proposed and baseline level of environmental quality. The specification in (11.29) and (11.30) can be explained in that the impacts of all sociodemographic variables, X, are restricted. Therefore these variables are excluded from the utility difference specifications. Under this category of response function specification, the six functional forms for comparison are (11.21), (11.22), (11.23), (11.24), (11.29), and (11.30).

2.2 The Expenditure Difference Model

The other category of response function is the specification for the expenditure difference. Similar to the functional forms used for the direct specification of utility difference, four functional forms for the expenditure difference model are listed below

$$\Delta e = \alpha + \beta Q + \gamma Y + \delta X \qquad (11.31)$$

$$\Delta e = \alpha + \beta \ln Q + \gamma \ln Y + \delta \ln X \qquad (11.32)$$

$$\ln \Delta e = \alpha + \beta Q + \gamma Y + \delta X \qquad (11.33)$$

$$\ln \Delta e = \alpha + \beta \ln Q + \gamma \ln Y + \delta \ln X \qquad (11.34)$$

3 WELFARE MEASURES OF DICHOTOMOUS CHOICE MODELS

3.1 Mean Welfare Measures

Based upon the estimation results, the welfare measure can be calculated for each specification described above. If the response function is interpreted as the utility difference, then the calculation of welfare measures is circuitous. The mean value of the welfare measure can be calculated as follows

$$E(WTP) = \int_0^\infty [1 - F(-\Delta V)] dT - \int_{-\infty}^0 F(-\Delta V) dT \qquad (11.35)$$

where $F(-\Delta V)$ is the cumulative density function for the stochastic component appended for the utility difference function ΔV. Assuming that the willingness to pay is nonnegative, then the mean willingness to pay is modified as

$$E(WTP) = \int_0^\infty [1 - F(-\Delta V)] dT \qquad (11.36)$$

In practice, a limited maximum offered-price T_{max} replaces the ∞. Boyle, Welsh, and Bishop (1988) have argued that the adjustment of the truncated cumulative density function is needed. The expected willingness to pay for the truncated distribution should be modified as

$$E(WTP) = \int_0^{T_{max}} [1 - F(-\Delta V)/k] dT \qquad (11.37)$$

where k is a normalized constant, which is the probabilities of willingness to pay falling in the range of $-\infty$ to the maximum truncated price T_{max}, and is calculated by substituting T_{max} for T in the utility difference function ΔV. If the error component follows a logistic distribution, then the normalized factor k is calculated as

$$k = \frac{1}{1 + \exp(\Delta V(T_{max}))} \qquad (11.38)$$

The expected willingness to pay under the logistic distribution assumption can therefore be calculated using the formula below

$$E(WTP) = T_{max} - \int_0^{T_{max}} \frac{1}{1 + \exp(\Delta V)} dT \qquad (11.39)$$

The mean willingness to pay for the expenditure difference specification can be calculated directly as an ordinary regression model. It is the expected value of estimated expenditure difference, denoted as $\Delta e^*(\cdot)$, from equations (11.31), (11.32), (11.33), and (11.34) and expressed as

$$E(WTP) = E(\Delta e^*(\cdot)) \qquad (11.40)$$

3.2 Confidence Interval of Mean Welfare Measures

Bockstael and Strand (1987) have emphasized that the parameter estimates used to calculate welfare measures are themselves random variables. The calculation of the confidence intervals for mean welfare measures will account for the variability associated with the estimated coefficients. Difference in welfare measures due to different functional specifications and different interpretations of response functions may not result consistently. Therefore, construction of confidence intervals for mean welfare measure is especially important for comparison across specifications.

The technique developed by Krinsky and Robb (1986) is one method of constructing confidence intervals for welfare measures. The approach involves repeatedly sampling from the estimated asymptotic bivariate normal distribution of the estimated parameters. Alternatively, a nonparametric approach proposed by Duffield and Patterson (1991), which involves no function form specification and does not rely on the asymptotic distribution of the parameter estimators, will be computed for the sample.

For the nonparametric approach, the $1-\alpha$ percent confidence interval for the truncated mean willingness to pay from the observed data is computed as follows

$$CI_{1-\alpha}[M(WTP)] = M(WTP) \pm t_{\alpha/2}[Var(M(WTP))]^{1/2} \qquad (11.41)$$

where:

$M(WTP) = \Sigma_{j=1}^{n} \Delta T_j P_j$

$Var(M(WTP)) = \Sigma_{j=1}^{n} (\Delta T_j)^2 P_j(1-P_j)/N_j$

T_j: offered-price level, $j=1,2,...,n$

N_j: total number of respondents' responses to offered-price level T_j

P_j: probability of willingness to pay for offered-price level T_j

$\Delta T_j = (T_{j+1}-T_{j-1})/2$, $\qquad j=2,3,...,n-1$

$\Delta T_1 = T_1 + (T_2-T_1)/2$

$\Delta T_n = (T_n-T_{n-1})/2 + (T_{max}-T_n)$

The comparison of confidence intervals can be made between this nonparametric approach and all other parametric estimations.

While the response function is specified as the expenditure difference, the derivation of confidence intervals for mean willingness to pay is analogous to the construction of confidence intervals for the generalized least square. The confidence interval of mean willingness to pay, according to the formula proposed by Cameron (1991), can be computed as follows

$$CI_{1-\alpha}[E(WTP)] = E(\Delta e^*) \pm t_{\alpha/2}(X\Sigma_{\theta} X')^{1/2} \qquad (11.42)$$

where

X: all the explanatory variables in the variation function

Σ_{θ}: variance-covariance matrix of all the estimated parameters θ.

3.3 Demand Functions for Environmental Goods

To find the marginal willingness to pay for the change of environmental goods is to derive the expression for $\partial E(WTP)/\partial Q$. The result is considered to be $P(Q)$. The presumed demand relationship, which is the Hicksian demand function, for environmental goods Q can be found by rearranging the terms. For the utility difference formulation of the response function, this derivative can be expressed as

$$\frac{\partial E(WTP)}{\partial Q} = \frac{-\partial}{\partial Q}\int_0^{T_{max}}\frac{1}{1+\exp(\Delta V)}dT \qquad (11.43)$$

ΔV comes from the specific forms in (11.21), (11.22), (11.23), (11.24), (11.29), or (11.30). For the expenditure difference specification, derivation of the demand function is straightforward. It is a direct derivative of the estimated expenditure difference function with respect to environmental goods Q, i.e. $\partial \Delta e(Y,Q;X)/\partial Q$. The functional form for Δe is a choice of (11.31), (11.32), (11.33), or (11.34).

The theoretical framework and model specifications will be applied to a case in which benefits of the improvement of water quality are concerned. Before the estimation results are presented and all the related empirical issues discussed, a brief description of the study area and the sample used for this research are presented.

4   APPLICATION TO WATER QUALITY IMPROVEMENT

4.1 The Study Area

Ping-tung County, with 7,883 hog farms, or 23.71% of the hog farms in the country and with 2,130,921 hogs, or 21.85% of the hog population of the country, is the number one hog production area in Taiwan (Chen, L.J., 1992). Tung-kang Creek and its tributaries, flowing through 14 districts in Ping-tung County, flow by 51.72% of the hog farms and 58.23% of the hog production in the area (Chen, L.J., 1992). Due to point and nonpoint source pollution along the creek, water quality in Tung-kang Creek has deteriorated in recent years (Chen, L.J., 1992; Wen, Kuo and Hsu, 1989). The pollutants include organic and inorganic chemicals from nearby industrial waste water, animal husbandry production and household sewage disposal. Of all sources of pollution, hog manure and waste water from animal production comprise the greatest volume.

One of the main uses of the water from Tung-kang Creek is as the source of running water for the city of Kaohsiung and Ping-tung County. In recognition of the importance of the safety of running water quality in these areas, improvement of the water quality in Tung-kang Creek, thus, is the primary concern of pollution control agents.

4.2 The Sample

Data for the empirical analysis came from a contingent policy referendum experiment. The part of the sample used here was selected from 10 districts of the city of Kaohsiung. A total of 540 households were selected in February of 1993 to represent running water users in the area. Fifty-four households were chosen from each district. Data were collected by personal interview.

Respondents in the sample were asked to value the improvement of water quality in Tung-kang Creek. The proposed improvement was made from a baseline quality level, indicated by a biochemical oxygen demand (BOD) level of 7 mg/l, to some alternative levels of 4 mg/l, 2 mg/l, or 1 mg/l. In order to make the different levels of BOD more clear and meaningful to the respondents, their corresponding water uses were translated. Biochemical oxygen demand at levels of 7 mg/l, 4 mg/l, 2 mg/l, and 1 mg/l were therefore described as the standards for irrigation, industrial, fish farming and swimming uses, respectively. The examples were given with the hope that respondents would link industrial water use to a better drinking water quality than irrigation use water, a fish farming quality directly to a much better drinking water quality than industrial use water, and a swimmable quality directly to the best drinking water quality.

Referendum vote questions were designed for survey respondents to answer 'yes' or 'no' to a pre-assigned fixed payment level for one of the improvements described above. The threshold payment levels were selected so as to reflect the general pattern of the responses from a pretest, in which valuations were found to be relatively concentrated. Choice of payment vehicle was made under the criterion of credibility and realism of the payment for the subject to value. Improvement of the source water quality should give respondents a strong hint that an increase in their tap water bill is to be expected. Because water bills are due every two months in the city, a bimonthly payment and a permanent increase in the utility bill for water are therefore used. The fixed bimonthly payments used in the questionnaire are NT$30, $50, $100, $150, $200, $300, $400, $500, $800, and $1,000.

The questionnaire also contained questions regarding respondents' attitudes toward environmental issues, and their usage of running water in their households. Respondents' income, education, and other sociodemographic characteristics were recorded for use in subsequent econometric analyses. Detailed description of the data collection can be found in the study by Chen *et al.* (1993).

5   RESULTS AND ANALYSIS

The independent variables selected to explain respondents' *WTP* and probability are listed in Table 11.1. The standard logit method is used to estimate the utility difference specifications, equations (11.21), (11.22), (11.29), and (11.30). The estimates are presented in Table 11.2. Because of the logarithm taken for the left-hand-side variable, the likelihood functions for equations (11.23) and (11.24) need to be specified and are expressed as follows

$$\ln L = \sum (1-I)\ln\{1/[1+\exp(\exp(\Delta V(Y,Q,T;X)))]\}$$

$$- I \ln\{1-1/[1+\exp(\exp(\Delta V(Y,Q,T;X)))]\} \qquad (11.44)$$

where I is a discrete indicator and is defined to be 1 if the respondent consents to pay the price T and to be 0 otherwise. Under the logistic distribution, the log-likelihood function for the expenditure difference specification is specified as

$$\ln L = \sum (1-I)\ln\{\exp[(T-\Delta e(Y,Q;X))/s]/[1+\exp(T$$

$$- \Delta e(Y,Q;X))/s]\} - I \ln\{1+\exp[(T-\Delta e(Y,Q;X))/s]\} \quad (11.45)$$

The presence of T, which is varied across individuals and is excluded from the explanatory variable, allows the coefficient parameters and s to be estimated separately.

The estimated coefficients from the expenditure difference specification can roughly be interpreted as these from the ordinary least squares regression. Depending upon the functional specification, the magnitudes of the estimated coefficients indicate the percentage change or unit change in willingness to pay for one unit change or one percent change of a particular explanatory variable. For the utility difference specification, on the other hand, the effect of change in one of the explanatory variables on the probability is the derivative of the likelihood function with respect to that variable.

The coefficient estimates are not consistent across specifications for both types of models. Except for the variables of offered-price, *Off*, or an offered-price related variable, $\ln(1-Off/Inc)$, and expense on distilled, bottled water, or clearance of water filter, all the other explanatory variables are not significant at the conventional 5% and 1% levels. The chi-square statistics reported in Table 11.2 show that the null hypothesis of all nonintercept parameters being zero is rejected for all specifications. The

Table 11.1   Independent Variables Used in Estimation and Their Mean
Values

Variable Name	Mean Value[a]	Description
Q	4.645	change of BOD from baseline to
	(1.240)	alternative level, used to represent
		the level of water quality
Inc	53445	household monthly income from
	(31529)	all sources
Gen	0.489	1 for male
	(0.500)	0 for female
Age	41.252	age of the respondent
	(11.093)	
Edu	10.910	years of education of the
	(3.246)	respondent
Off	359.610	preassigned price level in
	(314.390)	referendum question
H	5.059	household size
	(2.225)	
Wf	565.410	bimonthly utility expense in water
	(343.470)	
Wp	240.960	monthly expenditure on distilled,
	(322.770)	bottled water and/or clearance
		of water filter

Note
a. Numbers in parentheses are standard derivations of sample means.

scalar criteria measured in percentages of correct prediction of the specification indicate that all utility difference specifications and expenditure difference speci-fications are indifferent in terms of goodness-of-fit, except for one case.

Based on the coefficient estimates and the formula specified in (11.39), compensating welfare measures are calculated by numerically integrating the area under each estimated specification over the range of offered amounts between NT\$0 and \$1,000. All explanatory variables other than offered-price, *Off*, are set at their sample means. Table 11.3 is the summary of these results. Since the direct specification of the linear utility difference functional form, the category of utility difference (1), the indirect specification of the linear and linear-log utility functions, and the category of utility difference (5) and (6), are all similar in form, the mean *WTP*s are

Table 11.2   Parameter Estimates[a] for Utility Difference and Expenditure Difference Response Function

Variable	Utility Difference[b]						Expenditure Difference[c]			
	(1)	(2)	(3)	(4)	(5)	(6)	(1)	(2)	(3)	(4)
Intercept	1.80 (2.05)*	10.12 (2.29)*	2.08 (2.13)*	8.93 (1.78)	2.41 (5.23)**	1.74 (6.29)**	466.08 (1.98)*	1144.50 (1.09)	6.25 (16.86)**	7.38 (4.21)**
Q	0.02 (0.02)		-0.06 (-0.66)		-0.002 (-0.03)		5.35 (0.22)		0.01 (0.31)	
$\ln Q$		0.22 (0.44)		-0.41 (-0.65)				53.59 (0.42)		0.12 (0.57)
$\ln(Q^1/Q^0)$						0.12 (0.64)				
Off	-0.01 (-10.25)**		-0.01 (-4.66)**		-0.004 (-10.24)**					
$\ln Off$		-1.48 (-7.70)**		-1.17 (-5.39)**						
Inc	5.01×10^{-8} (0.01)		-1.39×10^{-6} (-0.38)				1.26×10^{-5} (0.01)		-2.70×10^{-9} (-0.002)	
$\ln Inc$		-0.04 (-0.12)		-0.08 (-0.19)				-38.04 (-0.49)		-0.06 (-0.43)
Off/Inc						-110.83 (-8.36)**				
Gen	0.05 (0.19)	0.10 (0.33)	0.56 (1.79)	0.52 (1.03)			11.71 (0.19)	24.12 (0.31)	0.03 (0.29)	0.02 (0.17)
Age	0.001 (0.05)		-5.91×10^{-3} (-0.58)				0.14 (0.05)		-1.31×10^{-4} (-0.03)	

Table 11.2, continued

Variable	Utility Difference[b]						Expenditure Difference[c]			
	(1)	(2)	(3)	(4)	(5)	(6)	(1)	(2)	(3)	(4)
lnAge		-0.66 (-1.11)		-0.43 (-0.60)				-190.73 (-1.18)		-0.34 (-1.28)
Edu	2.35×10^{-4} (0.09)		0.004 (0.08)				0.06 (0.01)		-0.001 (-0.09)	
lnEdu		-0.64 (-1.20)		-0.57 (-0.77)				-191.44 (-1.24)		-0.37 (-1.42)
H	0.03 (0.45)		0.03 (0.40)				6.50 (0.48)		0.004 (0.21)	
lnH		0.01 (0.02)		0.41 (0.73)				-7.59 (-0.08)		4.35×10^{-4} (0.003)
Wf	0.001 (1.28)		-4.26×10^{-4} (-1.00)				0.13 (1.34)		1.96×10^{-4} (1.38)	
lnWf		0.07 (0.25)		-0.42 (-1.02)				50.32 (0.66)		0.07 (0.57)
Wp	3.82×10^{-4} (1.01)		5.52×10^{-4} (1.24)				0.10 (1.27)		9.80×10^{-5} (1.02)	
lnWp		0.45 (2.30)*		0.55 (2.04)*				112.14 (2.27)*		0.20 (2.32)*
k							259.05 (10.42)**	260.60 (8.68)**	261.10 (10.37)**	260.59 (8.76)**
Model χ^2(df)	139(9)	107(9)	3027(9)	1079(9)	135(2)	97(2)	237(9)	1092(9)	269(9)	422(9)
Correct prediction (%)	77	79	75	74	77	76	66	77	77	77

243

Table 11.2, continued

Variable	Utility Difference[b]						Expenditure Difference[c]			
	(1)	(2)	(3)	(4)	(5)	(6)	(1)	(2)	(3)	(4)
Log-likelihood	-249.38	-154.52	-246.57	-168.38	-251.44	-270.72	-249.38	-158.61	-249.68	-154.42
N	524	326	524	326	524	524	524	326	524	326

Notes

a. Numbers in parentheses are asymptotic t values of each parameter estimate. A single asterisk indicates significant at 5% level; double asterisk indicates significant at 1% levels.

b. Functional form specifications for the utility difference model are

(1) $V = \alpha + \beta Q + \gamma Inc + \delta X$

(2) $V = \alpha + \beta InQ + \gamma InInc + \delta InX$

(3) $lnV = \alpha + \beta Q + \gamma Inc + \delta X$

(4) $lnV = \alpha + \beta lnQ + \gamma lnInc + \delta lnX$

(5) $V = \alpha' + \beta' Q - \gamma' Off$

(6) $V = \alpha' + \beta' ln(Q'/Q^o) - \gamma'(Off/Inc)$

X includes variables *Gen, Age, Edu, H, Wf, Off,* and *Wp.*

c. Functional form specifications for the expenditure difference model are

(1) $e = \alpha + \beta Q + \gamma Inc + \delta X$

(2) $e = \alpha + \beta lnQ + \gamma lnInc + \delta lnX$

(3) $lne = \alpha + \beta Q + \gamma Inc + \delta X$

(4) $lne = \alpha + \beta lnQ + \gamma lnInc + \delta lnX$

X includes variables *Gen, Age, Edu, H, Wf,* and *Wp.*

244

indifferent. The mean welfare measure from the linear-log utility difference specification is the one which is close to that computed from the nonparametric model. For the expenditure difference model, mean *WTP* is taken directly from the estimated *WTP* equations specified in (11.31), (11.32),(11.33) and (11.34). The results do not reveal significant differences in any specification except for the double-log form.

For utility difference models, to calculate confidence intervals of mean willingness to pay, the Krinsky and Robb (1986) simulation technique is implemented. According to their experiments, 1000 drawings lead to a reasonably good estimate. Therefore, 1000 random drawings are made here from a multivariate normal distribution with means and variance – covariance of estimated parameters.

For each drawing, a new set of estimated parameters is created. The mean *WTP* for each utility difference functional specification is calculated accordingly. For each functional form, we sorted the 1000 mean *WTP*s by size and found the 2.5% tails of the distribution. The upper bound and lower bound of mean willingness to pay are therefore determined. The bounds of mean willingness to pay for specifications (2), (3), and (4) of the utility difference model are not computable due to the nonexistence of the closed form of integration for simulation.

The confidence intervals of mean willingness to pay for the expenditure difference specifications are computed using the formula defined in (11.42) directly. The results of mean welfare measures and 95% confidence intervals of mean welfare measures from all specifications for both types of models are presented in Table 11.3. The confidence intervals vary across specifications. However, all parametric specifications and the non-parametric model, except for specification (6) of the utility difference model, overlap in the range between \$583.22 and \$602.47.

According to the estimated coefficients, (inverse) Hicksian demand functions for expenditure difference specifications are derived directly as follows:

linear

$$\frac{\partial E(WTP)}{\partial Q} = P_l(Q) = 5.356 \qquad (11.46)$$

linear-log

$$\frac{\partial E(WTP)}{\partial Q} = P_{il}(Q) = \frac{53.592}{Q} \qquad (11.47)$$

Table 11.3 Mean and 95% Confidence Intervals on Willingness to Pay[a]

Model Specification	Mean *WTP*	Upper Bound of Mean *WTP*	Lower Bound of Mean *WTP*
Utility Difference[b]			
(1)	599.52	643.12	555.33
(2)	561.65	N/A[d]	N/A
(3)	640.56	N/A	N/A
(4)	N/A	N/A	N/A
(5)	598.64	647.02	553.89
(6)	686.86	727.28	644.33
Expenditure Difference[c]			
(1)	634.64	729.12	540.15
(2)	614.89	722.90	506.88
(3)	632.64	682.05	583.22
(4)	511.44	602.47	434.16
Nonparametric Model	563.55	610.39	516.72

Notes
a.   The willingness to pay is a bimonthly payment per household.
b,c. Definitions of functional forms are the same as those in Table 11.2.
d.   Due to lack of a closed form of integration, the mean willingness to pay is not computable for specification (4). The incompatibility of bounds of mean willingness to pay for specifications (2), (3), and (4) results from the nonexistence of a limited formula for simulation.

semi-log

$$\frac{\partial E(WTP)}{\partial Q} = P_{sl}(Q) = 7.153\exp(0.012Q) \qquad (11.48)$$

double-log

$$\frac{\partial E(WTP)}{\partial Q} = P_{dl}(Q) = \frac{61.994\exp(0.123\ln Q)}{Q} \qquad (11.49)$$

Figure 11.4 shows the marginal willingness to pay for different water quality levels measured in terms of the abatement of biochemical oxygen demand for the specifications stated above. The numbers denoted as (1), (2), (3), and (4) correspond to the linear, linear-log, semi-log, and double-log expenditure difference specifications respectively. For all the estimated willingness to pay functions but the linear case, the estimated Hicksian demand functions reveal negative slopes. The higher the water quality is, the less difference in marginal willingness to pay is derived from different specifications of the expenditure difference model.

The Hicksian demand function for utility difference specifications is derived by taking the derivative with respect to the water quality variable, Q, from the expected willingness to pay equation, i.e. (11.43). The estimated (inverse) Hicksian demand functions are expressed as follows:

linear utility difference

$$\frac{\partial E(WTP)}{\partial Q} = P_l(Q)$$

$$= \frac{5.25}{1+\exp(-2.65-0.02Q)} - \frac{5.25}{1+\exp(1.35-0.02Q)} \tag{11.50}$$

semi-log utility difference

$$\frac{\partial E(WTP)}{\partial Q} = P_{ls}(Q)$$

$$\tag{11.51}$$

$$= \frac{7.86}{1+\exp(-\exp(-4.9-0.06Q))} - \frac{7.86}{1+\exp(-\exp(2.1-0.06Q))}$$

linear utility function

$$\frac{\partial E(WTP)}{\partial Q} = P_{lu}(Q)$$

$$= \frac{-0.59}{1+\exp(-2.41+0.002Q)} + \frac{0.59}{1+\exp(1.34+0.002Q)} \tag{11.52}$$

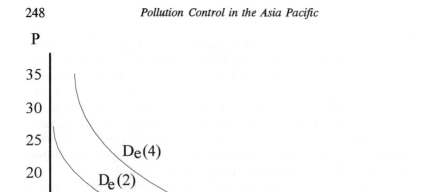

Figure 11.4 Hicksian Demand Curve for Water Quality Derived from Expenditure Difference Specification

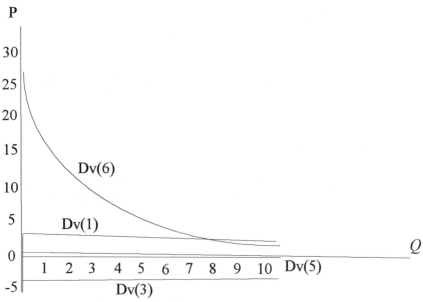

Figure 11.5 Hicksian Demand Curve for Water Quality Derived from Utility Difference Specification

linear-log utility function

$$\frac{\partial E(WTP)}{\partial Q} = P_{lg}(Q)$$

$$= \frac{59.31}{(1+\exp(-1.74-0.12\ln Q))Q} + \frac{59.31}{(1+\exp(0.33-0.12\ln Q))Q} \qquad (11.53)$$

Relatively complicated demand functional forms are derived from the utility difference model. For all three computable closed forms, the Hicksian demand functions are close to horizonal lines. Figure 11.5 is the presentation of these estimated Hicksian demand functions.

6   CONCLUDING   REMARKS

A comparison has been presented of Hanemann's utility difference and Cameron's expenditure difference models under various functional specifications for analyzing a set of contingent policy referendum data. The comparison is made specifically for the computation of mean willingness to pay and confidence intervals of mean willingness to pay and the derivation of the Hicksian demand function for each specification.

The results indicate that all the sociodemographic variables other than variable *Wp*, the amount spent on distilled, or bottled water or clearance of a water filter, are insignificant at the conventional 5% and 1% levels. An individual's different characteristics do not reflect a difference in *WTP*s for the case at hand.

The significance of the *Wp* variable could explain the insignificance of the income variable, a variable generally considered to be one of the most important variables affecting willingness to pay. Under a two-stage budgeting process, given a reasonable allocation of income, respondents are rational in a sense to compare their actual expenditure on bottled water and the price offered in the questionnaire. While evaluating the improved water quality, willingness to pay for the good to be valued will therefore be affected by a more directly related variable, *Wp*. The importance of income on willingness to pay for water quality improvement could thus be reduced.

Consistent with the findings from other studies, the mean welfare measures are different across models. However, the confidence intervals for all computable specifications and the nonparametric model, except for one case, overlap in the range of $583.22 to $602.47. The mean willingness to pay from the double-log expenditure difference specification, $511.44, is close to the average bimonthly expenditure on distilled, bottled water and/or clearance of a water filter, $481.92, which is consistent with the result implied in the significance of that variable.

A Hicksian demand function can easily be derived from the expenditure difference model for all four specifications estimated in the study. The estimated demand functions have shown that the higher the water quality is, the less difference there is in marginal willingness to pay for each functional specification. All but the linear case have revealed negative slopes of marginal benefit for water quality. Due to the lack of a limited form of integration for simulation, the derivation of the Hicksian demand function is not applicable in three out of six utility difference specifications.

Derivation of Hicksian demand functions of environmental goods in general, and for water quality in particular, is one of the purposes of this study. A continuous and measurable index of water quality is necessary for this purpose. Since a comprehensive indicator of water quality is not available, among the indicators of water quality, BOD, considered to be highly related to the pollution caused by manure and waste water of pig farms, is therefore used.

The results have shown that the water quality variable, Q, is insignificant in all cases. This may indicate that the description of each BOD level and its related water use does not convey the necessary message that the researchers optimistically aspired to convey in the questionnaire design. This could also imply that people do not in fact respond to the level of improvement. The derivation of the Hicksian demand function through the derivative taken for a continuous variable, Q, may not be adequate for this case. Nevertheless, the process demonstrated in this study illustrates that if there are Hicksian demand functions for some environmental goods then alternative ways of deriving these functions exist.

In summary, choice of models and functional specifications should consider not only the theoretical plausibility but also the empirical applicability and convenience. The specification of response function as expenditure difference and utility difference, though, results in similar outcomes in mean and confidence intervals of welfare measures. Nevertheless, for all functional forms specified in this research, interpretation of response function as expenditure difference results in a better performance in model estimation, mean welfare measure calculation, confidence intervals computation, and Hicksian demand function derivation.

REFERENCES

Bishop, R.C. and T.A. Heberlein (1979), 'Measuring Values of Extramarket Goods: Are Indirect Measures Biased?', *American Journal of Agricultural*

Economics, **61**(5), 926–30.

Bockstael, N.E. and I.E. Strand, Jr. (1987), 'The Effects of Common Sources of Regression Error on Benefit Estimates', *Land Economics*, **63**(1), 11–20.

Bowker, J.M. and J.R. Stoll (1988), 'Use of Dichotomous Choice Non-market Methods to Value the Whooping Crane Resource', *American Journal of Agricultural Economics*, **70**(2), 372–81.

Boyle, K.J., M.P. Welsh and R.C. Bishop (1988), 'Validation of Empirical Measures of Welfare Change: Comment', *Land Economics*, **64**(1), 94–8.

Bradford, D.F. (1970), 'Benefit-Cost Analysis and Demand Curves for Public Goods', *Kyklos*, **23**, 775–90.

Cameron, T.A. (1991), 'Interval Estimates of Nonmarket Resource Values from Referendum Contingent Valuation Surveys', *Land Economics*, **67**(4), 413–32.

Cameron, T.A. (1988), 'A New Paradigm for Valuing Nonmarket Goods Using Referendum Data: Maximum Likelihood Estimation by Censored Logistic Regression', *Journal of Environmental Economics and Management*, **15**(3), 355–79.

Cameron, T.D. and M.D. James (1987a), 'Estimating Willingness-to-pay from Survey Data: An Alternative Pre-test Market Evaluation Procedure', *Journal of Marketing Research*, **24**, 389–95.

Cameron, T.D. and M.D. James (1987b), 'Efficient Estimation Methods for Use with 'Closed-Ended' Contingent Valuation Survey Data', *Review of Economics and Statistics*, **69**(2), 269–76.

Chen, L.J. (1992), *A Report of Running Water and Pig Production Problems in Kaohsiung and Ping-tung Areas*, (in Chinese), Department of Agriculture and Forestry, Taiwan Provincial Government.

Chen, M.C., P.-I. Wu, H.-W. Tsai, I.-C. Chen and Y.-C. Chen, (1993), *Analysis of Social Costs of Pig Industry in Taiwan (2)*, (in Chinese), Report of the Environmental Protection Agency, EPA-82-E3E1-09-02, Department of Agricultural Economics, National Taiwan University.

Duffield, J.W. and D.A. Patterson (1991), 'Inference and Optimal Design for a Welfare Measure in Dichotomous Choice Contingent Valuation', *Land Economics*, **67**(2), 225–39.

Hanemann, W.M. (1984), 'Welfare Evaluations of Contingent Valuation Experiments with Discrete Responses', *American Journal of Agricultural Economics*, **74**(3), 332–41.

Hoehn, J.P. and A. Randall (1987), 'A Satisfactory Benefit Cost Indicator from Contingent Valuation', *Journal of Environmental Economics and Management*, **14**(3), 226–47.

Krinsky, I. and A.L. Robb (1986), 'On Approximating the Statistical Properties of Elasticities', *Review of Economics and Statistics*, **68**(4),

715–9.

Loehman, E. and V.H. De (1982), 'Application of Stochastic Choice Modeling to Policy Analysis of Public Goods: A Case Study of Air Quality Improvements', *Review of Economics and Statistics*, **64**(3), 474–80.

McConnell, K.E. (1990), 'Models for Referendum Data: The Structure of Discrete Choice Models for Contingent Valuation', *Journal of Environmental Economics and Management*, **18**(1), 19–34.

Park, T. and J. Loomis (1992), 'Comparing Models for Contingent Valuation Surveys: Statistical Efficiency and the Precision of Benefit Estimates', *Northeastern Journal of Agricultural and Resources Economics*, **21**(2), 170–6.

Park, T., J.B. Loomis and M. Creel (1991), 'Confidence Intervals for Evaluating Benefits Estimates from Dichotomous Choice Contingent Valuation Studies', *Land Economics*, **67**(1), 64–73.

Sellar, C., J.-P. Chavas and J.R. Stoll (1986), 'Specification of the Logit Model: The Case of Valuation of Nonmarket Goods', *Journal of Environmental Economics and Management*, **13**(4), 382–90.

Sellar, C., J.R. Stoll and J.-P. Chavas (1985), 'Validation of Empirical Measures of Welfare Change: A Comparison of Nonmarket Techniques', *Land Economics*, **61**(2), 156–75.

Wen, C.-K., C.-T. Kuo and H.-K. Hsu (1989), *Report of Comprehensive Planning of Water Pollution Prevention of Tung-kang Watershed*, (in Chinese), Report of Bureau of Environmental Protection, Taiwan Provincial Government, No. 88, Graduate Institute of Environmental Engineering, National Cheng Kung University.

12. Hierarchical Government, Environmental Regulations, Transfer Payments and Incomplete Enforcement

Chung-Huang Huang

1 INTRODUCTION

Issues of environmental regulations under incomplete enforcement have been discussed extensively in recent literature. Although not formally defined in the literature, incomplete enforcement may result from a firm's evasive behaviors (e.g., concealment and bribery), government hierarchy, high enforcement costs, uncertainty (or asymmetric information), penalty structures, etc.

Government hierarchy is an important factor in efficiency distortion that has received much attention in recent literature (Shavell, 1980; Demski and Sappington, 1987; Jones and Scotchmer, 1990; Spiller, 1990). Economists agree that every party under the present hierarchical system behaves in its own self-interest. As a result, the objective functions of the legislator and the regulator may be different to some extent. The transfer payment from the legislator to the regulator (hereafter referred to as the budget for pollution control) is considered a useful incentive mechanism by which the legislator can influence the regulator to correct inefficiencies or misallocations due to incomplete enforcement (Shavell, 1980; Demski and Sappington, 1987; Jones and Scotchmer, 1990; Spiller, 1990). It is also typically assumed that the budget for pollution control is exogenous to the regulator. However, in many cases, the optimal budget is likely to depend on the regulator's performance, and is not completely beyond the control of the regulator. Under this circumstance, the following questions are very important for optimizing budget allocations and improving environmental regulations: (1) How is the optimal budget for pollution control determined in a hierarchical political economy? (2) How is it possible that the standard enforced by the regulator diverges from the standard desired by the legislator? (3) Why is the regulator often unsatisfied with the budget from the legislator? Is a larger allocation to the regulator justifiable under this circumstance?

Firms' emissions violations and concealment are important factors that should be taken into account when modeling environmental regulations. Ignoring them may cause inefficiency and failure to meet the designated objectives of a particular environmental regulation (Downing and Watson, 1974; Harford, 1978; Viscusi and Zeckhauser, 1979; Linder and McBride, 1984; Kambhu, 1989). A firm's efforts to influence the regulator through various strategic behaviors such as lobbying and bribing are also important factors in modeling regulation enforcement. If bribery exists, the regulator's decision will be affected not only by the legislator, but also by the firm. Under this circumstance, it will be useful to know how the regulator's enforcement efforts may be affected by transfer payments from the firm to the regulator (hereafter referred to as bribes), and how a mutually acceptable bribe is determined between the firm and the regulator.

To consider such complex relationships between the regulator, the firm, and the legislator in a hierarchical system with incomplete enforcement, a multiple-principals agent approach is more appropriate than the conventional single-principal agent model (e.g., Shavell, 1980; Jones and Scotchmer, 1990; Malik, 1993). In this approach, both the firm and the legislator are considered principals of the regulator, who is considered an agent.

Furthermore, as noted by Roberts and Spence (1976), a mixed environmental policy can be an effective measure for mitigating the inefficiency of regulations under uncertainty. Both regulatory standards and emission charges have been jointly applied in many countries for years. A model with such mixed instruments will be more practical than one that deals with only one particular policy instrument. For this reason, this study incorporates both emission standards and emission taxes in the model to better reflect reality. The results will be compared to those derived from the studies on individual policy instruments (e.g., Harford, 1978; Jones, 1989; Linder and McBride, 1984; Shaffer, 1990).

As far as the firm's strategic response to pollution regulation is concerned, bribery is the main focus here. The reasons are threefold: (1) some firms benefit from bribery by receiving more lenient monitoring, (2) bribery is not unusual in many countries (developing countries in particular), and (3) the existence of bribes may be interpreted as an indication of incomplete markets or as a sort of market failure.

In this paper, the probability structure under incomplete enforcement is analyzed in Section 2. A multiple-principals agent model is developed in Section 3 to analyze behaviors of the regulator, the firm, and the legislator. The supply and demand response functions of transfer payments from the firm and the legislator to the regulator are derived in Section 4, where the determination of equilibrium payments and implications are also discussed. Section 5 concludes this paper.

2 PROBABILITY STRUCTURE UNDER INCOMPLETE ENFORCEMENT

2.1 Outcomes of Regulation Enforcement

Consider the following regulation setting: the firm is faced with emission standards set by the legislator and is required to report the volume of its own emissions, based on which emission charges are collected. The regulator attempts to determine whether or not the firm is in compliance. The firm will be prosecuted and fined if it is judged to be not in compliance.

The following notations are defined for expositional convenience:

V = the state when the firm is truly in violation;
NV = the state when the firm is not truly in violation;
D = the state when the regulator has determined that the firm is in violation;
ND = the state when the regulator has made 'no determination' of a violation;

In this situation, there are four possible outcomes, as defined by Linder and McBride (1984): $\alpha_1 = \Pr(V|D) =$ probability of discovering the violation, $\alpha_2 = \Pr(NV|D) =$ probability of a false alarm, $\alpha_3 = \Pr(V|ND) =$ probability of missing the violation, and $\alpha_4 = \Pr(NV|ND) =$ probability of a correct rejection (compliance is recognized). Suppose that the probabilities of compliance and noncompliance are, respectively, n and $1-n$. Let m denote the regulator's enforcement effort. It is then plausible to assume $\alpha_1 = \alpha_1(1-n, m)$ and $\alpha_4 = \alpha_4(n, m)$ such that:

(1) $\partial \alpha_i / \partial m > 0$ $(i=1,4)$, because the probability of a correct regulatory determination increases with enforcement efforts; and
(2) $\partial \alpha_1 / \partial(1-n) > 0$, and $\partial \alpha_4 / \partial n > 0$, because the probability of a correct determination of either type increases with the probability that the firm's status is, in fact, of that type.

Thus, the enforcement quality of the regulator may be defined as follows.

Definition. The enforcement quality of the regulator, denoted by α, is the

Probability

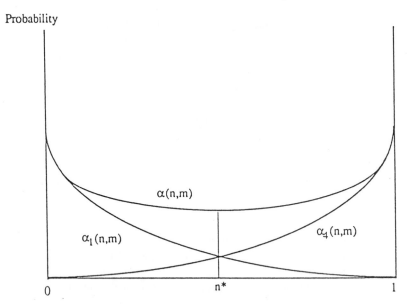

Figure 12.1   Enforcement Quality Function

probability that the regulator makes a correct regulatory determination with respect to the firm's compliance with environmental regulations, i.e., $\alpha(n, m) = \alpha_1 + \alpha_4$.

Note that $\partial\alpha/\partial m > 0$ and $\text{sign}(\partial\alpha/\partial n) = \text{sign}\{(\partial\alpha_4/\partial n) - (\partial\alpha_1/\partial(1-n))\}$. [1] Given an enforcement level, one example of the enforcement quality function $\alpha(n, m)$ is illustrated in Figure 12.1.

2.2 Outcomes of Pollution Abatement

The firm's compliance with the regulations depends not only on deterministic variables (e.g., output), but also on stochastic factors involved in pollution control, such as accidents, management capability, and the quality of treatment facilities. Under this consideration, the firm's abatement technology is assumed to be characterized by the following stochastic abatement frontier:

$$a = f(I) + u - v, \tag{12.1}$$

where a = volume of pollutants removed, I = vector of abatement inputs, $f(I)$ = deterministic effect of emission control, $u \approx N(0, \sigma_u^2)$, is a normally distributed random error, and v is assumed, as usual, to exhibit non-negative truncation of the $N(0, \sigma_v^2)$ distribution (e.g., half-normal distribution).

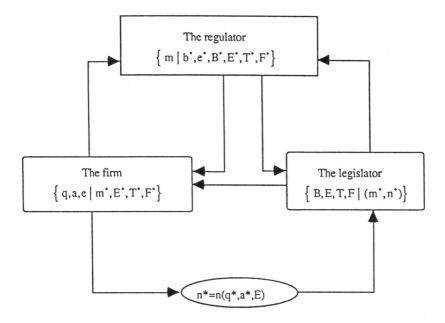

Figure 12.2   Flow chart of the Multiple-Principals Agent Model

Given the stochastic abatement frontier in (12.1), the probability of an emission violation $(1-n)$ is endogenized by its definition:

$$1-n = Pr[g(q) - a > E] = Pr[u - v < g(q) - k - E] \qquad (12.2)$$

where $g(q)$ is the pollution-generating function such that $g'=\partial g(q)/\partial q>0$, $g''=0, q=$output, $k=f(I)$, and $E=$the emission standard set by the legislator.

By the nature of the distribution function, it is straightforward to show that n, a function of $q, k,$ and E, exhibits the following properties:

(1) $\partial n/\partial q<0$ – probability of emission compliance decreases as the firm's output level increases;
(2) $\partial n/\partial k>0$ – probability of emission compliance increases with the firm's abatement level; and
(3) $\partial n/\partial E>0$ – probability of emission compliance decreases as the emission standard becomes stricter.

Now it becomes clear that enforcement quality is an endogenous variable, depending not only on the regulator's enforcement effort, but also on the firm and the legislator's decision variables.

3   THE MODEL

The modeling process is represented by Figure 12.2. The regulator is treated as an agent, because he is supervised by the legislator and influenced by the firms through bribery and through pressure on local politicians. Although the firm acts as one of the principals of the regulator, its behavior is also influenced by the legislator's policies. Such a relationship distinguishes the model from conventional multi-tier hierarchical frameworks (e.g., Bernheim and Whinston, 1986).

3.1 The Regulator

The objective function of the regulator can be formulated in various ways, e.g., maximizing net benefit or welfare (Linder and McBride, 1984; Lee, 1984; Jones and Scotchmer, 1990), maximizing utility (Shavell, 1980; Spiller, 1990), minimizing regulatory or social cost (Harford, 1991; Malik, 1993), maximizing compliance rate, maximizing enforcement effort, etc. While an objective formulation may have its own merits and demerits, it has, to a great extent, something to do with the environmental settings under discussion. Since the hierarchical system and the firm's bribery are considered here, the regulator's behavior is specified under the premise of self-interest, and he is assumed to seek the maximum net benefit by enforcing the regulations set by the legislator.

As an agent, the regulator is offered different schemes of transfer payments by two principals, the legislator and the firm. It is assumed that the budget $(B(\alpha))$ is strictly concave in α and that the bribe $(b(1-\alpha))$ is increasing with $1-\alpha$ at a constant rate.[2] Assume that the regulator is entitled to the penalties paid by the firm only when the firm's violation is discovered. The regulator is thus assumed to solve the following maximization problem by choosing an optimal level of enforcement effort:

$$MAX_{\{m\}}\ V = B(\alpha(m,1-n))+b(1-\alpha(m,1-n))-M(m)+T\cdot\hat{e}$$

$$+ \ \alpha_1(m,1-n)\cdot\{T\cdot(\bar{e}-\hat{e})+F_1\cdot(\bar{e}-E)+F_2\cdot(\bar{e}-\hat{e})\}$$

$$S.T.\ n = n(q,\ k,\ E) \tag{12.3}$$

where $M=$ enforcement cost (convex in m), $T=$ emission fees per unit of discharge, $\bar{e}=g(q)-k =$ expected emissions, $\hat{e}=$ emissions reported by the firm, and $F_i =$ unit penalty for i-th violation ($i=1$ represents emission violation and $i=2$ represents emission concealment).

It is worthwhile to point out that the regulator's objective function is based on the following considerations: (1) The regulator is assumed to retain all the revenues (the sum of budget, bribery, and fines) for his own pocket, since current environmental statutes prevent fines from being transferred to the legislator for general purposes. (2) Once the firm is found to be in violation, it will be charged a penalty proportional to the size of the violation (i.e., $F_1 \cdot (\bar{e} - E)$ for emission violation and $F_2 \cdot (\bar{e} - \hat{e})$ for emission concealment).[3] Meanwhile, the firm has to pay the evaded tax (equal to $T \cdot (\bar{e} - \hat{e})$. (3) The probability of discovering an emission violation is assumed to be equal to the probability of discovering emission concealment, because the regulator can determine whether the firm violates standards and underreports emissions as long as the true emission levels are uncovered. (4) Penalties for different types of violations are not necessarily identical. (5) There is no reward for firms whose abatement efforts are better than what is mandated. Therefore, individual rationality implies that $\bar{e} > E$ and $\bar{e} > \hat{e}$. (6) Because of the probability structure of α, the costs resulting from committing errors such as a false alarm and miss are incurred by the regulator and implicitly captured in the budget function $B(\alpha(m, 1-n))$ and bribe function $b(1-\alpha(m, 1-n))$.

The first-order necessary condition for the interior solution to the maximization problem is expressed as follows:

$$MBE + (MPE - MTE) = MCE \qquad (12.4)$$

where $MBE = B' \cdot (\partial \alpha / \partial m) > 0$, representing the incremental increase in the budget due to a marginal increase in enforcement effort; $MPE = R \cdot (\partial \alpha_1 / \partial m) > 0$, representing the incremental increase in penalty revenues due to a marginal increase in enforcement effort (hereafter referred to as the marginal penalty revenue of enforcement); $R = T \cdot (\bar{e} - \hat{e}) + F_1 \cdot (\bar{e} - E) + F_2 \cdot (\bar{e} - \hat{e}) > 0$; $MCE = \partial M / \partial m > 0$, representing marginal enforcement cost; and $MTE = b' \cdot (\partial \alpha / \partial m) > 0$, representing the decrease in bribes due to a marginal increase in enforcement effort (hereafter referred to as the marginal bribery loss of enforcement).

Note that the sign of $(MPE - MTE)$ can be positive, zero, or negative. The regulator's equilibrium effort in the case of $MPE - MTE > 0$ is represented by m^* in Figure 12.3.[4] It can be shown that the regulator's effort function $m^* = m^*(T, F_1, F_2, q, k, \hat{e}, E)$ is characterized by the following properties: Equilibrium effort will increase with emission tax rate, penalty rates for emission violation and concealment, and the firm's output level (i.e., $dm^*/dT > 0$, $dm^*/dF_1 > 0$, $dm^*/dF_2 > 0$, and $dm^*/dq > 0$), while it will decrease with the firm's abatement level, reported emissions k, and emission standard (i.e., $dm^*/dk < 0$, $dm^*/d\hat{e} < 0$ and $dm^*/dE < 0$).

(12.4) leads to the following conclusions:

(1) In a 'corrupt' society where $MTE > 0$, the regulator's enforcement effort in equilibrium will be less than in the case where the bribe is a lump sum payment or where bribery is not allowed (i.e., m' in Figure 12.3). In other words, $m^* = m'$ only if $MTE = 0$. This result explains why bribery exists in some developing countries, although it is prohibited by law.

(2) Whether m^* will be greater or smaller than the optimal effort under complete enforcement (i.e., m'' in Figure 12.3, characterized by $MBE = MCE$) depends on the difference between MTE and MPE. If and only if $MPE \geq MTE$, then $m^* \geq m''$ (as shown in Figure 12.3). The implications are twofold: (a) In a 'too corrupt' society where $MPE - MTE < 0$, the optimal enforcement effort under incomplete enforcement will be less than that under complete enforcement. (b) If greater enforcement effort than m'' is more desirable under incomplete enforcement, then the difference between MPE and MTE should be made as large as possible. This can be done according to the following principles:

(1) if $R = b'$, try to reduce b' and the marginal effects of enforcement effort on correct rejection (i.e., $\partial \alpha_4 / \partial m$);

(2) if $R > b'$, in addition to principle (1), one can also try to increase R and the marginal effects of enforcement effort on the probability of discovering violation (i.e., $\partial \alpha_1 / \partial m$); and

(3) if $R < b'$, in addition to principle (1), one can also try to decrease R and the marginal effects of enforcement effort on the probability of discovering violations (i.e., $\partial \alpha_1 / \partial m$).

3.2 The Firm

While engaging in two types of evasive activities (bribery and emission concealment), the firm is assumed to maximize expected profit ($E(\pi)$) by choosing optimal output (q), self-reported emissions ($\hat{e}$) and abatement level (k). That is,

$$\underset{\{q,\, k,\, \hat{e}\}}{MAX}\ E(\pi) = p \cdot q - C(q,\ k) - T \cdot \hat{e} - b(1 - \alpha(m^*, 1-n))$$

$$- \alpha_1(m^*, 1-n) \cdot \{T \cdot (\bar{e} - \hat{e}) + F_1 \cdot (\bar{e} - E) + F_2 \cdot (\bar{e} - \hat{e})\}$$

$$S.T. \quad m^* = argmax\{B(\alpha(m, 1-n)) + b(1 - \alpha(m, 1-n)) - M(m)$$

$$+ T \cdot \hat{e} + \alpha_1(m, 1-n) \cdot [T \cdot (\bar{e} - \hat{e}) + F_1 \cdot (\bar{e} - E) + F_2 \cdot (\bar{e} - \hat{e})]\}$$

$$n = (q,\ k,\ E)$$

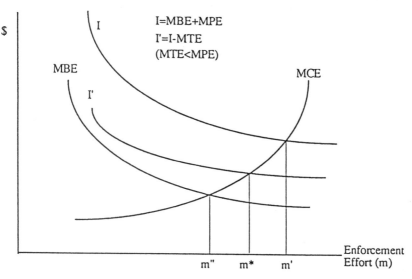

Figure 12.3 The Regulator's Optimal Enforcement Efforts

where p=output price, and $C(q,k)$=cost function such that $\partial C/\partial q>0$, $\partial^2 C/\partial q^2>0$, $\partial C/\partial k>0$, and $\partial^2 C/\partial k^2>0$.

3.3 The Legislator

The legislator is assumed to solve the following social-planning problem by choosing the optimal levels for environmental policy variables. That is,

$$\underset{\{E,\,T,\,F\}}{MAX} \quad W = U(\alpha(m^*,1-n^*))-M(m^*)-B(\alpha(m^*,1-n^*))$$

$$S.T. \quad m^* = argmax\{B(\alpha(m,1-n))+b(1-\alpha(m,1-n))-M(m)$$

$$+ \; T\cdot\hat{e}+\alpha_1(m,1-n)\cdot[T\cdot(\bar{e}-\hat{e})+F_1\cdot(e-E)+F_2\cdot(e-\hat{e})]\}$$

$$\{q^*,k^*,\hat{e}^*\} = argmax\{E(P) = p\cdot q-C(q,k)-T\cdot\hat{e}-b(1-\alpha(m^*,1-n^*))$$

$$- \; \alpha_1(m^*,1-n^*)\cdot[T\cdot(\bar{e}-\hat{e})+F_1\cdot(\bar{e}-E)+F_2(\bar{e}-\hat{e})]\}$$

$$n^* = n(q^*,k^*,E^*)$$

$$B(\alpha(m^*,1-n^*)) \geq \bar{B}$$

where $U(\cdot)$ is the regulator's utility function and $\bar{B}$ is the subsistence budget level required by the regulator.

Some features in the above setting deserve further explanation. (1) The pollution damage cost (DC) is implicitly incorporated in the utility function $U(\cdot)$, since DC is also dependent on enforcement quality. As usual, it is assumed that $U' = \partial U/\partial \alpha > 0$, and $U'' < 0$. (2) Despite the fact that enforcement cost is incurred by the regulator, it is still a component of the total social costs, and therefore, is taken into account by the legislator. (3) In general, the legislator may be faced with his or her own fiscal budget constraint. However, it is ignored in this case because the budget to the regulator for pollution control accounts for only a small portion of the total funds available to the legislator.

After some transformation, the first-order necessary conditions for interior solutions can be expressed by the following three equalities:

$$\{U'-(1+\lambda)B'\}\frac{\partial \alpha}{\partial m}=MCE, \tag{12.5}$$

$$\{U'-(1+\lambda)B'\}\{\frac{\partial \alpha}{\partial m}\frac{\partial m}{\partial E}+\frac{\partial \alpha}{\partial n}\frac{\partial n}{\partial E}\}=MCE\frac{\partial m}{\partial E}, \tag{12.6}$$

$$\lambda\{\bar{B}-B(\alpha(m^*,1-n^*))\}=0, \tag{12.7}$$

where λ is the Lagrangian multiplier of the minimal budget constraint.

These conditions provide the following insights:

(1) The first derivatives of the Lagrangian function with respect to T and F are all identical and represented by (12.5). This implies that the optimal combination of policy variables which can solve the maximization problem is no longer unique.[5] Any tax rate could be optimal as long as the associated fines and emission standards are properly chosen.

(2) The expressions (12.5) and (12.7) imply that it is necessary for the regulator's budget to exceed the subsistence level (i.e., $B^*=B(\alpha(m^*,1-n^*))>\bar{B}$) in order to obtain an enforcement quality better than the one that would prevail when the regulator receives $\bar{B}$ only from the legislator. Nevertheless, this does not imply that a greater budget to the regulator will be more socially optimal. Further exposition on an optimal budget allocation is made in the next section.

(3) (12.6) and (12.7) imply that $\partial \alpha/\partial n = 0$ is a necessary condition to achieve the legislator's optimality. This condition plays an important role in determining the legislator's budget allocation to the regulator.

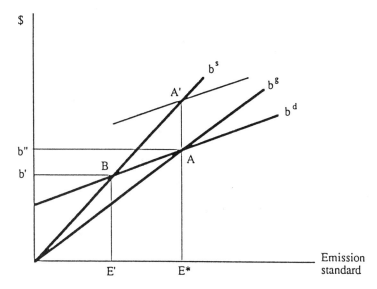

Figure 12.4(a)   Negotiated and Optimal Bribes When $\partial\alpha/\partial n < 0$

(4) Comparing (12.6) with (12.4), it is clear that the optimal enforcement effort desired by the legislator is likely to diverge from the regulator's optimal level. Environmental regulations can be made more effective if the mechanics and underpinnings for such divergence are understood. Divergence of this kind is discussed in more detail in the next section.

4   TRANSFER PAYMENTS IN EQUILIBRIUM

Two types of transfer payments are involved in our model, budgets (*B*) and bribes (*b*). The supply and demand response functions associated with each transfer payment can be identified by finding solutions to the equations above. The intersection point of the supply and demand response functions for bribes determines the optimal negotiated bribe, while the intersection point of the supply and demand response functions for the budget determines the optimal budget allocation.

4.1 Equilibrium Bribe to the Regulator

The regulator's demand for bribes is defined as the minimal payment that the regulator is willing to accept under a given emission standard, ceteris

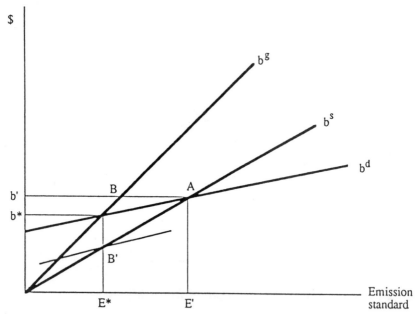

Figure 12.4(b)   *Negotiated and Optimal Bribes When $\partial\alpha/\partial n > 0$ and is*
                    Sufficiently Small

paribus. This demand response function can be obtained by substituting the
regulator's enforcement effort function into the payment equation, i.e.,

$$b^d = b(1 - \alpha(m^*, 1 - n)) \tag{12.8}$$

The slope of the regulator's demand function is given by

$$\frac{db^d}{dE} = -b'\{\frac{\partial\alpha}{\partial m}\frac{\partial m^*}{\partial E} + \frac{\partial\alpha}{\partial n}\frac{\partial n}{\partial E}\}, \tag{12.9}$$

where $(\partial\alpha/\partial m)(\partial m^*/\partial E)$ and $(\partial\alpha/\partial n)(\partial n/\partial E)$ represent, respectively, the
direct and indirect effects of emission standards on enforcement quality.
Whether the demand response will have a positive or negative slope
depends on the marginal effect of the probability of compliance on
enforcement quality (i.e., the sign and the size of $\partial\alpha/\partial n$). If $\partial\alpha/\partial n \leq 0$, the
demand response will always have a positive slope (e.g., the curve b^d in
Figure 12.4(a)). If $\partial\alpha/\partial n$ is positive but not large enough to make the
indirect effect outweigh the direct effect in (12.9), the demand response may
remain upward sloping; otherwise, it may become downward sloping as

shown in Figure 12.4(c).

The firm's supply of bribes (denoted by b^s) is defined as the maximal amount that the firm is willing to pay under a given emission standard, ceteris paribus. The supply response can be obtained by substituting $\alpha(m^*, 1-n^*)$ into the payment equation. That is,

$$b^s = b(1 - \alpha(m^*, 1-n^*)) \qquad (12.10)$$

Thus, the slope of the supply response function is given by:

$$\frac{db^s}{dE} = \frac{db^d}{dE} - b'\{\frac{\partial n}{\partial q}\frac{\partial q}{\partial E}\} \qquad (12.11)$$

As such, the supply response b^s will always have a greater slope than b^d.[6] Normally, the firm's bribe supply response will diverge from the socially optimal supply function unless $\partial\alpha/\partial n = 0$. The socially optimal supply function, denoted by b^g, is obtained by substituting the condition for optimality (i.e., $\partial\alpha/\partial n = 0$) into (12.11). The slope of b^g is expressed as:

$$\frac{db^g}{dE} = -b'\{\frac{\partial\alpha}{\partial m}\frac{\partial m^*}{\partial E} + \frac{\partial n}{\partial q}\frac{\partial q}{\partial E}\} > 0 \qquad (12.12)$$

Thus, b^g will always have a positive slope, regardless of the slopes of b^d and b^s. Since both b^s and b^g emanate from the origin, b^s will be sloping upward and steeper than b^g when $\partial\alpha/\partial n < 0$.[7]

The negotiated (or realized) bribe is determined by the equality $b^d = b^s$, while the socially optimal bribe is determined by the equality $b^d = b^g$. The implications of two interesting cases, $\partial\alpha/\partial n < 0$ and $\partial\alpha/\partial n > 0$, are discussed:

(1) $\partial\alpha/\partial n < 0$ – The demand response (b^d) is sloping upward, and the supply response (b^s) will have a steeper slope than b^d and b^g (see Figure 12.4(a)). Thus, the negotiated bribe is equal to b', which is less than the optimal level (i.e., b'' in Figure 12.4(a)). The emission standard corresponding to b' (i.e., E' in Figure 12.4(a)) may be regarded as the regulator's standard (or effective standard in Jones and Scotchmer's (1990) terminology). It also happens that the effective standard (E') is stricter than the optimal standard (E^*), where E^* is determined by the intersection of b^d and b^g. However, such an effective standard is neither stable (since, when approaching the optimal standard, the amount that the firm is willing to pay for extra emissions is greater than the amount that the regulator is willing to accept) nor Pareto optimal (since the less strict the effective standard is, the better off both the regulator and the firm will be). As compared to the bargaining solution (i.e., Point B in Figure (12.4(a)), the socially optimal

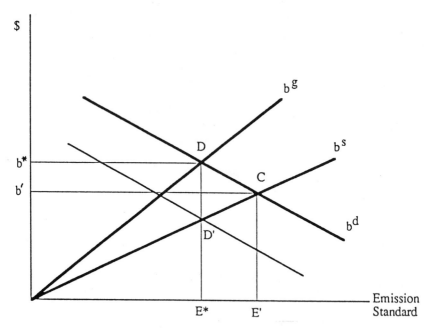

Figure 12.4(c)   *Negotiated and Optimal Bribes When ∂α/∂n > 0 and is*
                    Sufficiently Large

equilibrium (i.e., Point A in Figure (12.4(a)) represents a Pareto improvement for both the regulator and the firm.

The above result reveals that to achieve a stable bargaining solution it is
necessary (but not sufficient) that $\partial\alpha/\partial n \geq 0$, which implies that the
probability of discovering the non-compliance (i.e., α_1) is reduced by a
marginal increase in the probability of abatement success and should not
exceed the corresponding increase in the probability of correct rejection
(i.e., α_4). Examples of this kind are easy to find. For instance, $\partial\alpha/\partial n$ will be
zero if $\alpha_1 = m(1-n)$ and $\alpha_4 = mn$, and positive if $\alpha_1 = m(1-n)$ and $\alpha_4 = 2mn$.

(2) $\partial\alpha/\partial n > 0$ – There are two possibilities in this case: (a) $\partial\alpha/\partial n$ is not
sufficiently large so that the bribe demand response remains upward
sloping, and (b) $\partial\alpha/\partial n$ is sufficiently large so that the bribe demand
response becomes downward sloping. In each case, the slope of b^g is always
greater than the slope of b^s.

The equilibrium in the first case is represented by Point A in Figure
12.4(b), where the negotiated bribe (b') is higher than the socially optimal
bribe (b^*) and the effective standard (E') is less strict than the optimal
standard (E^*). In addition, it is unlikely that the firm and the regulator
would agree to move to the optimal standard since the bribe that the firm

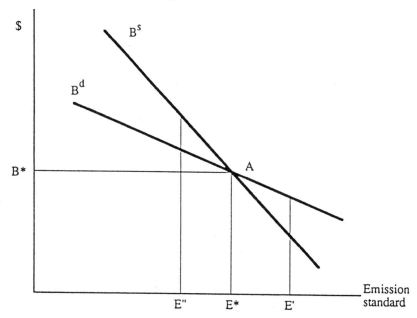

Figure 12.5(a)   Optimal Budget Allocations When Budget Demand Function is Downward Sloping

is willing to pay for extra emissions is less than the amount that the regulator is willing to accept. Such a divergence between effective and optimal standards constitutes one of the most typical consequences under hierarchical government and incomplete enforcement. In this circumstance, the socially optimal standard (E^*) can possibly be achieved by either making b^d shift downward so as to intersect b^s at Point B, or making b^s shift upward so as to intersect b^d at Point B.

In the case where $\partial\alpha/\partial n$ is sufficiently large to make the bribe demand response downward sloping, the equilibrium (i.e., Point C in Figure 12.4(c)) is quite similar to the first case, except that now the realized bribe (b') is less than the optimal level (b^*). Similarly, there is no incentive for the regulator and the firm to move toward the socially optimal solution. To attain the socially optimal standard (E^*), one can make b^d shift downward so as to intersect b^s at Point D' or make b^s shift upward so as to intersect b^d at Point D.

The above analysis contains three important implications worth noting. First, the more the firm is willing to pay for a given amount of emission, the stricter the effective standard will be, regardless of the slope of the demand response. The size of the negotiated bribe, however, will depend on the regulator's demand response. Second, if neither the firm nor the regulator

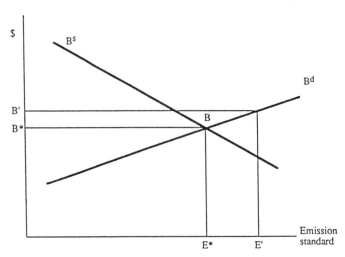

Figure 12.5(b)   Optimal Budget Allocations When Budget Demand Function is Upward Sloping

are confronted with emission standards set by the legislator, the bargaining solutions become neither stable nor desirable to both the firm and the regulator. This is because there are many cases in which the firm's willingness to pay for a specific emission level is always greater than the regulator's willingness to accept (see Figures 12.4(a)–12.4(c)). The construction of the function $b^g(\cdot)$ not only allows us to demonstrate how the negotiated bribe is determined, but also implies that mandating an emission standard is necessary for preventing emissions from getting out of control as well as avoiding excessive bribery. Third, in the case of $\partial\alpha/\partial n >$ 0, any measures that can reduce the regulator's bribe demand or increase the firm's bribe supply are applicable to attain the optimal emission standard. The demand-driving measures, however, will result in a smaller bribe than the supply-driving measures.

4.2 Equilibrium Payment from the Legislator

The regulator's budget demand (denoted by B^d) can be obtained by substituting m^* into $B(a(m, n))$. The slope of the demand response function is given by

$$\frac{dB^d}{dE}=B'\{\frac{\partial\alpha}{\partial m}\frac{\partial m^*}{\partial E}+\frac{\partial\alpha}{\partial n}\frac{\partial n}{\partial E}\}, \tag{12.13}$$

where the first and the second terms in the brackets represent, respectively, the direct and indirect effects of emission standards on enforcement quality.

Just as in the bribe demand response (b^d), the slope of B^d is dependent on the sign and the size of $\partial \alpha / \partial n$. The curve B^d will always slope downward if $\partial \alpha / \partial n < 0$ (e.g., B^d in Figure 12.5(a)). If $\partial \alpha / \partial n > 0$ and the direct effect outweighs the indirect effect in (12.13), B^d may become upward sloping (e.g., B^d in Figure (12.5(b)); otherwise, it remains downward sloping.

Similarly, the slope of the budget supply response function of the legislator is given by

$$\frac{dB^s}{dE} = B'\{\frac{\partial \alpha}{\partial m}\frac{\partial m^*}{\partial E} + \frac{\partial n^*}{\partial q}\frac{\partial q^*}{\partial E}\} < 0 \qquad (12.14)$$

That is, the budget supply response is always downward sloping. It will be steeper than B^d in the case of $\partial \alpha / \partial n > 0$ (as shown by Figure 12.5(a)). If $\partial \alpha / \partial n < 0$, both B^d and B^s will be negatively sloping. It is not obvious, however, which one will be steeper (as indicated by (12.13) and (12.14)).

Suppose that the budget demand response B^d is downward sloping in Figure 12.5(a), and upward sloping in Figure 12.5(b). In each case, a larger budget is necessary to reach the optimal emission standard (represented by the intersection of B^d and B^s) if the effective standard is less strict than the optimal standard (since there will exist excessive budget demand). The warranted budget, however, should be equal to or less than the level demanded by the regulator; it depends on the slope of the regulator's budget demand. For example, if the effective standard is given by E' in Figure 12.5(a), then the legislator should increase the budget according to the regulator's demand. If the prevailing standard is given by E' in Figure 12.5(b), the maximal payment should be no more than B' (the amount demanded by the regulator); otherwise, further divergence from the optimal standard may occur. This situation reflects the common observation that the regulator is always dissatisfied with current budget allocations.

On the other hand, if the effective standard is stricter than the optimal standard (recall that this can happen only when $\partial \alpha / \partial n < 0$, implying that B^d is downward sloping), it will be necessary to reduce the regulator's budget. For example, if the current standard is given by E'' in Figure 12.5(a), an excess budget supply will exist. To reach the optimal equilibrium (i.e., Point A), moderate budget cuts may turn out to be warranted.

In conclusion, whether a larger budget should be allocated to the regulator is closely related to the sign and the size of $\partial \alpha / \partial n$ (representing the marginal enforcement quality of successful abatement). In other words, the properties of the enforcement quality function are crucial in deciding whether and how large a budget should be allocated to the regulator.

5   CONCLUSIONS

This paper takes into account several important factors such as the government hierarchy in a political economy, the stochastic nature embedded in regulation enforcement and pollution control, and the firms' evasive activities (e.g., emission violation and concealment, bribing, and underreporting). To model the complex relationships between the regulator, the firm and the legislator, a multiple-principals agency model is developed to explore the principals' and agent's optimal behaviors, and to analyze the determination of equilibrium bribes and budget to the regulator under a mixture of emission standards and emission charges as instruments of environmental policy.

As for the regulator's behavior, the model demonstrates that the regulator's equilibrium effort will increase with emission tax rates, penalty rates for emission violation and concealment, and the firm's output level. The regulator's effort will decrease with the firm's abatement level, reported emissions, and emission standards.

As for the legislator, the optimal combination of environmental policy variables that can solve the maximization problem is no longer unique. The model indicates that it is necessary for the optimal enforcement budget to be greater than the regulator's subsistence level so as to obtain better enforcement quality. In most cases, the legislator's optimal standard tends to be stricter than the level actually enforced by the regulator. Such a divergence in emission standards constitutes the most typical result under hierarchical government and incomplete enforcement. Whether allocating a larger budget to the regulator is warranted to achieve the optimal standard is likely to depend on the properties of the enforcement quality function. If a larger budget is justifiable, the optimal amount would depend on the slope of the regulator's budget demand. It should be equal to the regulator's demand if the budget demand response is negatively sloped, and should be less than the regulator's demand if the budget demand response is positively sloped.

ACKNOWLEDGEMENTS

An earlier version of this paper, entitled 'Mixed Environmental Regulations and Transfer Payments under Incomplete Enforcement: A Multiple-Principals Agent Approach,' was presented at the Annual Meeting of Western Agricultural Economics Association, July 11–14, 1993, Edmonton, Canada. The revised version was also presented at the Fifth Annual Conference of the European Association of Environmental and Resource

Economists, June 21-June 24, 1994, Dublin, Ireland. Research grant NSC83-0301-H-007-009Z from the National Science Council in Taiwan is greatly appreciated. So are the constructive comments from Professor C.Y.C. Chu, the editors, and participants at the conferences.

NOTES

1. Since the probabilities are all endogenized in our model here, there is no prior information which could allow us to guess the sign of $\partial\alpha/\partial n$. However, it will become clear that $\partial\alpha/\partial n = 0$ is one of the necessary conditions for the legislator's optimality. Here it is assumed that $\partial^2\alpha_i/\partial m^2 < 0$, and $\partial^2\alpha_1/\partial(1-n)\partial m > 0$.
2. The assumption that the payment from the firm ($b(1-\alpha)$) is increasing with $1-\alpha$ at a constant rate will not jeopardize the existence of a stable equilibrium for the regulator and will simplify the analysis to a great extent.
3. It was argued that the penalty function has to be monotonic and nonlinear in relation to the size of the emission violation in order to induce more compliance by tightening emission standards (e.g., Harford, 1978; Viscusi and Zeckhauser, 1979; Jones, 1989; Shaffer, 1990, etc.). If enforcement quality is incorporated in the model, such requirements are no longer necessary (see Huang, 1993).
4. It can be shown that the curves *MBE*, *MPE* and *MTE* in Figure 12.2 are downward sloping with respect to m.
5. A similar conclusion was made by Lee (1984). He contended that any tax rate can be optimal as long as the corresponding enforcement effort is optimally chosen.
6. The condition $\partial q/\partial E > 0$ is assumed hereafter. It is equivalent to say that output will decrease when standards become stricter. It is plausible under perfect enforcement, even though it is not necessarily so in our model.
7. Since there will be no bribe when emissions are not allowed, both b^d and b^g emanate from the origin.

REFERENCES

Bernheim, B.D. and M.D. Whinston (1986), 'Common Agency', *Econometrica*, **54**(4), 923–42.

Demski, J.S. and D.E.M. Sappington (1987), 'Hierarchical Regulatory Control', *Rand Journal of Economics*, **18**, 369–83.

Downing, P. and W. Watson, Jr. (1974), 'The Economics of Enforcing Air Pollution Controls', *Journal of Environmental Economics and Management*, **1**, 219–36.

Harford, J.D. (1978), 'Firm Behavior under Imperfectly Enforceable Pollution Standards and Taxes', *Journal of Environmental Economics and Management*, **5**, 26–43.

Harford, J.D. (1991), 'Measurement Error and State-dependent Pollution

Control Enforcement', *Journal of Environmental Economics and Management,* **21**, 67–81.

Huang, Chung-Huang (1993), 'Effectiveness of Environmental Regulations with Incomplete Enforcement Quality', A paper presented at the Fourth Annual Conference of the European Association of Environmental and Resource Economists, June 30–July 3, Fontainebleau, France.

Jones, C.A. (1989), 'Standard Setting with Incomplete Enforcement Revisited', *Journal of Policy Analysis and Management,* **8**, 72–87.

Jones, C.A. and S. Scotchmer (1990), 'The Social Cost of Uniform Regulatory Standards in a Hierarchical Government', *Journal of Environmental Economics and Management,* **19**, 61–72.

Kambhu, J. (1989), 'Regulatory Standards, Noncompliance, and Enforcement', *Journal of Regulatory Economics,* **1**, 103–44.

Lee, D.R. (1984), 'The Economics of Enforcing Pollution Taxation', Journal of Environmental Economics and Management, **1**, 147–60.

Linder, S.H. and M.E. McBride (1984), 'Enforcement Costs and Regulatory Reform: the Agency and Firm Response', *Journal of Environmental Economics and Management,* **11**, 327–46.

Malik, A.S. (1993), 'Self-reporting and the Design of Policies for Regulating Stochastic Pollution', *Journal of Environmental Economics and Management,* **24**, 241–57.

Roberts, M.J. and M. Spence (1976), 'Effluent Charges and Licenses under Uncertainty', *Journal of Public Economics,* **5**, 193–208.

Shaffer, S. (1990), 'Regulatory Compliance with Nonlinear Penalties', *Journal of Regulatory Economics,* **2**, 99–103.

Shavell, S. (1980), 'Risk Sharing and Incentives in the Principal and Agent Relationship', *Bell Journal Economics,* **10**, 55–73.

Spiller, P.T. (1990), 'Politicians, Interest Groups, and Regulators: a Multiple-principals Agency Theory of Regulations, or "Let Them be Bribed"', *Journal of Law and Economics,* **33**, 65–101.

Viscusi, W.K. and R.J. Zeckhauser (1979), 'Optimal Standards with Incomplete Enforcement', *Public Policy,* **27**, 437–56.

13. Political Economy and Pollution Regulation: Price Regulation in Open Lobbying Economies

Kai-Lih Chen

1 INTRODUCTION

Pollution, in its many forms, is widely regarded as the major environmental problem. Pollution problems and their corresponding policies have been widely discussed in the literature. In principle, a government acting alone can successfully improve domestic environmental quality in a closed economy. However, unilateral environmental policies may not be efficient when trade occurs or when pollutants spread across national boundaries. The issues of pollution regulation in such open economies are rarely addressed in the literature.

The complexity of pollution problems in open economies motivates this research. In particular, pollution regulators in Pacific Rim countries should follow this line of discussions, since trade makes up a great portion of GNP in these countries. For example, the export/GNP and import/GNP ratios of Taiwan, Hong Kong, Singapore, and the Philippines are all much higher than those of the United States.[1] In addition, some export goods are highly polluting to their manufacturing countries, i.e., the goods are exported but the pollution remains in the producing countries.

Pork in Taiwan is one of those goods. Hog raising is an important industry in Taiwan with an export value of US$1,025 billion in 1992, which is 25.65% of the total value of agricultural exports from Taiwan. However, sewage from hog farms is one of the major sources of water pollution in Taiwan, especially in the southern counties where the majority of hog farms are located. Hsu (1992) pointed out that six of the ten most seriously polluted rivers in Taiwan are polluted by sewage from livestock farms, among which sewage from hog raising farms makes up the greatest proportion.

Also, some domestic industries are affected by foreign pollution. For example, fishing may be affected by water pollution from other countries.

Neoclassical environmental regulation literature has focused on the efficiency of policies and the choice of policy instruments. The discussions have ignored the political influence of interest groups. It is more realistic to take into consideration the fact that regulators are subject to political influences when they set regulations. However, most of the discussions on the political influence of interest groups are developed in trade models rather than environmental regulation models. In trade models, rent-seeking activities are to affect pre-existing distortionary policies such as tariffs and quotas, which are different from the distortion-correcting environmental regulations.

Chen et al. (1992) presented a closed lobbying model, which is a combination of two branches of economics, the theory of environmental policy and political economy. In that paper, we made the following comparisons: (1) competitive equilibrium (CE) vs. lobbying equilibrium (LE), (2) price vs. quantity regulations under first-best conditions, and (3) price vs. quantity regulations in the lobbying economy.

This paper extends that model to open models. The issues of different policy instruments are not addressed in this paper. Rather, I focus on the sources that affect the lobbying equilibria and the comparisons of the equilibria in closed and open models.

Open lobbying models for two countries are constructed. The two countries both produce pollution and the pollutants may cross the boundaries to the other country (this is called 'transfrontier pollution'). The lobbying equilibrium levels of emission charges are examined in both cases of localized pollution and transfrontier pollution. Each of the countries is a closed lobbying economy similar to the model in Chen et al. (1992).

In each country, agents have identical preferences defined over both market goods and environmental policy. Thus, agents are both 'consumers' and 'environmentalists'. Agents differ in their policy objectives because they differ in their sources of income: one set of individuals is endowed only with labor, while the other set is endowed with both labor and shares in the profits of firms. The instrument we study alters profits, and hence incomes, thereby differentially affecting the two groups. It is assumed that the government sets pollution regulations to maximize its own preferences, which are represented by a weighted sum of the utilities of the agents. Hence, distributional issues lie at the heart of the analysis. Agents 'lobby' in order to alter the parameters of the government's preference function, and therefore the regulatory choices made. We use the 'pressure function' introduced by Becker (1983) to provide a formal, if highly stylized, representation of the institutions through which political influence is exerted. This 'political economy' approach contrasts with much of the literature of public economics, in which the behavior of governments typically is posited to involve interventions to attain a Pareto optimal allocation, either by eliminating market failure or by redistributing income to maximize a social welfare function. Certainly, the vast majority of the research on environmental economics assumes 'benevolent' interventions. It is becoming increasing apparent, however, that these traditional approaches cannot provide adequate descriptive insight into how real political-economic systems operate. Hence, neither can these approaches provide a complete basis for designing policies for importing the performance of actual economies.

Specifically, two issues will be discussed in this paper. The first issue of concern is transfrontier pollution (TFP) problems, which involve the transportation of pollutants across national boundaries. We will assume that there is no trade in goods in this case. The efficient emission charge in this open (in terms of pollution) lobbying economy is compared to the efficient charge in a closed lobbying economy. The value of the conjectural variation (CV), the expected effect of a change in domestic emissions on foreign emissions, plays an important role in the comparison. With a zero CV, the decision rules are the same in both closed and open models. When the CV increases, the efficient regulation is tighter in the open economy than in the closed economy.

In the second model, the assumption of no trade in goods will be relaxed and only localized pollution will be considered. For simplicity, it will be assumed that trade barriers (tariffs or quotas) do not exist in any country. The equilibrium emission charge in this open (in terms of goods) lobbying economy is compared to that in the closed economy. Because the basic model is quite complex, analytical results are not forthcoming; we provide computed equilibria for an example economy. Hence, the discussion is more illustrative than definitive.

2   TRANSFRONTIER POLLUTION MODEL

The theoretical framework in this section follows the structure in Chen et al. (1992) but focuses on a domestic pollution control policy decision – an emission charge in the presence of transfrontier movement of pollutants. For simplicity, we assume that the total externality generated in a country is consumed in fixed proportions by domestic and foreign consumers and that there is no trade between countries.

2.1 The Model

There are two countries, domestic (A) and foreign (B). The economic
agents' behavior in each country is similar to that described in Chen et al.
(1992). There are two goods in each country. One good, indexed by $j = x$,
generates pollution when produced; the other good, indexed by $j = y$, is
pollution-free. For now, it is assumed that there is no trade in goods. The
only connection between these two countries is the pollutants transported
from one country to the other. There are n_x^A and n_y^A identical firms producing
goods x and y in Country A, and n_x^B and n_y^B identical firms producing goods
x and y industries in Country B. Each country has two types of agents. All
agents are endowed with an equal amount of labor, measured in time. In
addition, some agents receive a share of firm profits. Agents with only labor
are called laborers and are indexed by $i = c$ (consumers); those with profit
shares are called capitalists and are indexed by $i = f$ (firms). Countries A
and B are denoted by superscripts A and B. Hence, n_c^A is the number of
laborers (agents endowed with only labor) and n_f^A is the number of
capitalists (agents endowed with labor and profit shares) in Country A.
Each capitalist receives one n_fth of the total profits of firms. The only
factor, labor, indexed by L_x and L_y when used to produce x and y respectively, is supplied inelastically by consumers and is not mobile.

   Assume that good y is the numeraire in each country and let p^A be the
relative price of good x in Country A. Let t^A be the emission charge
imposed by the domestic government; t^B is the emission charge imposed
by the foreign government. We assume that the total emissions generated
in a country are consumed in fixed proportions by domestic and foreign
consumers. Let e_p^A denote the emissions generated by the representative firm
in the polluting industry in the domestic country and k^A, between 0 and 1,
be the ratio of emissions consumed relative to the emissions produced by
each firm in Country A, i.e., $(1 - k^A)$ is the spillover factor. If e_c^A denotes the
total emissions consumed in Country A, either from Country A or Country
B, then

$$e_C^A = k^A n_x^A e_P^A + (1 - k^B) n_x^B e_P^B$$

$$e_C^B = k^B n_x^B e_P^B + (1 - k^A) n_x^B e_x^P$$

(13.1)

2.1.1   Production Plans
The firms solve standard profit maximization problems. Competitive
conditions are assumed for both the input and output markets. A representative firm in the x industry in Country A chooses an input level to

maximize profits subject to the production function $x = f(L_x)$, an emission function, $e = e(L_x)$, and an environmental policy – an emission charge, t. The firm is assumed to take the regulation as given. The firms in Country B are similar to those in Country A. Therefore, superscripts will be dropped whenever there is no confusion. Hence, the representative firm in the x industry in each country solves the following problem:

$$\underset{x, L_x, e_p}{Max} \quad P_x x - w L_x - t e_p$$
$$s.t. \quad x = f(L_x)$$
$$e_p = e(L_x)$$

(13.2)

where w, t, f, and e are market wage rate, emission charge, production function and emission function, respectively. The production of y is not regulated since there is no market failure problem. Therefore, a representative firm in the y industry simply maximizes its profits subject to the production function: $y = g(L_y)$; the y industry is also assumed to be competitive.

2.1.2 Consumption Plans

Regarding consumers, we assume that they both consume and allocate resources to influence the government's environmental policy. For pedagogic purposes we take a two-stage approach to the consumer's problem. Initially, we treat the consumer's lobbying level, l^i, as a parameter and choose consumption; subsequently, we will study the lobbying decision. In each country, the representative consumer's optimization problem in the first stage is, for $i = c, f$:

$$\underset{x^i, y^i}{Max} \quad U^i(x^i, y^i, e_c)$$
$$s.t. \quad p_x x^i + p_y y^i \le m^i$$
$$= w(L^i - l^i) + n_x t e_p / (n_c + n_f)$$
$$+ J^i(n_x \pi_x + n_y \pi_y) / n_f$$

(13.3)

Here, x^i and y^i are i's consumption of the two goods; m^i is consumer type i's disposable income; e_c, defined in (13.1), is the total emissions consumed; L^i is the labor endowment; l^i is the time spent on lobbying; e_p is the emissions produced by the representative firm; and J^i is a characteristic function which equals zero if $i = c$ and equals one if $i = f$. The term $n_x t e_p / (n_c + n_f)$ represents each consumer's tax revenue rebate under the price instrument. π_x and π_y represent profits of the representative firm in x and y industries respectively. At this stage, consumers are assumed to act competitively, i.e., n_x, n_y, n_c, n_f, p_x, p_y, w, t, π_x, and π_y, are exogenous parameters. We let $V^i(p_x, p_y, w, m^i, e_c, t^i)$ be i's indirect utility function. Henceforth x^i and y^i will denote demands.

Before the consumers choose l^i, they form a hypothesis as to the effect of lobbying on the government's choice of levels for the instrument t. Following Becker (1983), let Ψ^i, be the pressure function of consumer type i and I^i be the influence yielded by Ψ^i, $i = c, f$. To simplify the notation, we replace $I^i(\Psi^c(l^c, l^f), \Psi^f(l^c, l^f))$ by $I^i(l^c, l^f)$.

In order to write the optimization problem for choosing a lobbying level, we need to specify the beliefs agents hold about the response of other agents to their lobbying. Here, we assume a one-shot, non-cooperative game between agents, using Nash conjectures about the behavior of others. The pressure function is taken as given by the consumers, and it is common knowledge. The agents are assumed to take the tax consequences of their actions into account when they lobby. We let $V^i(\,\cdot\,;l^i, l^i)$ summarize agent i's beliefs about the level of utility achieved when she lobbies at the level l^i and the other agent lobbies at level l^i. That is, V^i is agent i's indirect utility generated by her utility function.

Thus, the optimization problem in the second stage is, for $i = c, f$:

$$\underset{l^i}{Max}\ V^i(p_x,p_y,w,m^i,e_c;l^i,l^{-1}) \qquad (13.4)$$

where the consumer recognizes that p_x, p_y, w, m^i and e_c are affected by lobbying via the regulatory instrument, the level of which responds to lobbying.

2.1.3   The Government
In each country, we assume that regulation is set as if it maximizes preferences formed over the indirect utility levels of agents in the economy. The government's policy instrument is the emission charge. The regulations in each country are set as if they solve:

$$\underset{t}{Max}\ n_c I^c V^c + n_f I^f V^f \qquad (13.5)$$

The values I^i, $i=c, f$ are weights that define the government's preference ordering. These weights are influence functions whose arguments are determined by political pressure resulting from lobbying. From the first-order condition of the optimization problem for an emission charge and the definition of transfrontier pollution in (13.1), the terms $\partial e_p^A/\partial e_p^B$ and $\partial e_p^B/\partial e_p^A$, the expected reaction of the other country to the domestic emission charge (the conjectural variation, CV), is the key factor that affects the equilibrium and will be further discussed in the following subsection.

2.2 The Lobbying Equilibrium

The equilibrium emission charges in the lobbying economies in each country are determined by solving (13.5). In each country, the regulation is taken as given by the agents. The lobbying equilibrium is characterized by the solutions of problems (13.2)-(13.5) and the following market-clearing conditions:

$$n_c x^c + n_f x^f = n_x x \tag{13.6}$$

$$n_c y^c + n_f y^f = n_y y \tag{13.7}$$

$$n_x L_x + n_y L_y = n_c (L^f - l^f) \tag{13.8}$$

The lobbying equilibrium is found by the following process:
(1) The government chooses a value of CV:
   (a) Nash behavior – CV=0. In this case the consumer believes that the emission of the other country will not change with respect to a change in domestic emission.
   (b) Cooperative behavior – CV>0. There is a (possibly implicit) contract between the two countries such that one country agrees to reduce its domestic emission, which also affects the other country, provided that the other country does the same.
   (c) Non-cooperative, non-Nash behavior – CV<0.
(2) According to the chosen CV, the government determines the effluent charge rule, which is a function of the agents' relative influence, by maximizing the weighted average of the agents' indirect utilities with weights I^c and (n_f/n_c) I^f on laborers and capitalists, respectively. That is, the government in Country A solves:

$$\underset{t}{Max} \quad n_c I^c V^c + n_f I^f V^f$$

or equivalently,

$$\underset{t}{Max} \quad I^c V^c + (n_f/n_c) I^f v^f \tag{13.9}$$

(3) The agents determine, in addition to their consumption bundles, their optimal lobbying levels by maximizing their indirect utilities, i.e., they solve problems (13.3) and (13.4).

It is important to distinguish 'first-best', 'second-best', and 'third-best' outcomes in our model. A CE in an economy with externalities is, in general, inefficient in that the equilibrium production mix (x, y) is not on the production possibility frontier and the resulting indirect utility pair (V^c, V^f) is not on the utility possibility frontier.

For example, the CE might be at Point A in Figure 13.1. Supposing that policies are chosen to maximize a social welfare function, such as the weighted sum of indirect utilities, but without lobbying, then Pigovian taxation or an emission standard, combined with *lump-sum* redistribution of income, can move the society to the welfare-maximizing allocation, which perforce lies on the production possibility and utility possibility frontiers (e.g., Point B on U^1 in Figure 13.1). The economy now is in its first-best situation. In this model, instruments are set as if by a self-interested environmental regulator. The regulator's preferences take the form of a social welfare function (ignoring lobbying for the moment), but the outcomes cannot be first-best since redistribution does not take place in a lump-sum manner. Ignoring the resource cost of lobbying, a first-best outcome is achieved only when the weights used in the regulator's objective function happen to take on values such that only environmental regulation and not redistribution is needed. In general, the decentralized regulatory outcome is second-best.

When the political influences of agents are considered, the production and hence utility possibility frontiers shrink inward (e.g., to U^2 in Figure 13.1) because lobbying activities remove resources from production and because the government uses second-best redistributive instruments. A lobbying equilibrium (LE) is 'third-best' due to these two sources of inefficiency. If neither lump-sum instruments nor a 'political technology' that rules out lobbying are available, the LE is 'constrained efficient', since the regulation is maximizing the weighted sum of indirect utilities. Points such as B generally are unobtainable. Individuals may be better off or worse off in the LE relative to the CE, or they may be Pareto noncomparable. If the LE is represented by Points C or D, then one agent is better off while the other is worse off. If Point E is the LE utility pair, then both agents are better off in the lobbying economy than they are without the government.

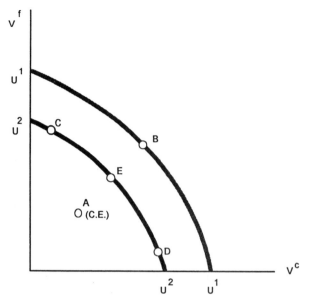

Figure 13.1 Utility Possibility Frontiers with and without Lobbying

2.3 Unilateral TFP and Bilateral TFP Problems

The TFP is unilateral when $k^B=1$ and $0<k^A<1$ (Country A's pollution spills into Country B but not vice versa) or $k^A=1$ and $0<k^B<1$ (Country B's pollution spills into Country A but not vice versa). In the former case (B is the victim), the domestic country (A) is not affected by the foreign (B) country's pollution. Since we have assumed that there is no trade in goods, the model is similar to the closed economy model, which has been discussed in Chen et al. (1992). The only difference is that now the total emissions consumed in the domestic country are $k^A n_x^A e_p^A$ with $k^A<1$ rather than $n_x e_p$ as in the closed model. In the latter case (A is the victim), the total emissions consumed in Country A are increased because of the spillover effects from Country B. Country A may propose to cooperate with Country B to reduce the emissions jointly. However, the polluting country (B) will have very little, if any, incentive to enter into any cooperative arrangement with the receptor nation (A) that would entail a voluntary (uncompensated) reduction in its levels of pollution. It is reasonable to assume that CV is zero when the regulator in Country A makes decisions; the equilibrium concept is Nash in this case, which is also the case in the closed model. The decision rules are not changed in the presence of TFP in Nash behavior, but the consumers' indirect utilities decrease as a result of TFP since $\partial V^i/\partial e_c<0$.

The pollution is bilateral if $0 < k^A, k^B < 1$. The value of CV plays an important role in determining the regulation level. Two interesting cases are CV$=0$ and CV>0.

When the amount of the externality from abroad is considered fixed by the regulator (the CVs in both countries are zero), the equilibrium in the domestic country is found by the same procedure as in the closed economy, except that the total pollution level is $k^A n_x^A e_p^A$ with $k^A < 1$ rather than $n_x e_p$. We have discussed the effects of lobbying activities and the welfare implications of different environmental regulations. However, the two countries are connected by TFP and may both be better off if they make an arrangement to reduce their pollution levels.

If Country A believes that Country B will reduce output of the externality provided Country A does the same and vice versa, then the amount of externality from abroad is a positive function of the domestic externality ($\partial e_p^B / \partial e_p^A > 0$ and $\partial e_p^A / \partial e_p^B > 0$). Intuitively, the efficient regulation in this case is tighter than when CV$=0$ in both countries. To state the proposition formally, we make the following assumptions:

(A1) The production function is continuously differentiable and concave, i.e., $f' > 0$, $f'' < 0$.

(A2) The emission function is continuously differentiable and convex, i.e., $e' > 0$, $e'' > 0$.

(A3) The utility functions are continuously differentiable and quasi-concave and are such that the indirect utility functions they generate satisfy the following conditions:
   (i) there exists a t^* such that $(dW/dt)|_{t*} = 0$ (the notation denotes (dW/dt) evaluated at t^*), and
   (ii) $d^2 W/dt^2 < 0$ for all t, where $W = n_c \beta_1 V^c + n_f \beta_2 V^f$ with $0 \leq \beta_1, \beta_2 \leq 1$.

Now, we are ready to state the following proposition:

Proposition 1. Let t_1^* and t_2^* be the efficient effluent charges associated with zero CV and positive CV, respectively. Under (A1)-(A3), $t_2^* > t_1^*$.

Proof. (See Appendix.)

The proposition implies that the equilibrium effluent charge is an increasing function of the CV in the bilateral TFP situation, i.e., the equilibrium regulation is tighter the greater the CV is. For a fixed positive CV, they also imply that the equilibrium effluent charge is an increasing function of the spillover factor $(1-k^B)$ since a greater $(1-k^B)$ implies a greater total emission consumption, which tightens the regulation.

2.4 An Example Economy

In this subsection we use an example economy to illustrate the game characteristics of the equilibrium in this TFP lobbying model. While the behavior of both Countries A and B is assumed to be symmetric, only Country A will be discussed in this example.

The production technologies of polluting industries in both countries are assumed to be the square roots of their labor inputs, and the emission functions are assumed to be their labor inputs. For the pollution-free industries in both countries, constant returns to scale technologies are assumed. As for consumers' utility functions, quasi-linear forms are assumed for both countries: $U = x + \ln x + y - \alpha\, e_c$, where e_c is the total emissions consumed in Country A, and $-\alpha < 0$ is the marginal disutility of total emissions. The maximization problems are summarized as follows:

Production of x:

$$\underset{x}{Max}\ \ p_x x - w L_x - t e_p$$
$$s.t.\ \ \ x = (L_x)^{1/2}$$
$$e_p = L_x$$

Production of y:

$$\underset{y}{Max}\ \ p_y y - w L_y$$
$$s.t.\ \ y = L_y$$

Consumption:

1st stage:

$$\underset{x^i,\, y^i}{Max}\ \ x^i + \ln x^i + y^i - \alpha n_x e_c$$
$$s.t.\ \ p_x x^i + p_y y^i = m^i$$

2nd stage:

$$\underset{l^i}{Max}\ \ V^i(\,p_x,\, p_y,\, w,\, m^i,\, e_c)$$

Government:

Table 13.1　Changes of Lobbying Equilibrium when CV, k^A, and k^B Changes

	t	x	p	e_p	e_c	l^c	l^f	V^c	V^f	SW
CV↑	↑	↓	↑	↓	↓	↓	↓	↑	↑↓	↑
k^A↑	↑	↓	↑	↓	↑↓	↓	↓	↓	↑↓	↑↓
k^B↑	↓	↑	↓	↑	↑↓	↑	↑	↑	↑	↑

Table 13.2　Lobbying Equilibria with $\alpha = 1$ and $k^A = k^B = 0.5$

	CV = 0	CV = 0.25	CV = 0.5	CV = 0.75	CV = 1
t	13.0329	16.3525	19.6772	23.0057	26.3373
x	0.3285	0.2937	0.2679	0.2478	0.2316
e_p	0.1079	0.08626	0.07177	0.06140	0.05362
e_c	1.0791	0.8626	0.7177	0.6140	0.5362
p	9.2194	10.1930	11.0786	11.8965	12.6602
l^c	0.004536	0.003654	0.003058	0.002628	0.002304
l^f	0.003053	0.002460	0.002058	0.001769	0.001551
V^c	1.3308	1.4377	1.4919	1.5181	1.5284
V^f	2.8465	2.9358	2.9768	2.9929	2.9949
SW	1.8922	1.9926	2.0419	2.0643	2.0715

$$\text{Max}_{t}\ n_c l^c V^c + n_f l^f V^f \tag{13.10}$$

We assume $n_x = 10, n_c = 17, n_f = 10, L^i = 5$ and $I^c/I^f = I = \ln[l^c/l^f]$, and calculate the lobbying equilibrium for the cases of $\alpha = 0.01, 0.5, 1$, and 2 when CV, k^A, and k^B take the values of 0, 0.25, 0.5, 0.75, and 1, i.e., $4 \times 5^3 = 500$ cases are computed. As a result, the lobbying equilibrium emission charge t increases as CV increases, k^A increases, or k^B decreases, while the equilibrium output levels of the polluting good, the emissions produced, and the lobbying time spent by both laborers and capitalists move in the opposite direction. Laborers are better off with greater CV since emissions are decreased. The effect of an increase of CV on capitalists is ambiguous because a tighter regulation will also decrease the profits of the industry. The impacts of changes of k^A and k^B are more complex because the emissions consumed domestically depend on the value of k^A and k^B. Table 13.1 shows the changes of lobbying equilibrium emission charge (t), output level (x), price (p), lobbying efforts (l^c and l^f), indirect utilities (V^c and V^f), and social welfare levels (SW, defined as $(n_c/(n_c + n_f))V^c + (n_f/(n_c + n_f))V^f$)

when CV, k^A and k^B change. The equilibria of 5 of the 500 cases are provided in Table 13.2 (a complete set of equilibria is available upon request).

We use CV $= 0$ and CV $= 1$ in Table 13.2 as an example to discuss the incentives of cooperation in Countries A and B. Consider a two-player, two-strategy game. Regulators in Countries A and B, denoted by I and II, respectively, are the two players. The regulation levels associated with CV $= 0$ and CV $= 1$, denoted by 0 and 1, respectively, are the two strategies. Let I_i and II_i, i=0, 1, be strategy i played by players I and II and let the social welfare levels when Country A plays strategy i and Country B plays strategy j, denoted by $U_I(I_i, II_j)$ and $U_{II}(I_i, II_j)$, be the payoffs. As shown in Table 13.2, $(U_I(I_0, II_0), U_{II}(I_0, II_0))$=(1.8922, 1.8922) and $(U_I(I_1, II_1), U_{II}(I_1, II_1))$ = (2.0715,2.0715). The payoffs associated with (I_1, II_0) and (I_0, II_1) can be calculated as follows. If the regulator in Country A believes that $\partial e^B_p / \partial e^A_p = 1$ but the regulator in Country B believes $\partial e^A_p / \partial e^B_p = 0$, then the equilibrium emissions per firm are 0.05362 in Country A and 0.1079 in Country B. The social welfare levels are:

$$U_1(I_1, II_0) = 2.0715 - 0.5 \times 10 \times (0.1079 - 0.05362) = 1.8001$$

and

$$U_{II}[I_1, II_0] = 1.8922 + 0.5 \times 10 \times [0.1079 - 0.05362] = 2.1636 \quad (13.11)$$

If, on the other hand, $\partial e^B_p / \partial e^A_p = 0$ and $\partial e^A_p / \partial e^B_p = 1$, then $U_I(I_0, II_1) = 2.1636$ and $U_{II}(I_0, II_1) = 1.8001$. To summarize, the payoff matrix is

	II_0	II_1
I_0	(1.8922, 1.8922)	(2.1636, 1.8001)
I_1	(1.8001, 2.1636)	(2.0715, 2.0715)

The unique Nash equilibrium of this game is (I_0, II_0). However, it is Pareto-dominated by (I_1, II_1). This game is a Prisoners' Dilemma game where a dominant strategy exists for each player and the equilibrium is Pareto inferior. In this example, it is obvious that if both players can cooperate on the 'CV $= 1$, CV $= 1$' strategy, they will do better than the 'CV $= 0$, CV $= 0$' solution of the non-cooperative game. Yet each is tempted to break any tacit agreement and knows the other player is also tempted to defect. The dilemma is whether each player is to trust the other; that is, the dilemma confronting each is whether to operate according to individual rationality or collective rationality (see, for example, Friedman, 1986). The main features of this paradox are (Sen, 1967; Runge, 1981):

(1) Pareto inferior outcome. Each player will choose independently 'CV = 0' strategy, leading to a situation in which both are made worse off.

(2) Strict dominance of individual strategy. The result of 'CV = 0, CV = 0' arises independently of the expectations of each player regarding the actions of others because of a strictly dominant strategy for each player.

(3) Need for enforcement. Even if an agreement is struck that both agree to play 'CV = 1', the strict dominance of individual strategy makes such an agreement unstable. Without compulsory enforcement imposed by an outside authority, any such agreement is unstable because nobody has an incentive to keep such agreements.

The example here is a Prisoners' Dilemma game, and strategy 0 is the dominant strategy for each player. It is possible that no dominant strategy exists for other examples. In these cases, a variety of alternative outcomes are possible, depending on the structure of mutual expectation and resulting patterns of strategic choice. In the context of international pollution, the role TFP plays is that it gives incentives to affected countries to cooperate. If they do cooperate, the output of emissions decreases as a result of tighter regulation, and so the agents are better off than if they do not cooperate. However, the existing incentives for coordination in international pollution regulation policies do not imply that such cooperation will actually occur. It requires the assurance that other countries comply with the agreement. Such an agreement represents a global public good. The assurance that everybody plays by the rules is crucial for the production of any public good (see, for example, Sen, 1967 and Runge, 1981).

2.5 A Summary

An open (in terms of pollution) lobbying economy is constructed and the lobbying equilibrium is defined in this section. The main source which affects the equilibrium is the expected effect of a change in domestic emissions on foreign emissions, i.e., the conjectural variation, or CV. Before we turn to the next issue, we summarize the results in the open lobbying economy (in terms of pollution) without trade in goods as follows:

(1) The decision rules for the unilateral TFP case and for CV = 0 under bilateral TFP are the same as in a closed economy where TFP is not present.

(2) CV > 0 results in tighter environmental regulation and higher indirect utilities as compared to the Nash equilibrium where CV = 0.

(3) Other things being equal, a greater CV results in tighter regulation.

(4) Other things being equal, a greater spillover effect $(1-k^B)$ results in tighter regulation.

(5) Other things being equal, laborers are better off with a greater CV, a smaller k^A, and a greater k^B; capitalists are better off with a greater k^B, but may be better off or worse off with a greater CV or a smaller k^A.

(6) The two-player, two-strategy game played by the two countries in the existence of transfrontier pollution is a Prisoners' Dilemma game in the example.

The conclusion of this model may be applied to the real world. For example, the industries in Taiwan and the Philippines may both pollute the Bashi Channel, and hence negatively affect the fisheries of both countries. That is, both countries are mutually affected by bilateral transfrontier pollution. If the environments are similar to the model described in this section, the government may set the emission charge according to the lobbying equilibrium. Cooperation will increase CV and hence both countries will tighten the emission charge, and, therefore, both countries may be better off. However, the characteristic of a Prisoners' Dilemma game may occur and cause such cooperation to be unstable.

3 OPEN LOBBYING MODEL

We now turn to the second major issue considered in this paper: the choice of environmental policy levels when trade occurs. The model is similar to that in Section 2, except that the assumption of no trade in goods is relaxed, and that the pollution is localized now. Specifically, the model in this section is as follows. There are two Countries, A and B, that produce two final goods, x and y, both of which are traded. The only factor of production, called labor, is supplied inelastically by consumers and is not traded. The export good of Country A is x and y is the export good of Country B. The production of x in Country A gives rise to a pure production externality, namely pollution, which is domestic in nature. The externality enters the utility functions of consumers in Country A.

Country A is a large economy, possessing some monopoly power in trade. Country B is assumed not to retaliate in any way against Country A's domestic policies which have trade implications. For simplicity, we assume that there are no tariffs or quotas in any country. Because the model with trade in goods is much more complicated than the previous model, we utilize a sample economy as an example and compute competitive equilibria (CE) and lobbying equilibria (LE) for eight hypothetical cases in order to make comparisons between CE and LE in closed and open economies.

There are two goods in Countries A and B. The production and utility functions are assumed to be identical in both countries and are those assumed in the example economy in (10) in Section 2, except that the production of good x, the polluting goods, in Country B costs more, probably because of a higher emission charge, which is exogenously determined by Country B. Therefore, Country A exports good x and imports good y.

The demand functions of x and y of representative consumers can be derived from their utility maximization problems. The supply functions of x, on the other hand, can be derived from producers' maximization problems. Because of the specification technology of y, $p_y = w = 1$, since the price of labor, w, is normalized to be unity. Therefore, the equilibrium price function can be solved by the market-clearing condition, which is

$$\frac{n_c^A + n_f^A + n_c^B + n_f^B}{P-1} = \frac{n_x^A p}{2(1+t^A)} + \frac{n_x^B p}{2(1+t^B)} \quad (13.12)$$

where $p = p^A = p^B$.

The indirect utility functions are derived by substituting the demand functions into the utility functions and are:

$$V^i = 1/(p-1) + \ln[1/(p-1)] + m^i$$
$$- p/(p-1) - \alpha n_x e \quad (13.13)$$

We assume $n_x^A = n_x^B = 10$, $n_c^A = n_c^B = 17$, and $n_f^A = n_f^B = 10$. We calculate competitive equilibria and lobbying equilibria of Country A for eight different combinations of exogenous variables – domestic marginal disutility of pollution α and foreign emission charge t^B: $(\alpha, t^B) = (0.01, 0.3)$, $(0.5, 15)$, $(1, 30)$, $(2, 60)$, $(0.01, 50)$, $(0.5, 50)$, $(1, 50)$, and $(2, 50)$.

3.1 The Competitive Equilibrium (CE)

In the example economy, the CE price level p is determined by the market-clearing condition in the open economy:

$$\frac{n_c^A + n_f^A + n_c^B + n_f^B}{p-1} = \frac{n_x^A p}{2} + \frac{n_x^B p}{2(1+t^B)} \quad (13.14)$$

The only factor that affects the price level is the emission tax of foreign country. The calculated values of CE price level (p), per-firm output (x), and per-firm emissions (e), are summarized in Table 13.3 for $t^B = 0.3, 15$,

Table 13.3   Competitive Equilibria in Open and Closed Economies

| | | t^B | | | |
	0.3	15	30	50	60	Closed
p	3.02078	3.72718	3.77300	3.79277	3.79785	2.87697
x	1.51093	1.86359	1.88650	1.89638	1.8989	1.43849
e	2.28128	3.47297	3.55887	3.59627	3.60591	2.06924

Table 13.4   Indirect Utilities and Social Welfare in Open and Closed Competitive Equilibria

	α	0.3	15	t^B 30	60	50	closed
	0.01	(3.068,5.350)				(2.613,6.210)	(3.163,5.233)
(V^c, V^f)	0.5		(-14.81,-10.90)			(-15.00,-11.41)	(-6.97,-4.91)
	1			(-32.61,-29.05)		(-32.99,-29.39)	(-17.32,-15.25)
	2				(-69.15,-65.54)	(-68.95,-615.36)	(-38.01,-35.94)
	0.01	3.913				3.945	3.930
	0.5		-13.082			-13.723	-6.207
SW	1			-31.291		-31.752	-16.555
	2				-67.812	-67.620	-37.247

30, 50, and 60. The resulting indirect utilities, (V^c, V^f), and social welfare, SW, are shown in Table 13.4.

In the comparisons of open and closed CE, the price level and hence the output level of the polluting good and the emissions are higher in the open economy than in the closed economy. The CE in the closed economy Pareto-dominates the CE in the open economy except for the case of $(\alpha, t^B) = (0.01, 0.3)$ and $(0.01, 50)$, in which cases they are Pareto-noncompara-ble, while the social welfare level is higher in the open economy when $t^B = 50$, and is lower in the open economy than in the closed economy. The CE in the closed economy Pareto-dominates the CE in the open economy except for the case of $(\alpha, t^B) = (0.01, 0.3)$ and $(0.01, 50)$, in which cases they are Pareto-noncomparable while the social welfare level is higher in the open economy when $t^B = 50$ and is lower in the open economy when $t^B = 0.3$.

Opening up the economy has a positive effect on the output level of the exporting good – the polluting good, x. This, in turn, has a negative effect on consumers' utilities. However, it also has a positive effect on the profit of this industry, and hence increases the disposable income of capitalists. When the positive income effect exceeds the negative externality effect, capitalists are better off. On the other hand, if the negative effect of the externality is relative large, both laborers and capitalists are worse off, and this results in a Pareto-dominated outcome. It is clear from this example that the CE in the open and closed economies may be Pareto noncomparable.

3.2 The Lobbying Equilibrium (LE)

Using a procedure similar to that described in Section 2, LE are calculated. The equilibrium emission charge t, per-firm output level of polluting good (x), relative price of polluting good (p), lobbying efforts of laborers and capitalists (l^c, l^f), indirect utility levels of laborers and capitalists (V^c, V^f), and social welfare (SW) are summarized in Tables 13.5 and 13.6.

In the open lobbying economy, the equilibrium emission charge is affected by the emission charge of the foreign country (t^B) and the domestic marginal disutility of pollution ($-\alpha$). The LE emission charge increases when t^B increases for fixed α's, and when α increases for fixed t^B's. The effects of changes of t^B's and α's on equilibrium emission charges t, output levels x, emissions produced e, output prices p, lobbying efforts l^c and l^f, indirect utilities V^c and V^f, and social welfare SW, are summarized in Table 13.7.

An interesting comparison is the relationship between the open LE and the closed LE. Table 13.8, summarized from Tables 13.5 and 13.6, shows the differences of closed and open LE. It is not definite that the equilibrium emission charge in the closed model is higher than in the open model or vice versa. For two cases, (t^B, α)=(50, 0.01) and (50, 0.5), equilibrium emission charges in the open model, t^0, are greater than the equilibrium emission charges in the closed model, t^c. For the other six cases, $t^c > t^0$. It is also ambiguous when equilibrium price levels are compared. Price levels in the open economy p^0 are less than the closed economy price level p^c when (t^B, α)=(30, 1), (50, 2), and (60, 2). As for equilibrium output levels, lobbying efforts, and indirect utilities, opening up the economy has positive effects on them. From Table 13.8, it is clear that agents are better off in the open LE than in the closed LE, which is the advantage of trade, even though more resources are spent on the unproductive activities – lobbying. However, the advantage of trade is not clear in the competition world, where open CE may be Pareto-dominated by the closed CE, or they may be Pareto-noncomparable, depending on the magnitudes of positive income effect and negative externality effect. This is not surprising since, in general, CE is not efficient in a world with externalities. The LE, on the

Table 13.5 Equilibrium Emission Charges, Per-firm Output, Price Levels and Lobbying Efforts in Open and Closed Lobbying Economies

	α	t^B					Closed
		0.3	15	30	60	50	
t	0.01	0.06379				0.769824	0.1537
	0.51		11.5260			14.6025	13.0329
	1			23.2626		25.5754	26.3373
	2				46.7619	45.3385	53.0570
x	0.01	1.43962				1.36370	1.3199
	0.5		0.3682			0.38040	0.3285
	1			0.2604		0.26802	0.2316
	2				0.18337	0.18020	0.1627
p	0.01	3.06291				4.82701	3.0456
	0.5		9.2251			11.8702	9.2194
	1			12.6343		14.2456	12.6602
	2				17.5164	16.7007	17.5926
(l^c, l^f)	0.01	(0.320,0.215)				(0.087,0.059)	(0.060,0.040)
	0.5		(0.184,0.124)			(0.111,0.075)	(0.005,0.003)
	1			(0.172,0.116)		(0.144,0.097)	(0.002,0.002)
	2				(0.164,0.110)	(0.171,0.115)	(0.001,0.001)

Table 13.6 Indirect Utilities and Social Welfare in Open and Closed Lobbying Economies

	α	t^B					Closed
		0.3	15	30	60	50	
(V^c, V^f)	0.01	(3.798,6.107)				(3.915,7.235)	(3.149,5.179)
	0.5		(2.610,4.368)			(2.562,4.856)	(1.870,3.386)
	1			(2.280,3.981)		(2.234,4.191)	(1.528,2.995)
	2				(1.942,3.601)	(1.971,3.532)	(1.181,2.612)
SW	0.01	4.653				3.145	3.901
	0.5		3.261			3.412	2.431
	1		2.91			2.959	2.071
	2				2.556	2.549	1.711

other hand, is an efficient outcome in the economy with lobbying inefficiency and non-lump-sum redistributive effects. The advantage of trade occurs in an efficient world, but not necessarily in an inefficient world.

Another interesting comparison is the relationship between LE and CE. In the closed model, LE may Pareto-dominate or be Pareto-dominated by CE. Suppose that the closed CE is Point A in Figure 13.1, the possible

Table 13.7   Changes of Lobbying Equilibrium when T and α Change

	t	x	e	p	l^c	l^f	V^c	V^f	SW
α = 0.01	↑	↑	↓	↑	↓	↓	↑	↑	↑
T↑ α = 0.5, 1,and 2	↑	↓	↑	↑	↓	↓	↓	↑	↑
α↑ open	↑	↓	↑	↑	↑	↑	↓	↓	↓
closed	↑	↓	↑	↑	↓	↓	↓	↓	↓

Table 13.8   Changes of Lobbying Equilibria from Closed Model to Open Model

	t	x	p	l^c	l^f	V^c	V^f	SW
closed –> open	↑↓	↑	↑↓	↑	↑	↑	↑	↑

locations of closed LE in our example are points such as E or F. However, in the open model, LE Pareto-dominates CE which implies that the open LE is located at the northeast of open CE (assumed to be Point A) such as Point E.

3.3 A Summary

In this section, we focus our attention on the price instrument for an open lobbying economy with trade in goods and localized pollution in production of the exporting good. To avoid complexity, we assume that there are no trade barriers in any country. A sample economy is used to compare (1) CE in the open vs. closed economies, (2) LE in the open vs. closed economies, and (3) LE vs. CE in an open economy. The comparisons depend on two exogenous variables – domestic marginal disutility of pollution α and foreign emission charge T. The results of this example can be summarized as follows:

(1) Open CE (OCE) and Closed CE (CCE):
  (a) It is possible that OCE is Pareto-dominated by CCE and that OCE and CCE are Pareto noncomparable.
  (b) Except when the marginal disutility of pollution is very small and the foreign emission charge is very large, society as a whole is worse off in OCE.
  (c) The results of (a) and (b) suggest that the advantage of trade does not necessarily occur in the competitive world since, in general, CE is not

efficient in an economy with externalities.

(2) Open LE (OLE) and Closed LE (CLE): CLE is Pareto-dominated by OLE which implies the occurrence of the advantage of trade.

(3) OLE and OCE: OCE is Pareto-dominated by OLE.

(4) CLE may Pareto-dominate or be Pareto-dominated by CCE. However, in the open economy example, OLE Pareto-dominates OCE.

The model may be applied to a real world situation if the production function and utility functions of the trading countries are known to the governments. Even though LE is not first-best, it is efficient, given that lobbying activities exist and that the redistribution effect of the instrument is not lump-sum. The model in this section provides a new approach in determining an emission charge and it is not limited to the price instrument. For example, it is straightforward to turn it to an emission standard instrument.

4 CONCLUSIONS

In this paper we have discussed an environmental policy instrument – emission charges – in two open economies when agents lobby regarding their implementation, which can be easily extended to an emission standard instrument. The first economy is 'open' in terms of pollution but not goods. The value of the expected effect of a change in domestic emissions on foreign emissions (the conjectural variation CV) plays an important role. The lobbying equilibrium emission charge is higher in the open economy than in the closed economy when the CV increases. In the second open model, trade in goods occurs but transfrontier pollution is assumed away.

Here, we have simply discussed, in a very limited number of simulations, the impact of opening up an economy in an economy embodying both lobbying inefficiencies and second-best redistributive impacts. The results, obtained via an example, are far from definitive, and thus, this model is very restricted. However, it is worth noting that the advantage of trade does not necessarily occur in the competitive world, while it does occur in the lobbying world.

We have not incorporated many of the potential sources of differences between agents in their preferences and their endowments. Since the example demand system did not exhibit income effects in the demand for polluting good, differences between agents also had minimal impacts on the resulting equilibria. Nor have we explored important power differentials between them.

The model has assumed full and symmetric information among agents. It would be of some interest to compare efficiency losses of instruments across sources of inefficiency in more 'realistic' settings. However, the results of this paper seem to indicate that the lobbying equilibrium concept can be extended to more complicated models. Thus, it appears that further research along these lines may be warranted.

ACKNOWLEDGEMENTS

Special thanks go to Professors Jack Knetsch, Jerome Geaun, and an anonymous referee for their comments on earlier versions.

APPENDIX

Proof of Proposition 1

Proposition 1. Let t_1^* and t_2^* be the efficient effluent charges associated with zero CV and positive CV, respectively. Under (A1)–(A3), $t_2^* > t_1^*$.

Proof. Let W_1 and W_2 be the government object functions for $CV=0$ and $CV>0$, respectively. First note that

$$dW_2/dt - dW_1/dt = (\partial W_2/\partial e_c)(1-K)N_x(\partial E_p/\partial e_p)(\partial e_p/\partial t)$$

$$- (\partial W_1/\partial e_c)(1-K)N_x(\partial E_p/\partial e_p)(\partial e_p/\partial t)$$

$$= (\partial W_2/\partial e_c)(1-K)N_x(\partial E_p/\partial e_p)(\partial e_p/\partial t)$$

$$> 0 \text{ for all } t,$$

since $\partial W_i/\partial e_c < 0$, $i = 1,2$ (by the fact that pollution is a negative externality) and $\partial e_p/\partial t < 0$. Also note that

$$(dW_i \,/\, dt)\,|\,t_i^* = 0.$$

The conclusion follows from the fact that $(dW_2/dt)\,|\,t_1^* > (dW_1/dt)\,|\,t_1^* = 0 = (dW_2/dt)\,|\,t_2^*$ and the assumption that dW_i/dt is a decreasing function of t. **Q.E.D.**

NOTES

1. For the Pacific Rim countries listed in the text, exports comprise anywhere from 18.30% to 134.96% of GNP, while imports make up between 27.35% and 136.10% of their GNP. For comparison, exports from the United States in 1992 made up 7.12% of GNP, while imports comprised 8.44% of GNP.

REFERENCES

Becker, G.S. (1983), 'A Theory of Competition among Pressure Groups for Political Influence', *Quarterly Journal of Economics*, **98**, 371–400.

Chen, Kai-Lih, T. Graham-Tomasi and T. Roe (1992), 'Political Economy and Pollution Regulation: Instrument Choice in a Lobbying Economy', paper presented at the Conference on Water Quantity/Quality Disputes and their Resolution, May 1992, Washington, DC.

Friedman, J.W. (1986), *Game Theory with Applications to Economics,* Oxford, UK: Oxford University Press, Inc.

Hsu, Mei-Lin (1992), 'Present Phenomena of River Pollution and Sources of River Pollution in Taiwan' (in Chinese), *China Environmental Protection*.

International Economic Weekly, No.969–987, Taiwan Economic Research Center.

Runge, C.F. (1981), 'Common Property Externalities: Isolation, Assurance, and Resources Depletion in a Traditional Grazing Context', *American Journal of Agricultural Economics,* **63**, 595–606.

Runge, C.F. (1984), 'Institutions and the Free Rider: the Assurance Problem in Collective Action', *Journal of Politics*, **46**, 154–81.

Sen, A.K. (1967), 'Isolation, Assurance, and the Social Rate of Discount', *Quarterly Journal of Economics,* **81**, 112–24.

14. Doubtful Merits of Equal-rate Pigovian Taxes and Tradable Permits in Controlling Global Pollution

Hirofumi Shibata

1 INTRODUCTION

Today, interest is strong in quasi-price mechanisms through which countries in the world are expected to achieve global environmental objectives, particularly control of the emission of greenhouse gases. Proposals for equal-rate Pigovian effluent taxes and tradable pollution permits are notable examples. Cited most often as justifications for these quasi-market mechanisms are (1) minimization of the aggregate cost of abatements of the world as a whole through equalization of marginal emission abatement costs across countries, and (2) the favorable income prospects for developing countries that could be produced by lump-sum redistribution of the revenues that these mechanisms generate.

In this paper we attempt to argue that these two justifications do not hold generally. First, the rates of Pigovian effluent tax must be differentiated individually to take account of individual differences in utilities of the pollution abatement that the polluters themselves experience, just in the same way that Lindahl prices of a public good must be differentiated individually, to achieve a Pareto optimal solution. Second, lump-sum transfers of the proceeds of effluent taxes or of permit sales will not produce favorable income distribution prospects for developing countries.

Before presenting our arguments, let us summarize the 'standard' version of the theory supporting equal-rate Pigovian environmental taxes and tradable pollution permits. It is argued that if pollution is the only defect in an otherwise perfectly competitive world, equalization of the marginal costs of emission abatement at the social marginal external effect across all polluters is the first best solution. It minimizes global aggregate abatement costs to achieve a given environmental standard, even if the marginal cost is not set equal to the social marginal external effect. Equal-rate Pigovian effluent taxes or uniformly priced tradable pollution permits are recommended as a means of equalizing pollution abatement costs across all polluters, provided that the tax revenues or the proceeds of the auction of pollution permits are redistributed by lump-sum transfers.[1]

Under the Pigovian effluent tax scheme, a polluter will emit pollutants as long as the marginal profit that he can earn by emitting an extra unit of pollutant exceeds the amount of effluent tax that he has to pay for producing products that entail emission of that extra unit of pollutant. He reaches the equilibrium level of emission when the earnings made possible by the marginal unit of pollutant emitted decline to the size of the effluent tax. The earnings that he loses by not emitting the marginal unit of pollutant are his marginal pollution abatement cost. Thus a uniform rate of the Pigovian effluent tax equalizes all polluters' marginal costs of abatement.

Alternatively, in the tradable pollution permits scheme, a permit giving an entitlement to discharge a given amount of environmentally undesirable emissions can be bought and sold in a market. Through competition among the demanders for and the suppliers of the permits in a single market, a uniform price emerges for a permit. This price equalizes the marginal costs of pollution abatement for all the pollutant emitters as they attempt to maximize their private profits. By not emitting a unit of pollutant and selling the pollution permit thus saved (or by not buying a permit to produce an extra unit of pollutant), a polluter can earn the price of the permit. He will, therefore, reduce emissions until the marginal cost of abatement becomes equal to the price of a permit.[2]

Redistribution prospects of the revenues to be generated by these methods are also cited as another reason for recommending them. Pigovian effluent taxes obviously generate revenues to the taxing authority through the proceeds of the taxes assessed. The tradable pollution permits can also generate revenues to the permit-managing authority if it auctions off a given quantity of permits in an open market. The amount of revenue to be generated is expected to be enormous if the rate of the tax or the price of permits is high enough to produce a meaningful degree of reduction in the world pollution level;[3] hence it is argued that Pigovian tax or permit trading schemes could be used to achieve income redistribution, which, it is alleged, is likely to improve the welfare of developing economies.[4]

Against the above standard arguments, we raise the following issues:

First, Much global environmental pollution, such as global warming, represents 'negative public goods' or 'reciprocal external diseconomies'. Individuals producing greenhouse gases, which cause the global warming, are simultaneously both the generators and the victims of the global warming. Schemes controlling environmental pollution of this nature should be different from those controlling one-directional external diseconomies. Acid rain, for example, brought by north winds across polluted Canadian lakes, damages forests mostly located in the United States but not those located in Canada, and thus the generators and victims of this particular environmental pollution are different. We contend that the standard recommendations are appropriate for controlling one-directional externalities, such as the above particular type of acid rain, but are not appropriate for controlling reciprocal external diseconomies such as global warming.

For example, assume smoke pollution in a closed room. One's own emission of pollutants hurts not only others but also the smoker himself. Hence, even in the absence of external interventions, a polluter will voluntarily reduce his own emission when he considers the quantities of others' emission as given. In other words, the existing equilibrium as well as the equilibrium to be reached after imposition of effluent taxes are Nash equilibria with a privately provided public good, namely pollution abatement. Therefore, the rates of Pigovian effluent tax must be differentiated individually to take account of individual differences in utilities of the pollution abatement that the polluters themselves experience. Having a uniform rate Pigovian effluent tax imposed internationally or allowing the international trade of uniformly priced pollution permits will produce a non-Pareto optimal, not to speak of the socially optimal, solution.[5]

Second, we also contend that the existing equilibrium in the absence of interventions by a world authority and the equilibrium to be reached by its intervention through the Pigovian tax or the tradable pollution permits are both Nash type equilibria. But the Nash equilibrium with a voluntarily provided public good is independent of income distribution patterns. It is generally understood that the revenues collected by the Pigovian tax must be returned to the economy in a lump-sum manner whether or not redistribution of income is intended, otherwise the returned revenues would cause another distortion in resource allocations. Hence whenever the revenues collected are returned to the economy in a lump-sum manner, the equilibrium solution reached under either the Pigovian taxes or sales of pollution permits is independent of the distribution of income. It is, therefore, not possible to make developing countries any better off by lump-sum transfers of the revenues obtainable by either one of these control measures.

2 SHORTCOMINGS OF THE STANDARD ARGUMENTS

Assume for simplicity a world consisting of two decision-making agents: Individual A and Individual B or alternatively Country A and Country B, assuming that each country has a well-defined social utility function and behaves as if it were a consistent decision-making unit striving to maximize its own social utility function like an individual. Henceforth, we shall simply refer to these agents as Country A and Country B, bearing in mind that each is assumed to act like a utility-maximizing individual.[6]

In Figure 14.1, Curve AE is the schedule of the monetary expression of the marginal utility (MU_A) or the value of marginal product (VMP_A) that the consumption activities entailing emission of pollutants bring to Country A. It is Country A's demand curve for pollution. Curve BF is similarly the schedule of Country B's marginal utility (MU_B) (alternatively, the value of the marginal product of emissions (VMP_B)) or its demand curve for pollution. The horizontal sum of the two curves (ACG) is the world demand curve for pollution. Curve OL and Curve OM are the schedules of monetary expression of the marginal disutilities of pollution suffered by residents of Country A and Country B, respectively. The vertical sum of the two curves, Curve ON, is the schedule of aggregate marginal damages that the world suffers from the pollution. A Pareto optimum level of pollution is OH, where the two aggregate curves, ACG and ON, cross each other.

It is argued that this optimum level of pollution will be supported if the world authority imposes a Pigovian tax equal to OP on each unit of pollutant emitted. Because all countries will emit pollutants until their marginal benefits derivable from the emission become equal to this tax rate, their marginal costs of abatement (the marginal benefits foregone), JP_A and KP_B for Countries A and B, respectively, are equalized and consequently the global aggregate abatement cost will be minimized. Such a situation implies that production activities entailing pollutants emission are allocated optimally between the two countries: OJ for Country A and OK for Country B in terms of pollutants emitted.[7]

The same result can be obtained, it is argued, by the world government auctioning off pollution permits of the quantity equal to OH in a worldwide open market. Since the aggregate demand schedule for pollution permits is curve ACG, the market-clearing price of a pollution permit will be established, and a permit will be traded, at price OP. Hence utility-maximizing Countries A and B will reach their equilibria when they emit quantities of pollutants equal to OJ and OK, respectively. The sum of these two quantities equals OH. The same results can also be obtained, it is argued, if the world government gives a subsidy equal to OP per unit of pollutant abated so that each polluter equates its marginal cost of abatement with the

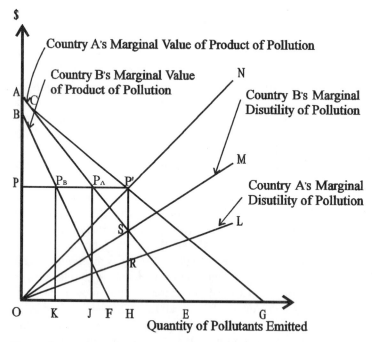

*Figure 14.1   The Standard Geometry of the Pareto Optimal Quantity of
Pollution*

opportunity cost of not abating, namely the subsidy foregone.

It is important to notice that the above standard arguments are based on an implicit assumption that each country behaves as if it were unwilling to voluntarily reduce emission of pollutants in its own country. Hence, it is assumed that each country emits pollutant, in the absence of the control by a world authority, up to the quantity at which its marginal utility (or the value of marginal product) of pollutant emission becomes equal to zero.

This implicit assumption, we observe, does not seem appropriate. If we assume that each country is rational, as an individual (as we have assumed), in the absence of game-theoretic strategic behavior, it must adjust its own pollutant emission so as to maximize its own welfare, regardless of the presence or absence of external control by a world authority. If it were to emit pollutants to such an extent that the marginal utility (or the value of marginal product) that the pollution entails is zero, because its marginal disutility is non-zero at that level of pollution, it would amount to deliberately reducing its own welfare level below that which is attainable unilaterally.

In fact, in the real world, the most advanced countries usually do take measures voluntarily to reduce the emission of pollutants in their own territories to improve their citizens' welfare even in the absence of a world government. Worldwide pollution such as global warming and depletion of the ozone layer by chlorofluorocarbons (CFCs) is universally regarded as a public bad. But all countries realize that the pollutants (greenhouse gases and CFCs) that they emit will harm not only other country's residents but also their own. Hence responsible governments of countries emitting them usually introduce their own measures to reduce emissions of these gases.[8] Therefore, even in the absence of intervention by a world authority, the global pollution level is most likely be lower than the level that would prevail had no countries taken abatement measures at all, that is the level of pollution equal to Quantity OG in Figure 14.1.

The question is then, what level of pollution would prevail in the absence of intervention by a world government and in the presence of intervention by responsible national governments. We argue that the appropriate assumption for our policy analysis should be that the equilibrium under these conditions is a Nash-type equilibrium. That is, in the absence of negotiation among the countries about the individual levels of pollutant emission permitted, the best each country can do is to take the other country's emission as given and to adjust its own emission so as to maximize its own welfare.

3 THE NASH EQUILIBRIUM

Assume that two countries (or individuals) are situated on the banks of a lake. The lake is owned by no one, and there is no world government. Both countries' consumption activities entail discharge of their waste into the lake freely, but at the same time both suffer from deterioration of the environment if the lake is polluted. Therefore, the government of each will restrain the quantity of waste that its residents discharge into the lake. But each country is unable to influence the amount of waste that the other country discharges, in the absence of negotiation or trade on pollution-reducing actions between the two. Each will take the quantity of the other's discharge as given and will adjust its own quantity of discharge so as to maximize its own welfare. The equilibrium outcome of these interactions is illustrated in Figure 14.2.

The vertical axis measures the quantity of consumption in terms of the numeraire good, Good Y, and the horizontal axis, the quantity of pollutants that consumption activities necessarily discharge into the lake from Point O, measuring pollution quantities to the left (because pollution is a negative public good). Point O represents zero discharge of pollutants. Assume for

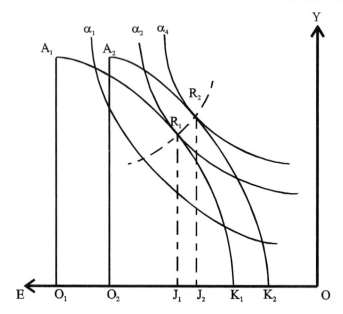

*Figure 14.2   Country A's Reactions to Change in Country B's Emission
           Levels*

a moment that the quantity of pollutants discharged by Country B is OK_1.
The consumption possibility set $K_1A_1O_1$ shows the attainable set for Country
A of vectors of the quantities of pollutants emitted and the quantity of
Good Y consumable. For example, when the quantity O_1A_1 of Good Y is
consumed, Country A must discharge the quantity of pollutants that equals
K_1O_1. When the country's emission is reduced to K_1J_1, the maximum
amount of consumption in terms of the numeraire good is reduced to J_1R_1,
and so on. The total quantity of pollutants emitted into the lake is the sum
of Country B's emission, OK_1, and Country A's emission. Thus curve
$K_1R_1A_1$ shows Country A's frontier of trade-off between the total amounts
of pollutants emitted and the consumption in terms of the numeraire good
(Y) when Country B's emission level is fixed at OK_1. Curves α_1, α_2,... are
Country A's indifference curves between the consumption in terms of Good
Y and the aggregate quantity of pollutants in the lake emitted by both
Country A and Country B.
    Given Country B's emission level at OK_1, Country A maximizes its utility

when it consumes J_1R_1 of Good Y and discharges K_1J_1 of pollutants, for at Point R_1 (vector $[OJ_1, J_1R_1]$), Country A's consumption possibility frontier $(A_1R_1K_1)$ is tangent to one of its indifference curves, α_2. When Country B reduces its emission level to OK_2, Country A's consumption possibility set shifts rightward to the location indicated by $K_2A_2O_2$. Country A finds that this time its utility is maximized at Point R_2, where its shifted consumption possibility frontier is tangent to one of its indifference curves, α_4, representing a higher welfare level than α_2.

As Country B's quantity of pollutants emitted is continuously reduced, tangency points between Country A's consumption possibility frontier, which is continuously shifting to the right, and its successively higher levels of indifference curves generate a 'consumption expansion path' akin to an 'income consumption curve', R_1,R_2,R_3....It is akin to an income consumption curve because, from Country A's point of view, Country B's emission reduction is equivalent to an increase in its own income by the amount that would be lost had Country A reduced that quantity of pollutants by itself. Corresponding to each point on the consumption expansion path, $R_1,R_2,...$, there exists Country A's optimum quantity of emission, such as Quantity K_1J_1, Quantity K_2J_2, and so on. Thus there is a one-to-one relationship between the quantity of Country B's emission and the quantity of Country A's emission when Country A reacts to Country B's emission level optimally. This relationship is shown as Country A's reaction curve AA in Figure 14.3, where the horizontal and vertical axes measure the quantities of emission by Country A and Country B, respectively.

A similar reaction curve can be drawn with respect to Country B, showing a one-to-one relationship between the quantity of Country A's emission and the quantity of Country B's when the latter reacts optimally to the former. When Country B's reaction curve BB is drawn on the same Figure 14.3, the intersection of the two reaction curves shows the Nash equilibrium set of quantities of the two countries' emission, OJ for Country A and OK for Country B, that will prevail in the absence of a world government.

As shown in Figure 14.2, when enjoying the good environment of an unpolluted lake is an income-elastic good, as it is likely to be, the consumption expansion path of each country has a positive slope (assuming no corner solutions) and hence the reaction curves of both have negative slopes. The greater the income elasticity of the good environment, the steeper the slope of Country A's reaction curve and the less steep the slope of Country B's reaction curve. Therefore, in Figure 14.3, Reaction Curve AA can be expected to cross Reaction Curve BB from above and hence a stable Nash equilibrium exists.

Quantity of Emission by Country B

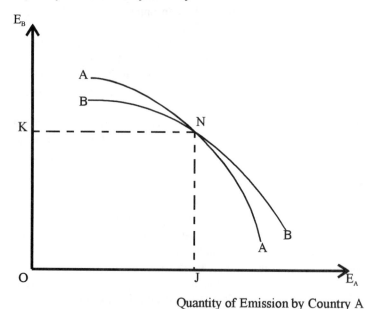

Quantity of Emission by Country A

Figure 14.3   Nash Equilibrium as an Intersection of Reaction Curves
of Countries A and B

4   A NASH EQUILIBRIUM AND A PARETO OPTIMAL SOLUTION: A NEED FOR DIFFERENTIATED PIGOVIAN TAXES

Let us show the Nash equilibrium depicted above by a partial equilibrium diagram. We measure in Figure 14.4 from Point O the quantities of pollutants emitted by Country A to the right and Country B to the left. Curve AE and Curve BF are Country A's and Country B's demand curves for pollution, respectively, reproduced from the corresponding curves in Figure 14.1. Assume that Country B emits a quantity of pollutants equal to OK'. Being a pure public bad, this quantity of pollutants enters Country A's utility function in the same amount. Therefore, Country A's marginal disutility of pollution schedule is Curve K'L, which originates at Point K' (to the left of Origin O by an amount equal to Country B's emission). The vertical line erected at Point K' can be viewed as Country A's vertical axis when we visualize Country A's disutility schedule. When Country A considers the amount of Country B's emission (OK') as given and maximizes its own welfare, it adjusts its own emission level to Quantity OJ', where its

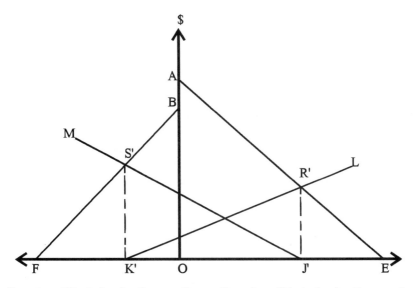

Quantity of Emission by Country B   Quantity of Emission by Country A

*Figure 14.4   Partial Equilibrium Geometry of the Nash Equilibrium
          Pollution Level*

demand curve for pollution (AE) intersects its own marginal disutility
schedule, K'L. Country A's marginal disutility (J'R') at the pollution level
where the quantity of global pollution is K'J'(=OK'+OJ') equals the
marginal utility (or the value of marginal product) to be gained by its own
emission of pollutants (OJ').

Similarly, when Country B considers Country A's pollution level (OJ') as
given and attempts to maximize in own welfare, it restrains its own
emissions to the level at which its marginal disutility curve (J'M) intersects
its own demand curve for pollution (BF) at Point S'. Pollution quantities
(OJ' for Country A and OK' for Country B) that satisfy quantitative
relationships as shown by Figure 14.4 may not be achieved instantly but
they will eventually prevail after a series of adjustments, and as such they
represent a Nash equilibrium. We consider the Nash equilibrium shown in
Figure 14.4 to be the equilibrium situation existing in the absence of
intervention by a world authority when each country independently attempts
to maximize its own welfare.[9]

The above-depicted Nash equilibrium situation is, of course, not a Pareto
optimal situation. A Pareto optimal Nash equilibrium is depicted in Figure
14.5 which reproduces Figure 14.4, except for the locations of the origins of
the two countries' marginal disutility schedules. Quantities OJ and OK are

the emission quantities of Country A and Country B, respectively. The line erected vertically at Point J cuts Country A's marginal disutility curve (KL) at Point R and Country A's demand curve for pollutant emission (AE) at Point P_A. The vertical line erected at Point K cuts Country B's marginal disutility curve (JM) at Point S and its demand curve for pollutant emission (BF) at Point P_B. If this situation is Pareto optimal, Distance JP_A must be equal to Distance KP_B. This implies that Distance KS must be equal to Distance RP_A and Distance JR equal to Distance SP_B. In other words, the marginal utility that resulted from allowing the pollutant to be emitted in each country (the marginal costs of abatement) (JP_A for Country A and KP_B for Country B) must be equal to each other and in turn these values must be equal to the sum of the marginal disutility of Country A (JR) and that of Country B (KS).

As seen in Figure 14.5, if the world authority wishes to attain a Pareto optimum solution it must impose a Pigovian tax of a rate equal to RP_A on each unit of pollutants emitted by Country A and SP_B on each unit of pollutants emitted by Country B. The two Pigovian tax rates are generally not equal ($SP_B \neq RP_A$).[10] (They are equal only when both countries experience an identical disutility from the same amount of pollution at a Pareto optimum solution.[11]) Thus differential Pigovian tax rates are generally called for to achieve a Pareto optimal solution. One can see from Figure 14.5 that, in the two-country case, the tax that should be imposed on Country A (RP_A) must be equal to the external diseconomy (disutility) that Country A imposes on Country B (KS), and the tax that should be imposed on Country B (SP_B) must be equal to the external diseconomy that Country B imposes on Country A (JR).

Notice that the configuration of the set of variables depicted by Points J, K, R, S, P_A and P_B in Figure 14.5 satisfies the Samuelsonian condition for a public good (that is, pollution abatement). The marginal cost of abatement (the foregone marginal utility or marginal value of emission's products), namely JP_A ($=KP_B$) equals the sum of marginal utility of abatement of Country A ($=JR$) and that of Country B ($=KS$), for $JR + KS = JP_A = KP_B$ when $KS = RP_A$ and $JR = SP_B$. Notice the correspondence between Figure 14.5 and Figure 14.1: The distances JP_A, KP_B, KJ, JR and KS in our Figure 14.5 are equal to the distances JP_A, KP_B, OH, HR and HS, respectively, in Figure 14.1, which is the 'standard' geometry depicting the Samuelsonian condition for a public good.

The same Figure 14.5 also shows that a tradable pollution permits system will not succeed in achieving a Pareto optimal solution because the differential pricing of pollution permits (RP_A for Country A and SP_B for Country B) is not generally possible in a single competitive market of pollution permits.

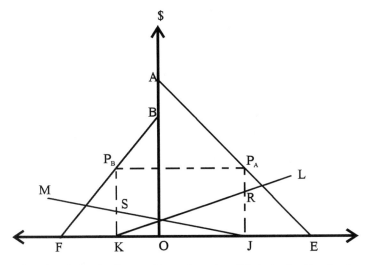

Quantity of Emission by Country B   Quantity of Emission by Country A

Figure 14.5 Partial Equilibrium Geometry of a Pareto Optimal Configuration of Pollution Levels under Optimally Differentiated Pigovian Taxes

Let us summarize our arguments above. Country A's marginal pollutant emission produces marginal utility (or value of marginal product) for Country A but at the same time it inflicts marginal disutilities on the global society (MDU_S) which equal the sum of the marginal disutilities experienced by the members of the society ($MDU_S = MDU_A + MDU_B$). But because Country A itself is one of the members of the society who suffer from the pollution, it adjusts its own emission so that its own marginal utility (MU_A) (or the value of marginal product (VMP_A)) of emission of pollutants equals its own marginal disutility of pollution or $MU_A = (VMP_A) = MDU_A$; but it neglects the marginal damages that it imposes on Country B (MDU_B). To force Country A to adjust its emission by taking into account not only the marginal diseconomy that it inflicts upon itself but also the marginal damages it imposes on Country B, it is suggested that a Pigovian tax applicable in Country A, t_A, be introduced in such a way that $t_A = MDU_B$. Country A then reaches its equilibrium level of emission when $MU_A = MDU_A + t_A$. It is also suggested that a similar Pigovian tax, t_B, which is equal to the external diseconomy that Country B imposes on Country A (MDU_A) be introduced in Country B so that Country B reaches its equilibrium level of pollution at $MU_B = MDU_B + t_B$, where $t_B = MDU_A$.

Minimization of the aggregate abatement costs of all polluters requires equalization of the marginal costs of abatement for them all. The marginal cost of abatement in this context is, obviously, the value of marginal utility (or the value of marginal product) foregone by not emitting pollutants. Accordingly, minimization requires $MU_A = MU_B = MSC$ (marginal social cost of abatement). This means that in each individual country the following condition must hold: for Country A, $MSC = MU_A = MDU_A + t_A$, and for Country B, $MSC = MU_B = MDU_B + t_B$. Since the marginal disutility that one country suffers from the aggregate pollution is generally different from that the other $(MDU_A \neq MDU_B)$, and minimization of the aggregate costs of abatement requires $MU_A = MU_B$, Pigovian taxes (t_A and t_B) to be imposed must be different from country to country $(t_A \neq t_B)$.

Moreover, since the Pareto optimum condition of a public bad requires $MDU_A^* + MDU_B^* = MSC^*$ (where MSC^* is a Pareto optimal marginal social cost), if we wish to establish a Pareto optimal level of pollution, in addition to minimization of aggregate costs of abatement, we must set the Pigovian tax rate of Country A equal to Country B's marginal disutility at a Pareto optimal solution, for $MDU_A^* + MDU_B^* = MSC^* = MDU_A^* + t_A$ implies that $t_A = MDU_B^*$; and we must set the Pigovian tax rate of Country B equal to Country A's marginal disutility at a Pareto optimal solution $(t_B = MDU_A^*)$.

When the emission of pollutants is taxed at correctly differentiated Pigovian tax rates, the Nash equilibrium then established satisfies the Pareto optimal condition. The Nash equilibrium that will emerge as a consequence of imposition of the Pigovian taxes with correctly differentiated tax rates is depicted in Figure 14.6. Given an amount of pollutant that Country B discharges (say, OK_1), Country A maximizes its utility at a consumption vector such as Point R_2'. A gap exists at Point R_1' between the slope of Country A's consumption possibility frontier $K_1R_1'A_1$ and the slope of one of its indifference curves (α_1) containing Point R_1'. The gap equals the Pigovian tax rate applicable to Country A. As Country B reduces its emission level to OK_2, Country A finds that its utility-maximizing vector shifts to a new point, R_2'. In response to changes in Country B's emission levels, the locus of utility-maximizing vectors of Country A such as Point R_1', generates a 'tax-adjusted consumption expansion path', R_1', R_2',... (At each point on the consumption expansion curve, the gap between the slope curve equals the tax rate.) From this consumption expansion path, the reaction curve of Country A prevailing under a Pigovian tax applicable to of Country A's indifference curve and that of its consumption possibility Country A can be generated and is shown by curve $A'A'$ in Figure 14.7. The reaction curve of Country B under the Pigovian tax applicable to Country B, the rate of which is generally different from the rate applicable to Country A, can similarly be generated as Curve $B'B'$ in Figure 14.7. The intersection of the

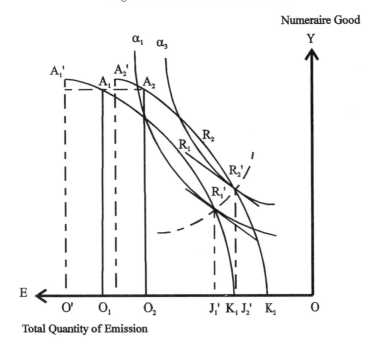

Figure 14.6 Derivation of Country A's Reaction Curve under a Pigovian Tax and Effects of Changes in Income on the Reaction Curve

two tax-adjusted reaction curves (Point P) gives the Nash equilibrium that prevails under the system of Pigovian taxes with correctly differentiated tax rates. The equilibrium satisfies the Samuelsonian public good conditions, for it satisfies the configuration of valuables that is depicted in Figure 14.5.

5 EQUILIBRIUM UNDER UNIFORM PIGOVIAN TAXES (OR TRADABLE EMISSION PERMITS)

When each unit of pollutants emitted is taxed at a uniform rate (or alternatively, when polluters must pay a uniform market price for a tradable emission permit), a Nash equilibrium which is different from a Pareto optimum emerges. (Henceforth 'the Pigovian tax rate' should be read as 'the uniform market price of a permit', if one is interested in the case of marketable emission permits.) From the consumption expansion path, generated in the same way as explained in Figure 14.6, the reaction curve under a given Pigovian tax rate is derived and is shown by the dotted curve A″A″ in Figure 14.7 for Country A. The reaction curve of Country B under

Quantity of Emission by Country B

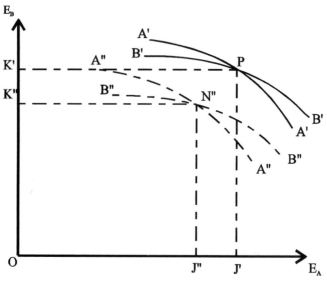

*Figure 14.7   Pareto Optimal Nash Equilibrium under Differentiated
Pigovian Taxes and Nash Equilibrium under Uniform
Rate Pigovian Tax*

the Pigovian tax with the *same* rate can be similarly derived: Dotted curve
B"B" in Figure 14.7. The intersection of the two dotted curves gives the
Nash equilibrium under the equal-rate Pigovian tax (Point N").[12]   The
nature of the equilibrium is the same as the Nash equilibrium that prevailed
under the non-tax situation, and hence the equilibrium would not be Pareto
optimal.

Figure 14.8 depicts the post-equal-rate Pigovian tax Nash equilibrium in
a partial equilibrium diagram. Each country equates its marginal abatement
cost with the sum of its own disutility and the tax that it has to pay to the
world authority. Hence at equilibrium, Country A's marginal abatement
cost is $J''T_A$ and Country B's is $K''T_B$. Even though the rate of taxes they
have to pay is the same ($R''T_A$ for Country A and $S''T_B$ for Country B), the
marginal abatement costs of the two countries are not equal as long as the
marginal disutilities that the two countries suffer from the same amount of
global emission ($J''K''$) are not equal. Because the marginal abatement costs
are not equalized, the global cost of pollution abatement is not minimized.
Surely, an equal-rate Pigovian tax will reduce the global pollution level below

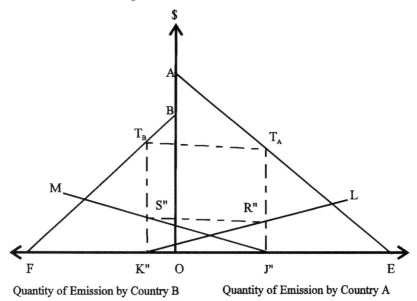

Figure 14.8 Nash Equilibrium under Equal-Rate Pigovian Taxes

that of the no-tax situation. But it is uncertain whether the tax improves the world's welfare, let alone that of the individual countries. For example, if the tax forces the high marginal abatement cost country to reduce pollution greatly while it does little to the low marginal abatement cost country, an equilibrium with inefficient resource allocation will be reached at a vector located inside the world consumption possibility frontier.

6 WELFARE NEUTRALITY OF REVENUE REDISTRIBUTION

The revenues accruing to a world authority are expected to be enormous if the authority were authorized to impose a worldwide Pigovian tax, or auction off pollution permits in a single worldwide market, to the extent that either one of the methods produces a meaningful reduction in a global pollution, such as CO_2 emissions. Some authors claim that such revenue prospects are a good aspect of the schemes proposed to establish a world authority to impose a global emission tax or to administer the sale of global pollution permits, for the revenues collected could be redistributed to developing countries. But we contend that this view is not generally correct.

First, opposition might come from the developed countries to the institution of a worldwide Pigovian tax precisely because of these enormous revenue implications.[13] But even if such opposition were overcome and the revenue redistribution was in fact done by lump-sum transfers, as it is recommended to achieve the first best solution, the redistributed incomes would be dissipated in pollution abatement activities by the recipients without improving their welfare.

Recall that the post-Pigovian tax equilibrium is represented by the Nash equilibrium that is identified as the intersection of the two countries' reaction curves generated in the presence of the Pigovian taxes (Figure 14.7). But the individual country's consumption expansion path remains unaffected by a change in the aggregate amount of income that the country receives. Therefore the reaction curves of countries (under a given set of Pigovian taxes, either a uniform rate or differentiated rates) also remain unaffected and so does the location of the Nash equilibrium.

Assume, for example, in Figure 14.6, Country B's emission level is OK_1 and Country A's consumption possibility set is given initially as $K_1A_1O_1$. Let a lump-sum subsidy of the quantity corresponding to the vertical distance between Point A_1 and Point A_1' be given to Country A in terms of the numeraire Good (Y). This subsidy enlarges Country A's consumption possibility set from $K_1A_1O_1$ to $K_1A_1A_1'O'$, but does not change the location of the consumption possibility frontier A_1K_1; it only extends the frontier by a length equal to the A_1A_1' section. This is explained below:

An income augmented by the lump-sum subsidy itself does not bring utility to the consumers of this country. The 'consumption' of that income brings utility to them. But consumption activities necessarily entail emission of pollutants, under the given available set of technologies. In Figure 14.9, let a lump-sum subsidy equal to size OO', which is equal to the vertical distance between Points A_1 and A_1', be given to Country A. It might be thought that the subsidy would shift the country's consumption possibility frontier K_1A_1 upward by a distance equal to OO' to the location $K_1''A_1''$. But such a shift does not occur. Consumption activities necessarily discharge pollutants when the income is consumed, and hence possible consumption vectors will be located to the left side of the corresponding unconsumed income vectors. Let a lump-sum subsidy equal to K_1K_1'' ($=OO'$) be received by Country A while Country B's emission level remains unchanged as OK_1. Country A's consumption of K_1K_1'' of income entails discharge of a quantity of pollutants equal to $K_1''M$. Hence this country's 'consumption-pollutants emitted' vector is represented by Point M. Similarly, when Country A consumes an income equal to the vertical distance between A_1 and A_1'' ($=K_1K_1''$) in addition to its previous consumption quantity O_1A_1, an additional quantity of pollutants equal to $A_1'A_1'$ will be discharged, and hence the consumption-pollutants emitted vector must be represented by Point A_1'

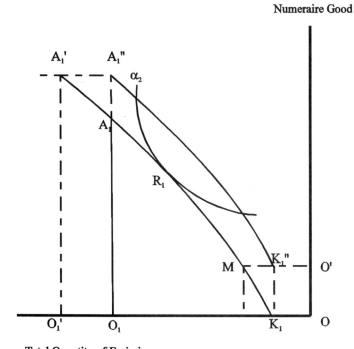

Numeraire Good

Total Quantity of Emission

Figure 14.9 Consumption Possibility Frontier and a Change in Income

and not by Point A_1''. Thus when a lump-sum subsidy equal to OO' ($=A_1'A_1'$) is given, the K_1A_1 section of the original 'consumption' possibility frontier does not shift upward to $K_1''A_1''$, but remains unchanged at the location of Curve $K_1R_1A_1$. The subsidy simply adds the section A_1A' to the original frontier as the country acquires an additional consumption possibility set equal to $O_1A_1A_1'O_1'$.

It is clear that this type of extension of the consumption possibility frontier does not change the location of Country A's welfare-maximizing consumption vector from Point R_1' (assuming the previous equilibrium was not a corner solution), because the country's consumption possibility frontier of the relevant range remains unchanged. Hence Country A's consumption expansion path also remains unchanged. Consequently, the reaction curves corresponding to the respective countries' tax-adjusted consumption expansion paths also remain unaffected when they receive lump-sum transfers. Therefore, each country's post-revenue-redistribution welfare remains at the same level as that it enjoyed before a lump-sum transfer was given.

In short, because the location of a Nash equilibrium of a public good is neutral with respect to the income distribution pattern among countries,[14] lump-sum transfers of the revenues of the taxes or of the proceeds from the auction of pollution permits will not cause any effects, favorable or unfavorable, on the welfare of the positive or negative recipients of the proceeds (income). Advocates of Pigovian effluent taxes or tradable pollution permits who base their support on the grounds of the favorable revenue implications of these schemes are thus mislead.

7   SUMMARY AND CONCLUSIONS

The proposition that minimization of the aggregate cost of abatement to achieve a given level of pollution (or a Pareto optimal level of pollution) requires equalization of marginal costs of abatement across all polluters holds even for the cases of a public bad. Obviously, the marginal costs of abatement in this context are the utility or the value of marginal products lost in the society by not emitting pollutants, which may be termed the *social* marginal cost.

It is widely alleged that imposition of equal-rate Pigovian taxes on pollutants emitted (or uniformly priced tradable pollution permits) automatically brings a state of equality in the marginal costs of abatement across all polluters. However, pollution of a public bad type inflicts damages on the polluters themselves and hence the polluter will adjust his own emission so as to reduce the damages that he otherwise inflicts upon himself. Consequently, a polluter's marginal utility from the consumption entailing pollution at the equilibrium is made equal to the marginal disutility that he suffers from the pollution. The correct Pigovian tax must, therefore, be adjusted individually so that the tax imposed on a polluter is equal to the difference between the social marginal cost of abatement and the private marginal cost of abatement, namely, the marginal disutility that he suffers from the pollution. In other words the rates of Pigovian taxes should be differentiated to account for individual differences in disutilities that polluters experience from the same aggregate quantity of pollution.

Currently, we observe that many advanced countries voluntarily undertake at least some direct or indirect measures to reduce their emission of pollutants, while assuming the pollution levels and abatement actions undertaken by others as given. Hence, the existing international equilibrium will be best characterized by a Nash-type equilibrium. The Nash equilibrium reached after imposition of an equal-rate Pigovian tax or of uniformly priced tradable pollution permits with the consequences of unequalized marginal costs of abatement among countries will be neither a Pareto optimum nor the aggregate cost minimizing solution to achieve a given standard level of pollution.

Equal-rate Pigovian taxes or uniformly priced tradable permits might succeed in achieving an efficient outcome if all countries and all polluters were to behave as if they disregarded the disutilities that their own emissions impose upon themselves (as they do correctly in a case of one-directional externalities). Indeed, this may be the case when all countries' emissions are equally small relative to the global sum of their emissions and each country believes that its own adjustment in its quantity of emissions would not change the global aggregate quantity of emissions appreciably. But it is most unlikely that they would surrender their own ability to reduce pollution when they see that they can improve their own welfare unilaterally. Consequently, when a relatively small number of large polluters are involved, as in the case of disposal of nuclear wastes, an equal-rate Pigovian tax or tradable pollution permits will not succeed in minimizing aggregate costs of abatement of all polluters (countries), let alone in achieving a Pareto optimum.[15]

The location of a Nash equilibrium involving the provision of a public good (that is, elimination of a public bad) is independent of the pattern of distribution of income among the constituents. Hence redistribution of the revenues from the tax or the proceeds of the sales of pollution permits by lump-sum transfers will not alter the distribution of welfare among countries. Therefore, recommendations in favor of a Pigovian tax or tradable pollution permits advanced on the grounds of favorable income redistribution prospects for developing countries are based on misguided logic.

ACKNOWLEDGEMENTS

The author is grateful to Professors Robert Mendelsohn (Yale University), Daigee Shaw and C.C. Yang (both of IEAS), Hiromitsu Ishi (Hitotsubashi University), Masako Murakami (Tokyo Christian University), and Akira Yokoyama (Chuo University) for their most valuable comments on an earlier draft.

NOTES

1. Proposals for equal-rate Pigovian effluent taxes as a solution for global environmental pollution originates apparently from the minimum cost theorem of W. Baumol and W. Oates. See Baumol and Oates (1971, 1975).

2. This idea originated in Dales (1968).
3. Various estimates of the total revenue which would be collected by Pigovian effluent taxes are that 'a (global) carbon tax large enough to significantly slow carbon dioxide emission would collect revenues equal to several percent of world GDP' (Poterba, 1991); 'could well account for 10 percent of global income' (Whally and Wigle, 1991); and 'about 6 percent as a percentage of (the Japanese) national tax in 1992' (Ishi, 1994).
4. See, for example, United Nations Symposia on Transnational Cooperation (1991); Dudek (1989); and Dasgupta and Maler (1990).
5. A situation can be readily conceived of such that non-equalization of Pigovian tax rates among countries becomes an optimal solution in the second-best world, that is, in the presence of many other distortions. Our argument for differential tax rates is, however, not based on the second-best argument. We assume here a situation where no other distortions but the pollution externality exist; hence if it were possible by either equal-rate Pigovian tax or tradable permits to internalize the pollution externality completely, it would bring forth the first-best solution.
6. Our argument applies better to the situation involving two individuals, for one may object to the assumption that a country has a consistent utility function. However, for expository convenience, we use countries by assuming, following the standard practice of international trade theory, that each country has a consistent utility function and utility-maximizing decision-making ability.
7. I believe this is the current standard argument for the optimal Pigovian effluent taxes. For example, Wallace Oates (1993, p.146) recently described the tax as follows:

> Figure 14.1 [our] depicts the key relationships. The aggregate marginal benefit curves (MB_W) [our Curve ON] is simply (á la Samuelson) the vertical summation of the benefit curves over the individuals in the two countries (where MB_r [our Curve OM] and MB_D [our Curve OL] are the aggregate benefit curves for the individual countries). The global marginal abatement cost curves (MAC_W) [our Curve ACG] is the horizontal summation of individual abatement cost curves...The Pareto efficient level of emissions reductions in this highly simplified setting is OA [our OH] where $MB_W = MAC_W$. *A first-best policy response would be a global effluent charge equal to* OB *[our* OP].

(Italics are mine.) See also Cropper and Oates (1992).
8. For example, currently, Sweden, Norway, Finland and the Netherlands have voluntarily enacted 'carbon taxes' to reduce CO_2 emissions in their own territories. Although these countries may be partly motivated to induce other countries to follow their leads in introducing anti-CO_2 emission rules. See Peter Bohm (1994 and 1995).

    Ozone depletion is said to result in the suppression of immune systems, plus effects on plant yields and on aquatic systems. The US banned the use of CFCs in aerosols voluntarily in 1978 before the Montreal Protocol was signed by major CFC-producing countries in 1987.
9. Many authors implicitly assume that the situation existing before introduction of a world authority is such that each country emits pollutants up to the level where its marginal utility or value of the marginal product of pollution is zero: namely, quantities OE and OF for Country A and B, respectively, in Figure 14.4. Hence, the origin of Country A's marginal disutility schedule is Point F and that of country B's is Point E. Obviously, these emission quantities are not the respective countries' equilibria because if they were, it implies that each country would emit pollutants beyond the level where its activities entailing emission would produce marginal utility (or value of marginal product) less than the marginal disutility that their emission would generate.

This 'standard' implicit assumption is appropriate only when each polluting country believes that its own emission quantity is so small relative to that of the world that consequently its pollution reduction would not alter the global emission level at all. This, however, hardly represents the beliefs of many countries of the present-day world: The Nordic countries have imposed their own 'carbon taxes'; a number of countries have voluntarily banned the use of CFCs in the past; and many other countries have some kind of voluntarily imposed regulations to curb external diseconomy-creating activities like discharges of nuclear waste. Even an individual household takes voluntary actions to reduce its own smoke emissions, in the absence of carbon taxes or emission regulations, below the level at which its marginal utility of emissions of pollutants is zero lest the smoke reduce comfort in the household.

10. If the subsidy scheme is used, the subsidy per unit of pollutants should be different from polluter to polluter. Although it is not usually pointed out, the subsidy given must satisfy, in addition to this differentiated rate (the marginal condition), a total condition such that the total amount of subsidy given to each polluter is large enough so that the polluter would not find that the total earnings that he forgo due to emission reduction are larger than the total subsidies that he is expected to receive. Henceforth, we shall not mention the Pigovian subsidy scheme specifically, but our critical argument on the equal-rate Pigovian tax scheme will apply equally to the equal-rate Pigovian subsidy scheme as well.

11. One may argue that by redistributing revenues from Pigovian taxes among countries so as to make the marginal disutilities that all countries experience equal at a Pareto optimum, the equal-rate Pigovian tax scheme can achieve a Pareto optimum. But as we shall argue below, a lump-sum redistribution of tax revenues arising from equal-rate Pigovian taxes is not capable of producing such a solution.

12. The tax rate usually ascribed to the Pigovian effluent tax (HP$'$ in Figure 14.1) is larger than the correct (differentiated) Pigovian tax rate applicable to each country (RP$'$ and SP$'$ for Countries A and B, respectively in the same figure). Therefore, each country's reaction curve under the usually recommended Pigovian tax is located below the reaction curve of the respective country that would prevail if the correct Pigovian tax rate were applied.

13. T.C. Schelling argued, 'I utterly dismiss the possibility that the United States would contribute in any fashion; let alone through taxation, upwards of 100 billion per year, or the Senate would ratify a treaty incurring such financial commitments' (T.C. Schelling, 1991, p. 215).

14. 'Independence of the Nash equilibrium of a voluntarily provided public good from income distribution' was first shown by this author by Figure 6 in his 1971 article, 'A Bargaining Model of the Pure Theory of Public Expenditures' (Shibata, 1971, p. 22), and later rediscovered by Warr (1983) and publicized since. This author's discovery, however, was neglected until Sandler called attention to it some twenty years later (Sandler 1992, p. 77). Also see Bergstrom and Varian (1985) and Bergstrom, Blume and Varian (1985).

15. It should be noted that whether either the equal-rate Pigovian taxes scheme or the tradable pollution permits scheme would produce a more efficient outcome than other schemes such as quotas or regulations in the real world is a different question from the one we are addressing here. Our attempt is to examine the validity of the logic of arguments commonly used to justify the widely circulated claims that either equal-rate Pigovian taxes or tradable permits would minimize the aggregate costs of abatement of global environmental pollution.

REFERENCES

Baumol, W.J. and W.E. Oates (1971), 'The Use of Standards and Prices for Protection of the Environment', *Swedish Journal of Economics*, **73**.

Baumol, William and William Oates (1975), *The Theory of Environmental Policy*, Englewood Cliffs, N.J.: Prentice-Hall.

Bergstrom, T., L. Blume and H. Varian (1985), 'On the Private Provision of Public Good', *Journal of Political Economy*, **93**.

Bergstrom, T. and H. Varian (1985), 'When are Nash Equilibria independent of Distribution of Agents' Characteristics?', *Review of Economic Studies*, **52**.

Bohm, Peter (1995), 'Environmental Taxes, Carbon Taxes, Tax Recycling and Tax Distortions', A paper presented at the Conference on International Harmonization of Environmental Policy, Ministry of Finance, Tokyo, Japan, March 6, 1995.

Bohm, Peter (1994), 'Government Revenue Implications of Carbon Taxes and Tradable Carbon Permits: Efficiency Aspects', A paper presented at the International Institute of Public Finance 50th Congress, August 22–25, Cambridge, MA: Harvard University.

Cropper, M.L. and W.E. Oates (1992), 'Environmental Economics: A Survey', *Journal of Economic Literature*, **30** (June), 675–740.

Dales, J.H. (1968), *Pollution, Property and Prices*, Toronto: University of Toronto Press.

Dasgupta, P. and K. Maler (1990), 'The Environment and Emerging Development Issues', A paper presented at the World Bank Annual Conference on Development Economics, April.

Dudek, D. (1989), 'Marketable Instruments for Managing Global Environmental Problems', A paper presented at the Western Economic Association in Vancouver.

Ishi, H. (1994), 'A Design of Environmental Taxes in Japan', A paper presented at the International Institute of Public Finance 50th Congress, 22–25, August, Cambridge, MA: Harvard University.

Oates, W. (1993), 'Global Environmental Management: Towards an Open Economy Environmental Economics', *Ambiente Etica Economica e Istituzioni*, Milano: Cariplo.

Poterba, J. (1991), 'Tax Policy to Combat Global Warming: On Designing an Carbon Tax', in R. Dornbusch and J. Poterba (eds), *Global Warming*: *Economic Policy Responses*, Cambridge, MA: MIT Press.

Sandler, T. (1992), *Collective Action*: *Theory and Application*, Ann Arbor: The University of Michigan Press.

Schelling, Thomas C. (1991), 'Economic Responses to Global Warming: Prospects for Cooperative Approaches', in R. Dornbusch and J.M.

Poterba (eds), *Global Warming:Economic Policy Responses*, Cambridge, MA: MIT Press.

Shibata, Hirofumi (1971), 'A Bargaining Model of the Pure Theory of Public Expenditure', *Journal of Political Economy*, **79**(1).

United Nations Symposia on Transnational Cooperation (1991), 'Options to Increase Transfer of Environmentally Sound Technologies to Development Countries on Favorable Terms', Draft Document, New York.

Warr, Peter G. (1983), 'The Private Provision of a Public Good is Independent of Distribution of Income', *Economics Letters*, **13**: 207–11.

Whally, J. and R. Wigle (1991), 'The International Incidence of Carbon Taxes', in R. Dornbusch and J. Poterba (eds), *Global Warming: Economic Policy Responses*, Cambridge, MA: MIT Press.

15. Difficulty in Enforcing Efficient Prices for Regulating Shiftable Externalities

Jerome Geaun

1 INTRODUCTION

The debate concerning how to treat the victims of a depletable externality has generated some interesting results (Freeman, 1984; Bird, 1987; Baumol and Oates, 1975, 1988; Shaw and Shaw, 1991; Geaun, 1993). In particular, the literature has revealed the importance of shiftable externalities in both theory and practice. It appears that the policy that compensates victims for accepting the externality has been favored by previous studies. However, it also appears that, in the presence of shiftable externalities, the allocative aspects of efficient prices have been somewhat overlooked, as the emphasis has been placed mostly upon how to cure the external effect caused by pollutant emissions or shifting actions. Moreover, the victim's overall response to shiftable externalities probably has not been considered in a complete manner in the proposed efficient treatments. Conceivably, there exist some feasibility problems that deserve more careful study.

In the first place, the policy of compensating acceptance (and implicitly penalizing shifting actions) may become another source of inefficiency. The victim, in addition to shifting actions, may undertake other defensive measures that lessen his exposure to the externality. As the acceptance cannot be adequately measured or distinguished from the level of exposure, his cost of reducing the exposure can be raised by the compensation policy. The victim's response of defense that does not cause any external effect is then implicitly penalized, and is thus apparently distorted.

Secondly, to induce an optimal distribution of shiftable externality across victims, the policy may incur fairly high administration cost. Baumol and Oates (1988) argue that a Pigovian charge equal to marginal social damage (evaluated at the optimum) imposed on the polluter who can decide the amount emitted to each site leads to an optimal result; the shiftable externality, such as trash, will be disposed of among the alternative sites in the least costly way to the society. However, the constant unit efficient price or identical Pigovian charge implies the marginal penalty on the polluter's emissions to different victims is the same and constant, and presumably does not cause an efficient distribution of externality. Similarly, if the victim is regulated by a unit compensation rate (or a unit tax rate) that reflects the resulting marginal external damage at the optimum, his effort of shifting (and thus the amount shifted) to each site is usually inefficient. To correct such inefficiency, normally the regulator has to set up a schedule of compensation (or tax) rates for *each* receiving site that reflects the varying marginal external damages corresponding to different levels of externality experienced at that site.

In all, this paper plans to address the issues of possible distortionary effects of compensating prices due to inadequate measures of acceptance, and the inefficient externality distribution caused by a constant unit efficient price, both of which have implications for policy feasibility. In the following, Section 2 addresses the distortionary effects of compensation policy. Sections 3 and 4 deal with the problems of constant unit prices to, respectively, polluters and victims. Section 5 concludes the paper.

2   DISTORTIONARY   EFFECTS   OF COMPENSATORY   POLICY

This section presents a basic model to analyze the problem, in undertaking the compensating policy, arising from the lack of an obvious distinction between the victim's accepted amount of externality and his level of exposure. For simplicity, it is assumed that the economy, using only one resource, L, produces only one good, X, the production of which generates a depletable externality, S, which is shiftable. Thus, with shifting actions, the victim has some choice as to the accepted amount of externality. In addition to shifting actions that can influence the distribution of externality among victims, the model incorporates the victim's defensive response of taking mitigating measures of no distributional effect to lessen his exposure to the damaging effect of any given amount of accepted externality. Following Geaun's (1993) notation for the most part:

X_i	= the amount of X consumed by individual i ($i=1,...,n$),
$\alpha_i S$	= the initial amount of S dispersed to individual i, with α_i being a positive parameter and $\Sigma^n \alpha_i = 1$,
L_i	= the amount of resource employed by individual i to shift the externality,
L_i^d	= the amount of resource that i employs in his defensive

activities,

$H^i(L_1,\ldots,L_n)$ = the net amount of externality shifted away from individual i,

Z_i = the total amount of externality accepted by individual i,

$E^i(Z_i, L_i^d)$ = individual i's exposure function indicating the level of damaging effect he actually experiences,

$U^i(X_i, E^i(\cdot))$ = individual i's utility function, and

$F(X, L_x, S) \leq 0$ = the firms' production function as a whole.

Note that Z_i equals $\alpha_i S - H^i(\cdot)$. $E^i(Z_i, L_i^d)$ describes how individual i's exposure can be reduced by his defensive effort L_i^d, depending on his accepted amount of externality. Apparently, the defensive action is specified to be of no distributional effect; for our discussion, the paper does not consider other possible external effects that an individual's defensive measures may impose on others. For instance, instead of shifting, the victim may take measures, without any external effect, to eliminate a portion of the *accepted* externality such as waste or acid rain that has potential damages for him. In such an instance, a victim's level of exposure can be measured by the amount of externality that actually damages him:

$$E^i(Z_i, L_i^d) = \alpha_i S - H^i(\cdot) - R^i(L_i^d) \tag{15.1}$$

where $R^i(\cdot)$ represents the amount of eliminated externality. Consider the real world example of trash dumping. Presumably the amount of accepted externality during a particular time period can be represented by the amount of trash accumulated in a victim's site without defensive actions. While the receiving site has at hand some measures to process or reduce the accumulated trash, the level of exposure should be measured by the accepted amount minus the amount eliminated.

Further simplification is made by considering the case of two persons, 1 and 2; thus, the Pareto optimum can be described by the following constrained maximization:

$$
\begin{aligned}
Max \quad & U^1(X_1, E^1(Z_1, L_1^d)) \\
s.t. \quad & U^2(X_2, E^2(Z_2, L_2^d)) \geq U^{2^*} \\
& F(X, L_x, S) \leq 0 \\
& X_1 + X_2 \leq X \\
& L_1 + L_1^d + L_2 + L_2^d + L_x \leq L \\
& L_i, L_i^d, L_x, X, S \geq 0
\end{aligned} \tag{15.2}
$$

where Z_1 equals $\alpha S - H(L_1, L_2)$ while Z_2 equals $(1-\alpha)S + H(L_1, L_2)$; $U_x^i > 0$, $F_x > 0, E > 0$, and $F_l < 0$ as usual; $U_e^i < 0, E_l^i < 0, H_1 > 0, H_2 < 0$, and $F_s < 0$ as assumed for the case of negative externalities. Further assume that the sufficiency conditions of convexities for the Kuhn-Tucker theorem are all satisfied. The model will accommodate the possible corner solutions of optimal shifting efforts L_i^{*}, as argued by Geaun. But, for simplification, it is assumed that all the endogenous variables, other than L_i, take interior solutions; it is also assumed that the externality can be eliminated by some defensive measures, and thus the exposure can be explicitly measured as indicated by (15.1). Maximizing the Lagrangian function:

$$\mathcal{L} = U^1(\cdot) + \lambda_2(U^2(\cdot) - U^{2^{*}})$$

$$-\lambda_f F(\cdot) + \lambda_x(X - X_1 - X_2)$$

$$+\lambda_l(L - L_1 - L^d_{\;1} - L_2 - L^d_{\;2} - L_x)$$

yields the Pareto optimum conditions

$$U_x^1 = \lambda_x \tag{15.3}$$

$$\lambda_2 U_x^2 = \lambda_x \tag{15.4}$$

$$\lambda_f F_x = \lambda_x \tag{15.5}$$

$$-U_e^1 H_1 + \lambda_2 U_e^2 H_1 \leq \lambda_l,$$

$$(-U_e^1 H_1 + \lambda_2 U_e^2 H_1 - \lambda_l)L_1 = 0 \tag{15.6}$$

$$-U_e^1 H_2 + \lambda_2 U_e^2 H_2 \leq \lambda_l,$$

$$(-U_e^1 H_2 + \lambda_2 U_e^2 H_2 - \lambda_l)L_2 = 0 \tag{15.7}$$

$$-U_e^1 R_l^1 = \lambda_l \tag{15.8}$$

$$-\lambda_2 U_e^2 R_l^2 = \lambda_l \tag{15.9}$$

$$\alpha U_e^1 + \lambda_2(1-\alpha)U_e^2 = \lambda_f F_s \tag{15.10}$$

$$-\lambda_f F_l = \lambda_l \; . \tag{15.11}$$

Conditions (15.6) and (15.7) describe the optimal amount of shifting efforts, or alternatively, the efficient allocation of externality across victims, with the possibility of corner optimal solutions being admitted. It can be shown that, by (15.6) and (15.7), optimality requires the externality be distributed among victims such that the social damage minus shifting cost is minimized. To facilitate later discussion, we suppose initially $(-U_e^1 + \lambda_2 U_e^2)$ is sufficiently greater than zero, i.e., Victim 1's marginal external damage is significantly more severe than Victim 2's. Hence, at the optimum, $L_1^* > 0$, and $L_2^* = 0$ according to the above conditions.[1]

The efficient prices that compensate the victim to accept an optimal amount of shiftable externality can be derived by Baumol and Oates's approach, comparing the Pareto optimum conditions with the corresponding market equilibrium. First, suppose that the amount of acceptance could be measured adequately. Given the experimental prices, t_z and t_z^2, Victim 1 wishes to minimize

$$PX_1 + W(L_1 + L_1^d) + t_z^1(\alpha S - H(L_1,\ L_2)) + \delta_1(U^{1^*} - U^1(X_1,\ Z_1 - R^1(L_1^d)))$$

as Victim 2 wishes to minimize

$$PX_2 + W(L_2 + L^d_2) + t_z^2((1-\alpha)S + H(L_1,\ L_2)) + \delta_2(U^{2^*} - U^2(X_2,\ Z_2 - R^2(L^d_2))).$$

The resulting market equilibrium can be described by the necessary conditions of above minimizations. Table 15.1 summarizes these results. These equilibrium conditions are then compared with the Pareto optimum conditions to solve for the efficient compensatory prices for attaining Pareto optimality. Given the condition that $L_1^* > 0$ and $L_2^* = 0$, we conclude, for attaining optimality

$$t_z^1 = \delta_1 \lambda_2 U_e^2$$

$$t_z^2 \leq (\delta_2 U_e^2 H_2 - W) \cdot H_2^{-1} \tag{15.12}$$

Assuming Victim 2 would shift if he is not regulated, both t_z^1 and t_z^2 are then negative, meaning acceptance is to be compensated.[2] Victim 1's shifting will then be implicitly penalized according to the resulting external effect, while Victim 2's shifting cost will be raised such that he will refrain completely from shifting.

However, it should be of no surprise at all that the accepted amount of externality may turn out to be hardly distinguishable from the level of exposure, and thus cannot be easily measured in an adequate manner, especially when the shifting and defensive actions are not undertaken once for all, as when the externality is emitted rather constantly and continuously. It is very likely to be the case even when the victim only lessens his exposure by reducing the amount of damaging externality. Refer to the case

Table 15.1 Equilibrium Conditions with Adequate Measure of Acceptance

Agent 1	Agent 2
$P-\delta_1 U_x^1=0$	$P-\delta_1 U_x^2=0$
$W-t_z^1 H_1+\delta_1 U_e^1 H_1 \geq 0$	$W+t_z^2 H_2-\delta_2 U_e^2 H_2 \geq 0$
$(W-t_z^1 H_1+\delta_1 U_e^1 H_1) \cdot L_1=0$	$(W+t_z^2 H_2-\delta_2 U_e^2 H_2) \cdot L_2=0$
$W+\delta_1 U_e^1 R_l^1=0$	$W+\delta_2 U_e^2 R_l^2=0$

of waste dumping (or acid rain) for example. A receiving victim may off and on take measures to eliminate the waste (or acid rain) by himself. In such a particular case, it then does not appear easy to measure the accepted amount without incurring high monitoring cost.

Under such circumstances, the level of exposure is usually taken to be the tax base of the compensating policy, or the regulator may even use it as the substitute to save enforcement cost. As such, the market equilibrium should be derived from different minimizations. Victim 1 is now taken to minimize

$$PX_1+W(L_1+ L_1^d) + t_e^1(Z_1- R^1(\cdot)) + \delta_1[U^{1^*}- U^1(X_1, Z_1- R^1(L_1^d))]$$

while Victim 2 is taken to minimize

$$PX_2+W(L_2+L_2^d) + t_e^2(Z_2- R^1(\cdot)) + \delta_2[U^{2^*}- U^2(X_2, Z_2- R^2(L_2^d))]$$

where t_e^1 and t_e^2 are the experimental rates of compensation. Table 15.2 summarizes the necessary conditions of minimization as representative of market equilibrium. Comparing these conditions with (15.6) and (15.7), it turns out that, to induce optimal amounts of acceptance,

$$t_e^1 = \delta_1 \lambda_2 U_e^2$$

$$t_e^2 \leq (\delta_2 U_e^2 H_2 - W)H_2^{-1}.$$
(15.13)

But, comparing with conditions (15.8) and (15.9), optimality requires

$$t_e^1 = t_e^2 = 0$$
(15.14)

which contradicts the results in (15.13).

It appears that t_e^i in (15.13) is essentially the same as t_z^i in (15.12). However, the result in (15.14) indicates that the external damages provide sufficient incentives for the victim to take efficient defensive measures, and no price is necessary. Therefore, the regulatory prices, such as those in

Table 15.2 Equilibrium Conditions with Inadequate Measure of Acceptance

Agent 1	Agent 2
$P-\delta_1 U_x^1=0$	$P-\delta_1 U_x^2=0$
$W-t_e^1 H_1+\delta_1 U_e^1 H_1 \geq 0$	$W+t_e^2 H_2-\delta_2 U_e^2 H_2 \geq 0$
$(W-t_e^1 H_1+\delta_1 U_e^1 H_1)\cdot L_1=0$	$(W+t_e^2 H_2-\delta_2 U_e^2 H_2)\cdot L_2=0$
$W-t_e^1 R_l^1+\delta_1 U_e^1 R_l^1=0$	$W-t_e^2 R_l^2+\delta_2 U_e^2 R_l^2=0$

(15.13), that are imposed on the victims' exposure will distort their defensive choice. For instance, in the case of trash dumping, as the victim has at hand some measures to process and reduce the accumulated trash, his cost of such defensive actions can be raised by the policy that intends to compensate acceptance but is imposed on exposure. Hence, his defensive behavior will then be distorted.

Presumably, it is costly to measure the accepted amount, as acceptance is not easily distinguishable from exposure. It is worth noting that, with information cost taken into account, the state where the victim's defensive actions are distorted can be Pareto superior to that defined by the optimum model of (15.2). That is, whether the distortion problem should be of concern depends on the magnitude of the resulting efficiency loss relative to the corresponding information cost.

3   INEFFICIENT ALLOCATION OF EXTERNALITY BY POLLUTERS

The above analysis has revealed that optimality requires the shiftable externality be allocated among the victims in a manner that minimizes the total social damage minus shifting cost. As Baumol and Oates (1988) emphasize that efficiency requires the prices to cure the external effects due to the polluter's emission and the victim's shifting, they appear to have somewhat overlooked the allocative aspects of the efficient prices. In particular, in arguing that a Pigovian charge equal to marginal social damage leads to an optimal result (pp. 21–23), they seem to believe that the generator can be counted on to optimally allocate the shiftable externality.

This section shows that a Pigovian charge, imposed on the polluter, equal to marginal social damage, or a schedule of fees that reflects the varying marginal damages associated with the dumping of externality at alternative sites, may not be sufficient for attaining optimality. Normally, in the case

such as trash dumping (in Baumol and Oates's example), where the polluter
has choice over the amount he emits to each site, optimality requires a
schedule of fees for *each* alternative site, reflecting the corresponding
schedule of marginal external damages. The basic model is now slightly
modified to illustrate this point. Supposing the polluter has choice as to
where to dump the externality, the *initial* amount of externality dispersed to
each victim is no longer exogenous to him, as indicated by $\alpha_i S$. Instead,
recognizing the polluter's allocative capacity, Victim i's accepted amount Z_i
equals $S_i - H^i(\cdot)$, where S_i is endogenous to the polluter and exogenous to
the victim. Therefore, in a two-person world, the Pareto optimum can be
described by maximizing the following Lagrangian function

$$\mathcal{L} = U^1(X_1,\ S_1 - H(\cdot)) + \lambda_2(U^2(X_2,\ S_2 + H(\cdot)) - U^{2^*})$$

$$-\lambda_f\ F(X,\ L_x,\ S_1 + S_2) + \lambda_x(X - X_1 - X_2)$$

$$+\lambda_l(L - L_1 - L_2 - L_x)$$

yielding the necessary conditions

$$U_x^1 = \lambda_x \tag{15.15}$$

$$\lambda_2 U_x^2 = \lambda_x \tag{15.16}$$

$$\lambda_f\ F_x = \lambda_x \tag{15.17}$$

$$-U_z^1 H_1 + \lambda_2 U_z^2 H_1 \le \lambda_P$$

$$(-U_z^1 H_1 + \lambda_2 U_z^2 H_1 - \lambda_P)L_1 = 0 \tag{15.18}$$

$$-U_z^1 H_2 + \lambda_2 U_z^2 H_2 \le \lambda_P$$

$$(-U_z^1 H_2 + \lambda_2 U_z^2 H_2 - \lambda_P)L_2 = 0 \tag{15.19}$$

$$-\lambda_f\ F_l = \lambda_l \tag{15.20}$$

$$U_z^1 = \lambda_f\ F_s \tag{15.21}$$

$$\lambda_2 U_z^2 = \lambda_f\ F_s. \tag{15.22}$$

Note that, for simplicity, the present model does not include the victim's defensive action.   By (15.18), (15.19), (15.21) and (15.22), optimality requires that the externality be allocated by the polluter among the victims such that their marginal external damages are equal, i.e., $U_z^1 = \lambda_2 U_z^2$, implying both victims are required not to shift, i.e., $L_1^* = L_2^* = 0$. That is, if the polluter has initially optimally allocated the externality, efficiency prohibits the victims from shifting. In addition, condition (15.21) or (15.22) implies that, for attaining optimality, the marginal product value of externality should equal each victim's marginal external damage.

The efficient prices to the polluter that induce him to emit an efficient amount of externality and to allocate it optimally can be solved for by using, again, Baumol and Oates's approach. With the experimental prices t_1 and t_2 imposed on the amounts emitted to the sites of Victims 1 and 2, the polluter is taken to maximize

$$PX_1 - WL_x - t_1 S_1 - t_2 S_2 - \delta_f F(X, L_x, S_1 + S_2).$$

Thus, the market equilibrium can be represented by the following necessary conditions

$$P = \delta_f F_x$$

$$-W = \delta_f F_l$$

$$-t_1 = \delta_f F_s$$

$$-t_2 = \delta_f F_s.$$

Comparing with the optimum conditions, efficiency requires

$$t_1 = t_2 = -U_z^1 = -\lambda_2 U_z^2.$$

Thus, it seems that the identical constant unit price (per unit of emitted pollutant) equal to the victim's marginal external damage evaluated at the optimum causes an efficient equilibrium.

However, such a scheme is presumably inefficient, because it provides no incentive for the polluter to emit an optimal amount of externality to *each* victim. Given the single constant price, the last two necessary conditions are in fact identical, not allowing the determination of both S_1^* and S_2^*. This point becomes even more obvious as the polluter's profit function is represented instead by

$$PX - WL_x - t_1(S_1 + S_2) - \delta_f F(X, L_x, S_1 + S_2).$$

The uniform constant price only leads to an optimal amount of $(S_1 + S_2)$. Intuitively, the identical unit charge for a polluter's emissions implies that the marginal penalty on his emissions to different victims is the same and constant, and thus provides no incentive for him to discriminate properly among the victims.

To remedy such a problem of inefficient externality distribution, the price scheme can impose on the amount of externality emitted to each site a list of charges that reflects the corresponding schedule of marginal external damages. With the penalty functions, $T^1(S_1)$ and $T^2(S_2)$, tentatively imposed on his emissions, the polluter is now taken to maximize

$$PX - WL_x - T^1(S_1) - T^2(S_2) - \delta_f F(X, L_x, S_1 + S_2)$$

yielding the following equilibrium conditions

$$P = \delta_f F_x$$

$$-W = \delta_f F_l$$

$$-T_s^1 = \delta_f F_s$$

$$-T_s^2 = \delta_f F_s \ .$$

Apparently, as T_s^1 and T_s^2 are specified to be, respectively, the functions U_z^1 and $\lambda_2 U_z^2$, i.e., the schedules of marginal external damages of Victims 1 and 2, rather than their values at the optimum, the policy scheme leads to an equilibrium that coincides with the optimum conditions. Hence, due to the necessity of estimating marginal damage functions, it appears very costly to induce an efficient equilibrium by regulating the polluter of a shiftable externality.

Note that, in addition to the polluter's emission, the distribution of externality depends also on the victim's shifting efforts. The constant polluter's price indeed cannot cause an equilibrium that accords with the Pareto optimum if the victims are not properly regulated. As the victim's shifting actions are regulated in a manner that leads to optimality, the efficiency loss due to the uniform polluter's price can be represented by their shifting costs. The problem of inefficient polluter's prices can be disregarded if the information cost of estimating penalty functions is greater than such an efficiency loss. But, note that whether the victim's shifting actions can result in an efficient equilibrium is another debatable issue.

4   INEFFICIENT SHIFTING BY VICTIMS

The result in the last section concerning the constant unit Pigovian charge to the polluter can be extended to the enforcement of the efficient price for regulating the victim's shifting actions. The optimal price for a victim's acceptance or shifting is supposed to induce optimal acceptance and/or shifting, and thus cause an efficient distribution of externality. However, in an economy of many persons, presumably a constant rate of unit compensation (or penalty) on a victim's acceptance (or shifting) for regulating his shifting to different sites does not lead to optimality. The basic reason is that the uniform constant price level implies an identical constant marginal penalty on the victim's shifting to different sites, and thus usually does not induce an optimal amount shifted to each site.

To illustrate this point, our model is enlarged to accommodate three victims, with H_i^j denoting the net amount of externality shifted from victim i to j. Of course, H_i^j depends on both i and j's efforts of shifting to each other. But, to simplify the model, it is assumed that optimality requires that $H_1^{2\,*}, H_1^{3\,*}$ and $H_2^{3\,*}$ be non-negative; thus, the victim's shifting efforts are not incorporated in the model. For example, Victim 1's final amount of accepted externality Z_1 now equals $\alpha_1 S - H_1^2 - H_1^3$, where α_1 is the dispersion parameter. Since the shifting inputs are omitted for convenience, all the resource is employed for the production of X. Hence, the Pareto optimum conditions for the case of three victims can be obtained by maximizing the following Lagrangian function

$$\mathcal{L} = U^1(X_1, \ \alpha_1 S - H_1^2 - H_1^3)$$

$$+ \lambda_2 (U^2(X_2, \ \alpha_2 S + H_1^2 - H_2^3) - U^{2^*})$$

$$+ \lambda_3 (U^3(X_3, \ \alpha_3 S + H_1^3 + H_2^3) - U^{3^*})$$

$$- \lambda_f \ F(X, \ L, \ S)$$

$$+ \lambda_x (X - X_1 - X_2 - X_3).$$

Note that the present model does not incorporate the polluter's allocative capacity and the victim's defensive action. The conditions in the following that govern the victim's optimal shifting are of particular interest to this section:

$$-U_z^1 + \lambda_2 U_z^2 \leq 0,$$

$$(-U_z^1 + \lambda_2 U_z^2) H_1^2 = 0 \qquad (15.23)$$

$$-U_z^1 + \lambda_3 U_z^3 \leq 0,$$

$$(-U_z^1 + \lambda_3 U_z^3) H_1^3 = 0 \qquad (15.24)$$

$$-\lambda_2 U_z^2 + \lambda_3 U_z^3 \leq 0,$$

$$(-\lambda_2 U_z^2 + \lambda_3 U_z^3) H_2^3 = 0. \tag{15.25}$$

If Victim 1's marginal external damage is more severe than that of other victims, he should shift away externality to the others, according to (15.23) and (15.24). That optimality requires $H_1^2{}^* > 0$ and $H_1^3{}^* > 0$ implies $(-U_z^1 + \lambda_2 U_z^2)$ $= 0$ and $(-U_z^1 + \lambda_3 U_z^3) = 0$, assuming $Z_i^* \geq 0$. It follows that $\lambda_2 U_z^2 = \lambda_3 U_z^3$, meaning Victim 1 should shift until the other two victims' marginal damages become equal.[3] Next, this section illustrates the difficulty caused by the constant rate of unit compensation for the victim's acceptance. With the tentative price t_z^1 imposed on his acceptance, Victim 1's optimal decision can be represented by minimizing

$$PX_1 + t_z^1(\alpha_1 S - H_1^2 - H_1^3) + \delta_1(U^{1^*} - U^1(\cdot))$$

yielding the following necessary conditions:

$$P = \delta_1 U_x^1$$

$$-t_z^1 + \delta_1 U_z^1 \geq 0,$$

$$(-t_z^1 + \delta_1 U_z^1) H_1^2 = 0 \tag{15.26}$$

$$-t_z^1 + \delta_1 U_z^1 \geq 0,$$

$$(-t_z^1 + \delta_1 U_z^1) H_1^3 = 0. \tag{15.27}$$

Suppose that Pareto efficiency requires Victim 1 shift to both Victims 2 and 3, and thus $\lambda_2 U_z^2 = \lambda_3 U_z^3$, as revealed by the above analysis. Compared with (15.23) and (15.24), for achieving optimality, conditions (15.26) and (15.27) imply $t_z^1 = \delta_1 \lambda_2 U_z^2 = \delta_1 \lambda_3 U_z^3$. Hence, it seems a constant rate of unit compensation, equal to the identical marginal damage evaluated at the optimum, is required for attaining optimality. However, in such a situation, conditions (15.26) and (15.27) are essentially identical, not allowing the optimal solution of both H_1^2 and H_1^3.

This argument certainly applies equally well to the other two victims' shifting actions. With the uniform constant unit price, a victim normally shifts an inefficient amount to each of the others. Thus, the optimal allocation of externality among the victims normally cannot be achieved. Of course, a reservation may be necessary due to the exclusion of shifting cost from the model. But, presumably with the shifting costs taken into account, the principal conclusion concerning the inefficiency due to a constant Pigovian charge still holds.[4] Intuitively speaking, an identical constant unit price level means that the marginal penalty (disregarding shifting costs for convenience) on a victim's shifting to different sites is the same and constant, and thus provides no incentive for him to properly discriminate among other victims. Such a point is obvious if Victim 1's optimization is alternatively represented by minimizing

$$PX_1 + t_z^1(\alpha_1 S - (H_1^2 + H_1^3)) + \delta_1(U^{1^*} - U^1(X_1, \alpha_1 S - (H_1^2 + H_1^3)))$$

of which the necessary conditions allow only the solution of optimal $(H_1^2 + H_1^3)$. The point can be generalized straightforwardly to other price schemes; and it implies the same enforcement difficulty as that in the case where the regulator intends to induce the polluter to optimally allocate the externality.

It is fairly costly to remedy such problems of inefficient externality allocation by victims. Just as in the case of the polluter's price, one alternative resolution would be imposing, on the net amount of externality that the victim has shifted to each site, a list of penalties reflecting the schedule of corresponding marginal external damages. Incorporating the penalty functions, $F^2(H_1^2)$ and $F^3(H_1^3)$, in the model, Victim 1 now wishes to minimize

$$PX_1 + F^2(H_1^2) + F^3(H_1^3) + \delta_1(U^{1^*} - U^1(X_1, \alpha_1 S - H_1^2 - H_1^3))$$

In a very similar manner, it can be shown that, as F_H^2 and F_H^3 are taken to be, respectively, the functions $\delta_1\lambda_2 U_z^2$ and $\delta_1\lambda_3 U_z^3$, the policy scheme will lead to efficient solutions of both H_1^2 and H_1^3. Hence, the attainment of optimality may require estimating the marginal damage function of each victim, which appears costly. Furthermore, such a resolution can hardly apply to the policy that compensates acceptance, unless it is possible to distinguish among the net amounts of accepted externality shifted from/to different sites.

On the other hand, instead of estimating the whole schedule of marginal external damages of each site, the regulator can still impose a constant efficient price, equal to $\delta_1\lambda_i U_z^i$ evaluated at the optimum, on the victim's acceptance, with the proviso that his efforts that shift externality to a resisting victim must receive additional penalty.[5] Since it may prevent Victim 1 from shifting an excessive amount to each site, such a scheme perhaps can induce him to discriminate among other victims properly, though the monitoring cost could be still very high and the resulting resistance incurs additional resource cost.

Of course, whether the inefficiency due to a uniform constant victim's price should be of concern depends to a great extent on the magnitude of the resulting efficiency loss. The inefficient externality distribution can be Pareto irrelevant if such efficiency loss is relatively minor compared to the enforcement cost of the above-mentioned alternatives. However, as each victim normally shifts an incorrect amount to any of the other victims, the resulting shifting war is presumably endless. Hence, the efficiency loss can hardly be minor and the enforcement difficulty matters.

5　CONCLUSIONS

The efficient treatment of shiftable externalities has attracted much attention since Bird first introduced the concept of shiftability (1987). It appears that, from the viewpoint of feasibility, the literature tends to favor the compensation policy that provides incentives to the victim for accepting an optimal amount of externality. Although an efficient treatment is supposed to induce optimal acceptance and/or shifting, and thus an efficient distribution of externality, the allocative aspects of efficient prices appear to have been somewhat overlooked in a two-person economy.

The analysis in this paper has shown that, in certain cases, the compensating policy may become another source of inefficiency, owing to the fact that the amount of accepted externality may not be adequately distinguishable from the level of the victim's exposure to externality. The shifting cost being omitted from the model for convenience, the analysis also concludes that the constant efficient unit price, equal to the corresponding marginal social damage evaluated at the optimum, that confronts the polluter or victim fails to achieve an efficient allocation of externality, which is presumably Pareto-relevant as the resulting efficiency loss is rarely minor. In summary, our analysis has indicated that the policy that compensates the victim's acceptance is not necessarily the most beneficial. It may distort the victim's defensive behavior. To cure the problem of inefficient externality distribution caused by a constant efficient price, a compensation policy normally requires no less administration cost.

So far, shiftable externalities appear to be quite common and significant phenomena. Take, for example, NIMBY (not in my backyard), LULU (locally unwanted land use) protests, and similar conflicts in siting of environmental hazards, which readily present themselves in the real world. The literature has also started to pay attention to the feasibility of enforcing efficient prices for regulating a shiftable externality. This paper merely represents another attempt to explore the genuine features of the efficient price and to investigate the enforcement difficulty. Evidently, enforcement difficulty is always an important issue in any policy proposal. The implications of shifting cost and, given the difficulties peculiar to the efficient price approach, the feasibility of a property rights approach would be among those topics that deserve further study.

NOTES

1. As $(-U_e^1 + \lambda_2 U_e^2)$ is initially greater then $\lambda_t\, H^{-1}$, Victim 1 should shift until both the equalities in (15.6) hold.
2. Such an assumption implies that $(\delta_2 U_e^2 H_2 - W)$ is positive according to the equilibrium conditions.
3. This result leads to the conclusion $H_2^{3*} \geq 0$. Assuming the opportunity cost of shifting efforts is positive, optimality then requires that $H_2^{3*} = 0$. Therefore, in this case, for the attainment of optimality, Victim 1 is supposed to be the only shifter.
4. In another manuscript, the author has reached the same result as a part of the conclusion obtained from a model incorporating shifting costs, which is rather cumbersome in its expression and covers certain different issues.
5. Simply referring to Table 15.1 for example, we see that as Victim 2 starts to resist, the equilibrium condition will violate condition (15.7).

REFERENCES

Baumol, W. and W. Oates (1975), *The Theory of Environmental Policy: Externalities, Public Outlays, and the Quality of Life*, Englewood Cliffs, NJ: Prentice-Hall.

Baumol, W. and W. Oates (1988), *The Theory of Environmental Policy*, 2nd ed., Cambridge, UK: Cambridge University Press.

Bird, P. (1987), 'The Transferability and Depletability of Externalities', *Journal of Environmental Economics and Management*, **14**, 54–57.

Cornes, R. and T. Sandler (1985), 'Externalities, Expectations, and Pigovian Taxes', *Journal of Environmental Economics and Management*, **12**, 1–13.

Freeman, A.M. III (1984), 'Depletable Externalities and Pigovian Taxation', *Journal of Environmental Economics and Management*, **11**, 173–9.

Geaun, J.C. (1993), 'On the Shiftable Externalities', *Journal of Environmental Economics and Management*, **24**, 30–44.

Oates, W. (1983), 'The Regulation of Externalities: Efficient Behavior by Sources and Victims', *Public Finance*, **38**, 425–37.

Shaw, D. and R.D. Shaw (1991), 'The Resistability and Shiftability of Depletable Externalities', *Journal of Environmental Economics and Management*, **20**, 224–33.

Shibata, H. and J. Winrich (1983), 'Control of Pollution When the Offended Defend Themselves', *Economica*, **50**, 425–37.

16. Optimal Environmental Quality Improvement in a Multi-Goods R&D Growth Model

Victor T.Y. Hung and Pamela Chang

1 INTRODUCTION

Pollution can impose both implicit costs, in the form of a lower quality of life, and explicit costs, such as damage to the environment and health, on a population. Formulating a coherent environmental policy to regulate industry necessitates a general equilibrium analysis. In particular, one of the most urgent issues is how to motivate market research and development of innovative new products that improve environmental quality. By using an intertemporal general equilibrium model, we are able to address some issues about environmental quality upgrading which may interest policy-makers.

Negative environmental externalities exist because firms and consumers do not take into account the damage to the environment caused by the actions of production and consumption. For example, production that involves the heavy use of coal leads to sulphur dioxide being emitted into the atmosphere through smokestacks. This is a production externality since the firms do not consider it a cost in production. To require firms to recognize this added expense is in general thought to raise their production costs, leading to higher prices, lower profits, less capital investment and slower growth. The question of how to improve environmental quality while sustaining economic growth has raised the interesting possibility that innovative activity might be able to mitigate the trade-off between the two goals. New production processes and new products have the potential of (1) reducing the amount of environmental damage caused during production and consumption and (2) raising the efficiency of production.

Recently there have been some growth models with pollution external-ities. Most of these models use a production externality which interacts with an environmental externality (Gradus and Smulders, 1993; Michel and Rotillon, 1993; Ploeg and Ligthart, 1993; Musu and Lines, 1993; Huang and

Cai, 1994). Very little work, however, has been done on incorporating environmental externalities into growth models along with endogenous technical progress. Since new technology can take into account environmental concerns and is able to be more environmentally friendly, allowing it to replace old and polluting technologies may be a better policy strategy. However, production based on new technology will still continue to generate pollution. As a result, it is crucial to link up technological development and environmental policies. Any environmental policy needs to take into account its effect on future technology development and feedback to the policy. Otherwise, we may either give up too much technological progress in order to preserve our environment or sacrifice too little to maintain it.

Without including technological progress, we may underestimate the impact of environmental regulations. The only significant piece of work which looks at the impact of environmental regulations on economic growth is by Jorgenson and Wilcoxen (1990). They use the Solow growth model with passive endogenous productivity growth to estimate the costs of such policies. They found only a 0.19% decline in the annual growth rate of the US. Liang (1994) uses a similar model to estimate the impacts on the Taiwanese economy. He also found a small effect on the growth rate. The Solow growth model is based on a perfectly competitive market structure. However, the energy sector and some polluting sectors of the industrial world are not competitive at all. We may have to reinterpret the estimates if we wish to take into account the market structure of those sectors.

Recent research on growth models has attempted to isolate and examine the effects of aggregate innovative activity and the development of new products on economic growth. In particular, Stokey (1992) uses a single-good model showing that even with different cost structures and preferences, and thus different market rates of R&D, economies will have the same socially optimal rate of R&D. Our paper extends her model with consideration of endogenous technical progress of the economy and environmental quality. We apply it to examine the trade-off between product innovations and improvement of pollution abatement technology. Firms pollute the environment through waste disposal or the emission of polluting chemicals into the air or water. This production externality problem can be alleviated by installing pollution abatement equipment. The abatement technology can be improved upon with adequate R&D. However, at the same time, firms are interested in spending their resources on developing new products, creating new markets and reaping monopoly profits in these new product markets. It can be shown that markets do not provide enough incentive for environmental improvement and instead may encourage too much growth relative to the social optimum if the pollution damage is large.

Given that in the presence of a production externality such as pollution, the market will not generate the socially optimal rate of R&D in the pollution abatement technology sector, governmental intervention could theoretically be used to correct this deviation which has been perceived as a market failure. However insufficient resources and low efficiency of R&D in abatement technology can prevent social planners from investing in environmental improvement. Therefore a government can only optimally invest in R&D on environmental quality once its resources reach a minimum threshold. Besides, we found that the optimal rate of R&D in abatement technology also increases as resources increase. This explains the recent stylized facts of environmental improvement along with economic development which are documented by Holtz-Eakin and Selden (1992), Grossman (1993), Baldwin (1993) and Grossman and Krueger (1994). These researchers all found that the environment deteriorates in the beginning of economic development and then begins to improve after some minimum level of income per capita has been achieved. In Section 2, we describe the model, and we solve the market and social planner (government intervention) equilibria in Section 3. We compare the two equilibria in Section 4. We discuss the policy implications in Section 5 and include an appendix at the end.

2   THE MODEL

We use a product variety R&D growth model similar to that of Grossman and Helpman (1989) and Romer (1990), with the additional feature of quality upgrading.[1] The utility function of the representative household is as follows:

$$\sum_{t=0}^{\infty} \exp(-\rho t) \; u(x_t, E_t) \qquad (16.1)$$

where ρ is the subjective discount rate and $u(x_t, E_t)$ is the instantaneous utility function defined over the consumption bundle $x_t = [x_{1,t}, x_{2,t}, ..., x_{K,t}]$ and the pollution emissions $E_t = [E_{1,t}, E_{2,t}, ..., E_{K,t}]$, K is the number of products in the economy, $x_{i,t}$ is the consumption of the ith good at time t, and $E_{i,t}$ is the effective (or net) pollution emissions from firm i in the economy at time t. With variables like $x_{i,t}(j)$, the subscripts, i and t, label the firm index and time period respectively, whereas the bracket index j denotes the state of technology. In order to simplify the notation, we omit the firm index and the time subscripts when they are obvious.

$$u(x,E) = \frac{\{(\sum_{i=1}^{K} x_i^{\alpha})^{\frac{1}{\alpha}} (\sum_{i=1}^{K} E_i)^{-\lambda}\}^{1-\sigma} - 1}{1 - \sigma} \tag{16.2}$$

where α relates the elasticity across the goods x_i (it is smaller than one), λ is the proxy for pollution damage (the higher the λ, the larger the damage) and $1/\sigma$ is the intertemporal elasticity of substitution. The budget constraint is

$$L + \exp(r_t) W_t = W_{t+1} + Y_t$$
$$Y_t = \sum_{i=1}^{K} p_{i,t} \, x_{i,t} \tag{16.3}$$

where L is the labor endowment, which is constant over time, r_t is the interest rate, W_t is wealth and Y_t is the expenditure at time t.

The production function is $x_i = l_i \, \psi(E_i \, A)$, where l_i = labor input and $E_i A = e_i$ with $\psi'(e_i) > 0$ for $e_i < \tilde{e}$ and $\psi'(e_i) = 0$ for $e_i \geq \tilde{e}$ for all i. A is the pollution abatement technology, e_i is the pollution generated by the firm prior to any abatement which we define with the assumption $A = 1$; and as noted before, E_i is the net emission level of firm i after abatement. Given technology A, the more emissions generated by the production process, the higher is the productivity of the input l_i. This leads to an $\tilde{e}$, the maximum emission level obtained from a firm's profit-maximizing behavior.

Since the endowment L is fixed, there is no loss of generality in noting that E_i is independent of x_i. With diminishing returns to emissions, we assume that the elasticity of ψ is decreasing with respect to e. Furthermore, we assume that ψ and $\tilde{e}$ are the same for all firms i and that there exists a general pollution abatement technology A for all industries. As a result, each firm's effective emission level is $E_i = \tilde{e}/A$. We normalize the wage rate to one, so the marginal cost of producing x_i is $1/\psi(\tilde{e})$ without government intervention.

With the constant elasticity of substitution (CES) utility function of (16.2) and the budget constraint (16.3), the demand for x_i is $p_i^{-1/(1-\alpha)} Y / [\Sigma_{i=1}^{K} p_i^{-1/(1-\alpha)}]$. Given the existence of Bertrand price competition between K firms,[2] we have constant mark-up price equilibrium: each firm sets price $p_i = 1/[\alpha\psi(\tilde{e}_i)]$. By symmetry, $x_i = x$, $\forall i$ and $x = \alpha \, \psi(\tilde{e}) \, Y/K$. This implies that the profits of all firms π_K are $(1-\alpha)Y/K$.

Suppose R&D firms can either undertake research to invent a new product x or lower the pollution emissions of firms by increasing the efficiency of the abatement technology A. A improves multiplicatively: $A(j+1) = \gamma \, A(j)$. K, the number of products, on the other hand, by definition can only increase arithmetically. We further assume that the probability function of a successful innovation of A is state-independent

$p_A(z_A)$ and that of a new product is state-dependent and linear: $p(z_K, K) = \phi_K K z_K$, where z_A and z_K are the research inputs for the abatement technology and product innovations respectively. The intuition behind the specifications above is that both R&D on abatement and new products have intertemporal knowledge spillovers. By investing in R&D this period, one increases the probability of a successful innovation in products the next period and increases the improvement that will occur in abatement technology in the future. We impose additional regularity conditions on the function $p_A(z_A)$, i.e., $p_A(0) = 0, p_A' > 0$ and $p_A'' \leq 0$ and we assume $\phi_K > 0$.

Due to monopolistic competition in the goods market, the existence of knowledge spillovers in the R&D sector, and of the pollution externality in production, the market equilibrium is not optimal. We define the growth of the economy as the growth in utility derived from private consumption: $[\Sigma_{i=1}^{K} x_i^{\alpha}]^{1/\alpha}$, and environment degradation as the decrease in utility derived from pollution damage: $[\Sigma_{i=1}^{K} E_i]^{\lambda}$. In the following sections, we solve both market and social planner equilibria, compare them, and discuss environment improvement and economic growth in a later section.

3 MARKET AND SOCIAL PLANNER EQUILIBRIA

Without any government-mandated control over pollution, firms will not pay to install the pollution-abatement technology A. In the absence of regulations, improvements in A do not affect the marginal cost of the firms because $\tilde{e} = E(0)A(0)$ when the technology is $A(0)$, or equal to $E(1)A(1)$, when the technology is $A(1)$. Since firms are not constrained by their effective emissions E, they will not pay to install A to lower emission to $E(1)$. Therefore, given that it requires resources to do R&D, there is no private incentive to improve the pollution abatement technology because improving pollution abatement technology only leads to negative profits. The market rate of $\tilde{z}_A$ will be zero. On the contrary, new products create their own markets and generate monopoly profits. With property rights protection, firms will do R&D to search for new products. The sum of present discounted profits from the new product is $\Sigma_{t=0}^{\infty} \exp\{-\int_0^t r_s \, ds\} \pi_t$. Given that the probability of success is $p_K(z_K, K)$ and the cost of R&D is z_K, the first-order condition for profit maximization of R&D firms at the steady state (with a constant interest rate r and $\Delta K/K$) is

$$\pi_0 \, (\partial p_K(z_K, K)/\partial z_K)/(r + \Delta K/K) = 1$$

$$\Rightarrow (1-\alpha)(L - z_K)\phi_K/(r + \Delta K/K) = 1 \qquad (16.4)$$

where profits $\pi_0 = (1-\alpha)Y/K$ and Y equals $L - z_K$ because aggregate saving equals investment in R&D.[3]

Under the intertemporal optimization conditions, the rate of change of the marginal utility of expenditure Y equals $\rho - r$. With the Euler equation and the marginal utility:[4]

$$\Delta \ln \left(\frac{\partial u}{\partial Y} \right) = \rho - r$$

$$\frac{\partial u(Y,K,A)}{\partial Y} = [K^{\alpha^{-1}-1-\lambda} \alpha \psi(\tilde{e}) \tilde{e}^{-\lambda} A^{\lambda}]^{1-\sigma} Y^{-\sigma} \tag{16.5}$$

The market interest rate at the steady state can be written as

$$r = \rho - (1-\sigma) \left[(\alpha^{-1}-1-\lambda) \frac{\Delta K}{K} + \lambda \frac{\Delta A}{A} \right] \tag{16.6}$$

The second term in the right-hand side of (16.6) indicates that more variety increases the utility but also generates new pollution from the new products. The net effect can be negative if $\alpha^{-1} < 1 + \lambda$. The third term is the increase in marginal utility due to the decrease in pollution emissions from the technical progress of A. Substituting r of (16.6) into (16.4) together with

$$\Delta K = p_K(z_K, K) = \phi_K z_K K; \quad \frac{\Delta A}{A} = p_A(z_A)(\gamma - 1) \tag{16.7}$$

and the assumption of $p_A(0) = 0$, we can solve for the market rate of R&D for product innovation

$$\tilde{z}_K = \frac{(1-\alpha)L - \rho / \phi_K}{2 - \alpha - (1-\sigma)(\alpha^{-1}-1-\lambda)} \tag{16.8}$$

In solving for the social planner's equilibrium (or the governmental policy-maker's equilibrium), as in the case of the market solution, firms have the same abatement technology and all x_i and E_i are equal across firms in equilibrium. Since the unit input is $\psi(e)$, the social planner will choose x equal to $\psi(e)$ multiplied by the input for each industry i, which is the endowment L minus the total R&D inputs divided by the number of firms K. This restores the static efficiency where price equals marginal cost. Total emissions is $\Sigma_{i=1}^{K} E_i = Ke/A$. Therefore the social planner maximizes the objective function

$$\sum_{t=0}^{\infty} \exp(-\rho t) \; \frac{\{K_t^{\alpha^{-1}} \; [(L - z_A - z_K/K_t) \; \psi(e)] \; [K_t \; (e/A_t)]^{-\lambda} \}^{1-\sigma} - 1}{1 - \sigma} \quad (16.9)$$

with respect to e, the rates of R&D expenditure on product innovation and abatement technology, z_K and z_A respectively.

There are two static inefficient problems in the market equilibrium. The first one is that firms in choosing a larger $\tilde{e}$ neglect the negative externality $\tilde{e}^{-\lambda}$ to consumers, whereas the social planner takes into account the cost of production $\psi(e)$ and the cost of pollution $e^{-\lambda}$ in choosing an optimal e^*. The second problem in the market equilibrium is that there is inefficient production under monopoly pricing in the market solution. These two problems affect the welfare of the consumer and also alter the rate of growth of welfare in the market equilibrium. However, the optimal choice of e^* and the restoring of marginal cost pricing will not affect the social choices of z_K and z_A in our model. This is due to the assumptions of a homothetic utility function and of constant returns to scale production. This has the attractive property that static pollution control can be separated from R&D intervention in a planned economy.

Proposition 1: The social planner's choices of z_K and z_A are independent of the function $\psi(e)$ and of the optimal choice of e^*.

Proof: (in Appendix).

4   COMPARING MARKET EQUILIBRIUM AND SOCIAL OPTIMUM

In the product variety model, the market gives a sub-optimal growth rate relative to the social planner's solution. This is due to the knowledge spillover's effect on product innovation and the 'appropriability' effect or consumer surplus effect.[5] Both effects tend to make the private sector under-invest in product innovation. Firms do not see this because they only care about their profits and not the social welfare of the economy. But if there is a pollution externality in producing new products, it will not be necessarily true that a market economy under-invests in product innovation and therefore grows too slowly. In the extreme case, when $\alpha^{-1} \leq 1 + \lambda$ with the constraint $z_K \geq 0$, product innovation leads to greater disutility from more pollution and the increase in the variety of newer products does not fully compensate for the increased pollution. The socially optimal rate of R&D for product innovation will thus be zero. Therefore the problem reduces to a one-dimensional multiplicative R&D growth model, like Grossman and Helpman's (1991) quality upgrading model. If $p_A(\cdot) = \phi_A z_A$, then the socially optimal rate of z_A^* is: [6]

$$z_A^* = \frac{L}{\sigma} - \frac{\rho}{\phi_A \Omega \sigma} \; ; \; \Omega \equiv \frac{\gamma^{\lambda(1-\sigma)} - 1}{1 - \sigma} \; ; \; \lim_{\sigma \to 1} \Omega = \lambda \ln \gamma. \qquad (16.10)$$

But when $\alpha^{-1} > 1 + \lambda$, it can be shown that the market still will provide sub-optimal growth if the pollution damage is small. The intuition is very simple. The social planner sets z_K by trading off the damage of the pollution against the gain from knowledge spillovers and from the 'appropriability' effect. As a result, it is not always true that when individuals ignore the pollution damage caused by growth, the social planner should slow the growth of the economy.

Proposition 2: Given $\alpha^{-1} > 1 + \lambda$ and assuming $z_A^* = 0$ and $z_K^* > 0$, if $\sigma \geq 1$ and λ is smaller than $(1-\alpha)^2/\alpha$, then z_K^* will be greater than $\tilde{z}_K$.

Proof: (in Appendix).

In general, market economies without government intervention in environmental policy tend to devote too few resources to upgrading environmental quality. This is because the social planner cares about the general welfare, whereas firms only care about profits. If there is no profit incentive, the private sector will not invest in R&D for abatement technology. Since the social planner has to sacrifice consumption today to invest in improving environment quality, as long as the efficiency of R&D in abatement is high enough, the social planner will want to invest. In the following proposition, we show that with low efficiency of R&D in abatement and insufficient endowment L, even the social planner may not devote resources to improve environmental quality.

Lemma 1: Given $\alpha^{-1} > 1 + \lambda$ and assuming $\sigma \geq 1 - p_A'(0)\Omega/[(\alpha^{-1} - 1 - \lambda)\phi_K]$, if $\rho/[(\alpha^{-1}-1-\lambda)\phi_K] < L < \rho/[p_A'(0)\Omega]$, then $z_K^* > 0$ and $z_A^* = 0$.

Proof: (in appendix).

The function $u(x,E)$ implies that better environmental quality is more attractive with more goods available. If the elasticity of intertemporal substitution is greater than one, new products will increase the marginal utility of expenditure (from equation (16.5)) which will lower the social discount rate. This increases the incentive to invest in R&D for abatement technology. We call this intertemporal complementarity. On the other hand, when the elasticity of intertemporal substitution is smaller than one, we have intertemporal substitutability. However, both types of R&D compete with the product market for the same resource L. The condition for $\sigma \geq 1 - p_A'(0)\Omega/[(\alpha^{-1} -1-\lambda)\phi_K]$ is to ensure that the elasticity of intertemporal substitution is not so large that the competition effect between product innovation and environmental improvement still dominates the intertemporal complementary effect.

Lemma 1 and Proposition 3 below illustrate that larger quantities of the resource L encourage both product innovation and abatement process innovation. If we interpret L as human capital, then as the economy accumulates human capital over time, there will be more and more incentive for the government (social planner) to improve the environment even when the efficiency of R&D in abatement is very low, i.e., $p_A'(0)$ is very small. As L reaches $\rho/[p_A'(0)\Omega]$, the government will start to care about environmental improvement. This result can explain the findings of recent studies that look at the relationship between economic growth and the environment: Holtz-Eakin and Selden (1992), Grossman (1993), Baldwin (1993), and Grossman and Krueger (1994). They all found that the environment deteriorates in the beginning of economic development and then begins to improve after some level of income has been achieved.

Proposition 3: Given $\alpha^{-1} > 1 + \lambda$, if $L > \rho/[(\alpha^{-1}-1-\lambda)\phi_K]$ and $L > \rho/[p_A'(0)\Omega]$, the optimal solutions of z_A^* and z_K^* will both be positive and with some regularity conditions, $\partial z_A^*/\partial L > 0$ and $\partial z_K^*/\partial L > 0$. Besides, with linear function of $p_A(z_A)$, $\partial(z_A^*/z_K^*)/\partial L > 0$.

Proof: (in appendix).

5 CONCLUSIONS

It is not surprising that markets do not provide enough incentive for environmental improvement and instead sometimes promote too much growth, as we have shown above. This suggests that some government intervention is needed to restore optimality. For example, governments could subsidize environmental research activities but tax the environmentally unfriendly research of polluting industries. However these policies are only helpful in restoring intertemporal efficiency. They do not affect static efficiency. On the contrary, the static control of pollution emissions E will affect the market rates of R&D, $\tilde{z}_A$ and $\tilde{z}_K$. Different policy instruments affect the rates of R&D of $\tilde{z}_A$ and $\tilde{z}_K$ differently.

In the theoretical literature, instruments in environmental policy include non-technological effluent standards, technological standards, effluent charges, marketable permits and subsidies or financial incentives for capital expenditures on pollution abatement equipment. Different countries have tended to favor different mixes of these instruments. One of the most important questions regarding any instrument should be its impact on innovation in pollution control technology. In this vein, one must address the issue of how successful any instrument has been in stimulating R&D in pollution abatement technology or more specifically, the type of effect that any instrument has on the amount of R&D investment. Innovations can theoretically be divided into those that affect output production technology and those that affect pollution control technology. In our model, we can interpret the product innovation K as a proxy for improvement in productivity[7] and define the abatement technology A as pollution control technology. In this set-up, improvements in productivity reflected through K are assumed not to affect the emissions of pollutants from production at the firm level directly. In Section 4, we looked at whether firms over- or under-invest in R&D on pollution abatement technology and product innovation relative to the social optimum in the presence of a production externality (pollution). Some instruments may correct the deviation of the market R&D rates from the socially optimum ones, while others may exacerbate this deviation. One must surely consider how varying instruments affect the market R&D rates differently. One can then also examine the implications of any of these policy instruments on the long run growth rate of the economy. We address those questions in a separate paper (Hung and Chang, 1994).

There, we show that in the case where there is no growth in K, both the technological standard and the emission allowance yield only a one-time improvement in environmental quality and the steady-state R&D rate in pollution abatement technology is zero. The emission tax rate and the marketable permit also only give one-time improvements in environmental quality but maintain a positive growth rate in pollution abatement innovations over time. The difference between these instruments is more noticeable when we allow for economic growth, i.e., growth in number of product K. With economic growth, the environment worsens under the technology standard and the emission allowance system. This is because the increase in the number of firms does not influence each individual firm's choice of optimal emission level. On the other hand, under the tax rate policy and the marketable permit system, the environment does maintain its one-time improvement in the steady state. With a subsidy, the environmental improvement is dictated by the size of the subsidy.

In this paper, we provide some new insights into the trade-off between resources allocated to environmental improvement and resources allocated to economic growth. Both R&D rates in pollution abatement technology and in product innovation are endogenously determined in our growth model. While one is more likely to expect that the market will over-invest in product innovation and neglect the environment, we find that it is not always true that the market rate of product innovation exceeds the socially optimal rate. When the pollution damage effect on social welfare is small, the market may still under-invest because it ignores the knowledge spillover effect in the product innovation sector and the consumer surplus effect.

This paper shows that introducing endogenous technical progress can definitely provide a greater understanding of the environmental policy debate. There is no doubt that imperfect competition between firms and the possibility of new entries into polluting industries complicate the issue. Future empirical research will be needed to consider the feedback from industrial structure to pollution regulation and to re-evaluate policy strategies.

APPENDIX

Proof of Proposition 1:

Since the probabilities of successful R&D in new products and abatement technology are independent, we formulate the Bellman equation by the social planner's objective function (equation (16.9) in text) as

$$
\begin{aligned}
\{W\, &[K(i), A\,(j)] \\
&= \max_{z_K,\, z_A} \Big\{ \frac{[K(i)^{\alpha^{-1}-1-\lambda}\,(L-z_K-z_A)\,\psi(e^*)e^{*-\lambda}A\,(j)^{-\lambda}]^{1-\sigma}-1}{1-\sigma} \\
&\quad + \exp(-\rho)\,[p_K(z_K,K)p_A(z_A)\,W\,[K(i+1),A\,(j+1)] \\
&\quad + p_K(z_K,K)[1-p_A(z_A)]\,W\,[K(i+1),A\,(j)] \\
&\quad + [1-p_K(z_K,K)]p_A(z_A)\,W\,[K(i),A\,(j+1)] \\
&\quad + [1-p_K(z_K,K)][1-p_A(z_A)]\,W\,[K(i),A\,(j)]]\} \quad (16A.1)
\end{aligned}
$$

where $W[K(i), A(j)]$ is the maximum expected discounted utility when the current number of products and abatement technologies are $K(i)$ and $A(j)$ respectively. The maximum is subject to the constraints $z_K + z_A \leq L$, and z_K and z_A are non-negative. $K(i+1) = K(i) + 1, A(j+1) = \gamma A(j)$ and $e^* = $ argmax $\psi(e)e^{-\lambda}$.

Postulate the solution of $W[K(i), A(j)]$ as

$$K(i)^{(\alpha^{-1}-1-\lambda)(1-\sigma)} A(j)^{\lambda(1-\sigma)} w_0 + B \qquad (16A.2)$$

Substituting the solution into the Bellman equation gives us $B = (1+\rho)/[\rho(\sigma-1)]$. Since the utility function is time–separable, with linear probability function of $p_K[z_K, K(i)] = \phi_K z_K K(i)$, the social planner can decentralize the R&D in product innovation. Given a large K, this eliminates all aggregate risk in product innovation by using the law of large numbers. This yields $K(i+1) = p_K[z_K, K(i)] + K(i) = K(i)[1+\phi_K z_K]$. The simplified Bellman equation in terms of w_0 is

$$w_0 = \max_{z_K, z_A} \frac{[\psi(e^*)e^{*-\lambda}(L - z_K - z_A)]^{1-\sigma}}{1-\sigma}$$

$$+ \frac{w_0 [p_A(z_A)(\gamma^{\lambda(1-\sigma)} - 1) + 1][1+\phi_K z_K]^{(\alpha^{-1}-1-\lambda)(1-\sigma)}}{\exp(\rho)} \qquad (16A.3)$$

Here are the first-order conditions of z_K^* and z_A^*:

$$z_K^* \{ -g(e^*)(L - z_K^* - z_A^*)^{-\sigma}$$
$$+ \exp(-\rho) w_0 [p_A(z_A^*)(\gamma^{\lambda(1-\sigma)} - 1) + 1] \qquad (16A.4)$$
$$[1 + \phi_K z_K^*]^{(\alpha^{-1}-1-\lambda)(1-\sigma)-1}(\alpha^{-1} - 1 - \lambda)(1-\sigma)\phi_K \} = 0$$

and

$$z_A^* \{ -g(e^*)(L - z_K^* - z_A^*)^{-\sigma}$$
$$+ \exp(-\rho) w_0 [1 + \phi_K z_K^*]^{(\alpha^{-1}-1-\lambda)(1-\sigma)} \qquad (16A.5)$$
$$+ \frac{\partial p_A(z_A^*)}{\partial z_A^*}(\gamma^{\lambda(1-\sigma)} - 1) \} = 0$$

where $g(e^*) \equiv [\psi(e^*)e^{*-\lambda}]^{1-\sigma}$. For $z_A^* = 0$ or $z_K^* = 0$, the corresponding brackets $\{\}$ of (16A.4) and (16A.5) should be nonpositive. With (16A.3), (16A.4) and (16A.5), one can deduce that z_K^* and z_A^* are independent of the function $\psi(e)$, e^*, $K(i)$ and $A(j)$. Q.E.D.

Proof of Proposition 2:

Suppose $z_A^* = 0$ and $z_K^* > 0$. From (16A.3) and (16A.4) we obtain

$$\exp(\rho) = \{1 + L(\alpha^{-1} - 1 - \lambda)\phi_K + z_K\phi_K[1 - (\alpha^{-1} - 1 - \lambda)]\} \quad (16A.6)$$
$$\times [1 + \phi_K z_K]^{(\alpha^{-1} - 1 - \lambda)(1 - \sigma) - 1}$$

By taking natural logs on both sides of (16A.6) and using the approximation $\ln(1 + x) \approx x$ when x is small, we solve for z_K^* as

$$z_K^* = \frac{L}{\sigma} - \frac{\rho}{\sigma\phi_K(\alpha^{-1} - 1 - \lambda)} \quad (16A.7)$$

In comparison, the market rate $\tilde{z}_K$ is

$$\tilde{z}_K = \frac{(1 - \alpha)L - \rho/\phi_K}{2 - \alpha - (1 - \sigma)(\alpha^{-1} - 1 - \lambda)} \quad (16A.8)$$

If $(1 - \alpha)^2/\alpha > \lambda$ and $\sigma \geq 1$, then $\partial z_K^*/\partial L > \partial \tilde{z}_K/\partial L$ and $L(\tilde{z}_K = 0) > L^*(z_K^* = 0)$. As a result, $z_K^*(L) > \tilde{z}_K(L)$ for all L.   Q.E.D.

Proof of Lemma 1:

First, suppose $\rho/[(\alpha^{-1} - 1 - \lambda)\phi_K] < L$ and $z_A^* = z_K^* = 0$. If both z_A^* and z_K^* are zero, this reduces the first-order condition of (16A.4) to

$$-g(e^*) L^{-\sigma} + \exp(-\rho)w_0(\alpha^{-1} - 1 - \lambda)(1 - \sigma)\phi_K \leq 0 \quad (16A.9)$$

where $g(e^*) \equiv [\psi(e^*)e^{*-\lambda}]^{1-\sigma}$. $w_0 = g(e)L^{1-\sigma}/[(1-\sigma)(1-\exp(-\rho))]$ from (16A.3). We approximate $\exp(\rho)$ as $1 + \rho$. Given $g(e) > 0$ for all $e > 0$ and also $\alpha^{-1} > 1 + \lambda$, it implies that $\rho/[(\alpha^{-1} - 1 - \lambda)\phi_K] \geq L$, which contradicts the above.

Secondly, suppose $L < \rho/[p_A'(0)\Omega]$ and $z_A^* > 0$. Let $\hat{L} \equiv L - z_K^*$. From (16A.3), we can get

$$w_0 = \frac{g(e)(\hat{L} - z_A^*)^{1-\sigma}}{(1 - \sigma)\{1 - \exp(-\rho)[p_A(z_A^*)(\gamma^{\lambda(1-\sigma)} - 1) + 1]\Lambda\}} \quad (16A.10)$$

where $\Lambda \equiv [1 + \phi_K z_K]^{(1/\alpha - 1 - \lambda)(1-\sigma)}$. Given $z_A^* > 0$, the bracket of (16A.5) is zero. Substituting (16A.7) into it reduces to

$$\frac{\hat{L} - z_A^*}{1 - \sigma} \frac{p_A'(z_A^*)(\gamma^{\lambda(1-\sigma)} - 1)}{\exp(\rho)\Lambda^{-1} - [p_A(z_A^*)(\gamma^{\lambda(1-\sigma)} - 1) + 1]} = 1 \quad (16A.11)$$

Let $\hat{\rho} \equiv \rho + \phi_K z_K^*(\sigma - 1)(\alpha^{-1} - 1 - \lambda) \approx \ln\{\exp(\rho)\Lambda^{-1}\}$. Remembering that $\Omega \equiv [\gamma^{\lambda(1-\sigma)} - 1]/(1 - \sigma)$, (16A.11) becomes

$$\frac{\hat{L} - z_A^*}{1 - \sigma} \frac{p_A'(z_A^*)(\gamma^{\lambda(1-\sigma)} - 1)}{\hat{\rho} - p_A(z_A^*)(\gamma^{\lambda(1-\sigma)} - 1)} = 1 \qquad (16A.12)$$

Given $\rho > Lp_A'(0)\Omega$, it implies $\rho > Lp_A'(0)\Omega - z_K^*[p_A'(0)\Omega + (\sigma-1)(\alpha^{-1}-1-\lambda)\phi_K]$ when $p_K'(0)\Omega + (\sigma-1)(\alpha^{-1}-1-\lambda)\phi_K > 0$. It is equivalent to $\hat{\rho}/\Omega > \hat{L}p_A'(0)$. Since from (16A.12), $\hat{\rho}/\Omega = (\hat{L} - z_A^*)p_A'(z_A^*) + p_A(z_A^*)(1-\sigma)$, with $\partial^2 p_A/\partial z_A^2 \leq 0$, we deduce that

$$p_A(z_A^*)(1 - \sigma) - z_A^* p_A'(0) > (\hat{L} - z_A^*)[p_A'(0) - p_A'(z_A^*)] > 0 \qquad (16A.13)$$

But we know $p_A'(0) > p_A(z_A)/z_A$ for all z_A, so it is contradictory. Given the first and the second suppositions, by counter-positive arguments, the lemma is proven.   Q.E.D.

Proof of Proposition 3:

First, suppose $z_A^* = 0$ and $z_K^* > 0$ and $\rho/[(\alpha^{-1}-1-\lambda)\phi_K] \geq L$. From (16A.7), $z_K^* > 0$ implies $\rho/[(\alpha^{-1}-1-\lambda)\phi_K] < L$, which is contradictory. Secondly, suppose $z_A^* > 0$ and $z_K^* = 0$ and $L \leq \rho/[p_A'(0)\Omega]$. From (16A.5), we obtain

$$\frac{L - z_A^*}{1 - \sigma} \frac{p_A'(z_A^*)(\gamma^{\lambda(1-\sigma)} - 1)}{\rho - p_A(z_A^*)(\gamma^{\lambda(1-\sigma)} - 1)} = 1 \qquad (16A.14)$$

Since $z_A^* > 0$ implies $L > \rho/[p_A'(0)\Omega]$, it is contradictory again. Together with the first part of the proof of Proposition 3, by counter-positive arguments, if $\rho/[(\alpha^{-1}-1-\lambda)\phi_K] < L$ and $\rho/[p_A'(0)\Omega] < L$, then $z_A^* > 0$ and $z_K^* > 0$.

Given $z_A^* > 0$ and $z_K^* > 0$, from (16A.4) and (16A.5):

$$\frac{p_A'(z_A^*)[\gamma^{\lambda(1-\sigma)} - 1]}{p_A(z_A^*)[\gamma^{\lambda(1-\sigma)} - 1] + 1} = (\alpha^{-1} - 1 - \lambda)(1 - \sigma)[1 + \phi_K z_K^*]^{-1}\phi_K \qquad (16A.15)$$

which implies $z_K^* = Z(z_A^*)$, $\partial Z/\partial z_A^* > 0$. From (16A.11), we can obtain

$$\rho + \phi_K z_K^*(\sigma - 1)(\alpha^{-1} - 1 - \lambda) - p_A(z_A^*)[\gamma^{\lambda(1-\sigma)} - 1]$$
$$= (L - z_K^* - z_A)p_A'(z_A^*)\Omega \qquad (16A.16)$$

Therefore

$$\frac{\partial z_A^*}{\partial L} = \{Z'(z_A^*)[p'(z_A^*)\Omega + (\sigma-1)(\alpha^{-1}-1-\lambda)\phi_K]$$
$$+ \Omega[p_A''(z_K^* + z_A^*) + p_A'\sigma]\}^{-1} \quad (16A.17)$$

Assuming that $p_A'(L)\Omega + (\sigma-1)(\alpha^{-1}-1-\lambda)\phi_K > 0$ and $p_A''L + p_A'\sigma > 0$, they imply $p_A'(z_A^*)\Omega + (\sigma-1)(\alpha^{-1}-1-\lambda)\phi_K > 0$ and $p_A''(z_K^* + z_A^*) + p_A'\sigma > 0$ respectively. As a result, $\partial z_A^*/\partial L > 0$, so $\partial z_K^*/\partial L > 0 \because Z' > 0$. With $p_A(z_A) = \phi_A z_A$ and

$$\frac{(\alpha^{-1}-1-\lambda)(1-\sigma)\phi_K}{\phi_A(\gamma^{\lambda(1-\sigma)}-1)} > 1 \quad (16A.18)$$

so $\partial[z_A^*/z_K^*]/\partial L > 0$. \hfill Q.E.D.

NOTES

1. For more on this form of upgrading, see Grossman and Helpman (1991) and Aghion and Howitt (1992).
2. With large K, we ignore the own-price effect on the price aggregate $\Sigma_{i=1}^{K} p_i^{-\alpha/(1-\alpha)}$.
3. We assume away other types of capital accumulation.
4. Given the demand of x, K and A, with symmetry, the $u(x,E)$ can be written as
$$\frac{[K^{\alpha^{-1}-1-\lambda}\alpha\psi(\bar{e})(\bar{e}A^{-1})^{-\lambda}Y]^{1-\sigma} - 1}{1-\sigma}$$
5. Private firms only consider the benefit of the profit $(1-\alpha)Y/K$ rather than the total consumer surplus generated by the new product.
6. One can find the solution in the case of $\alpha^{-1} < 1 + \lambda$ from equation (16A.14) in the appendix.
7. The result will qualitatively be the same if we reinterpret the new product as intermediate goods which can enhance the productivity of the final goods production (e.g., Romer, 1990).

REFERENCES

Aghion, P. and P. Howitt (1992), 'A Model of Growth Through Creative Destruction', *Econometrica*, **60**, 323–51.

Baldwin, R. (1993), 'Does Sustainability Require Growth?', Working Paper. GIIS, Geneva, CEPR and NBER.

Gradus, Raymond and Sjak Smulders (1993), 'The Trade-off Between Environmental Care and Long-term Growth: Pollution in Three Prototype Growth Models', *Journal of Economics*, **58**, 25–51.

Grossman, G.M. (1993), 'Pollution and Growth: What Do We Know?', Working Paper 93–4,Woodrow Wilson School of Public and International Affairs, Princeton University, Princeton, NJ.

Grossman, G.M. and E. Helpman (1989), 'Product Development and International Trade', *Journal of Political Economy*, **97**, 1261–83.

Grossman, G.M. and E. Helpman (1991), 'Quality Ladders in the Theory of Growth', *Review of Economic Studies*, **58**, 43–61.

Grossman, G.M. and A.B. Krueger (1994), 'Economic Growth and the Environment', Working Paper No. 4634, Cambridge, Massachusetts: National Bureau of Economic Research (NBER).

Holtz-Eakin, D. and T.M. Selden (1992), 'Stoking the Fires? CO_2 Emissions and Economic Growth', Working Paper No. 4248, Cambridge, MA: NBER.

Huang, Chung-huang and Deqin Cai (1994), 'Constant-Returns Endogenous Growth with Pollution Control', *Environmental and Resource Economics*, **4**, 1–18.

Hung, T.Y.V., and P. Chang (1994), 'Technical Progress, Environmental Improvement and Growth: How Does the Choice of Instruments Matter?', mimeo, Dept. of Economics, Wellesley College, Wellesley, MA.

Jorgenson, D.W. and P.J. Wilcoxen (1990), 'Environmental Regulation and U.S. Economic Growth', *Rand Journal of Economics*, **21**, 314–40.

Liang, Chi-Yuan (1994), 'Macroeconomic Effects of Environmental Regulations in Taiwan', a paper presented at the Institute of Economics of Academia Sinica (IEAS) International Conference on Economic Perspectives of Pollution Control in the Pacific Rim Countries, March 18-19,Taipei.

Michel, P. and G. Rotillon (1993), 'Pollution Disutility and Endogenous Growth', mimeo, Dept. of Economics, CME Université Paris I, Paris, France.

Musu, I. and M. Lines (1993), 'Endogenous Growth and Environmental Preservation,' mimeo, Dept. of Economics, University of Venice, Venice, Italy.

Ploeg, F. van der and J. Ligthart (1993), 'Sustainable Growth and Renewable Resources in the Global Economy', mimeo, Dept. of Economics, University of Amsterdam, Amsterdam.

Romer, P. (1990), 'Endogenous Technical Change', *Journal of Political Economy*, **98**, 71–102.

Stokey, N. (1992), 'R&D and Economic Growth', mimeo, Dept. of Economics, University of Chicago, Chicago, IL.

Index